Churchill and Stalin

Churchill and Stalin

Comrades-in-Arms during the Second World War

Martin Folly, Geoffrey Roberts & Oleg Rzheshevsky

Pen & Sword
MILITARY

First published in Great Britain in 2019 by
PEN & SWORD MILITARY
An imprint of Pen & Sword Books Ltd
Yorkshire – Philadelphia

ISBN 978-1-78159-049-2

Typeset by Concept, Huddersfield, West Yorkshire, HD4 5JL.
Printed and bound in England by TJ International Ltd, Padstow, Cornwall.

Pen & Sword Books Ltd incorporates the imprints of Aviation, Atlas,
Family History, Fiction, Maritime, Military, Discovery, Politics, History,
Archaeology, Select, Wharncliffe Local History, Wharncliffe True Crime,
Military Classics, Wharncliffe Transport, Leo Cooper, The Praetorian Press,
Remember When, White Owl, Seaforth Publishing and Frontline Publishing.

For a complete list of Pen & Sword titles please contact
PEN & SWORD BOOKS LTD
47 Church Street, Barnsley, South Yorkshire, S70 2AS, England
E-mail: enquiries@pen-and-sword.co.uk
Website: www.pen-and-sword.co.uk
or
PEN & SWORD BOOKS
1950 Lawrence Rd, Havertown, PA 19083, USA
E-mail: uspen-and-sword@casematepublishers.com
Website: www.penandswordbooks.com

In Memory of Janice,
1954–2018

Contents

List of Plates

Signed photograph presented by Churchill to Stalin.

Stalin in his Marshal's uniform.

People's Commissar for Foreign Affairs, Vyacheslav Molotov.

British Foreign Secretary, Anthony Eden.

Averell Harriman, American Ambassador in Moscow, 1943–5.

Ivan Maisky, Soviet Ambassador to Great Britain, 1932–43.

Churchill and Stalin in Moscow, August 1942.

Presentation of King George VI's Sword of Stalingrad to Stalin at the Tehran conference.

The Sword of Stalingrad to shown to the seated Roosevelt at the Tehran conference.

Stalin talking to Sarah Churchill at the Tehran conference.

Churchill, Molotov and Field Marshal Alan Brooke in Moscow, October 1944.

Churchill, Stalin and Soviet interpreter Vladimir Pavlov at the Yalta conference.

Stalin, Roosevelt and Churchill at the Yalta conference.

Eden and Molotov at the Potsdam conference.

Stalin at the Potsdam conference.

Churchill, Truman and Stalin at the Potsdam conference.

Stalin, Truman and Churchill at the Potsdam conference.

List of Key Characters

Attlee, Clement (1883–1967): Leader of the Labour Party (1935–55), Deputy Prime Minister and Prime Minister of Great Britain (1940–5, 1945–51).

Beaverbrook, Lord (Max Aitken) (1879–1964): variously British Minister of Aircraft Production, Supply, and War Production (1940–2).

Bevin, Ernest (1881–1951): British Foreign Secretary (1945–51).

Bierut, Bolesław (1892–1956): Polish communist, leader of the Polish Committee of National Liberation (1944–5), President of Poland (1947–52).

Bór-Komorowski, Tadeusz (General) (1895–1966): Polish commander of the Warsaw Rising of August 1944.

Byrnes, James F. (1882–1972): US Secretary of State (1945–7).

Cadogan, Alexander (1884–1968): British civil servant, Permanent Under-Secretary for Foreign Affairs (1938–46).

Churchill, Winston S. (1874–1965): British Prime Minister (May 1940–July 1945).

Clark Kerr, Archibald (1882–1951): British Ambassador to the Soviet Union (1942–6).

Cripps, Stafford (1889–1952): British Ambassador to the Soviet Union (1940–2).

Curzon, Lord (George) (1859–1925): British Foreign Secretary (1919–24).

De Gaulle, Charles (General) (1890–1970): Leader of the Free French Forces, Head of the Provisional Government of the French Republic (1944–7), President of France (1958–69).

Eden, Anthony (1897–1977): British Foreign Secretary (1940–5, 1951–5), Prime Minister (1955–7).

Harriman, William Averell (1891–1986): US Ambassador to the Soviet Union (1943–5).

Hess, Rudolf (1894–1987): Deputy Führer to Adolf Hitler (1933–41).

Hopkins, Harry L. (1890–1946): President Roosevelt's Chief Diplomatic Advisor and Personal Emissary.

Maisky, Ivan M. (1884–1975): Soviet Ambassador to Great Britain (1932–43), Deputy People's Commissar for Foreign Affairs (1943–5).

Mikołajczyk, Stanisław (1901–66): Leader of the Polish People's Party, Prime Minister of the Polish Government-in-Exile (1943–4), Deputy Prime Minister of Poland (1945–7).

Molotov, Vyacheslav M. (1890–1986): People's Commissar for Foreign Affairs (1939–46), Soviet Foreign Minister (1946–9, 1953–6).

Osóbka-Morawski, Edward (1909–97): Chair of the Polish Committee of National Liberation, Prime Minister, Polish People's Republic (1944–7).

Roosevelt, Franklin D. (1882–1945): President of the United States (1933–45).

Sikorski, Władysław Eugeniusz (General) (1881–1943): Prime Minister of the Polish Government-in-Exile (1939–43); killed in an air crash.

Stalin, Joseph V. (1878–1953): General Secretary of the Soviet Communist Party (1922–53).

Truman, Harry S. (1884–1972): President of the United States (1945–53).

Introduction

The Big Two

It is often said that the Grand Alliance was forced into existence by Hitler and fell apart as soon as Nazi Germany was defeated. But neither the formation of the Grand Alliance nor its collapse was inevitable. The Grand Alliance was willed into existence by its leaders and sustained through four years of total war. To achieve victory, it was necessary to develop deep and far-reaching economic, military and political cooperation. It was one of the most successful alliances in history and each of the major partners in the coalition – Britain, the Soviet Union and the United States – made significant contributions to the common cause.

An old saying about the Second World War is that to beat the Nazis the Russians gave their blood, the Americans their money and the British the time they bought by refusing to capitulate to Hitler after the fall of France in summer 1940 – an historical fact that Churchill was fond of reciting to Stalin. Had Britain sued for peace or succumbed to invasion in 1940 it is possible the Red Army would have been defeated by the Germans when they invaded the USSR in summer 1941. The United States, with no European platform from which to project its industrial and military might, would perforce have pivoted to Asia and focussed on the Japanese threat, leaving Hitler as the unchallengeable master of Europe. Nazi genocide and ethnic cleansing on a continental scale would have been the fate of European states from the Atlantic to the Urals.

When the Grand Alliance – as Churchill later called it – emerged in the latter half of 1941 it was not clear the Anglo-American-Soviet coalition could survive the vicissitudes of war. The three countries had very different socio-political systems and there was a bitter history of ideological conflict between Soviet communism and Western liberal democracy. Within Western states there were anti-communists hostile to an alliance with an ideological enemy, while on the Soviet side there were deep suspicions of Western capitalist leaders, not least of Churchill, who had tried to strangle Bolshevism at birth by massive military intervention in the Russian Civil War. The Grand Alliance also had to deal with Hitler's efforts to sow seeds of doubt by spreading rumours that each of the allies was negotiating a separate peace with the Germans.

Significant internal tensions existed during the coalition's early years when most of the fighting was being done by the Red Army while the British and Americans fought on the margins of the conflict. But increasing amounts of Allied material aid did reach the USSR from 1943, and in June 1944 the Western Allies invaded northern France – an operation Moscow had been demanding since July 1941.

The Grand Alliance overcame these difficulties because the so-called Big Three – Winston Churchill, Franklin Delano Roosevelt and Joseph Stalin – put aside ideological differences in the interests of a greater cause. At Yalta in 1945 the Big Three proclaimed their commitment to a peacetime Grand Alliance that would prevent war and provide peace, security and prosperity for all states – a goal reaffirmed that same year at the Potsdam summit and at the founding conference of the United Nations in San Francisco.

After the war Soviet-Western collaboration continued. Major Nazi war criminals were tried at Nuremburg and convicted of crimes against humanity and of conspiracy to wage aggressive war. A peace conference was convened in Paris in summer 1946, and in 1947 peace treaties were signed with the Nazis' wartime allies – Bulgaria, Finland, Hungary, Italy and Romania. In spring 1947 the inter-Allied Council of Foreign Ministers met in Moscow to negotiate Germany's future. These negotiations were inconclusive but Stalin remained optimistic: 'Don't despair', he told the American Secretary of State, George C. Marshall, 'results can be achieved at the next session. On all the main questions – democratisation, political organisation, economic unity and reparations – it is possible to achieve compromise.'[1] However, negotiations about a German peace treaty soon collapsed and the Grand Alliance disintegrated. The failure of the Grand Alliance led to the Cold War and to decades of division, conflict and rivalry between the Soviet Union and its erstwhile Western allies.

The social background, personalities, politics, leadership styles and working methods of the Big Three were diverse. But they had one important trait in common: they were men of long political experience who placed a high premium on personal relations with each other. As Frank Costigliola has put it:

> Roosevelt, Churchill and, perhaps to a lesser extent, Stalin operated on the belief that the attitudes, feelings, demeanour, and body language displayed by statesmen in face-to-face meetings could reveal inner thoughts and ultimate intentions ... Even acrimonious interactions could clarify differences ... Despite the differences in their personal backgrounds, each of the three leaders had developed confidence in his interpersonal skills. Roosevelt's talent for charm and guileful manoeuvre had fuelled his rise to the presidency. Churchill could usually sway a room with his rhetoric and marshalling of history ... Stalin was a master of charm, feint, and argument.[2]

The response of the Big Three to the supreme crisis and challenge of war was broadly similar: each actively assumed the mantle of commander-in-chief, thereby concentrating, centralising and personalising military as well as political decision-making.

In the diplomatic sphere the Big Three each had their own trusted confidants who accompanied them or represented them in important and intimate negotiations. Vyacheslav Molotov, Stalin's foreign commissar, drafted his correspondence with Churchill and Roosevelt, carried out important diplomatic missions at home and abroad, and acted as his deputy in face-to-face negotiations with the British and Americans. Harry Hopkins was President Roosevelt's chief diplomatic advisor and personal envoy. Important, too, was Averell Harriman, Roosevelt's Lend-Lease coordinator in London and his ambassador in Moscow from October 1943. Churchill liked to keep his own counsel and preferred personal diplomacy rather than that conducted via intermediaries. During the war he travelled more than 100,000 miles, meeting Roosevelt eleven times and Stalin twice, as well as taking part in tripartite summits at Tehran, Yalta and Potsdam. But it was Churchill's Foreign Secretary, Anthony Eden, who travelled to Moscow in December 1941 for the first wartime summit with Stalin and he attended most of Churchill's bilateral meetings with Stalin and Molotov.

Personal contact between the three leaders – at meetings, through correspondence and via intermediaries – convinced them they could work together and trust each other. At times that trust and friendship was strained but difficulties were overcome and differences resolved through compromises that respected honour and protected vital interests. The Grand Alliance as it developed during the war is unimaginable without this personal bond between Churchill, Roosevelt and Stalin.

Power in the Grand Alliance lay with Roosevelt and Stalin. As Churchill famously said, it was the Red Army that tore the guts out of Hitler's war machine, while it was American industrial strength and manpower that tipped the balance of forces decisively in the Allies' favour. But the beating heart of the Grand Alliance was Churchill's relationship with Stalin. As Averell Harriman recalled, while Stalin admired and respected Roosevelt and praised him as a 'great man for war and a great man for peace', Churchill he toasted as 'my comrade-in-arms'.[3] Churchill and Stalin were the Big Two of the Grand Alliance, the personal axis around which it revolved.

Stalin's relations with Churchill were fragile but intimate and intense. Churchill was a mercurial personality and his relations with Stalin were volatile. He had a history of militant anti-Bolshevism and was unapologetic about it. Yet Stalin, a dedicated communist, hoped Churchill would win the 1945 British General Election and was shocked when he lost in a landslide to the Labour Party. During the war the two men conducted a 500-message correspondence (two-thirds of the messages were Churchill's) and Churchill travelled twice to Moscow – in August 1942 and October 1944 – for crucial bilateral meetings with Stalin. The only time Stalin met Roosevelt was at the Tehran and Yalta conferences, though he did send Molotov to Washington in June 1942. After the war Stalin clashed publicly with Churchill following the now ex-Premier's 'Iron Curtain' speech in Fulton, Missouri in March 1946, but the two men never lost their affection for each other.

It is commonly assumed the Cold War was inevitable, that once Hitler was defeated the conflicting interests and ideologies of the Soviet Union and the Western Powers inexorably drove the two sides apart. His reputation as an early Cold Warrior notwithstanding, that was not Churchill's view at the time; indeed, even in his 'Iron Curtain' speech he said there was a need for a good understanding with Russia.

The Cold War was not Stalin's choice. Throughout the war the Soviet dictator had stressed the long-term common interests – economic, political and military – of the partners in the Grand Alliance. An avid reader of historical works, Stalin told Churchill and Roosevelt at Yalta that 'in the history of diplomacy I know of no such close alliance of three Great Powers as this'.[4] After the war Stalin clung to the hope the Grand Alliance could endure in some form. Not until the founding of the Communist Information Bureau (Cominform) in September 1947 did the Soviets declare that the post-war world had definitively split into two camps.[5]

In the end the story of the Grand Alliance and its denouement is quite simple. During the war its leaders choose to ally against a common enemy and then carry the coalition forward into peacetime political collaboration. After the war different choices were made – to pursue the separate as opposed to the common interests of the Grand Alliance. The result was the Cold War. The first set of choices saved the world from Hitler and the Nazis. The second set of choices plunged the world into decades of a potentially catastrophic conflict, whose vast nuclear arsenals continue to pose an existential threat to humanity.

This book was inspired by the late Professor Oleg Rzheshevsky's prodigious work on Churchill and Stalin during the war. Many of the documents it contains first appeared in his books.[6] Based on Russian archives,[7] it analyses and documents Churchill's personal and political relationship with Stalin. It contains the essential correspondence between the two leaders[8] and records of all their bilateral meetings, many translated into English for the first time, including the complete Soviet report of the notorious meeting in October 1944 at which Stalin and Churchill discussed dividing south-eastern Europe into percentage-based spheres of influence.[9]

The authors of this book have different national backgrounds, come from different historiographical traditions and hold different political views. We had many disagreements about Churchill, Stalin and the history of the Second World War. None of us agreed with every interpretation proposed in this book. But, like Churchill and Stalin during the war, what united us was more important than the differences.

The authors are grateful to Professor Ged Martin for his contribution on Churchill's wartime travels.

Professor Rzheshevsky indicated a desire to express his gratitude for the comments and evaluations of his work on Churchill and Stalin by V.A. Zolotarev, M.Yu. Myagkov, A.V. Panshin, V.O. Pechatnov, N.M. Barinova, Yu.V. Kudrina , Yu.A. Nikiforov, and other Russian and foreign specialists.

Geoffrey Roberts would like to acknowledge the funding received from University College Cork and the Helsinki Collegium for Advanced Studies.

All the documents in this book were translated from Russian originals by Geoffrey Roberts and Svetlana Frolova.

The index was compiled by Susan Certo of Mark Your Words and she did her usual brilliant job.

The book is dedicated to the memory of Geoffrey Roberts' younger sister, Janice, who died on 26 December 2018.

Maps

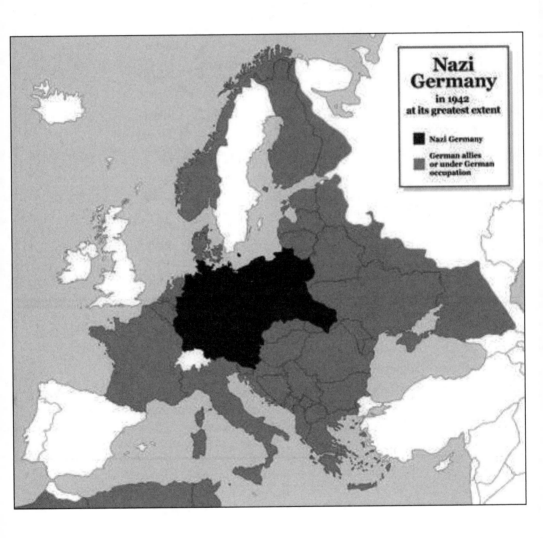

Poland's Frontiers 1939-45

— · — · —   Pre-war frontiers

●●●●●●●   Soviet-German demarcation line 28 Sept 1939

━ ▪ ━ ▪ ━ ▪   Polish-Soviet frontier from 1945

●●●●●●●●   Anglo-US proposed Polish-German frontier on Eastern Neisse river

━ ━ ━ ━   Polish-German frontier from 1945

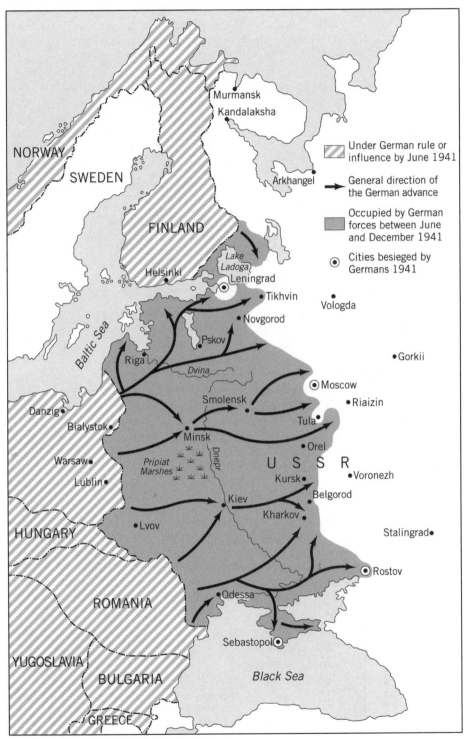

Operation Barbarossa: The German Invasion of the Soviet Union, June–December 1941.

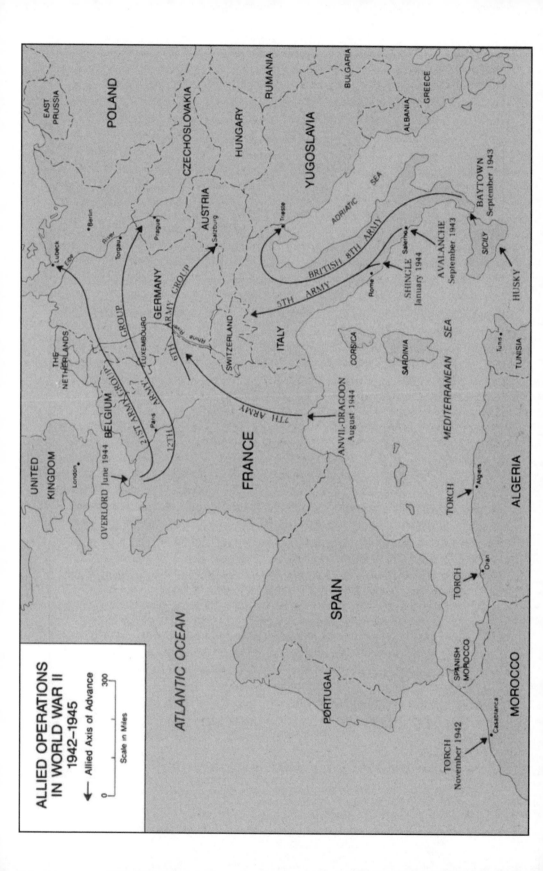

ALLIED OPERATIONS
IN WORLD WAR II
1942–1945

→ Allied Axis of Advance

0   300
Scale in Miles

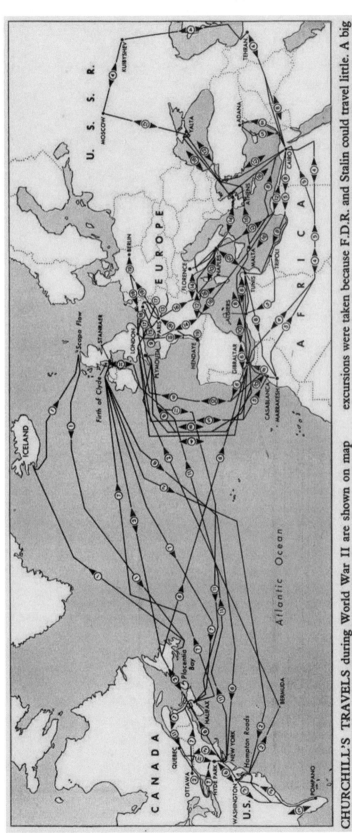

CHURCHILL'S TRAVELS during World War II are shown on map with numbers denoting chronological order of his trips and arrows showing direction. (Double arrow is round trip over same route.) His many excursions were taken because F.D.R. and Stalin could travel little. A big obstacle to allied unity, he once said, "is geography. We stand around the circumference of the circle. The main enemy lies at the centre."

Chapter 1

Big Game: Churchill and Stalin before Barbarossa

The accepted idea that the Grand Alliance only came into existence after Hitler attacked the Soviet Union in June 1941 requires some amendment. For a start, the formation of coalitions against German aggression date to the beginning of the twentieth century. The Anglo-Franco-Russian Entente was formed in 1904–7 and during the First World War this military-political alliance united more than twenty states (including the USA, Italy and Japan) against Germany and its allies. At the end of August 1939, after the failure of the Anglo-Soviet-French triple alliance negotiations, Britain, France and Poland united against German aggression. The signature of the Soviet-German non-aggression treaty (23 August 1939) and the Soviet-German friendship and boundary treaty (28 September) undermined Churchill's pre-war campaign for a Soviet-Western Grand Alliance but it did not end his efforts in that regard. This much is evident from direct and indirect contacts between Churchill and Stalin before the German invasion of the USSR in June 1941.

The European situation was complicated in autumn 1939. Poland had been defeated by the Wehrmacht in two weeks. German troops were on the Soviet Union's new frontier and only Hitler's intervention stopped them crossing the demarcation line in Poland agreed between Berlin and Moscow. It was assumed the war would be prolonged and would be fought on land along the Western Front, as well as in the air and at sea, with the outcome determined by the impact of the Allied economic blockade of Germany as much as the military and political strength of the two sides. The success of Germany's war with Poland demonstrated the military prowess of the Nazi regime and highlighted the danger that Hitler represented not just to Britain and France but to the Soviet Union and United States as well.

In this complex situation the first steps along the path to the Grand Alliance were taken by Churchill. On 1 October 1939, Churchill, who had returned to government as First Lord of the Admiralty (i.e. Britain's navy minister), spoke on the radio:

> Russia had pursued a cold policy of self-interest. We could have wished that the Russian armies should be standing on their present line as the friends and allies of Poland instead of as invaders. But that the Russian armies should stand on this line was clearly necessary for the safety of Russia against the Nazi menace. I cannot forecast to you the action of Russia. It is a riddle

wrapped in a mystery inside an enigma; but perhaps there is a key. That key is Russian national interest. It cannot be in accordance with the interest or the safety of Russia that Germany should plant itself upon the shores of the Black Sea, or that it should overrun the Balkan States and subjugate the Slavonic peoples of south-eastern Europe. That would be contrary to the historic life-interests of Russia.[1]

On 6 October Churchill invited the Soviet ambassador in London, Ivan Maisky, to see him at the Admiralty. As Maisky recorded in his diary, Churchill wanted to talk about Anglo-Soviet relations, which he said had

always been poisoned by the venom of mutual suspicion, today more than ever before. What are these suspicions? Britain suspects the USSR of having concluded a military alliance with Germany and that it will openly come out, one fine day, on Hitler's side against the Western Powers. Churchill himself does not believe this, but many (including some in government circles) do. This circumstance cannot but affect the general tone of Britain's attitude to the USSR. On the other hand, the USSR suspects Britain of pursing a hostile policy against the USSR and of various machinations against it in the Baltic, Turkey, the Balkans and elsewhere. This condition cannot but affect the general tone of the Soviet attitude to Britain. Churchill understands why our suspicions are especially acute today. The Anglo-Franco-Soviet pact negotiations were conducted in a repulsive way ... and have left bad memories in Moscow's mind. But let the dead bury the dead. The present and future are more important than the past ... His starting point is that the basic interests of Britain and the USSR do not collide anywhere ... We should not take too much to heart the criticism and indignation with which the Soviet-German non-aggression pact and the subsequent moves of the Soviet Government have been met in Britain. This was due to their unexpectedness.

Churchill then told Maisky that if the Baltic States were to lose their independence it was better that they be brought into the Soviet state system rather than the German one and that Britain and the USSR had a common interest in stopping Germany from reaching the Black Sea. Britain viewed Soviet neutrality positively, said Churchill, and merely wished it to be a friendly neutrality. Churchill then asked Maisky what steps could be taken to improve Anglo-Soviet relations. Maisky remained silent but that did not stop Churchill from stating that 'Stalin is playing a big game at the moment and is doing so felicitously. He can be satisfied. But I fail to see why we should be dissatisfied.'[2]

On 21 February 1940 Foreign Commissar Vyacheslav Molotov sent Maisky some guidelines about Soviet policy towards Germany. Firstly, the idea that the USSR would enter into a military alliance with Germany was 'ridiculous and insulting'. Secondly, the value of Soviet-German trade only amounted to 500 million marks. Thirdly, the Soviet Union was neutral and would remain so, as long as Britain and France did not attack it. Rumours of a Soviet-German military alliance were being spread for domestic political purposes in Britain and France as well as by those in Germany striving to unsettle the British and French.[3]

Table 2

colunm one	colunm two	column three
colunm one	colunm two	column three
colunm one	colunm two	column three
colunm one	colunm two	column three
colunm one	colunm two	column three

The Winter War with Finland (November 1939–March 1940) interrupted this incipient tendency towards rapprochement in Anglo-Soviet relations and created new dangers for the USSR. The Soviet Union was excluded from the League of Nations and the United States declared a 'moral embargo' which in effect prohibited trade with the USSR. In his memoirs Churchill noted how heated his personal support for the Finns had been, while the French journalist K.A. Frankais noted that the idea of a crusade against Russia was in the air and those in France who insisted on sitting defensively on the Maginot Line now wanted to send armies to do battle in northern lands.[4]

The Hitlerite leadership supported this anti-Soviet campaign as a means to distract the Western Powers from invading Germany. The most important part of this German propaganda campaign was a supposed schema for peace with Germany. 'Peace would be achieved at the expense of Russia', recalled French diplomat, J. Bardoux. 'England would get Turkistan. The border between Iran and Turkey would shift to the Caspian Sea. Italy would get a share of the oil, while Germany annexed Ukraine.'[5]

The British Chiefs of Staff examined the pros and cons of declaring war on Russia. In one document they pointed out that Russia had three centres of oil production: Baku, Grozny and Maikop. To destroy Russia's oil supplies Baku was to be bombed for fifteen days, Grozny for twelve days and Batumi for six days.[6] At the end of December, the Chief of the Imperial General Staff, General Ironside, noted in his diary that there was an opportunity to turn the tables against both the Germans and the Russians, but the British had to proceed carefully in order to avoid surprises; constructing the necessary aerodromes and preparing the planes required would take until summer 1940.[7]

On 5 February the Anglo-French Supreme War Council decided to send a 150,000-strong military expedition to Finland. The Polish Government-in-Exile was also prepared to send a brigade of its forces to Finland. In London and Paris plans were drawn up to attack Leningrad and Baku, followed by a march on Moscow.[8] In the far north, Anglo-French occupation of Petsamo was envisaged together with a joint Western-Finnish advance to cut the Murmansk-Leningrad rail link. In the south, the aim of French General Maxime Weygand, commander-in-chief of the Eastern Theatre of Operations (Syria and Lebanon), was to 'break the back of the USSR'.[9]

There was a real danger of the USSR becoming involved in the wider war between Britain, France and Germany. Standing in the way was Norway and Sweden's refusal to allow the transit of Allied troops across their territory. Nor were the Finns willing to accede to British and French demands that they end peace negotiations with the Soviets. The Finns thought the Western Powers were bluffing, given that they had betrayed Czechoslovakia and done little to aid Poland directly when it was attacked by Germany. So, with the military situation turning against them, the Finns negotiated a peace treaty with the USSR – signed on 12 March 1940 – that ended the so-called Winter War.

On 10 May 1940 the German offensive in Western Europe began. France capitulated forty-four days later as Denmark, Norway, the Netherlands, Belgium and Luxemburg also fell to the Germans. Anglo-French military forces in Europe were heavily defeated and only a major evacuation operation at Dunkirk saved the British from complete disaster. It was a glorious moment in British history but as Churchill said, wars are not won by retreats. By this time Churchill had become Britain's Prime Minister, in succession to Neville Chamberlin. He rejected German peace overtures – though not without opposition from within his own cabinet – and announced publicly that with the end of the battle for France the battle of Britain would begin. In summer 1940 there took place in the skies above Great Britain a decisive air battle that saved the country from invasion by Hitler.

In this new situation British policy towards the Soviet Union took on a different complexion from that during the Winter War. An early sign was recorded by Maisky in his diary on 18 June 1940:

> I spent the afternoon in Parliament. Today's speech by Churchill has lifted morale. His firm statement that England, regardless of France's defeat, will fight to the end was met with loud applause from all the benches ... The end of today's sitting was marked by a rather unusual demonstration. The Labourite John Morgan took the floor and suggested that the House should

mark the fact of Cripps' arrival in Moscow and his accession to the post of ambassador. The suggestion was welcomed with cheers from all sides. Furthermore, members of Parliament turned their faces to the diplomatic gallery, where I was sitting in the front row. Morgan then wished Cripps every success in his new job. Friendly approval echoed round the chamber once more and Churchill ... looking in my direction waved his hand in salutation.[10]

In Moscow, Stafford Cripps, a supporter of Anglo-Soviet rapprochement, sought a meeting with Stalin and sent Molotov a note stating that he had been instructed to present to Stalin personally a message from Churchill. Cripps met Stalin on 1 July. Churchill's message to Stalin observed that although Britain and the Soviet Union were on opposite sides of Europe and had very different political systems, the two countries had a common interest in opposing German domination of the continent.[11] In response, Stalin told Cripps that while Moscow was not allied with Germany against Britain, Soviet relations with Hitler were governed by the terms of the non-aggression treaty. The Soviet Union had no interest in restoring the status quo in Europe, a balance of power that had worked against Soviet interests. Cripps replied that the task was not to restore the old balance of power but to prevent German domination of Europe. When Cripps observed that in the West only Britain stood in the way of German hegemony Stalin remarked that he had forgotten about the United States, a point the ambassador parried by noting the Americans had made no commitment to intervene in the European situation. Stalin also cast doubt on the idea that the Nazis aspired to global hegemony.[12]

After his conversation with Stalin, Cripps reported home that while the meeting had been friendly and open, cooperation between the Soviet Union and Germany would continue.[13] Indeed, Count Friedrich von der Schulenburg, the German ambassador in Moscow, was informed about the meeting and provided with a sanitised but not inaccurate report of the exchanges between Stalin and Cripps. On 1 August, Molotov told the Supreme Soviet that the non-aggression treaty with Germany was based not on 'fortuitous considerations of a transient nature, but on the fundamental political interests of both countries'.[14]

Molotov's signal to both Berlin and London that there would be no changes in Soviet-German relations did not deter the British from undertaking a rather dramatic initiative in autumn 1940. As Maisky noted in his diary:

On behalf of the British Government, Cripps has asked Molotov for an audience on a matter of 'paramount political importance'. Molotov could not receive Cripps so instead Cripps met Vyshinsky to whom he submitted a special memorandum. Its concluding part contained three points:
1. The British Government announces its readiness to recognise 'de facto' the changes in the Baltic so as to settle 'de jure' the whole issue later, probably after the war.
2. The British Government declares itself prepared to ensure the participation of the USSR, on an equal basis, in the settlement of European affairs after the war.

3. The British Government promises not to participate in any military
actions against the USSR

Vyshinsky told Cripps that he would report the matter to the Soviet Government.[15]

At the heart of the British memorandum was a proposal for a non-aggression pact between Great Britain and the Soviet Union. The Soviet Union would remain neutral but would be benevolent towards Britain in exchange for a British promise to refrain from entering alliances directed against the USSR. Britain would *de facto* recognise Soviet territorial gains in relation to Estonia, Latvia, Lithuania, Bessarabia, North Bukovina and eastern Poland (i.e. Western Belorussia and Western Ukraine) while the USSR would continue to support China in its struggle against Japan and would not do anything to facilitate Japanese aggression against British interests in the Far East.[16]

As Academician A.O. Chubaryan has observed, acceptance of the British proposal would have entailed a radical change in Soviet foreign policy, one that would have magnified greatly the danger of war with Germany.[17] While Moscow wanted to prevent any further deterioration in Anglo-Soviet relations, its rejection of the British proposal came as no surprise. When, in February 1941, the British wanted to send their Foreign Secretary, Anthony Eden, to meet Stalin in Moscow, Vyshinsky told Cripps 'the time for resolving the big issues has yet to come'.[18]

On 3 April, Churchill sent Stalin a message warning of the growing danger of Germany attacking the USSR, which reinforced Soviet intelligence on the build-up of German forces along the frontiers of the USSR. However, in May 1941 Anglo-Soviet relations took another turn for the worse. On 10 May, Rudolf Hess, Hitler's deputy, flew to Britain and landed by parachute 20 miles from the estate of the Duke of Hamilton in Scotland, who was well-known for his pro-German activity. Soviet suspicions were aroused; Moscow's intelligence agencies had been reporting for years on secret negotiations between London and Berlin. Maybe this was a renewed attempt at an Anglo-German peace at the USSR's expense.

Moscow was also alarmed by information that while the United States and Britain would support the USSR in the event of a German attack on the Soviet Union, they would do so only under certain conditions. One source reported that in May 1941 President Roosevelt told his chiefs of staff that if Stalin did not provoke an attack by Germany, the United States would support the USSR; otherwise, they would not get involved.[19] Hess's arrival in Britain heightened Soviet fears about the unreliability of its potential allies, while the intensification of anti-communist propaganda that the USSR was striving for world revolution through the unleashing of a new world war showed that the ground was being prepared to blame the Soviets for the coming German attack.

Stalin was desperate to delay war for as long as possible, not least because he did not trust what the British and Americans would do when the Germans attacked. In early June he ordered the NKVD to create a special group (headed by P.A. Sudoplatov) to prevent German saboteurs from conducting provocations in the area of the Soviet border, similar to that carried out before the beginning of the invasion of Poland in 1939. He also banned Soviet aviation flights in the border area and cancelled an order of the commander of the Kiev Special Military District for troops to occupy advanced front-line positions.[20] On 13 June, the Soviet news agency, TASS, broadcast a statement that emphasised the USSR's fidelity to a policy of peace, its commitment to the Soviet-German non-aggression pact and its repudiation of false and provocative rumours that Moscow was preparing for war with Germany.[21] Actually, the Soviet Union was actively preparing for war with Germany and had been doing so for several months. Among the most, frequent visitors to Stalin's Kremlin office in the first half of 1941 were his Defence Commissar, Marshal Semyon Timoshenko, and Chief of the General Staff, General Georgy Zhukov.[22]

On 13 June, Eden informed Maisky of concentrations of German troops on Soviet frontiers and said that if the USSR was attacked Britain would send a military mission to Moscow and provide economic and military aid.[23] In Moscow, the reception of this information was coloured by the belief that the British were trying to provoke the Soviets into a premature war with Germany. On 15 June, Churchill informed Roosevelt of the UK's readiness to provide Russia with all possible assistance in the event of a German attack – a stance the American President endorsed. But neither Churchill nor Roosevelt informed Stalin of this decision.[24]

The uncertainty surrounding Anglo-Soviet relations continued until the day of the German attack on the USSR, 22 June 1941. But that same evening Churchill made his famous radio broadcast in which he pledged to support the Soviet Union with all the means at Britain's disposal. On 24 June President Roosevelt stated at a press conference, 'of course we are going to provide Russia with all the help we can'.[25] Stalin reciprocated in his radio address on 3 July, when he emphasised that the war against Germany would be fought alongside Britain and the United States.

On 12 July, Britain and the Soviet Union signed an agreement on joint action against Germany and in May 1942 agreed an Anglo-Soviet treaty of alliance. The United States did not actually enter the war until December 1941 but in October 1941 it signed a supply agreement with the Soviets, and American aid was already beginning to flow into the USSR – a trickle that became a flood as the war progressed. The Grand Alliance that Churchill dreamed of before the Second World War had come into being, though perhaps not in the manner and form he had expected.

Chapter 2

Comrades-in-Arms: Churchill and Stalin at War

There continues to be enormous interest in and fascination with Winston Churchill and Joseph Stalin. They are discussed a great deal in accounts of the Second World War and their relationship is extensively documented in the official papers available from the archives of both their governments, and from the private papers of participants. With the availability now of documents from the Soviet archives, moreover, a more rounded and complete picture can be presented and a fuller analysis achieved. The Soviet records of meetings, in particular, give a quite different and often less dramatic perspective than the British ones that have been the standard fare for assessing Churchill's interactions with Stalin for years.

The personal interactions between Churchill and Stalin have always had a problematic place in the traditional, but enduring, narrative of Churchill's wartime views of the USSR, and of Churchill himself as war leader. The prominent theme of that narrative, established by Churchill himself, was his 'eyes-open' attitude: open to wartime cooperation, but without letting delusions about the USSR or Stalin get in the way, and always aware of Stalin's designs on Eastern Europe. Historians who have devoted serious attention to Churchill's attitudes have preferred not to present them in quite so stark a form as this narrative, even though it remains potent in accounts of Churchill for a general readership. What tends to divide such historians is the degree to which they find consistency in Churchill's views and attitudes. There are those who find Churchill influenced by his long-standing hatred of Bolshevism.[1] Others find Churchill more inconsistent, as wavering between that view and a readiness to see cooperation with the Soviets as a realistic possibility.[2] Churchill's attitudes were certainly neither straightforward nor consistent, but the result of conflicting elements in his attitudes to communism (domestic and Soviet), to the USSR and to Stalin, magnified by, but not entirely created by, the conditions of co-belligerency. Examination of Churchill's contacts with Stalin in person demonstrate that though his attitudes to Bolshevism were immutable, his attitudes to *Stalin* were not.[3] Appreciation of the degree to which Stalin was significantly distinct from being simply a personification for Churchill of Bolshevism's worst excesses is central to understanding the paradoxical nature of his attitudes as they developed in the period of the alliance, 1941–5. In engaging with Stalin as a (fellow) warlord, Churchill was able to reconcile his conflicting impulses to simultaneously embrace the Soviets as powerful and significant partners in his self-defined mission to crush Hitler, and to recoil from them out of suspicion about their methods, their past and their objectives.

To an extent, Churchill operated on the basis of a specific conceptualisation of both his great allies: he constructed an image of Franklin Roosevelt that only partly reflected the reality of that complex individual (and contained a certain element of romanticisation and wishful thinking).[4] Roosevelt became the personification to Churchill of the America that Britain needed America to be, and there are good grounds for arguing that Churchill did the same with regard to Stalin. In Stalin's case, Churchill came to alight on an image of Stalin as warrior-leader, and then proceed to conceive of their relationship as a 'comradeship-in-arms' (reflecting his own self-image too), a term he never used in association with Roosevelt.

As much as Churchill, Stalin's earlier career gave no hint that there was a possibility of any kind of cordial relationship between the two. Britain was regarded in the 1920s as the main threat to the fledgling USSR. Churchill had been one of the prime moving forces behind the Allied intervention in Russia, 1919–20, waging his own 'little private war', as he described it to Stalin later.[5] Churchill was well-qualified to be the archetype of the British imperialist. There is some suggestion that there was curiosity on Stalin's part about Churchill when his vocal opposition to appeasement emerged in the mid-1930s. It was known that Prime Minister Neville Chamberlain was hostile to the USSR, and Churchill appeared in a better light by contrast with his political opponent. However, the traditional view of Stalin in Western historiography presents him as a man driven by ideology, unaffected by personality. He would see people as types whose behaviour was predictable by applying the tenets of Marxism-Leninism. A variation on this has been to emphasise Stalin's dark and suspicious mind, bordering on paranoia. Under either interpretation, there could be no real personal relationship between the two statesmen, beyond Stalin's single-minded and cold-blooded manipulation. This has been a highly enduring image: in a recent biography of Churchill, Max Hastings has depicted Stalin as machine-like in his diplomacy.[6]

However, Stalin appreciated the personal importance of Churchill, and as we shall see, approached his relationship with him in a way that cannot be reduced to such a simple formula. The historiography that has emerged since the partial opening of Soviet-era archives suggests that while ideology was the basis of Stalin's view of the world, he also had a well-refined sense of what he called 'the correlation of forces'.[7] If his domestic power was all-encompassing, in international affairs it was more conditional, requiring active diplomacy and flexibility – indeed, an alternative to the traditional interpretation sees Stalin as primarily an extremely flexible opportunist.[8] For many years the main sources for Stalin's personal attitudes to Churchill came from a handful of second- or third-hand sources, all of them problematical in some way. By far the most often cited was the disillusioned Yugoslav communist Milovan Djilas's recollections of conversations with Stalin. His notes of Stalin's remarks about Churchill became definitive: Churchill as a man who would pick your pocket for a kopeck, and Djilas's own judgment that Stalin saw him as a dangerous bourgeois statesman.[9] However, Djilas was hardly an objective observer, and the materials now available give a fuller and more nuanced picture of Stalin's view of Churchill, in the context of Stalin's desire for continued cooperation and clearly shaped by emotional responses as well as calculation. He approached the issue of relations with Churchill influenced by the interaction of his ideological world-picture, his shifting sense of the interests and needs of the Soviet state, and his reading of Churchill himself. This reading was certainly influenced to a degree by his view of Churchill as a 'dangerous bourgeois statesmen', but also by his perception of Churchill's specific attitudes to the USSR and to the key issues of the war, such as the future of Germany and the commitment of British forces in battle. These were influenced not only by his preconceptions but by the information received from sources like the ambassador in London, Ivan Maisky, and not least in his own interactions, both in person and also in their extended and at times very frank correspondence. The care taken in composing messages certainly shows Stalin saw Churchill as a man who could be influenced and his behaviour modified by persuasion or by playing on his emotions of guilt or gratitude – and playing off Churchill's soldier's instincts for offensive action which were conflicting with his politician's instincts to conserve Britain's strength and human resources.

Thus, emotion and the attempted manipulation of emotion were a central element of the Churchill-Stalin relationship in both its forms, face-to-face and on paper. The evident perceptions one of the other indicate the bounded rationality within which each formed his perceptions and which prompted the formulation of the correspondence and the attempt of each to squeeze out advantage, in a way more complex, and indeed interesting, than were one simply to focus on the fundamental ideologies that for many superficial studies appear to be the key factor to consider when addressing the relationship between these two leaders.

Antecedents

Russia had always exercised a certain fascination for Winston Churchill. He welcomed the apparent move towards democracy inaugurated by the February Revolution. He condemned the October Revolution of the same year, 1917, taking up an anti-communist stance from which he never deviated, once describing Bolshevism as 'foul baboonery', and on another as a pestilence akin to typhus. It was notable that he never used such extreme language in his condemnations of Fascism or Nazism.[10] In a statement in 1936 he went so far as to say that if he had to choose between Communism and Nazism, he would not chose Communism.[11] It is a matter of more debate, however, as to how far that hostility was always replicated in his attitude to the USSR as a state. Certainly, for much of the time, Churchill would not have distinguished between the two: yet there is evidence that at times he did so – that he detected in the Soviet Union in essence the old Russia. In particular, as the threat from Nazi Germany grew during the 1930s, so he saw the possibilities of the USSR playing a more traditional role in the balance of power. This perception was no doubt strengthened by the obvious danger that Hitler posed to the USSR and influenced by the more 'civilised' diplomatic behaviour of Foreign Commissar Maxim Litvinov from 1933 to 1939. Churchill was among the wide circle of opposition and anti-appeasement figures cultivated by Ambassador Maisky.[12]

His attitudes towards the Soviet Union, even if it was the fountainhead of Bolshevism, were clearly changeable according to developments in international politics, and to this extent it is clear that he regarded the Soviet leadership in a sense as realists. He had, in fact, had no contact with that leadership. He had said little about Stalin himself, though it is highly suggestive, given his later wartime attitudes, that in commenting on the growth of the Terror in the USSR in 1936, he depicted Stalin as acting against the Old Guard Bolsheviks, implying that Churchill accepted the idea that some derived from the slogan 'socialism in one country' that Stalin was not a proponent of world revolution. In November 1937, Churchill remarked to Maisky, at Buckingham Palace of all places, 'we need a strong, a very strong Russia', and after calling Trotsky 'a perfect devil', declared 'I'm wholly for Stalin'.[13]

In the face of the rising threat of Nazi Germany, Churchill became a strong advocate of closer cooperation with the Soviets, even to the extent of renewing the pre-1914 alliance. The great upheavals of Stalin's crash industrialisation pro- gramme and collectivisation of agriculture, followed by the purge first of political figures and then of the military, brought into question in the West the effective- ness of any Soviet contribution against Germany, but to Churchill it was essential that all help, however dubious, be enlisted. As early as 1936, Lord Hankey found in a conversation with Churchill that he had buried his violent anti-Soviet complex of former days, but was doubtful about 'how far Russia could be relied upon as an ally'.[14] This latter feeling was widely shared in the Government. It was felt that no reliance could be placed on the USSR, both out of doubt about its military strength and also about the reliability of its motives. Members of Stanley Baldwin's and later Chamberlain's governments shared Churchill's dislike of the Soviet Union, but were less inclined than he to bury their prejudices in the face of the threat of Germany. In March 1939, when Britain gave guarantees to Poland and Romania, which could only really be effective with Soviet help, Chamberlain wrote that he had no faith in Soviet military abilities and had 'most profound distrust of Russia'.[15]

Churchill entertained no such fastidiousness. His thoughts now dominated by the threat of Germany, he advocated an alliance with the USSR, because he saw it as the only way to deter Germany from going to war and to make the British guarantee to Poland an effective reality and generally increase British chances of resisting German power. He took every opportunity to make his views public. For instance, in the *Daily Mirror* he criticised the 'unaccountable delay' in con- cluding 'a solid, binding all-in alliance between Britain, France and Russia'.[16] Churchill based his arguments not on a different assessment of Soviet military strength than the government's military advisors, nor on a specific appraisal of the policies of the Soviet leadership, but on broad geopolitics and an assumption of Soviet realism. As he was to demonstrate during the wartime alliance period, Churchill tended to build an image of other states that fitted his needs and overall vision, rather than basing them on deductive reasoning, which, given Churchill's enthusiasm for secret intelligence, is paradoxical.

When the war broke out, and especially after its invasion of Poland on 17 September, the USSR was firmly aligned in most British minds with Nazi Germany. There were even those who felt that Britain should declare war on the USSR. Churchill, now in the War Cabinet, did not share such views, regarding Germany as quite enough enemy for the time being. He resisted the tendency of many at this time to bracket the USSR and Germany together as ideological twins, emphasising instead the self-interested nature of Soviet foreign policy – the 'realist' line that he had been arguing for some time.[17] He publicly stated that there was a good possibility that British and Soviet interests would coincide.[18] It was soon after this that he made his often-quoted remark about Soviet policy being a mystery inside a riddle, wrapped in an enigma.[19] What is often over-looked is that at that time, most observers, including leading figures in the British and French Governments, found Soviet policy far from enigmatic – indeed they saw the Soviets as acting clearly and unambiguously in cahoots with the Nazis. Churchill was, by contrast, suggesting that there was a distance between the two, that the Soviets and Nazis were not the same – as many people were saying – and that they could easily realign in a way more favourable to Britain.

Churchill's own realism shaped his response when the USSR attacked Finland on 30 November 1939. Though, as Conservative MP Henry Channon wrote, he 'only a few weeks ago was campaigning for an alliance with Russia', he now allowed his anti-Bolshevism full rein in an effort to drum up support for action in Scandinavia.[20] In a broadcast he said:

> Many illusions about Soviet Russia have been dispelled in these few fierce weeks of fighting in the Arctic Circle. Everyone can see how Communism rots the soul of a nation – how it makes it abject and hungry in peace and proves it base and abominable in war.[21]

The opportunity to strike a blow at German economic resources overrode for Churchill any reservations about adding the USSR to Britain's active enemies. Churchill reverted to the kind of anti-Bolshevik rhetoric he had eschewed since 1936, but his motivation had nothing to do with the USSR, and everything to do with using operations in the Arctic as a pretext to interrupt the ore traffic from Sweden to Germany that ran through the north Norwegian port of Narvik. Churchill also shared French fears that the Western Front would develop into a bloody stalemate, and sought other ways of striking at Germany on its peripheries.

The Norwegian and Swedish refusal to allow passage of Allied troops, and the capitulation of Finland on 13 March 1940, put a stop to plans for an expeditionary force of 100,000 men, though Churchill still hoped to carry out the part of the operation which interested him most, the occupation of Narvik.[22] Ironically, it was the failure of this and the fiasco of the whole Norwegian campaign which provided the catalyst to sweep Chamberlain out of 10 Downing Street, and Churchill in.

Churchill's First Message to Stalin

With the Battle of France, the collapse of that country and the Battle of Britain, the new prime minister had more pressing matters to attend to than relations with the Soviet Union. It has been suggested, however, that the appointment of the left-wing MP Sir Stafford Cripps as the new ambassador to Moscow is an indication that Churchill immediately sought to improve relations with the USSR by indicating that the old Chamberlainite hostilities were no longer a guiding influence in the British Government. Back in October 1939 Cripps noted in his diary that he had spent an hour with Churchill discussing the Soviet Union and found they had much in common. He noted that Churchill 'thought it would be a good thing if I could go to Russia, and eagerly threw out the suggestion I might go as Ambassador – which I did not encourage as it would be, I think, of little help'.[23] The initiative in May 1940 for Cripps' appointment, however, came from elsewhere – and in any case it was not intended that he would be the permanent British representative in Moscow.

It was Labour leader Clement Attlee who suggested on 15 May that a minister on a special mission be sent to Moscow to follow up hints that Cripps had reported from a meeting he had had with the Soviet Commissar for Foreign Affairs, Vyacheslav Molotov, back in February, and subsequently reiterated by Maisky, that the Soviets were ready to negotiate a trade agreement. Attlee's proposal was made at least partly to balance the despatch of Samuel Hoare to Madrid, which would inevitably arouse criticism from Attlee's own party. Cripps himself was not Attlee's choice, nor was he favoured by the new Minister of Economic Warfare, Labour's Hugh Dalton. The Foreign Office had a career diplomat, Maurice Peterson, in mind for the Moscow post.[24] Foreign Secretary Lord Halifax was the one who approached Cripps to undertake a mission to Moscow, feeling that he would be fresh and *persona grata* there.[25] Cripps was invited to go as a special envoy to discuss Soviet attitudes on various questions of interest to the Ministry of Economic Warfare and other departments, but he was not to reach any agreements.[26] The Soviet Government insisted that Cripps be appointed as full ambassador or they would not accept him at all. The Cabinet was serious enough in its desire to improve relations – or at least reach an economic agreement that restricted Soviet trade with Germany – to bow to this pressure and allow the Soviet government to effectively decide who was British ambassador in Moscow.[27] The Soviets for their part wanted to de-emphasise the 'specialness' of the Cripps mission: the appointment of a new ambassador could be presented to their German ally as merely routine and not signifying any desire to re-orient the relationship with Germany.

While Cripps' appointment itself did not signify anything significant with regards to Churchill's policy to the USSR, he did seize the opportunity offered by the high profile of Cripps' mission to open communications directly with Stalin. Cripps was given a message to him, although at this point Stalin occupied no official position in the Soviet Government. Churchill had been communicating directly with the US President, Franklin D. Roosevelt, since September 1939.

Whereas with Roosevelt, Churchill appealed to sentiment and common cultural connections as well as to issues of national security, Churchill from the start approached Stalin in terms of realism.

It is tempting to see Churchill's first message to Stalin as an attempt by him to open a similar connection to the Soviet leader as the one he had forged with Roosevelt. While the link with Roosevelt had been very much on Churchill's own initiative, his first contact with Stalin was made at the suggestion of the Foreign Office. It was put forward by an official, Fitzroy Maclean, who was a leading sceptic on Soviet policy and who felt the best way to influence Stalin was by threats. Maclean firmly believed that the Soviet aim was to achieve mutual exhaustion of the belligerents. Maclean thought that it might be worth trying a combination of a promise to 'take legitimate Soviet requirements into consideration' were the Soviets to help defeat Germany, with the threat of attacks on the oil in the Caucasus if they continued their present policy. Maclean's proposal developed into the draft message for Churchill to send to Stalin through Cripps, suggesting Stalin re-examine his position with regards to German hegemony in Europe. Maclean argued that Stalin, who he characterised as 'shrewd and on the whole open-minded', would be prepared to consider the arguments fairly, if put to him in a cogent form by Churchill, whom he no doubt realised meant business.[28]

Churchill was probably less cynical than Maclean, and certainly maintained a less rigid attitude with regards to the immutability of Soviet relations with Germany. He accepted the idea of opening communications with Stalin, and the message he sent was lacking in any element of threat. Churchill did not intend to go further without a sign from the Soviets. He did no more than state in clear, unequivocal terms his view of events, with little optimism that Stalin's attitude would be appreciably altered, though it was a test of sorts to see how worried the Soviet leadership was about the extent of German triumphs. In that sense, it was an appeal to Stalin's self-interest, couched in terms of the realities of power. It pointed out that a new situation had arisen, and suggested that the two powers take cognisance of this and be prepared to consult together. Churchill tried to use geopolitical concepts to bridge the ideological gap he saw no sense in hiding or ignoring. Britain and the USSR lay on the extremities of Europe and were therefore in a position to resist Germany. British policy was to resist, and to free the rest of Europe. Churchill hoped that this would make it plain to Stalin that though Britain was not 'running after him in order to pull its chestnuts out of the fire', the Government *had* changed its ideas and was now ready to discuss with the Soviets the defeat of Germany's ambitions. Stalin was left to draw his own conclusion as to how his interests were affected by Germany's bid for European hegemony.[29]

There were no concrete proposals, nor offers of concessions, and any potential improvement was linked specifically to the matter of common interest against Germany. To this kind of communication Stalin rarely gave satisfactory answers – he responded better to firm proposals. Cripps' interview with Stalin followed different lines to those proposed, as the Soviet leader affected to see in

Churchill's message a desire to enlist the Soviet Union in an attempt to re-establish the 'old equilibrium' in Europe.[30]

There was no follow-up from Churchill. The message was only a new start in policy in so far as it contained the precept which was to be the basis of Churchill's attitude after the Soviet Union entered the war, namely that ideological differences need not stand in the way of a coming-together in the face of the German danger. This did not bear immediate fruit on either the Soviet or the British side. The aim had been to help Cripps – and the message at least enabled him to make contact with Stalin. It was consistent with Churchill's style of government to start some sort of personal contact with the leader of a large and potentially important country, though he was not yet taken with the idea of any kind of relationship with Stalin based on that contact, such as he was later to attempt. The policy that followed was one of reserve.

The obvious fact, reiterated by Molotov on 1 August, that Soviet-German relations were too firm to be shaken meant that Cripps' work in Moscow was fruitless and Anglo-Soviet relations remained on the icy side of cool. The Soviet Union continued to trade with Germany and maintained what amounted to hostile neutrality towards Britain. An approach by Cripps to the Soviet Government to make a wide political agreement was ignored, and Molotov's visit to Berlin in the same month, November, seemed to herald even closer ties between Germany and the USSR. (Though this was not actually the case, as Molotov refused a number of German requests, intended to turn Soviet interest away from the Balkans to the Middle East and India.)[31]

Churchill's Second Message to Stalin

Unlike most of his military advisors, Churchill did consider that a breach between Germany and the USSR might come as a result of a German decision to end it by attacking. This derived from his views of German-Soviet relations as inherently unstable. As early as June 1940, he had told Jan Smuts, 'if Hitler fails to beat us here he will probably recoil eastwards. Indeed he may do this without attempting an invasion [of Britain] ...'[32] In October, Churchill took the view at a Defence Committee meeting that Germany would inevitably turn on the USSR in 1941, and that the USSR, needing its oil for agriculture, would have to fight or starve.[33] Although he saw Britain as Germany's main enemy, Churchill was flexible enough to see the probability of an attack on the USSR before Britain was defeated, which was at odds with the views of his own military intelligence departments. That he did so was not the result of his having different sources of information but because of his assumptions about the mutability of the German-Soviet relationship.[34]

Thus, in January 1941, in the face of judgments by the military intelligence departments and the Foreign Office that Soviet-German relations 'appeared to be as close as at any time' since summer 1939, he again referred to the chances of a conflict in the east. A month later he concluded that the Soviets were in an unenviable position and that their current policy was to make concessions to gain time.[35] He saw their attitude as 'uncertain', but hoped it would remain 'loyal and friendly' – an odd formulation for the time, by which he meant giving no aid to German attempts to increase their influence in the Balkans. Soviet fear of Germany, he told Turkish president Ismet Inönu, could be balanced by the presence of British bomber squadrons capable of threatening the oil in Baku and Romania. The Soviets, Churchill continued to believe, responded to realities of power – though the reality at this point was that any British threat was an empty one, since no such bomber force was available.[36]

Churchill was more receptive than many when evidence began to appear that an attack might well happen, and to read it correctly. He did expect Hitler to make far-reaching demands first. Since he saw Hitler's main aim still to be the defeat of Britain, these demands would serve a twofold aim of building up his strength and removing the threat in his rear. His forces were being deployed to increase the pressure, with the plan that they would then be relocated westwards. Churchill expected a German ultimatum to the USSR, but also clearly saw in the meticulous preparations, involving support units as well as front-line divisions, that Hitler was prepared to attack should his pressure not attain the desired results. In this he was more clear-sighted than many of his advisors. Where he was mistaken was in seeing it in terms of Hitler's war with Britain, rather than as Hitler's new and overriding aim.[37]

It was difficult for outside observers to tell from the actions of the Soviet Government whether they expected an attack and were playing for time, or whether they did not see it coming at all and believed their own protestations that Soviet-German relations were as cordial as ever. Not enough was known of their military movements to indicate whether they were taking any defensive precautions. They did seem to be making every effort to be friendly to the Germans – intelligence suggested that supply of war materials from the USSR was on the increase. Churchill's view was that Soviet policy was aimed at preventing involvement in the war by any means. He was quick to attach significance to German troop movements in Poland, which had been reported without comment in the Chiefs of Staff (COS) résumé of 27 March 1941.[38] He later said that this came like a 'lightning flash', but actually it took him some days to react. On 30 March he noted to Foreign Secretary Anthony Eden that 'the moment he [Hitler] was sure Yugoslavia was in the Axis he moved three of the five Panzers towards the Bear'.[39] Churchill resolved to send a warning and he drafted it on 3 April. He hoped he would achieve some credit with the Soviet leader by warning Stalin that his appeasement policy was not working, and that this might eventually lead to regular contact. Once again, his message was made short and factual, leaving Stalin to draw his own conclusions. Churchill described the movement of the German divisions, and concluded 'Your Excellency will readily appreciate the significance of these facts'.[40]

Churchill hoped that this would come as a 'lightning flash' to Stalin as it had to him. If so, it might convince him of Britain's goodwill and desire to help the Soviets now they were threatened by the enemy. Churchill was encouraged by the Soviet response towards the anti-Nazi coup in Belgrade, which he later described as 'the one flash of sentiment from the usual cold-blooded, crafty, immoral, sub-human calculation of self-interest'.[41]

The handling of Churchill's message, and its impact – or lack of it – has been subject to controversy, fanned by Churchill's own later complaints about Cripps' actions. The fact is that it got caught up with initiatives by both Eden and Cripps. These were also intended to bring about a shift in Soviet attitudes, but the result was confusion.[42] Ultimately, though, whatever Churchill later wrote, the lack of progress was the result of the rapid collapse of the Yugoslav regime, rather than mishandling by the ambassador in Moscow.

The lack of political content or weighty propositions in Churchill's message led Cripps, unaware that it was based on intercepted German air force signals, to regard it as less significant than a complex approach he had designed to exploit apparent Soviet concerns about German penetration into the Balkans. The Soviet government had cut its shipments of oil to Germany and was making supportive gestures towards the new regime in Belgrade that had overthrown Prince Paul after he had succumbed to German pressure and agreed to join the Axis.[43] Cripps took the view that his approach, being more comprehensive, should have prece-dence, and failed to deliver the PM's message until pressed to do so.[44] By that time, 19 April, the situation in Yugoslavia had changed and the Soviet govern-ment was frantically trying to restore its previous relationship with Germany.

Churchill was annoyed the ambassador took so long to hand over his message and that when he did so spoke in such a way (to Deputy Foreign Commissar Andrei Vyshinsky) that suggested it was of little significance. To the Soviets the delay would seem as if the British attached no importance to the message whereas Churchill, typically, was trying to reach Stalin on a personal level by this offer of gratuitous information.[45] Later in the year, Churchill meditated on what he saw as a lost opportunity. He regarded as amazing 'effrontery' Cripps' action in delaying the message because he had sent his own discourse on the Balkans to Vyshinsky. It showed, Churchill believed, that he had no sense of proportion. 'Sir Stafford Cripps had great responsibility for his obstinate, obstructive handling of this matter. If he had obeyed his instructions, it is more than possible that some kind of relationship would have been constructed between me and Stalin.'[46]

While it is doubtful that Cripps' actions mattered that much, the remark is revealing as to what was in Churchill's mind. At the time, Churchill expressed the point in a different way, but which still gives a foretaste of his attitude towards Stalin throughout the war. Eden and some of his officials had made tentative steps towards trying to use the Yugoslav situation to alter Anglo-Soviet relations on political matters.[47] For Churchill, the basis for progress should be the hard facts of the war situation, and the person to deal with was Stalin. It was no use getting embroiled in trying to build a political relationship separate from and in advance of progress in that area.[48] He restated his realist interpretation by com-menting to Eden that the Soviets

> know perfectly well their danger and also that we need their aid. You will get
> more out of them by letting forces work than by frantic efforts to assure

them of your love. This only looks like weakness and encourages them to believe that they are stronger than they really are. Now is the moment for a sombre restraint on our part, and let them do the worrying.[49]

No such relationship was constructed before the German invasion of the USSR: indeed, it is difficult to see on what it would have been based. Churchill's interest was, if not to gain an ally against Germany, to at least bring the USSR to a state of true neutrality, whereas Stalin was anxious to avoid war with Germany for as long as possible, and would do anything to achieve that end short of jeopardising Soviet ability to resist when that attack might come. Stalin was well aware of Britain's situation and had a long-standing view that the British were cunning practitioners of foreign policy moves that drew others into defending their own interests ('pulling their chestnuts out of the fire').[50] He therefore discounted warnings received from British sources (even his own agents) on the grounds that they were designed to embroil the USSR in the war with Germany that the British had failed to bring about in the Moscow negotiations of 1939. Soviet officials maintained an uncommunicative attitude to the British Government and media outlets presented a pose of unconcern despite the warnings. Churchill's message would have confirmed such an interpretation, and in doing so given the opposite impression to that intended by Churchill.[51] Thus on 14 June, a day after Eden had seen Maisky and offered help to the USSR with arms and a military mission when it was attacked (which Maisky denied would happen), a public refutation was published by TASS of rumours that Germany was about to attack. It declared that such rumours were made by certain powers interested in damaging German-Soviet relations, which however remained as solid as ever, based on mutual self-interest.[52]

On 15 June, Churchill told Roosevelt in a telegram:

It looks as if a vast German onslaught on Russia is imminent. Should this new war break out we shall of course give all encouragement and any help we can spare to the Russians, following the principle that Hitler is the foe that we have to beat.[53]

To many commentators, this principle mattered more to Churchill than other ones for most of the war. He reiterated it to his secretary Jock Colville on 21 June, when Colville asked him, remembering the part he had played in inspiring the intervention in 1919–20 and his detestation of Communism, whether the German invasion of the USSR might not put him in an awkward predicament. He replied 'If Hitler invaded Hell, I would at least make a favourable reference to the Devil in the House of Commons'.[54] There is certainly no record of Churchill expressing the sentiment to be heard in some right-wing circles and the expression of which earned Moore-Brabazon, Minister of Aircraft Production, his dismissal in the autumn, that it would be a good thing if Germany and Russia fought each other to exhaustion leaving Britain and America dominant in Europe. However, as we will see, it was a view ascribed to him by Maisky and by Stalin.

It is sometimes asserted that Churchill's decision to go to the aid of the USSR was a spontaneous one, made on the day of the invasion. However, discussions with Maisky by both Eden and Cripps in the days before Barbarossa clearly fore-shadowed it. Moreover, on 22 June itself, before Churchill's broadcast in the evening, Maisky called at the Foreign Office and Eden reiterated the offer of a military mission to be sent to Moscow.[55] There has been some speculation about who may have influenced the actual wording of the broadcast. Churchill was at the prime minister's country house, Chequers. He saw many people there during the course of that day: Sir John Dill (Chief of the Imperial General Staff), 'Gil' Winant (the US Ambassador) and Cripps were staying for the weekend. Eden and Lord Beaverbrook, Minister of Supply, arrived during the day. Though his speech apparently was not ready until twenty minutes before it was broadcast at nine o'clock on the evening of 22 June, this may only have been a matter of revision, not indecision.[56] The policy in the speech was undoubtedly Churchill's own, and though he may have sought the advice of those at Chequers, Colville asserts that he kept his speech away from Eden and Cadogan, the Permanent Under-secretary at the Foreign Office, in case they should want to tone it down – it was likely that they would have done so, as Churchill rather carelessly left some political hostages to fortune in his rhetorical flourishes. His statement that the 'Russians' were standing on the 'threshold of their land' seemed to accept the conquests of the Nazi-Soviet pact era as legitimate parts of 'Russia' (let alone the USSR). His statement that all who marched with Hitler were Britain's enemies came back to haunt him when later in the year Stalin demanded declarations of war on the other Axis states that had joined with the Germans in their invasion. Specifics of rhetoric apart, it seems very likely that Churchill had already decided upon the line it would take some time before. His broadcast to the nation left no doubt where Britain stood:

> The Nazi regime is indistinguishable from the worst features of Communism. It is devoid of all ... principle except appetite and racial domination. It excels all forms of human wickedness in the efficiency of its cruel and ferocious aggression. No one has been a more consistent opponent of Communism than I have for the last twenty-five years, I will unsay no word that I have said about it. But all this fades away before the spectacle which is now unfolding. The past with its crimes, its follies, its tragedies flashes away. I see the Russian soldiers standing on the threshold of their native land, guarding the fields which their fathers have tilled from time immemorial. I see them guarding their homes where mothers and wives pray – ah yes, for there are times when all pray – for the safety of their loved ones, for the return of the breadwinner, of their champion, of their protector. I see, then, ten thousand villages of Russia, where the means of existence was wrung so hardly from the soil, but where there are still primordial human joys, where maidens laugh and children play.
>
> ... I have to make the declaration, but can you doubt what our policy will be? We have but one aim and one single irrevocable purpose. We are resolved to destroy Hitler and every vestige of the Nazi regime. From this nothing will turn us – nothing ...

... Any man or state who fights on against Nazidom will have our aid. Any man or state who marches with Hitler is our foe ...

... The Russian danger is therefore our danger, and the danger of the United States, just as the cause of any Russian fighting for his hearth and home is the cause of free men and free peoples in every quarter of the globe. Let us learn the lessons already taught by such cruel experience. Let us re-double our exertions and strike with united strength while life and power remain.[57]

Churchill chose the heightened, archaic and romanticised language of the broadcast carefully. He had shown in his communications with Roosevelt that he was sensitive to the domestic political issues raised by aligning with the USSR, as well as the likely reaction of significant elements of American opinion. He thus avoided describing the Soviets as 'allies', and interestingly set 'Communism' as the benchmark of a terrible regime, to which level the Nazis had sunk.

The emphasis on 'Russia' was quite deliberate, as a political device. It also reflected the way that Churchill had come already to separate out the Communist Soviet Union as a political entity and actor in international relations through the Comintern, from the geopolitical entity of the USSR – as essentially Russia by another name. It was domestically important to do this, and Churchill was very much at pains to make clear that it did not change his hostility to Communism. He was saying that one could support the Soviet Union (as 'Russia') and not be at the same time favouring Communism. He had already attempted (unsuccessfully) to forge a connection with Stalin as the leader of the latter entity, appealing solely along such lines. There is little evidence that Churchill had thought extensively about Stalin himself and reached this characterisation of him through analysis, though this did square with his earlier thoughts about Stalin's purges being an attempt at crushing hard-line Bolsheviks in favour of a more realist approach – it was rather that if the geopolitical USSR did exist, then it was in Stalin that its leadership would repose. It was only subsequently that this became developed into an attitude based upon deductive reasoning, from interactions with Stalin, and even then, as we shall see, an element of wish-fulfilment was to remain. It might also be argued, right from the start of Churchill's initiatives towards Stalin, incorporating both the two initial messages and the broadcast of 22 June, that Churchill was attempting to draw such an entity – Stalin the war-lord comrade-in-arms, motivated by geopolitical concern to defeat Hitler – into being by effectively inviting Stalin into participating in such a relationship. It could be argued that he had already embarked on a similar project to create a Roosevelt as 'friend-of-the-British-Empire'.

The Churchill-Stalin Correspondence Begins

Churchill's message to Roosevelt of 15 June had flagged up the issue of political alliance with the USSR, and this was to be a matter that attracted some attention immediately. The first problem in Anglo-Soviet relations was how Britain was to help its new-found ally. Churchill's heightened language in the broadcast masked the fact that he was careful to offer no specific aid or name any actions that Britain would take. The day after Churchill's statement aligning Britain with the Soviet fight, discussion with ministers revealed the misgivings many had on both right and left with regard to British public reactions to a close relationship with the USSR. Eden and the Minister of Information, Alfred Duff Cooper, argued that 50 per cent of British public opinion would be hostile to an alliance.[58] On 27 June, Molotov raised with Cripps the issue of a political alliance, and was told that military and economic arrangements were all that was necessary. A political agreement could come at the peace conference, when 'we had all learnt to trust each other'.[59] This accurately reflected the approach that Churchill followed as he began to try and build a working relationship with Stalin, and indeed it was to remain central to Churchill's attitude for some time after Eden and the Foreign Office and some other colleagues in the government, such as Lord Beaverbrook, as well as Cripps himself, had abandoned it.

Stalin repeated Molotov's request for a political arrangement when he met Cripps on 8 July, though he indicated that all he had in mind was a declaration that the two states would aid each other and not make a separate peace. Churchill was pleased with this, while indicating to Eden that he would be happy with a mention of a more specific political matter – namely the Soviet frontiers, enlarged as they had been under the secret protocol of the Nazi-Soviet Pact. He proposed a statement that frontiers should be based on ethnicity, and settled on the basis of the wishes of the peoples, who should be free to choose their own form of government. Eden warned him off such a statement, which clearly challenged the legitimacy of the Soviet annexations of 1939–40, and the Cabinet agreed to the mutual assistance agreement along the lines Stalin had proposed. The declaration was signed in Moscow on 12 July.[60]

Churchill had already composed his first message to Stalin in the new context. He immediately set the tone he would follow consistently throughout this correspondence. He praised the 'bravery and tenacity of the Soviet soldiers and people' and promised to do everything to help that 'time, geography and our growing resources allow'. A typical combination of a statement of the limits and hints at future *largesse* and action. This was followed by a fulsome account of RAF activity over Germany, which asserted that the main way that Britain would draw German strength away from the Soviet front would be by bombing. Churchill concluded 'we have only to go on fighting to beat the life out of these villains'.[61] Having received as yet no hint of a communication from Stalin, this was a shot in the dark by Churchill, an attempt at establishing some kind of warlord relationship – the beginning of a process that he was to describe in February 1943 as 'wooing Stalin like a maid' – though it bore closer relation to trying to bond with him as a fellow warrior.[62] Stalin did not reply, though he did see Cripps that day.[63]

The outcome was the Anglo-Soviet mutual assistance agreement, and Churchill's second message reported the War Cabinet's concurrence.[64] It was not until 18 July that Stalin eventually responded, with a message that began by identifying Britain and the Soviet Union now as 'fighting allies'. With the situation on the Soviet-German front deteriorating catastrophically, Stalin adopted a frank, frantic tone, seeking to make the promises in the agreement concrete and immediate, and involving operations as well as supply of munitions. He made no bones about admitting the USSR's serious position, while taking the opportunity to justify the 1939–40 annexations by pointing out how it would have been still worse if the Soviet forces had started by defending 'the region of Odessa, Kamenets Podolski, Minsk and the environs of Leningrad'. He pressed for the opening of fronts in northern France and Norway. Churchill responded regretfully but in matter-of-fact terms, claiming the French coast had been fortified 'diligently' by the Germans for over a year, and that a landing would only lead to a 'bloody defeat', without drawing any force away from the Soviet Front.[65]

Eden pressed on Churchill the need for some action rather than words, while the COS counselled caution and were opposed to any dissipation of British resources, either as supplies or as expeditions to fight alongside the Soviets. Much as he regretted not being able to answer Stalin's pleas for the establishment of fronts in North France and the Arctic with anything more than the RAF's (rather meagre at this time) bombing of Germany and a flow of words, Churchill too believed that Operation Sealion had merely been postponed, and knew full well that there was little within Britain's means that it could do materially to affect the course of fighting in the USSR that summer. The only answer was to exhort resistance and promise aid from what the Americans were supplying to Britain. What Churchill did do was attempt immediately to open his own regular line of communication with Stalin, much as he had done, very successfully, with Roosevelt. Eden was disturbed by Churchill's evident intention to do this, and accused him of trying to become involved in day-to-day diplomacy. He was: Churchill subsequently apologised for being 'tiresome' – but did not alter his approach.[66] Eden was often consulted, but the main channel to the top of the Soviet Government was throughout the war to be Churchill-Stalin, rather than Eden-Molotov. Eden was left to rue what he saw as Churchill's 'emotional' approach to foreign relations.[67] Oliver Harvey, Eden's Private Secretary, noted in his diary on 28 July:

> P.M. is developing a regular correspondence with Stalin by private telegraph – much to A.E's concern. P.M's style is becoming so sentimental and florid that Cripps has telegraphed privately to A.E. to try and restrain him. We fear that it will have the worst effect on Stalin who will think guff no substitute for guns.[68]

Harvey, like Beaverbrook, the Minister of Supply, was to be almost continually frustrated by the apparent lack of eagerness to help the USSR. Eden, on whom he had some influence, also at this time took a stand in favour of helping the USSR. Churchill listened to Eden, and he listened to Beaverbrook, also to the less enthusiastic Labour ministers, Attlee and Bevin, and to the COS who were not enthusiastic at all. As a result, Churchill moved to a position that sat between all these positions (and attracted criticism from both sides). Thus, while delivering the flattery that Harvey characterised as 'guff', Churchill was also prepared to be frank. His early correspondence with Stalin therefore contained a mixture of fulsome compliments and hard-nosed military realism.

The challenge for Churchill was to try to assure the Soviet leader that the British commitment to his cause was a genuine one, and at the same time establish the limits of what was possible, without revealing more information than was felt to be prudent. The military missions in Moscow and London, which might have been the conduits for the frank provision of detailed information, never fulfilled this function. Instead, Churchill sought to present his case in carefully-chosen words, appealing to Stalin as a realist while being niggardly with detailed substantiation. Churchill sought to use his skill with the written word to bridge the gap. The result was often the over-flowery language that Harvey derided as 'guff' not guns. The problem with the method was that Stalin's own taste was for detailed picking-over of language and disputation of theses and the detail of exposition and the result was that the relationship between 'Churchill-on-paper' and 'Stalin-on-paper' was to follow a quite different trajectory and to involve levels of tension that were quite at odds with the way that their relationship developed in their face-to-face personal contacts. Both worked on their style and approach, attempting to manipulate and persuade the other on paper, over the course of the next four years, with limited success.[69]

The immediate problem, though, was the desperation of the Soviet situation. Cripps argued repeatedly that the Soviet leaders were deeply suspicious of British motives, and that this prompted Stalin's increasingly caustic tone. If it did, it was ill-advised, for Maisky should have reported from his own knowledge of Churchill that this was quite the wrong way to get a positive response. Instead, Maisky was misinterpreting the caution of the British military about what they regarded as wasting resources on a front the outcome of which they could not affect. Maisky always had a tendency to magnify the importance of anti-Soviet figures – the so-called 'Cliveden set'. The ambassador fed back to Moscow an exaggerated estimate of the prevalence of the view that Britain should watch on the sidelines while Germany and the USSR mutually destroyed each other: a school of thought, moreover, which preferred an intact Germany, rid of Hitler, to a powerful Soviet Union.[70]

Maisky also reported Churchill's reservations about the readiness – and indeed ability – of Britain's army to engage with the Wehrmacht. Stalin's message to Churchill, handed by Vyshinsky to Cripps on 3 September for onward transmission, reflected the desperate situation on the Soviet front. Once again, Stalin frankly admitted the USSR faced mortal danger and warned that without a second front it might be defeated completely, or at the least left so weak as to be unable to keep on with active operations. He did so now in a tone of complaint at British inaction, the clear message being that the British could act if they wanted, or if they had the courage. If the British really could not open a front in the West, Stalin proposed the despatch of forces to fight in the USSR, and declarations of war on Romania, Hungary and Finland.[71]

While Churchill might press his COS for more action, he responded badly to such promptings from others: Maisky may have misjudged his man, though the ambassador's diary reveals that although he knew such a goading message might not get any progress on the main issue, he hoped that it would lead the British to make bigger efforts on what Maisky called 'secondary' matters, such as supplies. Churchill spoke rebukingly to the ambassador and initially framed a very sharp reply, which he put to the Cabinet.[72] He thought better of this, and toned it down, but it was still robust, emphasising the impossibility of opening a second front.[73]

Cripps saw Stalin on 7 September and reported him to be tired and depressed, suspicious and pessimistic.[74] To Cripps, Churchill said that what Stalin was demanding meant 'an effort rising superior to space, time and geography' and 'these attributes are denied us'.[75]

Aid to the Soviet Union

Even as he made his justifications to Stalin, Churchill was hectoring the COS about providing help for the Soviets. Churchill supported Beaverbrook when he started to press the Soviet cause. At Beaverbrook's suggestion, supplies were promised instead of military operations, despite the protests of the War Office and the Air Ministry.[76] This was a political decision, since the munitions would not arrive in time to help in the Soviet Union's immediate plight. Stalin's request, made on 13 September, for a British army of twenty-five to thirty divisions to serve on the Soviet front, was not immediately answered, with Churchill pleading shipping difficulties and raising a favourite side-issue of relations with Turkey.[77] Churchill's reply of 17 September had avoided specifically mentioning sending troops to the Soviet southern front, and Maisky reproached Eden with this, since Britain had 600,000 men in the Middle East. When the British did consider the idea, it was in terms of sending troops into the Caucasus, which was not what Stalin had in mind.[78]

It was agreed in late August that Beaverbrook should go to Moscow in September to reach agreement over what supplies the Soviets needed and what Britain could spare. Churchill later claimed that he saw Beaverbrook's role in the Cabinet as balancing, along with Eden, the views of the Service ministers and the COS and went on to greatly overstate the alterations to British plans that resulted: 'I tried to keep the main proportion evenly presented in my own mind . . . we endured the unpleasant stresses of exposing our own vital security and projects to failure for the sake of our new ally – surly, snarly, grasping and so lately indifferent to our survival.'[79]

Beaverbrook's advocacy of the Soviet cause was useful to Churchill in his own tussles with the military chiefs. On the other hand, Churchill had no intention of allowing himself to be dominated by his old friend's view. Before Beaverbrook's mission to Moscow, he told him:

> It is our duty and our interest to give the utmost possible aid to the Russians even at risk of serious sacrifices by ourselves. However, no large flow can begin till the middle or end of 1942, and the main planning will relate to 1943. Your function will be not only to aid in the forming of the plans to

help Russia, but to make sure we are not bled white in the process, and even if you find yourself affected by the Russian atmosphere, I shall be quite stiff about it here. I am sure however that you are the man for the job, and the public instinct has already endorsed this.[80]

Thus, while pressing his own military to find ways to help the Soviet war effort, Churchill remained sensitive to what he regarded as insults or unacceptable Soviet claims about the unimpeachable nature of their own attitude. He had no sympathy for those who argued that Britain had to make the active moves, and act as if their previous attitudes had been wrong. Coming on the top of Soviet gripes about what they were being given – when Churchill had gone out on a limb with his own military – he was provoked to respond to both Cripps and Stalin explosively. It is possible also that Churchill felt less need to accommodate the Soviets since their resistance had won the necessary breathing space: Britain could be sure by mid-September that it would not face a German invasion that year. He felt no moral obligation to Stalin, and brutally stated in a letter to Cripps in October, 'They brought their own fate upon themselves when by their Pact with Ribbentrop they let Hitler loose on Poland and so started the war'.[81] With regard to military liaison, Churchill remarked '[T]hey are far more dependent on us than we on them', a view not reflected in his hyperbolic statement to Stalin soon after: 'Words are useless to express what we feel about your vast, heroic struggle. We hope presently to testify by action.'[82]

The most strident demands from the Soviet Government were for immediate military aid – either attacks on the Germans in the West, or despatch of large-scale fighting forces to the Soviet front and supply of munitions and other war materiel. Stalin also raised political issues, anxious to ascertain how much he could count on his new allies. Having already asked for declarations of war on Finland, Hungary and Romania, when he met Beaverbrook he suggested a formal alliance. Cripps, Eden and Beaverbrook, albeit from differing perspectives, thought that the impracticality of satisfying Stalin on military issues meant that focus should be on building better political relations by conceding on some of these issues. As Eden argued to Ambassador Winant, the Soviets needed to be drawn out of their suspicions and brought into regular cooperation. Otherwise prospects for the future were bleak.[83]

In October and November 1941, when the war situation became acute, Churchill's relations with Stalin came close to breaking down. Eden had raised the issue of an alliance with the War Cabinet on 13 October.[84] He was authorised to discuss it with Maisky, which he did, but discussions quickly became bogged down on the issue of declaration of war on Finland, Hungary and Romania.[85] Beaverbrook and Eden favoured this, as a substitute for sending troops to the USSR or opening a second front. Churchill and the Labour ministers opposed it, on the grounds that it would simply drive the three countries further into coalition with Hitler.[86]

The Stalin-Churchill correspondence had already become distinctly direct and undiplomatic in tone and content. Churchill saw Stalin as a realist who could face

facts, but was also considerably riled by Cripps' arguments about Soviet suspicions of British motives and his continued refrain that the fault lay on the British
side. Churchill answered him robustly that the guilt was mainly Soviet, and while
his comments were made to Cripps (and the sharpest were not even actually
sent[87]), they tended to be reflected in the tone of his messages to Stalin. Stalin
responded in kind. When Churchill refused to declare war on the satellites, and
acted on Cripps' view that the Soviets needed to be involved in full and frank
discussions of strategy by offering to send two generals to Moscow, Stalin sent a
direct and bitter message. Alongside a number of complaints, made in the
brusquest tone, Stalin raised once again the question of a post-war arrangement
and complained about the lack of clarity in Anglo-Soviet relations, pointing to
the absence of agreed war aims or strategy.[88]

While making some allowance for the desperate military situation on the
approaches to Moscow and Leningrad, Churchill himself was deeply annoyed.[89]
Fortunately, perhaps, Cripps intervened in a series of long, whining telegrams,
reiterating his points and apologias for Soviet behaviour and diverting Churchill's
anger towards himself.[90] Meanwhile, Eden took the matter up with Maisky.[91] The
ambassador was prevailed upon to present a gloss on Stalin's message that
mollified Churchill while not actually losing Stalin any face by being a direct
retraction of anything he had said. Maisky said, for the record, that Stalin was very
preoccupied with the defence of Moscow and had been depressed by press leaks
about the declaration-of-war request, but he had not meant to offend or insult
anyone, especially not the Prime Minister.[92] This was as close to a direct apology
as might be expected, and was carefully orchestrated between Eden and Maisky.[93]

Mollified, Churchill then put forward his own olive branch on 21 November,
after a special Cabinet on the USSR, saying,

> The fact that Russia is a Communist State and that Britain and the USA are
> not and do not intend to be, is not any obstacle to our making a good plan
> for our mutual safety and rightful interests.

Now, Churchill agreed to the declaration of war on Finland, if Stalin really
thought it would help (for the Soviets it had clearly become a symbol, as Cripps
argued, of British willingness to cooperate with them), and to the exploration of
political issues that he had previously avoided. In place of the generals, Eden was
offered as an envoy, whose status it was hoped would indicate British seriousness.
Churchill noted that he had started a personal correspondence with Roosevelt at
the start of the war, and hoped for similar with Stalin, a conscious attempt to both
raise Stalin to the level of friend and also induct him into a 'Big Three'.[94] Stalin
responded in kind, and agreed that the differences in political systems need not
stand in the way of a political alliance based on the need to deal with the possibility of German (or Prussian, as Churchill liked to put it) resurgence.[95] Seven
days later, in an unprecedented gesture, Stalin wished Churchill a happy birthday.[96] The 'guff' element of communication had been restored, to be maintained
as a key lubricant of the relationship through to the end of the war. Not that the
'guff' element had disappeared: a couple of days before his birthday, Cadogan

noted that according to Beaverbrook, Churchill was still in an anti-Russian defeatist frame of mind.[97] Further evidence of how difficult it is to put a simple label on Churchill's views on Stalin and the Soviet Union is his decision to over-ride COS objections to sending the new Churchill tank to the Soviets. The Chiefs feared this new design falling prematurely into German hands: Churchill ruled that political grounds (servicing the alliance) took precedence.[98]

Stalin's Desire for a Political Alliance

Stalin's insistence on a political dimension to the alliance inevitably meant it was impossible to avoid confronting the Soviet demand for British recognition of its 1941 frontiers. In the absence of any means to give direct military aid, and concerned to bolster the Soviet will to resist, Eden went to Moscow to follow up the alliance suggestion Stalin had first made to Beaverbrook and then reiterated in his angry message of 8 November.[99] At the same time, Churchill travelled to the United States as a response to the Japanese attack on Pearl Harbor and on the British Empire in the East. Stalin demanded of Eden that the British recognise the annexations made by the Soviets during 1939–41 (Lithuania, Latvia, Estonia, Eastern Poland, Bessarabia, Northern Bukovina and parts of Finnish Karelia). Eden stalled him, but on his return to London argued that these demands should be conceded, in order to assuage Soviet suspicions, keep them fighting until Germany was completely defeated, and to build a post-war alliance to contain Germany.[100]

Churchill shared the views of his American hosts that such a concession was inadvisable, claiming that what mattered to the Soviets were not political issues but military assistance and supplies of munitions. Full of the first flush of opti-mism now that the USA was in the war, he asserted that the Soviets would have vast reconstruction needs after the war and would be faced with an economically strong Anglo-American bloc.[101] It was not long before it became evident that such simple assumptions about the solidarity and unanimity of Anglo-American cooperation were premature, and this may have been a factor in subsequent modifications in Churchill's attitude towards handling the Soviets and in partic-ular the relationship he attempted to construct with Stalin.

The War Cabinet debated the Soviet frontier demands in February, with Beaverbrook and Attlee lining up against each other.[102] When he failed to per-suade Churchill to make the concession, Beaverbrook resigned.[103] However, within a month, Churchill had changed his mind.[104] There is no clearly-stated and authoritative reason for this *volte-face* in the documentary record. David Carlton's view is that Churchill was influenced by the growing pro-Soviet tide in British public opinion, and also that he was now considering the unwelcome prospect that the Soviets, not the Anglo-Americans, would be the principal victors in Europe. Eden was certainly arguing that US involvement in post-war European affairs should not be taken for granted, and that if one posited an Allied victory then one had to face the reality of increased Soviet influence.[105] There is no direct evidence, however, that Churchill was thinking along these lines. Indeed, he is often represented as influenced not by apprehension of early Soviet victory, but by a fear they would suffer further catastrophic defeats. In March 1942, it was very unclear to British observers what the future held on the Soviet-German front. There were some signs that the Soviet winter counter-offensive, which had produced prematurely optimistic public statements by Stalin, had run out of momentum, but it was not clear where that would leave Germany in terms of its ability to launch another massive offensive in the summer. There was no reason as yet for the British to consider drastic concessions to try to keep the Soviets in the war.[106]

While he had ordered an investigation into the feasibility of an invasion of Western Europe, such as the Soviets were demanding, Churchill had deep reservations about the strategic wisdom of such a move. His first flush of enthusiasm for his new American allies had also been diminished by their evident optimism about the possibilities of such an operation during 1942 – an operation that would predominantly involve British units. It may well have been these factors that brought him to the conclusion to which Eden had come earlier, namely that political concessions were preferable to military operations he thought would be a disaster. An Anglo-Soviet alliance would not, as Cadogan said, prevent Stalin doing a 'double-cross' if he wanted to, but it might relieve some of his evident suspicions that the British were not committed to Soviet victory. Oliver Harvey and new CIGS General Alan Brooke both noted at the start of March that Churchill was talking about going to see Stalin, and Brooke mentioned specifically that the purpose would be to discuss post-war frontiers.[107]

A final element might have been pique with the Americans. Roosevelt had weighed in with the comment that Stalin distrusted the British, but liked him better, so perhaps things could be settled between the two of them.[108] Despite his determination to be the best of friends with Roosevelt, Churchill was not prepared to concede to him the leadership in relations with Stalin, and Roosevelt's attitude may well have strengthened Churchill's readiness to seize the initiative in order to achieve a closer Anglo-Soviet relationship. Roosevelt's evident intention not only to forge his own personal relationship with Stalin but also to speak for the British as well certainly seems to have struck Churchill, for even though he had indicated to the War Cabinet on 16 March that he agreed with Roosevelt, he made his own bid to play that role when he asked Maisky whether Stalin would welcome a visit from himself.[109] He was thinking of somewhere like Baku or Astrakhan. Maisky thought Stalin would come and meet him, but the idea was not taken further until the end of July 1942.

By then, the alliance had been formally established in the Anglo-Soviet Treaty, though without an agreement on frontiers. Churchill felt torn between his desire to improve relations with Stalin, who at the time was doing all the fighting, and also to work together with Roosevelt in building the special Anglo-American relationship which he saw as the key to winning the war. This dilemma was voiced by him to the Cabinet on 7 May, talking of the proposed draft treaty which at that point contained recognition of the 1941 Soviet frontiers: 'we ought to remember that this is a bad thing: we ought not to do it, and I shall not be sorry if we do not'.[110] Any idea that this comment reflected Churchill's moral objections to the 1941 frontiers is qualified a little by what he had said to Maisky a year earlier. On 20 July 1941 Maisky had visited Chequers to deliver Stalin's first message to the Prime Minister. Upon reading Stalin's statement about how much worse the Soviet position would have been had the attack come across the old frontiers, much further east, the ambassador noted Churchill as exclaiming, 'Quite right! I've always understood and sought to justify the policy of "limited expansion" which Stalin has pursued in the last two years.'[111] This, of course, was prior to the commitment made in the Atlantic Charter not to recognise territorial changes made during the war, unless made with the consent of the peoples involved.

Molotov came to London in May, and agreed to a 20-year treaty of cooperation in place of an overtly political arrangement, but he thought he had secured what the Soviets primarily wanted: a promise from Roosevelt of a second front in 1942. Churchill was at pains to point out to him that no promise had been made, only a statement that they would urgently investigate the possibilities.[112] It is often overlooked that before meeting with Stalin, Churchill had a series of meetings with Molotov. Many of the themes that subsequently arose in the meetings in Moscow were foreshadowed. In particular, Molotov repeatedly emphasised the view that the second front, while a military operation, was a political issue, and that the decision of when and where to do it was political.[113] This remained the Soviet position and both Molotov and Stalin staunchly resisted the repeated attempt by Churchill to have the focus shifted to discussion of military practicalities between the generals. As Stalin later said to him, the soldiers were merely consultants, not decision-makers (when he said this, in Moscow, Churchill agreed with him, though he might perhaps have wished for more of Stalin's dominance over his strategists, for he found it difficult to impose his will on his own 'consultants').[114]

Although Eden was present, and did the detailed negotiation on the Treaty, Churchill took the lead. He attempted to put across the potential problems with British public opinion and with the US people and government if the 1941 frontiers were recognised. Molotov answered by claiming Soviet public opinion was on his side. Churchill was also determined to put his views across on the difficulties of invading France in 1942 and found Molotov's determination to disregard all the practical considerations by continually reiterating that it was a political decision to be trying. The general atmosphere conveyed in the record is friendly enough, though the recorder (Maisky) made a point of noting Churchill's perpetual consumption of cigars and whisky.[115] The meetings were interrupted by Molotov's journey to Washington D.C. When they resumed, on 9 June, Churchill was at pains to qualify Roosevelt's rather loose statements about the desirability of a second front in France in 1942 and his willingness to accept the risk of high casualties and another Dunkirk. Since these casualties would be British, Churchill demurred. He also sharply dismissed Roosevelt's musings on the post-war world, most especially the 'world policemen' idea that would impose disarmament not only on defeated enemies, but on allies and neutrals. Churchill did make positive noises about a small-scale landing in France (six divisions), though the sharp Molotov picked up on his contradictions on this issue. More importantly, while he made clear that whatever Roosevelt had said, Britain had not promised a second front in France in 1942, he did make firm statements that they intended to do so in 1943.[116] The meetings ended with the appearance of cordiality and Churchill, who had told Molotov at one point that he wished to visit Stalin, wired to him that 'we have done a great deal towards beating down the barriers between the two countries'.[117]

The British then proceeded to persuade the Americans that even a large-scale raid, codenamed Sledgehammer, was out of the question in 1942. Churchill and Roosevelt agreed instead, against the inclinations of American military advisors, to launch an invasion of French North Africa, codenamed Gymnast (later changed to Torch).[118] The decision unfortunately coincided with the disaster of PQ17, the latest Anglo-American convoy bringing supplies to the USSR, which left Iceland on 27 June. Fearing attack by the German battleship *Tirpitz*, the Royal Navy escort had been withdrawn and the ships ordered to proceed independently. German submarines and aircraft took a terrible toll; only nine out of thirty-four vessels reached Soviet ports. Churchill's first response was to cancel further convoys until the end of the year. Moreover, the German offensive had material-ised and the Soviet armies were in full retreat to the Caucasus.[119] Stalin's reaction to Churchill's news was bitter and reproachful. He described the arguments of British experts as 'untenable', and implied that what was lacking was the will, willingness to risk losses, and the readiness to honour obligations. He went on,

As to ... opening a second front in Europe, I fear the matter is not being treated with the seriousness it deserves. In view of the situation on the Soviet-German front, I state most emphatically that the Soviet Government cannot tolerate the postponement of the second front in Europe until 1943.

I hope you will not take it amiss that I have seen fit to give you my frank and honest opinion and that of my colleagues on the points raised in your message.[120]

Stalin was (correctly) reading between the lines of Churchill's telegram of 18 July (as well as ignoring Churchill's statement to Molotov on 9 June): Churchill spoke of 'preparations going forward on a vast scale for Anglo-American mass invasion of the Continent'. But he had gone on to say 'Believe me, there is nothing that is useful and sensible that we and the Americans will not do to help you in your grand struggle. The President and I are ceaselessly searching for means of over-coming the extraordinary difficulties which the geography, sea-water and the enemy's air power interpose.' In justifying the suspension of the convoys to Arkhangelsk, he slipped in the comment that loss of command of the Atlantic would affect the build-up of US forces in Britain and a 'really strong second front in 1943' would be rendered impossible.[121] It is thus incorrect to depict Churchill's task when he went to Moscow in August as 'breaking the news' about the second front to Stalin.[122] Stalin knew, and not only from the accurate report he had received of Allied strategic decisions from the NKVD.[123] Churchill's reaction to the 23 July telegram from Stalin was angry, aggravated by bad news from the battlefield in Egypt, where the Eighth Army was in retreat. Maisky found Churchill drunk, depressed and offended all at the same time. The ambassador, however, thought the telegram was good tactics: 'Churchill is hot-tempered, but he is easily appeased. The stronger the shock, the greater the chances that Churchill will do the right thing.'[124]

Churchill's First Trip to Moscow

Typically, Churchill decided to go in person to Egypt and address what he suspected was a problem in the high command of the British forces. Without knowing of Churchill's plans, Sir Archibald Clark Kerr, who had replaced Cripps in Moscow in March 1942, wrote of his concern at Soviet reactions to the news concerning the second front and the convoys. Clark Kerr was an eccentric and unconventional diplomat, who attached great importance to personal interactions and emotional responses. Unlike Cripps, he had got on well in his first meeting with Stalin (the political situation having changed greatly) and felt that in a similar face-to-face meeting, Churchill would be able to impress Stalin with his fighting spirit and thereby modify the impression given by the recent decisions that the British were not prepared to engage the enemy to help the Soviets.[125] He suggested that Molotov might well have failed to convey this fighting spirit when he reported back to Stalin after his London mission. Clark Kerr suggested that a personal visit was the only way to explain the second front decision to Stalin, and thought it would be beneficial for the alliance as a whole for the two men finally to meet each other. Eden showed the telegram to Churchill, who was immediately taken with the idea and resolved to go on from Egypt to meet Stalin.[126]

Churchill wired to Stalin:

> We could survey the war together and take decisions hand-in-hand. I could then tell you plans we have made with President Roosevelt for offensive action in 1942.[127]

The idea appealed to Churchill for the same reasons that he had been considering such a trip earlier, now revived in his mind by Clark Kerr's suggestion. He later described his mission as 'like carrying a large lump of ice to the North Pole', but his aim was never simply to break the news that the second front would be in French North Africa, not Northern France.[128] That could be done by telegram and to go in person would only expose Churchill directly to Soviet reproaches. Neither before nor later was there any reluctance to send Stalin bad news either by telegram or by ambassadorial interview.

Churchill's decision to make this dangerous journey, about which he was clearly apprehensive, was based on his desire to do more than simply be an unwelcome messenger. Talking to Stalin in person was something he had been wishing to do since March, when it became obvious that strategic planning with the Americans would not be the smooth matter he originally anticipated. Success in persuading Stalin of the wisdom of Operation Torch would open up the possibilities of persuading him to share Churchill's overall strategic vision: 'closing the ring' by operations on the Axis periphery (notably the Mediterranean, Norway and bringing Turkey into the war) combined with relentless strategic bombing of Germany. Stalin's telegram of 20 June gave some grounds for hope that he recognised the benefits of operations on these two fronts.[129] This would have the further effect of starting meaningful Big Three cooperation with a bias towards Churchill's own strategic inclinations.

He was going to Moscow fresh from discovering that American planners had quite different strategic views, which meant that the reality of the Anglo-American part of Big Three cooperation was not going to be the smooth process, based on shared culture and values, that he had anticipated. Even though they had not been followed up beyond a conversation with Maxim Litvinov, the Soviet Ambassador in Washington, Roosevelt's suggestions that he should handle Stalin for the two of them led Churchill to seek to mould the still-undefined Allied relationship with the Soviets.

Churchill asked again for a meeting in Astrakhan or the Caucasus: Stalin insisted that he could not leave Moscow during the 'tense struggle' on the Soviet front. This is often depicted as typical Stalin callousness, exposing the 67-year-old Churchill to an extra 800 miles of hazardous flying, but Stalin had genuine reason to wish to keep at the centre of the direction of the war, quite apart from his own aversion to flying, with his vital southern front collapsing before his eyes. Churchill left for Egypt on 1 August, having written to King George VI that his hope for the Moscow leg of the trip was that 'I may perhaps make the situation less edged'. There were no preparatory briefs from either Foreign Office or the Chiefs of Staff Committee. This reflected both the rather *ad hoc* nature of the mission and also Churchill's main purpose, which was personally to engage with Stalin. For that he needed no advisors present. Rather belatedly he decided he would like an American representative and with Roosevelt's permission Averell Harriman joined the mission while Churchill was in Cairo. This may well have been influenced by the fact that Churchill found Harriman, Roosevelt's personal envoy in London, a most congenial travelling companion. Accompanied by his somewhat lightweight team of Harriman, Cadogan, Air Marshal Tedder of the Desert Air Force and Generals Brooke and Wavell, Churchill set off for Moscow via Tehran, arriving, with only his entourage and Harriman, on 12 August.[130]

This was a mission that Churchill's wife, Clementine, described to him as a 'visit to the Ogre in his Den'.[131] In most histories of the wartime coalition of Britain, the United States and the Soviet Union, it plays a small and insignificant part.[132] However, Churchill's mission should not be dismissed so lightly when examining the early development of the coalition: Churchill's meetings with Stalin established – despite great setbacks in the middle period of the mission – that this alliance could function as a viable entity, so long as all parties agreed tacitly to certain rules of engagement.

The first meeting between Churchill and Stalin took place the day he arrived. It was a small-scale, intimate affair, with Churchill accompanied only by Clark

Kerr, Harriman and the embassy interpreter, Charles Dunlop.[133] For such an important meeting, Churchill had done little preparation (it was not his habit to seek much in the way of briefing from his experts, particularly the diplomatic ones) and was relying on his personality to win over Stalin, who at this point he still rather underestimated as a simple-minded 'peasant'. It is a common criticism of Roosevelt that he placed too much reliance on his ability to 'charm' Stalin: Churchill's approach to this mission suggests that reliance on charm was not confined to Roosevelt, and indeed later in the mission, Stalin himself made an attempt (ultimately quite successful) to 'charm' his guest.

In addressing his task, Churchill adopted a tactic he had used before, with Roosevelt.[134] He began by stating the worst aspect to a problem, and then gave his compromise solution, which if presented at the start would have seemed inadequate. This approach appeared to bear fruit in this opening meeting. Churchill delivered the bad news immediately and without equivocation, telling Stalin that Anglo-American planners had ruled out a cross-Channel invasion in 1942. Stalin again expressed his disappointment with this decision, but Churchill sweetened the pill with a somewhat exaggerated description of the destruction being caused by British strategic bombing of Germany. He then sprang on the Soviet leader the plan to land in French North Africa. According to the British record, he drew a crocodile and said they would attack its soft belly as well as the hard snout. Stalin responded, 'may God help this enterprise to succeed'. Stalin quickly identified four reasons why this operation was advantageous: that it would attack the enemy in his undefended rear, it would make the Germans and French fight each other, it would put Italy out of action and it would keep the Spaniards neutral.[135] From these remarks it would appear that Stalin anticipated that the operations in the Mediterranean would expand beyond Torch's ostensible objective of the liberation of North Africa, though the Soviet record does not list these four advantages with the same emphasis. Nor does it mention the crocodile.[136]

Clark Kerr took the British official minutes, and in addition left in his private office papers a colourful eyewitness account of Churchill and Stalin's first meeting. He emphasised the cut and thrust of the exchanges and the directness with which each spoke. He concluded '[n]ow the two men know each other and each one will be able to put the right value on the messages – and they are very frequent – that pass between them. At times both were very blunt, as if each one sought by his bluntness to make a dint upon the other. I think that each succeeded and that the dints were deep.' He noted that afterwards the 'PM was in very good humour, he felt that he had got away with it ...'.[137]

Churchill came away from the meeting believing that he had managed to carry it off. He telegrammed to the War Cabinet that 'courtesy and dignity had failed', but that Stalin's four points in favour of Torch had shown his 'swift and complete mastery of a hitherto novel problem'. He concluded optimistically, 'I expect I shall establish a solid and sincere relationship with this man'.[138]

The self-congratulation was premature, however, and may have had an effect on what followed. Churchill was accommodated at State Villa Number Seven,

Stalin's *dacha*, rather than at the British Embassy. Churchill gloated to the newly-arrived British military representatives that Stalin was a peasant whom he knew how to handle. Too late did Tedder warn of the likelihood that the *dacha* was bugged.[139]

Whether such eavesdropping had an effect on Soviet attitudes is unclear, but certainly the mood had changed by the next day, and an issue Churchill thought had been resolved was revealed to be very much still in dispute. Warning signs were evident in the morning when Molotov observed to Churchill that there was no certainty the North African operation would go ahead – after all, the second front was not going to, despite Roosevelt's statement in June that it would.[140] This was just a prelude to the storm that Stalin unleashed later. He presented a memorandum criticising not only the decision not to open a second front, but also the delivery of equipment to the Red Army and its quality.[141] He then released a stream of invective at Churchill, accusing the British Army and Navy of cowardice and the Allies of breaking faith and of failing to acknowledge the significance of the Soviet struggle. According to Colonel Ian Jacob, who took the minutes for the British, the effect of this was made even worse by the crude English of Vladimir Pavlov, Stalin's interpreter. In Jacob's record, Churchill is noted as saying, 'he earnestly desired to hear the ring of comradeship in the discussions. He well knew what the Russians were going through: we ourselves had fought alone for a year ... He had come a long way in the hope that he would receive the hand of comradeship and that he would be believed in a spirit of loyalty and friendship ... It grieved his heart that the Russians did not think we were doing our utmost in the common cause.' Stalin replied that 'it was not a case of mistrust, but only of a divergence of view ... He felt that if the British army had been fighting the Germans as much as the Russian Army, it would not be so frightened of them.'[142]

Churchill described this as 'a most unpleasant discussion'. Stalin, he wrote, had said a great many insulting things:

> I repulsed these squarely, but without taunts. I suppose he is not used to being contradicted repeatedly, but he did not become at all angry or animated. He kept his eyes half closed, always avoiding mine, uttering at intervals a string of insults ... He will have to go a long way to do any good with me.[143]

In launching this attack, it is generally assumed that Stalin, like Churchill the previous day, was following a favourite tactic, the so-called 'second-session ploy'. This involved appearing conciliatory at the first meeting, raising expectations in those he was dealing with, then taking an obstructionist stance, to be followed at the right moment by a slight softening of attitude that would come as such a relief that it would be seen to be praiseworthy statesmanship. Stalin may well have felt that he had missed a trick by being too understanding at the first meeting, and he now wished to build up some negotiating capital by not accepting the Anglo-American plan without gaining something in return.[144] Churchill speculated that he did so to satisfy hard-liners in the Politburo.[145] Stalin was certainly acting on what Maisky had reported to him: that Churchill was indeed apprehensive about British forces' prospects in battle with the German army. Maisky had suggested that doing this could leverage some concession on issues like supplies, if not on the main matter.[146]

Maisky had taken the liberty of expounding at length his reading of Churchill prior to the Bracelet meetings, and Stalin's tactics suggest that he was in agreement with the fundamentals. After emphasising the domestic pressures on Churchill caused by British public sympathies for the USSR, Maisky stressed Churchill's hesitancies about the offensive capabilities of British forces – which ran quite counter to the assumptions the British made about how the Soviets would see Churchill (that they would recognise his 'fighting spirit'). He also argued that Churchill shared the views of 'bourgeois Britain' that wanted Hitler's defeat but did not want the USSR to emerge too strong.[147]

Whatever Stalin's motivation, all it did was draw forth a bullish response from Churchill, who, like Stalin, dropped diplomatic form and delivered an eloquent and rhetorical speech. Dunlop, the interpreter, proved as inadequate for the task as Pavlov had been, and stumbled in translating Churchill's words (though in his defence, Churchill tended to take little account of the needs of the translator once he had launched into full-blown rhetoric). At one point, according to Jacob's later recollections (though not the Soviet record), Stalin stopped Churchill and said that he did not understand the words but admired the fighting spirit evident in Churchill's tone. The Soviet record makes clear the frank statements of opinion from Stalin, and Churchill's emotional response – that his heart was 'aching for the burden that Russia has to bear'. However, it does not record any breakdown in interpretation, nor Stalin's alleged remark concerning Churchill's fighting spirit. Indeed, subsequent evidence suggests that, despite the image the British tried to present of the 'bulldog spirit' of Churchill, this was a continued matter of doubt for Stalin.[148] Both men having vented their spleen, the mood calmed a little. The discussion shifted to the situation in the Caucasus and Stalin offered the British soldiers who were present a demonstration of the *Katyusha* rocket launcher.[149]

During the meeting, Harriman had passed Churchill a note that a similar change in mood had been evident in the second meeting with Stalin in October 1941, implying that this may have been either a tactic or a result of pressure from behind the scenes.[150] This suggestion did not mollify Churchill, however, and he came away from the meeting deeply disgruntled. He was inclined not to attend the state dinner, since Stalin had been so offensive. When Clark Kerr called at the *dacha* the following morning, he found Churchill to be like a

wounded lion. He declaimed against Stalin in ponderous Gibbonesque periods ... He declared he was damned if he would keep his engagement to dine with Stalin tonight.[151]

His method of handling Stalin had failed, but once again his lack of diplomatic finesse may have saved the day. His mood would have been evident to any of the Soviet listeners of the goings-on at the *dacha*, and he made little attempt to hide it at the lavish Kremlin banquet given in his honour, which Churchill finally did grudgingly agree to attend. He chose, however to dress in his remarkable one-piece garment that was sometimes called his 'siren suit'. The Soviets, who were punctilious with regard to etiquette, were all in formal dress or uniform and must have been greatly taken aback, if not insulted. However, perhaps himself perceiving that his own tactics had gone awry, Stalin had reverted to his congenial persona, making toasts and sharing humorous remarks with his colleagues. For a time, Churchill cheered up under Stalin's flattery, but the mood faded when Churchill asked if he was forgiven for his past (meaning his efforts to defeat the Bolshevik revolution) and Stalin replied 'Who am I to forgive. Only God can forgive'.[152] Stalin continued in party mood, but his *bonhomie* increasingly grated on Churchill. Stalin's dig at British intelligence failure in Churchill's First World War Dardanelles operation did not help. Stalin's habit of moving around the room to clink glasses with people he was toasting, and the restrictions of interpretation, magnified Churchill's grumpy mood. Though normally such lavish food and drink would have appealed to him, he now seemed to find it distasteful.[153] He perked up for a photograph session, but when Stalin suggested watching a film, Churchill abruptly took his leave. Stalin followed Churchill to the door, jogging to keep up; an unprecedented gesture.[154]

Back at the *dacha*, Churchill voiced his discontent eloquently, saying he would leave Stalin to fight his own battles. 'I ought not to have come', he said, though he added that he might be able to work with 'that man', but for the language barrier. But, he told Wilson, his doctor, he had deliberately said, 'Goodbye', not 'Good evening', and said 'I am going to leave this man to fight his own battles'.[155] According to Clark Kerr and Wilson, the mood was no better the following day. The ambassador has left a detailed account of his attempt to persuade Churchill to make one more effort to get on with Stalin (again confirming that this was one of the ostensible purposes of the mission). Clark Kerr's account of the conversation is typically colourful and cannot be verified, but there is no reason to doubt its general veracity. According to the ambassador, he argued to Churchill that the Soviets were indeed rough and inexperienced, fresh from the plough or the lathe. They said what they thought. However, that was just their manner, and too much should not be read into it. Churchill could not afford to risk the Soviets going their own way in the war, and it would play badly with British public opinion. He should use all his personal charm to overcome Stalin's unfortunate manner. Churchill muttered that he had been insulted, but Clark Kerr pressed that he could not risk the USSR being defeated as a result of his inaction, and it was up to him to use his skills to patch things up. It was in his power, said Clark Kerr, to 'nobble Stalin'. According to the ambassador's account, Churchill was persuaded by these arguments not to leave in a huff, but to give Stalin one more chance. Whether Churchill ever seriously intended leaving early, we cannot know. Wilson and Clark Kerr thought his threat genuine.[156]

Jacob's account makes much less of Churchill's mood, saying that Churchill was already reconsidering the implications of the second meeting with Stalin before Clark Kerr arrived at the *dacha*. Jacob noted in his diary that it was he who suggested that Churchill meet Stalin again. He also suggested using the inter-preter who had done the job at the military meetings, Major Arthur Birse.[157] Clark Kerr arrived after Jacob had left for a meeting, so it is possible that the ambassador gave parallel advice. It is tempting to think that Churchill was making a show for the microphones, and did not seriously intend to leave without another attempt at winning Stalin over to his point of view. None of the accounts written at the time suggests this, but Cadogan had been involved in just such a ruse during Eden's visit in December.[158] It is perhaps suggestive that when Clark Kerr arrived to speak to him they went outside and walked in the garden, away from prying ears – even though it was an unsatisfactory place to hold a conver-sation because of the need to walk in single file. On the other hand, Clark Kerr clearly thought Churchill needed to be persuaded.[159]

The result was that Cadogan sought out Molotov to arrange a further meeting. He was stalled for hours: this seems to have been a deliberate Soviet ploy, for some time in the afternoon Stalin's daughter Svetlana was told to prepare to have Churchill over for dinner – even though when the meeting was finally arranged there was no mention of dinner, and indeed Churchill made arrangements to dine with the Polish General Anders after he had spoken for an hour or so with Stalin. He left, however, with the parting words that he would not leave the Kremlin until Stalin was 'in his pocket'.[160]

As it happened, the meeting, as Stalin seems to have intended, lasted for over seven hours, from 7pm to 3am, even though neither man had any particular objective in mind. Accounts of the meeting are limited to those of Churchill himself, his new interpreter, Arthur Birse, and Pavlov.[161] Stalin once again turned on the charm. Both had made their points in their earlier meetings, and now relaxed somewhat in each other's company. They had no agenda and no burning issues on which they needed to take a stand or produce agreements. Conse-quently, the discussion was wide-ranging, of a kind that Churchill always seemed to enjoy. Churchill began by saying 'I hope that nothing stands between us. I came, apart from direct business, with the earnest wish for a personal under-standing.'[162] According to the Soviet record, Stalin said in reply, 'The fact that he and Churchill had met, got to know each other [literally 'friend to friend'] and had prepared the basis for future agreements is of great importance. He was inclined to look at the matter more optimistically.'[163] After a while, Stalin sprang his invitation to 'go for a drink' in his flat. Churchill replied that he was in principle always in favour of such a policy. They then made the short journey through the Kremlin to Stalin's modest personal apartments. There they ate a fork buffet, served by Stalin's housekeeper and by Svetlana, and joined at Stalin's suggestion by Molotov. Jibes were made at Molotov's expense: Churchill said that while in the US, Molotov had secretly gone off to see New York City. No, said Stalin, it had been Chicago, 'where the other gangsters live'. Stalin excused the Nazi-Soviet pact of August 1939 on the grounds that it was made to buy time and because he felt the British and French were not sincere in their own proposals for an agreement. Churchill even got him talking about collectivisation and the fate of the kulaks.[164] Cadogan was also summoned, and found Churchill and Stalin sitting amidst innumerable bottles and a suckling pig:

> Winston, who by that time was complaining of a slight headache, seemed wisely to be confining himself to a comparatively innocuous effervescent Caucasian red wine. Everyone seemed to be as merry as a marriage bell.[165]

Back at the *dacha*, while his bath was run (to prevent electronic eavesdropping?), Churchill spoke to Clark Kerr and Jacob and expressed his satisfaction with the outcome of his trip. He felt he had reached a personal relationship with Stalin similar to that with Roosevelt (an indication, like his 'comradeship' remark to Stalin, that this was all along a prime objective of his).[166] He telegraphed to Attlee that he and Stalin had got on easy and friendly terms – 'I feel I have established a personal relationship which will be helpful'.[167] Clark Kerr agreed: Jacob was more dubious. He did concede that Churchill had got further with Stalin than anyone else could have, but actually to make friends with Stalin would be equivalent to making friends with a python.[168] At 5.30 in the morning, with Molotov having come to see him off, Churchill and his party flew back to Tehran.

Churchill had activated the personal element of the second wing of the war-winning Grand Alliance. Indeed, the meeting was to remain the sole face-to-face contact of either Churchill or Roosevelt with Stalin until November 1943. It is easy to dismiss it as of no significance.[169] The Soviets went on to fight, and win, their own battles, and it is unlikely that another way of conveying Churchill's bad news would have produced a different military outcome. No formal agreements were reached, except a vague one on the principle of sharing information and another on the deployment of Anglo-American aircraft squadrons in the Caucasus.[170] No progress was made on political issues. Topics like the Soviet frontiers and Poland that were still major subjects of contention were not even touched upon.

To leave it at that, however, may be to miss the more intangible, but perhaps significant, aspects of the meetings in Moscow. The objective was never to reach firm agreements on substantive matters, but to test whether the two leaders, and their two states, could find some common foundations on which to build an alliance and overcome the sense of disconnectedness between their various war efforts that had become evident in the light of recent events. Despite their deep differences of background and ideology, Churchill and Stalin had found common ground, as evidenced in their discussion of the relative merits of Churchill's ancestor the Duke of Marlborough and the Duke of Wellington as military commanders.[171] In addition, and of some importance for Churchill, Stalin had seemed enthusiastic about Churchill's pet scheme of a joint invasion of north Norway, and agreed with him about the desirability of getting Turkey into the war (though he was not optimistic it could be achieved).[172] In this sense, Churchill might well have felt that Stalin's views of future strategy were preferable to those of some of the Americans, hence his declaration of respect for Stalin's 'sure-footed and quick military judgement' and his sense of achievement at the end of the mission. He was not above also exaggerating Stalin's statements about Torch into unqualified support, to give him ammunition on the ongoing strategic debates with Washington.[173]

Churchill was not a naïve or simplistic statesman and as with his personal relationship with Roosevelt, he remained aware that political differences had not been expunged by inter-personal cordiality. He had been trusting in his ability to win over a supposedly simple, peasant-minded Soviet leader by strength of rhetoric. Stalin's initial refusal to be charmed left him frustrated and angry. Stalin's tactics also led to a dead end. Both then made a renewed attempt to find common ground separate from discussion of specific issues, and found that they could in fact do so. The final result, the last meeting, when the air had been cleared and the reality of mutual need had dawned on both leaders, produced a long-lasting sense for Churchill that at the heart of the impersonal, grim and ruthless Soviet state was a human figure capable of frankness and humour, and who appeared in the last resort to attach importance to Churchill and his continuing good opinion. Similarly, Stalin's ploy of goading Churchill by impugning his fighting spirit had failed, but the fall-back of hospitality and comradeship had worked. Churchill returned with an attitude to Stalin that was if anything more full of ambiguities than before, but one which, right to the end of the war, contained the sense that Stalin was a rational, intelligent man with whom deals could be struck. Eden told Maisky that Churchill felt that at the final meeting he had 'met the real Stalin'. Churchill later said that if he could dine with Stalin once a week then all difficulties would be capable of resolution. On the Soviet side, there were similar feelings: Molotov reported to Maisky that the extensive conversations in Stalin's apartment had 'made for a close personal rapport with the guest'.[174]

With regard to the meeting's impact on Stalin's attitudes, Clark Kerr concluded that Stalin actually enjoyed Churchill's company, since there were few in the USSR with whom he could converse on such terms, and that Churchill by the force of his personality had dispelled the 'long-standing and tenacious suspicions which have clouded the judgement of Stalin'. He exaggerated: the conference clearly did not do that. However, Churchill and Stalin had been able to get the measure of each other, and each had made a contribution, difficult though they found it personally, to averting a disastrous breach in relations – and, more importantly, came intuitively to a basis on which the alliance could proceed.

The usually sceptical Cadogan's view was that 'I think the two great men really made contact and got on terms ... conditions have been established in which messages exchanged between the two will mean twice as much, or more, than they did before'.[175]

The Bracelet mission to Moscow represents a crucial first stage, in which the two leaders, neither conceding ground on an issue that divided them profoundly, concluded that notwithstanding this, they could find scope for cooperation and sensed that each valued the other's contribution to a common enterprise. This was implied in Churchill's key use of the term 'comradeship', which had practical as much as sentimental connotations. The essentially pragmatic basis for the conduct of the Grand Alliance – a way of managing potential disagreements by offsetting them and framing the relationship as primarily a warrior alliance – was established.[176]

As they left, the delegates felt the trip had raised the wartime relationship with the USSR to a new level of understanding and alliance. 'The Prime Minister', Harriman noted shortly afterwards, 'has been all for Uncle Joe ever since.'[177] In his account to the House of Commons of his trip, Churchill made the following striking statement about Stalin:

> It is very fortunate for Russia in her agony to have this great rugged war chief at her head. He is a man of massive outstanding personality, suited to the sombre and stormy times in which his life has been cast; a man of inexhaustible courage and will-power and a man direct and even blunt in speech, which, having been brought up in the House of Commons, I do not mind at all, especially when I have something to say of my own. Above all, he is a man with that saving sense of humour, which is of high importance to all men and all nations, but particularly to great men and great nations. Stalin also left upon me the impression of a cool deep wisdom and a complete absence of illusions of any kind. I believe I made him feel that we were good and faithful comrades in this war, but that after all is a matter which deeds, not words will prove.[178]

More 'guff', of course, this time for public consumption, and Churchill seems to have convinced himself that despite Stalin's barbed comments, he actually supported the Torch operation. The reality was quite different. He approved of Torch because some kind of Anglo-American military action in the European theatre was better than nothing. The main point though was that Stalin did not really think Torch would actually happen: he expressed doubts that it would ever take place right up to the moment that it did.

Relations Take a Turn for the Worst

For most of the time that they were run, the Arctic convoys to Murmansk and Arkhangelsk were of more importance politically than they were for the material they carried. The losses, suffering and inconvenience were not justified purely by the amounts that got through to the Soviet forces. They were begun to show the Soviets that the British and Americans were willing to help their fight, and for some time they were the only way, apart from the bombing of Germany, in which Britons and Americans were suffering and dying for their Soviet comrades. The numbers of tanks and aircraft, often of types ill-suited for use on the Soviet-German Front, though substantial in Western eyes, were insignificant in the great scale of that struggle. The really important Western contribution to the Soviet War effort were the jeeps, trucks and other soft-skinned vehicles, most of which reached the Red Army by the southern, Iranian, route not fully operational until 1943. For both sides the convoys' chief importance was political: a matter of prestige and trust.

There were times when military reasons meant that these political considerations had to be put aside. In September, following Churchill's visit to Moscow, a big combined effort was made for Convoy PQ18. Over seventy warships escorted the merchantmen, this time with help from Soviet submarines and aircraft. Even so, one-third of the convoy was lost. The Torch landings would make heavy demands on escort vessels, and since the Atlantic could not be denuded of them, Churchill informed Stalin that the convoys would have to cease for the duration of the operation. He tried to sweeten the pill by repeating the earlier offer to send RAF squadrons to the Caucasus.[179] It was hoped that since Stalin had made a few positive comments about the North African project in August, he would accept the convoy cancellation. He did not. He merely acknowledged receipt of the message. Churchill at first was worried by this lack of response. On 24 October he told Roosevelt that he was baffled and perplexed. He speculated once again on the possibilities of dissension within the Soviet ruling clique, still convinced of Stalin's sagacity: perhaps something had happened 'inside the Soviet animal to make it impossible for Stalin to give an effective reply' and pondering whether this indicated the Red Army had gained influence.[180]

If it was the Soviet 'machine' that was causing the problem, Churchill felt no need to make concessions to it, noting to Eden,

> I am sure it would be a great mistake to run after the Russians in their present mood; and still less to run around with them chasing a chimera ... I assure you that the only thing that will do any good is fighting hard and winning victories ... Should success crown our efforts you will find that we shall be in a very different position. Meanwhile, I should treat the Russians coolly, not getting excited about the lies they tell, but going on steadily with our task.[181]

This idea of a 'reserved' attitude was one Churchill returned to on a number of occasions, particularly in comments to Eden – the implication being that he thought the Foreign Office more likely to 'chase the Soviets'. This tended to annoy Eden because Churchill never found it easy himself to stick to this precept.

Maisky had been instructed to do all he could to counter with British formers of public opinion the impression that the Moscow meeting had resulted in Soviet acceptance of Torch as a second front. Likewise, he raised doubts about the mission of Rudolf Hess, connecting it with the idea, that seems to have become almost an obsession, that the British were seeking ways to negotiate with amenable Germans. Stalin complained to Maisky about Churchill's uncooperative attitude and motivations and repeated that Churchill opposed a second front as he wanted Germany to exhaust the USSR and then would come to terms with Hitler or Brüning.[182] The personal interaction that seems to have had an impact on Churchill – if only to confirm a view he was already inclined to take derived from his earlier characterisation of Stalin as a realist and his own need for a warrior comrade – clearly had had no corresponding effect on Stalin. Indeed, as with Churchill, it had simply reinforced his existing attitude. He suspected Churchill of seeking to avoid British losses, husbanding resources for the future, and of being prepared to make a deal with any successors to Hitler that might preserve Germany as a significant European power. He was deeply sceptical that even the limited Operation Torch would take place. On 28 October, in a note drafted by

Stalin in his own hand, he described Churchill to Maisky as 'the champion of an easy war' (for Britain). Although Churchill had predicted in Moscow that there would be about a million Anglo-American troops in Britain by spring 1943, ready to launch a second front, he was, said Stalin, one of those political figures who easily make a promise only to forget it or break it just as easily (which is ironic, given that one of the stereotypes of Bolshevik leaders in the West was that they were all liars). Churchill was, said Stalin, under the influence of those 'who are interested in the defeat of the Soviet Union'. He also, said Stalin, promised intensive bombing of Berlin in September and October and it had not happened. Churchill's strategy of exaggerating British activities was thus exposed and revealed to be counter-productive. Now, Stalin concluded 'we will know what kind of allies we have to deal with'.[183]

However, Stalin himself then changed the atmosphere. In his keynote speech celebrating the anniversary of the Bolshevik Revolution, on 6 November 1942, he went out of his way to mention the Anglo-Soviet-American coalition in positive terms, speaking of 'a steady rapprochement among the members of the coalition, and the development of it into a strong 'fighting alliance'.[184] Stalin went on to distinguish between 'Hitlerites' and ordinary Germans, and denied any intention to dismantle the German state.

Stalin followed up his speech with a further public statement on 13 November. This was in the form of an open letter to Henry Cassidy, the Associated Press correspondent in Moscow. In it, Stalin expressed a very positive opinion of the Allied invasion of North Africa, which contrasted with the earlier Soviet line that Operation Torch made little difference to the main conflict of the war on the Soviet-German front and that a second front was still not being delivered as promised. This can be taken as confirmation that Stalin's immediate reservations about Torch had derived from doubt that it would actually happen at all. On the other hand, Stalin remained alert for signs that Torch would be all that happened, rather than a prologue to the main task of invading Western Europe. Thus, on 27 November, he was very grateful that Churchill had promised a convoy and acknowledged how busy the Royal Navy was, but then showed he was still reading between the lines. Churchill had said how Anglo-American forces would take 'any favourable opportunity' for action against the Germans in France. Stalin asked whether than meant it was not definite that an invasion of France would happen in the spring, which he claimed Churchill had promised in Moscow.[185] Churchill did not directly contest this claim, nor the implications that Stalin was drawing, but said that he could not reply without consulting Roosevelt. He suggested a meeting of all three powers' military planners – though he was by no means keen on the idea of diluting Anglo-American planning (which the British were dominating at that time) with adding a representative from the USSR. He also suggested a Big Three meeting, which Stalin said he could not attend because of the pressure of the events at the front that were reaching their climax in the environs of Stalingrad.[186]

While the military side of the relationship remained tense as a result of Stalin's well-founded misgivings, Eden and the Foreign Office were keen to build on the political possibilities that they read in Stalin's public approbation of cooperation, and put together an approach for Clark Kerr to make to carry the matter further.[187] Clark Kerr duly raised the issue of the future treatment of Germany, and of the reorganisation of Eastern Europe into confederations. Stalin's response was positive, and he suggested full three-power talks to reach agreement on the political aims of the alliance, much as he had suggested back in 1941. Churchill had been out of the country while Eden and his officials were devising the approach, in conference with Roosevelt at Casablanca and then in Turkey. On his return he took to his bed for a week with a severe pneumonia. He read Stalin's letter on his sickbed and asked Eden tetchily, 'What brought this up?'.[188]

In his letter, Stalin wrote that

> only one correct method exists – that of a meeting between official representatives of both states and the reaching of an agreement, which would be binding on both parties ... Should ... the British Government now consider it necessary to arrange such a meeting and to come to an agreement with the Soviet Government on the question of the fate of Germany or of other states, the Soviet Government are prepared to meet them half way.[189]

Clark Kerr was told by a Foreign Office official that Churchill, on seeing Clark Kerr's report and this letter from Stalin, had 'emitted a series of the most vicious screams from his sickbed and ordained that the whole subject of post-war matters should be dropped at once like the hottest of hot bricks'.[190] Churchill's anger was directed at Eden, with whom he was at the same time having an argument over France.[191] This was not simply because Churchill had no interest in postwar issues: indeed one of Clark Kerr's tasks in his interview with Stalin had been to pass over the paper Churchill had penned himself, with no Foreign Office input, called 'Morning Thoughts'.[192] This paper had been given to Inönu, and Clark Kerr was instructed to reassure Stalin that it had been worded specifically to meet Turkish sensibilities, as part of Churchill's ongoing, and futile, attempt to draw Turkey into the war.[193] Churchill took a highly optimistic view that Turkey was moving away from neutrality, and tried to persuade Stalin that he could solidify this movement by friendly gestures. Stalin took the realistic line that the Turks had hedged their bets and were continuing to do so, and was sceptical of any change until Allied victory was assured. He also denied that any fault in Turkish-Soviet relations lay with the USSR.[194]

In fact, as Churchill himself had raised such matters in 'Morning Thoughts', what he had done was assert his own authority over post-war issues, as well as his preference for controlling the lines of communication with Stalin. Eden went to Washington in March, and Churchill took over the Foreign Office in his absence. As such, he agreed to the shutdown of any further discussion of post-war topics, and, not for the first time, recommended the ambassador in Moscow be reserved and not try to make any contacts, in connection with a dispute over military liaison.[195] Churchill was also very aware that Stalin would soon have to be told some very unpalatable news about Anglo-American strategic decisions, and about the suspension of convoys to the USSR in order to facilitate operations that they would regard as mere diversions. Raising political issues at such a time was hardly likely to be productive, nor conducive to diplomatic give-and-take.[196]

'Nul et Non Avenu'

Decisions taken at Casablanca earlier in the year, to follow up the Tunisian campaign with the invasion of Sicily, meant the effective postponement again of the second front in France. Once more, Churchill took on the role of principal communicator with Stalin, and it was his preoccupation with such issues that influenced his pique at Eden's attempt to deal with political issues. Stalin made his displeasure at the strategic decisions, and the way they were made in his absence, quite clear – he also made it plain that he did not consider that the Allied offensives in the Mediterranean constituted a second front.

Stalin suspected, correctly, that Churchill's was the dominant influence in prioritising the Mediterranean. While he kept his messages to Roosevelt cool and matter-of-fact, with Churchill he became increasingly frank. This also reflected the warlord relationship into which both had deliberately slipped, maintained by the steady flow of congratulatory telegrams that paralleled the more critical interchanges. Stalin started fairly cautiously. He had asked on 30 January for concrete details, including dates, of what had been agreed at Casablanca.[197] Churchill's reply was written when he was, as Maisky noted, feeling very positive about Red Army successes at Stalingrad, and relishing a British role as the bridge in the Big Three relationship. He left serious hostages to fortune by painting a very optimistic future of rapid success in North Africa, progress in the Mediterranean and a cross-Channel operation in August, or at the latest, September. Churchill himself was undoubtedly carried away with this vision, but he was surely aware of the many conditional factors – notably the tense situation in the Battle of the Atlantic and the poor progress in Tunisia – which he singularly failed to set out for Stalin, choosing instead to gain immediate positive gains but setting up future pain.[198]

By 11 March, reality had intruded and the error of Churchill's strategy towards Stalin began to appear. He tried to dampen Soviet expectations by outlining the range of conditional factors, especially the slow US build-up in Britain, but by doing so now rather than in his original message, he raised suspicion of backtracking. Molotov proposed to Stalin that he demand a proper clarification. Stalin for now moderated the response, by at least conceding the difficulties the Allies faced, but his reply still indicated his grave (and well-founded) apprehension.[199]

A few weeks later and Churchill was moved to tears again in Maisky's presence, this time about Stalin's appreciative comment about the film of the Eighth Army's success at Alamein, *Desert Victory*. He went on, however, to announce the suspension of the northern convoys. Stalin responded that this was 'catastrophic'. However, Churchill's apprehension of a worse reaction – he used the word 'divorce' to Maisky – did not transpire.[200] But Stalin's belief that Churchill sought to sit back while the USSR did the fighting, hoping they would defeat Germany but be weakened in the process, was undoubtedly confirmed. It was, as a matter of fact, inaccurate, but was certainly a rational deduction. As an immediate response to Stalin's 'guff' praising British fighting spirit and saying it had confounded the 'scoundrels' who doubted it, it would have inclined Stalin to switch to the more aggressive, frank, even bullying tone, that sought to shame Churchill, which he had used at the second Bracelet meeting.

Polish-Soviet relations began to deteriorate in February 1943 when the Polish Government in London headed by General Sikorski re-affirmed its right to the frontiers occupied by Poland on 1 September 1939. After some sharp exchanges, the Soviets made their disagreement clear. The Soviets wished for their frontier with Poland to be to the west of the line established by the Treaty of Riga (1921), essentially matching that established in the secret protocol to the 1939 Nazi-Soviet Pact, though they claimed this was the line drawn up by Lord Curzon in 1919 on ethnographic lines. The Soviets also protested about the anti-Soviet attitude of most of the Polish Government-in-Exile, especially the soldiers. Matters reached a climax in April with German revelations of what they discovered at Katyn, near Smolensk – the mass graves of Polish officers murdered by the NKVD in 1940.

The Sikorski Government's response to the German claim – to propose a Red Cross inquiry, which the Germans then endorsed – gave Stalin a chance to divert attention from the USSR's culpability to the Poles. He complained to Churchill of the way that Sikorski had publicised the allegations in the Polish press, and declared that it was a Nazi trap which Sikorski and his 'anti-Soviet government' deliberately and collusively agreed to support.[201] Churchill's comment on the Katyn massacre was 'Alas, the revelations are probably true. The Bolsheviks can be very cruel.'[202] He sent a soothing reply to Stalin, and Eden got the Poles to agree to withdraw the request for the Red Cross inquiry, but it was too late.[203] Stalin replied that he was breaking off relations with the Polish Government.[204] This he did, despite the further plea from Churchill that this simply aided German propaganda, and from then there were two questions to be settled in Soviet-Polish relations: Polish frontiers and the composition of the Polish Government.[205] The former proved capable of settlement (that is to say the Soviet view was finally reluctantly accepted), the latter not.

The temperature of Anglo-Soviet relations began to rise and fall almost daily in the confusion of events. Stalin's speech on 1 May was fulsome in its references to the alliance and its unity: Churchill wired to him on 2 May:

> I have just read with the utmost satisfaction and admiration your splendid speech on May Day and I particularly appreciate your reference to the united blow of the Allies and you can indeed count on me to do everything in my power to 'break the spine of the Fascist beast'.[206]

Then on 7 May Stalin reproached the British Government for not having warned him of the Polish press offensive and for not having stopped it. Simultaneously he and Churchill exchanged mutually congratulatory telegrams on military operations. On 22 May Stalin announced the dissolution of the Communist International. Although this agency was moribund and had ceased to be a useful instrument of Soviet foreign policy, a fact which many in the West knew, it was a considerable gesture to dispel distrust and help post-war cooperation. Stalin appeared to be using a mixture of the knout and the carrot to move things along in the way he wanted.[207]

What Stalin apprehended was finally revealed to him in early June, when Churchill and Roosevelt told him the second front was postponed until spring 1944.[208] His bitterness was focused at Churchill and he concluded his angry message of 24 June by depicting his allies as untrustworthy.[209] Churchill was stung by this. Maisky described him as 'nervous and confused', but he replied robustly: 'your reproaches leave me unmoved'. There was some confusion in the message, however, as Churchill tried to justify the decision both by the difficulties in getting US forces to Britain, but also by saying how a 'more fruitful policy' opened up in the Mediterranean. This of course was disingenuous, as he had the Mediterranean as the priority from the start – and he cheekily claimed that Stalin himself had seen the 'military correctness' of the strategy. To Maisky he said 'we are not gods: we make mistakes'. He thought the personal correspondence, on which he had had hopes, should cease. His resentment at Stalin's frankness was ironic, given his own tardiness in actually being honest about the situation and Allied intentions, confirming in the process the worst of Stalin's suspicions.[210]

There was indeed a long pause – but the channel was too useful to drop, and it was revived by a reasonably friendly message by Stalin on 9 August, as the prospects on the central Soviet front looked increasingly promising. Stalin was eager to be involved in the political decisions in the Mediterranean following the fall of Mussolini and was keen for a meeting of the Big Three leaders. He congratulated the Allies on invading Sicily and on the fall of Mussolini. Stalin had evidently become suspicious that Britain and the US were working together to the exclusion of the USSR, for he pressed for a three-power commission to deal with negotiations with former satellites of Germany, protesting about the handling of the Italian surrender and stating:

> To date it has been like this ... The USA and Britain reach agreement between themselves, while the USSR is informed of the deal ... I must say that this situation cannot be tolerated any longer.[211]

This probably had a profound effect on the President, for at Tehran and later at Yalta he went out of his way to disprove Stalin's allegation that Britain and the US were ganging up on the Soviet Union, much to the chagrin of Churchill, whose approach centred both on this 'ganging up' with the Americans, but also with Stalin. To the British it confirmed the view of some, such as Clark Kerr, that the USSR wanted to be part of international diplomatic 'society' – a member of the 'club', and not a pariah as it had been before and now Stalin feared might be happening again.[212] The idea of a commission was met with approval, but was stymied by the desire of the Allies to keep important decisions in the hands of the local commander, General Eisenhower. The exclusion of the Soviets from effective influence on the surrender negotiations, and from a say in administration of the occupied territory, was an unfortunate precedent which the Soviets were only too glad to emulate later in Eastern Europe.

Eden thought that Churchill was now getting dangerously anti-Russian, affected by the rude tone of Stalin's messages. On 24 August, for instance, Stalin wrote to both Churchill and Roosevelt:

I earnestly request you to appreciate my position at a time when our armies are exerting themselves to the utmost against the main forces of Hitler and when Hitler, far from having withdrawn a single division from our front has already transferred, and keeps transferring, fresh divisions to the Soviet-German front.[213]

Though Eden and General Ismay had said to Churchill while he and Roosevelt were meeting in Quebec that he could not complain about Stalin keeping aloof and then criticise him for rudely 'joining the party', Harriman reported that 'the P.M. would have none of it. After dinner when we were alone, he said he foresaw "bloody consequences in the future", using bloody in the literal sense. "Stalin is an unnatural man. There will be grave troubles".'[214]

His liking for Stalin seemed to wearing thin now, as a result of Stalin's direct language, his ingratitude at Allied efforts and his attempt to influence the situation in Italy, where, complained Churchill, no Soviet soldier had fought. The gruff 'Stalin-on-paper' had erased most of the residual comradely feeling from Moscow. Whatever the care with which Stalin's messages had been drafted by Molotov and amended by Stalin, as Vladimir Pechatnov has documented, their cumulative impact on Churchill was overwhelmingly negative.[215] The time was well overdue for a meeting of the Big Three.

Stalin suggested Moscow for a Foreign Secretaries' meeting and Tehran for the Big Three, both of which requests were eventually accepted.[216] Churchill remained annoyed. Harvey relates that in a Cabinet on 5 October:

P.M. talked for three hours without having read the papers: talked great nonsense: 'must not weaken Germany too much – we may need her against Russia'.[217]

On 13 October another offensive message from Stalin was received about convoys – probably the nastiest message Stalin sent to Churchill. Stalin asserted that the convoys were an obligation, and Churchill's statement that they would do their best to send them but could not promise, to be 'a kind of threat addressed against the USSR'.[218] Eden was on his way to Moscow, and Churchill took some pleasure in receiving the new Soviet ambassador, Fyodor Gusev, on 18 October and handing the message back to him unanswered, with the correct formal diplomatic phrase, '*nul et non avenu*' ('null and void'). Gusev noted later, 'he literally shoved the envelope into my hand, turned away and walked back to his desk'.[219]

Even if his feelings about Stalin had come under pressure, Churchill continued to nurse a crucial assumption. To Roosevelt, Churchill exonerated Stalin of the blame:

I have now received ... telegram from Uncle Joe which I think you will feel is not exactly all one might hope for from a gentleman for whose sake we are to make an inconvenient, extreme and costly exertion ... I think, or at least I hope, this message came from the machine rather than from Stalin as it took 12 days to prepare. The Soviet machine is quite convinced it can get everything by bullying, and I am sure it is a matter of some importance to show that this is not necessarily always true.[220]

He was quite wrong: evidence from the Soviet archives shows that Stalin himself added in some of the more astringent comments.[221]

Renewal of Personal Contact

The October Conference of Foreign Ministers in Moscow went surprisingly well. The European Advisory Commission was set up, to discuss and settle armistice questions. US Secretary of State Cordell Hull achieved his Four-Power Declaration on the founding of a new international security organisation, which was his main purpose. He also succeeded in preventing territorial questions being discussed, which also pleased the Poles. Eden had a talk with Stalin to clear up the quarrel over the convoys, and was on the whole well-pleased.[222] Stalin's amenability when approached in person on this issue could only further confirm the assumption that he was a moderating influence on the 'Soviet machine'.

Churchill's warning to Roosevelt to resist Soviet bullying and loud Soviet demands for a definite date for Overlord fell on deaf ears. The Tehran Conference at the end of November found the Americans, in Harry Hopkins' words, 'lining up with the Russians'.[223] Soviet-American relations were as cordial at Tehran as they were ever to be. Both sides knew that the war would be won, but still each needed the other in order to achieve it; the Soviets wanted a second front in France, and the Americans desired Soviet help against Japan. For the first time unable to play the role of link-man between Roosevelt and Stalin, Churchill instead felt like a gooseberry between the two leaders, and did not like it. He rationalised it by seeing himself dwarfed between the 'bear and the buffalo' – the poor little English donkey, was, he said, 'the only one who knew the right way home'.[224]

At the first meeting, after some exaggerated statements to butter up Stalin and Molotov, Churchill had a wrangle with them over Italy. Suvorov, Stalin said, had barked his shins on the Alps: there was no need to fight up Italy and Rome was of no importance. The Americans agreed, and were pleased when Stalin hinted the USSR would help against Japan after Germany was defeated.[225]

At the presentation by Churchill of the Sword of Stalingrad, Stalin turned on the emotion. However, Stalin would never allow such sentiments to get in the way of negotiating, and when the second session began he demanded to know the date of D-Day and the name of the commander. Only when he had this information would he believe the Allies meant business. Anxious to show that they did mean business, Roosevelt cut short a long monologue by Churchill on Turkey and Rhodes, saying that nothing must delay Overlord. Stalin looked at Churchill as if to say, well, what about that? and then rubbed it in by asking 'do the British believe in Overlord, or do they not?' He received the equivocal answer that they did, if the conditions were right. Churchill saw that if Turkey could be tempted into the war, then there might then be a reason to delay Overlord.[226] At midnight, after Stalin had spent the evening needling Churchill with remarks that Britain wanted a soft peace for Germany, Churchill voiced his fears to Eden, Clark Kerr and Wilson (now Lord Moran).[227]

Churchill shook off some of his black mood the following day. A one-on-one session with Stalin was more congenial for him than the conference round table. He was able to once more engage Stalin as warlord to warlord, and have strategic discussions of the broad-ranging kind he loved. While Stalin never let Overlord slip far from focus, he also expressed little demur to Churchill's enthusiastic discourse on the offensive possibilities in the Mediterranean theatre. This was the kind of conversation – in which he did most of the talking – that Churchill particularly enjoyed.[228]

The conference ended on a high note with the junketings of the final dinner, given in honour of Churchill's sixty-ninth birthday. Stalin was amiable – Churchill said 'he can be quite friendly when he gets what he wants' – and Roosevelt even more so. Churchill proposed a toast to the proletarian masses, and Stalin one to the Conservative Party. The Americans were highly delighted at the results of the conference. Churchill, however, was still uneasy. Stalin's leg-pulling, and more especially the American tactic of not consulting with the British, had not pleased him.[229] With the decisions on Overlord, he developed a strong impression that his own power and that of Britain was diminishing in comparison to the other two members of the Grand Alliance. This is not to say he had become anti-Stalin. Stalin still exercised a fascination for him. Seven years later he still did not regret that an anti-Soviet stand was not taken at Tehran:

> It would not have been right at Tehran for the Western democracies to found their plans upon suspicions of the Russian attitude in the hour of triumph and when all her dangers were removed.[230]

Though Churchill had become irritated by Stalin's obsession with 'this bloody Second Front' – Eden told Moran at Tehran that Stalin could talk of nothing else, and that was certainly in evidence in the record of his conversation with Churchill – Jock Colville noted that in December 1943 Churchill was still louder in his praise of 'Russian' courage than in his criticism of Stalin's surliness.[231] Colville believed that Churchill thought the Soviet Government (or at least the supposedly sagacious Stalin) was more aware than it showed of British efforts and losses on the convoys and of the unreciprocated willingness to keep the Soviets informed of British military plans. At Tehran, Churchill was the only one not sceptical about Soviet motives in inviting Roosevelt to stay at the Soviet Embassy on the pretext of an assassination plot. Most Britishers believed this was done to prevent the British and Americans colluding. Churchill saw it as just an indication of Stalin's hospitality. For his part, Stalin kept probing at Churchill with regard to his alleged 'soft spot' for Germany: this had clearly become something of an acid test for Stalin of Churchill's overall attitude.[232]

Churchill and Stalin Make Deals

Although he remained sensitive to the dangers of Communism, and had not lost his antipathy to the 'Soviet machine', Churchill seems to have absorbed at least some of the ideas that were emanating from the Moscow embassy and being peddled by E.H. Carr and others in *The Times* and other media, that the USSR was changing under stress of war, in a direction of convergence towards Western practices. Czechoslovak leader Eduard Beneš reported to him very positively on Stalin's intentions.[233] More significantly, however, he was influenced by his view of Stalin. In explaining why his view on the Soviet frontiers had changed since 1942, he said to Eden in January 1944,

> Undoubtedly my own feelings have changed in the two years that have passed since the topic was first raised during your first visit to Moscow. The tremendous victories of the Russian armies, the deep-seated changes that have taken place in the character of the Russian State and Government, the new confidence which has grown in our hearts towards Stalin – these have all had their effect.[234]

However, he had attempted a style of handling Stalin, by focusing on military issues and eschewing political ones, which developments early in 1944 revealed to be inadequate. Although the War Cabinet endorsed the future potential for cooperation with the USSR in January 1944, both Churchill and Eden reacted emotionally to the Soviet return to more brusque interactions rather than the overt cooperativeness of the direct contacts at Tehran.[235] This became evident when *Pravda* published a story in January 1944 that the British had been attempting to negotiate a separate peace with the Germans in Romania. The story deeply offended Churchill, calling into question as it did the 'warrior alliance, in it together until the death' approach to which he was committed.[236] General Brooke noted Churchill's reaction in his diary:

> Long Cabinet from 6 to 8.15pm with Winston in great form. He was discussing Stalin's latest iniquities in allowing *Pravda* to publish the bogus information that England was negotiating with Germany for a peace. He said 'Trying to maintain good relations with a Communist is like wooing a crocodile. You do not know whether to tickle it under the chin or beat it over the head. When it opens its mouth you cannot tell whether it is trying to smile or preparing to eat you up.'[237]

To Stalin, however, he tried to emphasise the personal relationship. He wrote 'I have been very much buoyed up with the feeling brought back from Tehran of our good relations ... if we had been together these difficulties would not have occurred'. He ended by appealing to the manly, comrade-in-arms relationship that he hoped they had established: 'We have always agreed to write frankly to each other so I do so now but I hope you will see Clark Kerr ... and let him explain more at length the position as between Allies not only fused together in war but linked by our twenty years' treaty.'[238]

The issue was, though, quickly overshadowed by failure in the next two months to make any progress in bringing together the London Polish Government-in-exile and the Soviets. The Poles would not accept the loss of eastern territory to the USSR, which had been agreed in their absence at Tehran, and the Soviets refused to restore relations with the Poles.[239]

On 7 February, Stalin told Clark Kerr that provided he got the Curzon Line and a new Polish Government, he would permit them to return to Warsaw and be free and independent. He telegrammed to Churchill that he wanted the Curzon Line, Königsberg and changes in the government.[240] Churchill told Stanislaw Mikołajczyk, the Polish premier, that this was the one and only chance to take Stalin's offer. Only the Soviets could liberate Poland. If they accepted, they had a decent prospect ahead of them. If they refused, the Russian steamroller would go over them. He, Churchill, did not, he said, intend to allow Anglo-Soviet relations to be wrecked by the Polish government. If they refused what he regarded as a reasonable offer he would then conclude a direct agreement with Stalin without them. The Poles were impressed and shaken, especially since they regarded Churchill as their friend.[241]

The Poles, however, decided to reject the offer. The Polish Peasant Party (Mikołajczyk's) was the only party even half supporting the proposal. The Polish Government was adamant it could not cede territory till it returned to Poland; all it would say was that it would accept the Curzon Line as an administrative line. Churchill sent a message to Stalin to this effect.[242] On 22 February Churchill spoke in the House of Commons, saying that Stalin had personally assured him that what he wanted was a 'strong independent Poland as one of the leading powers of Europe'. It was 'reasonable and just' that the USSR should have the Curzon Line and that Poland should obtain 'compensation at the expense of Germany both in the North and in the West'.[243]

Having gone out on a limb to support the Soviet line, Churchill then reacted when Stalin started to get tough in the face of the lack of movement by the Polish Government.[244] Harvey noted that Churchill's first reaction to Clark Kerr's report of his talk with Stalin was that he wanted to 'wash his hands of the Russians!'[245] Despite his Commons statement, and pressure on the Poles, Churchill was now bitter towards his Soviet ally, as was Eden.[246] The reply to Stalin, indicating their disappointment, spoke of the risks to the alliance non-agreement with the Poles posed and the British hope that they would after all reach a working agreement.[247] Stalin sent two rough replies, on 23 and 25 March, taking Churchill to task for threatening him, and for backing out of the Tehran agreements on the Curzon Line. He described the tone of Churchill's messages and Clark Kerr's statement to 'bristle with threats against the Soviet Union'. Threats, he said, 'are not only out of place in relations between Allies, but also harmful, for they may lead to contrary results'. He said that his quarrel was not with his ally Poland, but with the 'émigré' Polish Government in London. Stalin seemed extremely riled, to use such direct and offensive language. Simultaneously, though, cordial messages still passed between them on purely military matters. Even at the end of his angry telegram, Stalin said, 'as far as I am concerned, I stand and continue to stand for cooperation. But I fear that the method of threats and defamation, if continued, will not benefit our cooperation.'[248]

The British Government was left in an awkward position. Churchill had told Stalin he proposed to say in the House of Commons that territorial questions should be left until after the war. Stalin replied that this was his own affair, 'but if you make such a statement I will think that you have committed an unjust and unfriendly act in relation to the Soviet Union'.[249] Churchill did not make the speech, but Harriman reported him full of bitterness, frustrated by the stalemate. He said he had done a great deal for the Soviets as well as the Poles, getting temporary acceptance of the Curzon Line, and all he got was 'insults from Stalin – a barbarian'. However, his mood quickly changed and he asked Harriman (who was now the US ambassador in Moscow) to tell Stalin how hard he tried, and how hurt he was Stalin had not believed in his good intentions. Churchill's mood indeed varied wildly in this period.[250]

On 28 March Cordell Hull, who had been absent from Tehran, pressed for the formulation of a joint Anglo-American approach. Hull suggested that the time had come for a plain-speaking Anglo-American approach to Stalin, pointing out to him the consequences if he continued taking one-sided action.[251] Hull's emphasis on working together appealed to Churchill, and he suggested to Eden that an Anglo-American approach be made, while once again suggesting, as he had in March the previous year, lapsing into 'a moody silence' in diplomatic contacts more generally. He proposed, he said, to follow that principle in his own correspondence.[252]

Churchill never found it easy to maintain silence, 'moody' or otherwise. While Eden was on leave in April 1944, Churchill again took on the role of Foreign Secretary and allowed himself to be drawn into a fruitless dispute with Molotov. In December 1943, the British had parachuted some officers into Romania to contact opposition elements.[253] In April, the Soviets, whose troops were soon to enter Romania, cast aspersions on British motivations, implying once again that they were doing deals with the enemy. Churchill protested British innocence and accused Molotov of having 'got hold of a mare's nest'.

Molotov's response seemed to Churchill to be an attack on his good faith. He replied robustly. His first draft included the following: 'you are absolutely mad if you suppose . . .' and 'I trust you will send me an answer which I shall not have to hand back to your Ambassador'. He toned this down to read: 'Of course if you do not believe a single word we say it really would be better to leave things to run out as they will. But considering the tremendous business we have in hand together, I trust that you will consider carefully your answer before you send it.' One senses Churchill was seizing the opportunity to be as rude and offensive as Stalin, but not directly *to* Stalin, so not endangering his special relationship with him – and also taking the opportunity to speak sharply to the 'Soviet machine'.[254] When Eden returned from leave he commented, ruefully, and not for the first time, that he wished the prime minister would desist from such messages to the Soviets.[255]

Despite Churchill's angry invective, the Foreign Office was looking to develop a working cooperation along pragmatic lines with regards to Romania and Greece.[256] They made clear to the Soviets that Britain would follow their lead in the former. Furthermore, before the Romanian issue had blown up with Churchill, Molotov had made a point of stating his own ignorance on the Greek issue and explicitly invited the British to take the lead and provide guidance.[257] On 18 May Gusev reported that his government accepted the idea that they take the lead in Romania and Britain take the lead in Greece.[258]

The ambassador in the US, Lord Halifax, was told the idea of the Soviets 'taking the lead' in Romania and the British doing the same in Greece was a useful device for heading off divergence in the Balkans of which disquieting signs were emerging. It was not a matter of spheres of influence, Halifax was told, nor was the intention to exclude the US.[259] It was principally a statement of British interests, to provide a frank basis for realistic cooperation. It would also hopefully avoid a repetition of the kind of tetchy exchange in which Churchill and Molotov had recently indulged.

The American preferred all such discussion to take place in three-power committees. Churchill found this stultifying and wired to Halifax, 'There is no spheres of influence [sic]. We shall all have to act together, but someone must be playing the hand ... No fate could be worse for any country than to be subjected in these times to decisions reached by triangular or quadrangular telegraphing.'[260] In the face of this direct appeal from Churchill, Roosevelt assented to a three-month trial period, though the State Department's continued opposition was so obvious that the Soviets picked it up and, although it fitted with their objectives, themselves backed away for a while from the arrangement because of their own concern to maintain the alliance.[261] While Soviet motives came under increased suspicion when a mission was secretly dispatched from an Allied airfield in Italy to the Greek Communist resistance (EAM/ELAS), the main British displeasure was directed towards the Americans.[262]

With the belief that ELAS was already being more cooperative, Churchill's mood had changed: in the Commons debate on 24–25 May, Churchill spoke enthusiastically of the Soviet Union, and on 29 May Harriman informed Roosevelt, while passing back through London on his way to Moscow, that Churchill's rage had mostly blown itself out: 'due largely to Stalin's recent civil messages the sun is shining again on the Soviet horizon.' Churchill told Harriman that the Soviets were being so cooperative that he even hoped to solve the Polish problem.[263] David Reynolds aptly describes Churchill's attitude to the USSR at this time as 'mercurial'.[264] Stalin's glowing praise of Overlord added to this mood.[265]

In the Foreign Office, schemes for a post-war Western bloc were now being mooted, but Churchill viewed a Western bloc as so weak as to be a burden and preferred a close Anglo-American relationship, and saw that the way forward was to supplement this with interest-based arrangements with the USSR to reduce areas of conflict and preserve vital British interests in Greece and the Eastern Mediterranean. Churchill was looking to limit and define the area of Soviet influence, and to get Soviet acknowledgement of his own sphere of influence. Churchill had finally come to understand that the Soviets attached significance to formal written agreements: at last, Stalin's approach to diplomacy as essentially a matter of bargaining had been fully comprehended.[266]

At the beginning of August, with the Soviet armies approaching, the Polish *Armiya Kraiowa* (AK: Home Army) in Warsaw rose up against the German occupation forces in the hopes of liberating Warsaw before the Soviets arrived. Stalin denounced the Poles as 'bandits'. Despite pleas from the British and Americans, the Red Army did little to help them. Stalin took a similar attitude at the end of August when the Slovak rising took place. This revolt was led by Slovak and Czech Communists, hoping to link up with the Soviet advance, but the Red Army still halted as planned.[267] While there was some inclination in London and Washington to accept the Soviet argument that the Red Army was not actually in a position to help, there was anger at the refusal to drop supplies and arms to the beleaguered Poles, or even to allow Allied bombers to land on Soviet airfields after undertaking such missions.[268] When Harriman and Clark Kerr were finally authorised to make a joint approach to Stalin, they found his attitude much more helpful than expected. The Marshal said he did not realise the Allies felt so strongly, and gave his permission for the proposed supply missions. This response tended to confirm Churchill's inclination to blame the 'Kremlin gang', rather than Stalin himself, for the obstructionist attitude.[269] It was, however, far too late to make a difference, as Stalin surely knew – and Stalin's action could better be seen as an attempt to recover diplomatic ground now the outcome he wanted was assured.[270]

Churchill was in Quebec at the time, for the second Anglo-American Conference there. Encouraged by an unusually cordial message from Stalin, and the success of Clark Kerr and Harriman, he decided to go to Moscow and attempt to revive his role as alliance 'fixer', with the difference that this time he accepted political arrangements connected with the advance of forces should be confronted and settled on the basis of a realistic recognition of interests and the correlation of forces – the kind of thing that Stalin had pressed for since 1941.

There is no detailed documentation of Churchill's preparation for his meetings with Stalin, just as for the 1942 trip, and it is not precisely clear what he had as his agenda, if indeed he had one. That he was intending some kind of hard deal is suggested by the evasive way he informed Roosevelt of the mission and the ambiguous position of Harriman as a partial observer but not participant. Whatever the nebulousness of the precise plans, it is clear that the aim was to do what Churchill, Eden and the Foreign Office had wanted since Tehran – reach more precise agreement on the practical way that European issues were going to be handled, side-stepping the US inclination to delay untill the final peace conference.[271]

With the return to his fixer role, Churchill became quite optimistic. All would be well if he could win Stalin's friendship. Roosevelt, he felt, was wrong to think that only he could manage Stalin. He told Moran he could talk to Stalin as one human being to another – he was sure Stalin would be sensible. 'If we three come together' he said, 'everything is possible – absolutely anything.' Roosevelt could not do anything before the election, but the Red Army would not wait for that, so the Prime Minister decided to go alone:

> The atmosphere there is quite different since we brought off the landings in Normandy. I shall take advantage of it to come to an amicable settlement with Stalin about Poland. That is why I am going.[272]

Roosevelt did not approve of the bilateral talks and made it clear that he regarded them as only a preliminary to a Big Three meeting. Stalin was confused, telegraphing to Roosevelt:

> I am somewhat embarrassed by your message of October 5th. I had supposed that Mr. Churchill was coming to Moscow in accordance with agreement reached at Quebec. However, it happens that this supposition of mine does not appear to correspond to reality. I do not know with what questions Mr. Churchill and Mr. Eden are coming to Moscow. I have not so far been informed ...[273]

However, at the first opportunity, Stalin expressed his own annoyance with Roosevelt's attitude to Churchill's willing ears, in the process emphasising the Stalin-Churchill nexus:

> He [Stalin] had the impression ... that the President was worried. He has to say that he didn't like the message because the President demands a lot of rights for himself and doesn't leave many for England and the Soviet Union, who are bound to each other by a treaty of mutual assistance.[274]

At the first meeting, Mikołajczyk was called to Moscow to join in the discussion. It was at this meeting on 9 October 1944 that Churchill first raised the 'percentages' proposal, apportioning 'influence' in the Balkans, for which this conference (codenamed Tolstoy) is best known. For an issue that has attracted such historical attention, it was approached most casually. It is assumed that Churchill went to Moscow with the achievement of some kind of formal apportionment of influence in mind, though there is no evidence of any prior drafting of such an arrangement on his part. He knew from Ultra decrypts that a German withdrawal from Athens was imminent, so the time was 'ripe to do business', as he put it. His principal concern was to ensure a free hand to install his preferred regime in Greece. The uncertainty about the Romania-Greece arrangement that had been proposed in May, and frustration at the US lack of interest in the matter, caused Churchill to seek by a face-to-face meeting with Stalin to confirm what appeared to be the case, which was that the Soviet mission to ELAS was acting as a restraint on a Communist push for power. However, while the terms of the putative May agreement had implied something close to predominance (for the Soviets in Romania and for the British in Greece), Churchill wished to discuss the rest of south-eastern Europe too and reach a general *modus vivendi*. Nothing of this goal was leaked to his colleagues, let alone the Americans.

According to Churchill's published account, he wrote out percentages on a piece of paper with regard to Romania, Greece, Bulgaria, Hungary and Yugoslavia and Stalin ticked the document with his blue pencil and passed it back. Churchill suggested the document was 'naughty' and should be destroyed, but Stalin told him to keep it. According to the official British record, it was not as easily concluded as this, and not with the same purport and reservations as Churchill claimed. Moreover, the Soviet record indicates that there was much more discussion of the issue than Churchill acknowledged. Stalin immediately disputed the amount of influence (if this was what the percentage indicated: it was never clearly defined) Churchill claimed for Bulgaria.[275] His famous blue tick on the naughty document is over the percentage for Romania.[276] Churchill's paper was in English, so Stalin may or may not have known what he was putting his tick next to. It was never clearly established what the percentages were supposed to represent, and Harriman when he was finally told (he was not at the first meeting) was perplexed as to what Churchill hoped to accomplish. The only real concrete agreement was that Greece would be a predominantly British interest, as a Mediterranean country, and Romania, as a Black Sea country, mainly Soviet, the percentages being 90:10 in both cases. Possibly the 'percentages' part was for the benefit of the Americans, who would be shocked by mention of spheres of influence – though even this was not directly reported to them.[277] Another speculation is that Churchill thought reducing the concept to numbers would appeal to the materialist Marxists in the Kremlin, and Stalin himself, who was supposed to prefer arithmetic to algebra. Molotov obviously believed they signified something, for in a follow-up meeting he and Eden engaged in much argument over the figures for Hungary, Yugoslavia and Bulgaria. Molotov's comment at one point that in Yugoslavia the British were interested in the coastal area and the Soviets the interior implied that he saw the figure to signify actual territorial division, though that could have little meaning for 90:10 arrangements. Although Eden and Molotov finally reached consensus, no formal document was drawn up or signed.[278] Despite the constant reference in the literature to a 'percentages agreement', there was therefore actually nothing of the sort. Stalin in his letter to Clark Kerr back in February 1943 had made plain that only properly formulated and agreed documents could be regarded as binding agreements. On the other hand, Churchill referred to the matter as if it was indeed an agreed arrangement in subsequent messages, and mentioned the 50-50 approach to Yugoslavia in his talk with Stalin on 18 July 1945, and Stalin never contested this implication that there was actually such an arrangement.[279]

Churchill drafted a letter to Stalin on 11 October, which would have set in motion the next stage of formalisation, but then thought better of it. This is often ascribed to Harriman's intervention.[280] The draft letter contained the following passage reiterating the concept that the Soviet system under Stalin was reforming away from revolutionary communism. The dissolution of the Comintern was an indicator of this, wrote Churchill, going on to say,

> We have the feeling that, viewed from afar and on a grand scale, the differences between our two systems will tend to get smaller and smaller, and the

great common ground which we share of making life richer and happier for the mass of the people is growing every year.[281]

Churchill was clearly uncertain about what his conversation with Stalin amounted to. In reply to a Cabinet query, he said that the percentages were not about numbers of representatives on control commissions, but a 'general guide' expressing 'interests and sentiments' regarding the Balkan countries. It was not a rigid system but a guide for the immediate wartime period. Often seen as a cynical carve-up of Europe that formally conceded Eastern Europe to the Soviet Union, it was nothing of the kind. For one thing, there was no mention of the parts of Europe already in Anglo-American hands: Stalin made no attempt to raise 'division of influence' (the term the Soviet record uses[282]) in Italy, France or Belgium. For another, what Churchill was doing was not so much conceding influence as trying to secure the acknowledgement of some level of Allied interest. The statement in the draft letter suggested rather than a rigid division between two distinct spheres, a sort of gradual transition area that shaded off between the two. The percentage concept, far from a spheres of influence arrangement, suggested a moderation of the predominance brought by military occupation. It was an assertion that Britain retained interest in the affairs of Bulgaria, Yugoslavia and Hungary, whereas an agreement to 'take the lead', as previously proposed for Romania and Greece, did not.[283] But there was no actual agreement as to what that meant, and nothing followed from this assertion of interest. Romania and Greece were different: here Churchill achieved what he wanted, which was a reaffirmation of what had been established in the summer.

Moving on from percentages, Churchill made clear at this first meeting that if Stalin did not oppose British efforts to recover its colonies lost in the east to Japan, he would not oppose Stalin's efforts to realise the 'legitimate territorial ambitions' of the Soviet Union, or to revise the Montreux Convention. Most of the subsequent discussion for the rest of Churchill's visit was devoted to Poland. While the British Government had a moral commitment to Poland, Stalin held all the high cards: he had the Red Army and the Lublin Committee, comprised of the Moscow-based Union of Polish Patriots, actually on the ground in Poland. Stalin said to Churchill that military difficulties had prevented him helping Warsaw, but he could not say this publicly. Churchill said that he believed it. The prime minister stressed the need for a real Polish settlement because of the effect on Anglo-Soviet relations. If two sets of Poles could not agree, a settlement should be imposed.[284]

A settlement proved impossible. Mikołajczyk arrived, but with little or no authority to negotiate. He was bound by a cabinet memorandum that Poland must have as much territory as before the war, with the main cultural and raw material centres in the east included. Also, there was to be equal representation for the five political parties: the four in the London Government, and the Communists. If the attitude of the London Poles angered Churchill, the Lublin Poles also made a bad impression. He described Bierut, Osóbka-Morawski, Rola-Żymierski, Witos and Wassiliewska as a lot of 'inverted Quislings'.[285] Both the

British and the Soviets pressed the Curzon Line on the London Poles. Churchill said good relations were more important than mapping frontiers, and was apt to lose his temper when Mikołajczyk thought differently and could not be persuaded that Stalin was honourable.[286]

With the exception of Poland, on which Churchill's efforts failed to produce agreement, the Moscow talks produced a hopeful glow in the alliance. From the start, as Birse, once more Churchill's interpreter, noted, the atmosphere was less tense than on previous occasions. On 10 October Moran remarked to Churchill that Stalin looked much older: 'If anything happened to him it would be a disaster'. Churchill replied; 'God, yes, a catastrophe'.[287] Even in the wrangles over Bulgaria, the Soviets were fairly jocular.[288] At lunch, Stalin admitted that German fear of invasion of France in 1942 had kept fifty German divisions in the West which would have been crucial on the Soviet-German Front. The British soldiers were delighted at the Soviet openness, and the way they disclosed their military plans as never before.[289] Moran observed that whenever he saw Stalin, Churchill came back in a good mood. More than once, Churchill revealingly called Stalin his 'friend and war comrade'.[290]

At the end of the conference, Churchill said to his doctor, according to Moran's recollection:

> Stalin is more friendly these days. The invasion and the number of prisoners taken by us have sent us up in his eyes. He talks freely to me. Stalin's sense of humour is his strongest characteristic. He talked about my private war with Russia in 1919, all in a friendly way. I said, 'I'm glad now that I did not kill you. I hope that you are glad that you did not kill me?' Stalin agreed readily, quoting a Russian proverb; 'A man's eyes should be torn out if he can only see the past'. We all made a move at three in the morning, but Stalin would not let us go and kept us till four. All the time he got more animated and expansive.[291]

As he wrote to King George VI, Churchill was still impressed by the possibility of creating a lasting friendly relationship with Stalin. With the shared public appearance at the Bolshoi Theatre and Stalin's unprecedented luncheon at the British embassy, the atmosphere of goodwill was marked.[292]

On 3 December, Churchill described Stalin to Eden as 'that great and good man' and eight days later said he was impressed by Stalin's 'loyalty' (over Greece) in resisting considerable temptation to meddle.[293] Stalin kept Churchill informed of the visit to Moscow by the French leader Charles De Gaulle and showed a readiness to align with whatever Churchill's approach was on France.[294] They continued also to exchange little positive expressions of goodwill: noteworthy is Churchill's effusive encomium on the Soviet film about Marshal Kutuzov on 19 December.[295] On 25 December Churchill went to Athens to try to find a non-Communist settlement for Greece. He continued to feel that he was able to succeed in this because Stalin had made a promise in Moscow and had kept it, and meant perhaps that he did not pick up clearly how Stalin was moving towards recognition of the communist group based in Lublin as a Polish provisional government.[296] This belief regarding Stalin's good faith over Greece, he took with him to Yalta for the second Big Three Conference from 4 February to 11 February.

The Yalta Conference

The popular characterisation of the Yalta Conference is that it is the point where the division of Europe was sanctioned, and in particular where Eastern Europe was given up to Soviet control. This can obscure understanding of what was actually done at the conference – and what actually caused the division of Europe.

It is important that Yalta be set in its context. The prime result of doing so is to understand that it was not a peace conference, it was a war conference. It was a gathering of the anti-Axis coalition looking to renew and resolve and cement its connections under the pressures of the political issues the progress towards victory was raising, so that it could successfully complete the job. This job did not look quite over in February 1945, though generally the strategic part of the conference was frictionless.[297]

Apart from keeping the alliance together, the three leaders each came to Yalta with a set of primary and secondary objectives. For Roosevelt there were two main goals: to resolve issues left outstanding concerning the new world organisation, notably membership and veto powers, and to obtain a firm Soviet agreement and timetable to enter the war against Japan. In addition, and connected to the UN issues, he was concerned to bring home something tangible that he could use to counter a growing dissatisfaction in American public opinion concerning the actions and aims of his allies. He was in poor health, but on the issues that mattered to him he was still sharp: he just did not expend much effort on what was of secondary importance to him.

Stalin sought, as was his custom in such summits, to achieve concrete detailed agreements through bargaining. The two main areas he was concerned to get commitments from his allies were on reparations to pay the immense cost of reconstruction of the USSR, and on the dismemberment of Germany. In previous meetings, including the recent ones with Churchill in Moscow, there had been general agreement on breaking up the German state, but no firm plans had been made.[298] He did not intend to raise any Eastern European issues himself, having made his move in Poland at the start of the year by unilaterally declaring the Lublin Poles to be the Provisional Government – but if it were to come up, as he surely knew it would, he wanted endorsement of his actions and final agreement on the detail of the revision of Poland's frontiers that had been agreed in principle at the Tehran conference.

Churchill was concerned to have acknowledgement of a role for France in post-war Europe, and to get agreement that states not yet at war with the Axis (notably Turkey) should be allowed into the world organisation. He was also concerned to get an agreement on the repatriation of Allied prisoners-of-war being liberated in large numbers by the Red Army.[299] It is not clear what he was hoping to achieve with regards to Poland: for the rest of Eastern and South-eastern Europe, he had already set out with Stalin his views at the Tolstoy conference and showed no signs of wishing to return to the issue.

Both Roosevelt and Churchill seem to have been more concerned to get an agreement on Poland (principally the composition of a Provisional Government) that could be defended in their own domestic political arenas than they were actually expecting to get much alteration of Stalin's policies. While Churchill pressed harder for a time, Roosevelt revealed himself quite prepared to accept a trade-off over the UN question and Stalin linked the two issues explicitly on a number of occasions. Each party bargained, rather than appeased, and each came away from the conference having achieved some of their objectives. The big winner was Roosevelt, having gained his UN settlement and the clear commitment of the USSR to join the war against Japan. Churchill got his way over France and over the admission of states to the UN. While voicing disquiet over the casual attitude to the rights of small nations displayed by Stalin, he was happy that British actions in Greece had not been questioned. Stalin gained qualified commitment from his allies on both reparations (Churchill refused to agree a figure) and on dismemberment of Germany, but signs of softening in his allies' commitment to breaking Germany up were a matter of concern to him. At their meeting of 10 February, Stalin goaded Churchill once again for being soft on the Germans.[300]

Stalin's apprehension that the UN would turn out in practice to be an instrument of Western dominance over the USSR had not entirely gone away: the provision of two extra seats on the General Assembly hardly balanced the voting blocs that the US could be expected to command in Latin America and the British would have with their Dominions. Stalin had reason to be pleased with how he had come out on the Polish matter, as he had headed off the proposal to send in election observers and had gained an agreement on the government of Poland that could be interpreted as giving the Lublin Poles the central role. However, at the end, Roosevelt had then picked his pocket, getting his signature to the Polish agreement specifically mentioning free elections and the Declaration on Liberated Europe, which after most of the conference had passed with no discussion of eastern or southern Europe, suddenly at the end committed the USSR (and Britain) to an American liberal-democratic approach.

Yalta signalled a revived US interest in all of Europe and on the basis of a public commitment to a particular form of settlement, setting a yardstick of behaviour against which both Britain, and more importantly the Soviet Union, would be measured. Almost immediately it was found wanting, precipitating, in time, the onset of the Cold War.

In the short term, the conference achieved its main goal and the alliance held together to the end of the war. Despite misgivings, the British delegation left the Crimea feeling the conference had been a success, particularly from the point of view of the behaviour of the Soviets. Cadogan wrote:

> I have never known the Russians so easy and accommodating. In particular, Joe has been extremely good. He is a great man, and shows up very impressively against the background of the other two ageing statesmen.[301]

Churchill himself indulged in some 'guff': he wired to Stalin on 17 February; 'I pray that you may long be spared to preside over the destinies of your country, which has shown its full greatness under your leadership.'[302] His actual feelings about the conference were mixed. Even more than at Tehran, he felt Britain had been side-lined by the relationship between Roosevelt and Stalin, aggravated by Roosevelt's refusal to coordinate tactics in advance, even though they met at Malta on the way to the conference. Churchill's method of bilateral arrangements with each partner, so recently practised with success at Moscow, simply could not be maintained in the Big Three context, given Roosevelt's strategy of doing the same.

Churchill continued, however, to set some stock on his relationship with Stalin, which Stalin's apparently cooperative behaviour over Greece – he had not raised the issue at the conference at all – had reaffirmed. Hugh Dalton noted that Churchill said to him, 'Poor Neville Chamberlain believed he could trust Hitler. He was wrong. But I don't think I'm wrong about Stalin.' He thought a remark of Stalin's very significant – 'we are conscious of our great sins against Poland in the past, through occupation and oppression of that country'.[303] Churchill recalled later his pleasure at Stalin's words at the dinner on 8 February, 'In the history of diplomacy I know of no such close alliance of three Great Powers as this. May it be strong and stable; may we be as frank as possible.'[304]

On 27 and 28 February, the House of Commons debated the Yalta agreements. Harold Nicolson, who spoke for the government, had drinks with Churchill and noted that the Prime Minister was 'very sensible', saying that the Soviets were very powerful and on the spot.

> Moreover, it seemed to him a mistake to think that the Russians are going to behave badly. Ever since he had been in close relations with Stalin, the latter had kept his word with the utmost loyalty. During the three weeks of the Greek crisis, for instance, a single article in *Pravda*, would have tipped the whole balance, but Stalin kept an obstinate silence which was of immense value to us.[305]

Post-Yalta Tensions

On the Moscow committee to form a Polish provisional government, Molotov refused discussion of any of the nominees put forward by Harriman and Clark Kerr, while in Poland the Lublin group was busy consolidating its position behind the Red Army. Molotov held that at Yalta it had been agreed that the Lublin 'government' would form the core, with some additions, of the new Polish government. Churchill warned Roosevelt on 13 March:

> We are in the presence of a great failure and an utter breakdown of what was settled at Yalta, but ... we British have not the necessary strength to carry the matter further ... the limits of our capacity to act have been reached.[306]

Underlying this statement though were two considerations. First, that the bargain made at Moscow regarding influence in Romania and Greece was still being adhered to by Stalin, so that Britain could not really complain about what was being done in Bucharest: Churchill was trying to get Roosevelt to take the lead on this instead. Second, the blame tended to be ascribed to the likes of Molotov and Vyshinsky. Stalin was still envisaged as a moderate battling with shadowy, more hard-line forces, including the marshals of the Red Army. Given the apparent success of the bargaining done at Moscow in October, Churchill believed an opportunity was being wasted to acquire some more bargaining counters. He urged Eisenhower, the Supreme Commander of Allied forces in North-west Europe, to thrust as quickly as he could for Berlin.[307] Eisenhower ignored this and continued with his advance on a broad front through central Germany.

To the Anglo-American complaint of violation of the spirit of the Crimean agreements, Stalin gave an evasive reply, accusing the Allies of secretly negotiating with Germans in Bern, Switzerland concerning a surrender in Italy. He also insisted that they had agreed to build the Polish government around the Lublin Poles.[308] The good relations established at Yalta had deteriorated quickly into insults and suspicions. Removed from the pragmatic atmosphere of diplomatic interaction, the necessity of the bargains that had been struck no longer seemed so strong. However, Roosevelt's final message to Churchill, which he composed himself, showed the President's lack of concern about this state of affairs. Warren Kimball shows that Roosevelt may not have paid close attention to the drafts of messages to Churchill in March and April, which included strongly-worded protests about Stalin's allegations about the Berne talks. He did compose the message to Churchill of 11 April, writing in very typical Roosevelt vein, 'I would minimize the general Soviet problem as much as possible because these problems, in one form or another, seem to arise every day and most of them straighten out …'[309]

The death of Roosevelt came as a great shock to the Soviets.[310] Clementine Churchill, in Moscow at the time in connection with her Aid to Russia fund, witnessed a spontaneous two-minute silence. As a gesture Stalin decided to send Molotov to the San Francisco conference, having earlier appointed Andrei Gromyko, the ambassador in Washington, to be the head of delegation. The new US President, Harry S. Truman, while he may not have been so tough-talking as he later represented in his memoirs, to Churchill's pleasure appeared more responsive to the idea that firm handling was the way to deal with the Soviets, though he declared that he intended to follow his predecessor's policy.[311]

Though he was encouraged by this, Churchill was generally pessimistic about the future. Churchill appealed to Stalin not to 'smite down the hand of comradeship', still trying to get mileage out of the appeal to the soldierly relationship.[312] The attempt to reduce tension by agreement, which he had tried in Moscow, had deteriorated into what seemed like a free-for-all to grab influence as a result of the vaguer Yalta agreements. Churchill combined advocacy that the Anglo-Americans join in the free-for-all by pushing their forces as far east as possible, with an attempt to resuscitate the warrior relationship with Stalin, trying to use arguments that would balance the pressure Stalin was supposedly under from the 'shadowy figures' on the Politburo and over-zealous communists in the liberated countries. Eden made yet another attempt to curb Churchill's sending of messages in March 1945: depicting Soviet behaviour as abominable, he suggested 'you should cut down your personal messages to Marshal Stalin to a minimum'. Churchill noted that he quite agreed, but as before found it impossible to stick to that principle and was soon to be found sending messages as before.[313] Churchill retained his belief that he could still do business with Stalin himself. At the end of a message to Roosevelt on 19 March, he had added a typical Churchillian doggerel, 'UJ:OKAY:UK'.[314] On 28 April he wrote to Stalin:

> There is not much comfort in looking into a future where you and the countries you dominate, plus the Communist Parties in many other states, are all drawn up on one side, and those, who rally to the English-speaking nations and their allies or Dominions are on the other. It is quite obvious that their quarrel would tear the world to pieces, and we, the leaders on both sides, would be shamed before history.

Stalin's reply was, Churchill later recalled, 'most disheartening'. Stalin refused to shift his position that the only Poles that were acceptable in a government were those that had shown themselves actively friendly to the USSR, and did not respond at all to Churchill's attempt to play on his emotions by identifying the two of them as having the future of the world in their hands.[315] Churchill concluded that the only way to break through the impasse on Poland and other matters which soured great power relations, was another face-to-face meeting of the Big Three. He recommended this to Truman, who stalled.[316]

Three days after the German surrender on 8 May, Churchill talked to Cadogan of his fear of an 'aggressive Russia sprawling across Europe'.[317] He still felt that pressing Allied forces as far as they could get into Germany, and a delay in retiring to their agreed zones, would make the Soviets more amenable by giving the Western Allies something tangible with which to bargain. The Americans, however, disagreed; they were anxious to get their troops out of Europe as quickly as possible, wanted to avoid antagonising the Soviets unnecessarily when they still required Soviet aid in the war against Japan, and hoped for Soviet cooperation in the formation of the United Nations organisation. Churchill's strategy was on shaky ground: to hold position on the Elbe rather than retire to the zones arranged months before, would have left Berlin solely in the hands of the Soviets, with no reason for them to hand over half to the other Allies, since the British and Americans would have already broken the agreement, nor to allow in the Anglo-American teams that were poised to seek out as much as possible of German technical, scientific and administrative papers that would be found in the capital. Moreover, the zones had been deliberately arranged to give the Soviets a fairly large share, because there was some fear in the west as to the problems of feeding and maintaining the Germans after the surrender and the more the Soviets were responsible for, the better.[318]

Churchill wrote once more to Truman on 12 May regretting the withdrawal of the US armies and air force from Europe. He summed up the problem as he then saw it. Stating that an 'iron curtain is drawn down upon their front', Churchill asked

> what is to happen about Russia? I have always worked for friendship with Russia, but, like you, I feel deep anxiety because of their misinterpretation of the Yalta decisions, their attitude towards Poland, their overwhelming influence in the Balkans, excepting Greece, the difficulties they make about Vienna, the combination of Russian power and the territories under their control or occupied, coupled with the Communist technique in so many other countries, and above all their power to maintain very large armies in the field for a very long time.[319]

Churchill protested strongly at Truman's suggestion, conveyed to him by Joseph P. Davies, whom Churchill disliked, that the President should first meet Stalin alone. Such a suggestion denied the common interest of Britain and the United States and 'affronted the dignity of the British Empire and Commonwealth'. A Three-Power meeting was finally arranged for Potsdam near Berlin in the middle of July.[320]

Churchill was prepared himself both to speak bluntly to the Soviets, and to consider alternatives. On 18 May he treated Gusev to an extensive critical survey of Soviet policies in the territories they had occupied. He urged, as he had with Truman, the need for an early Big Three meeting, 'to discuss all problems in a friendly manner': correspondence by telegram, he observed, rarely worked. Churchill's language was direct: so direct in fact that he ordered all copies of Clark Kerr's minutes of the meeting to be returned to him for security reasons.[321] He asked rhetorically how the Soviets were facing the new condition of peace in Europe, and supplied the answer himself:

> ... By dropping an iron screen across Europe from Lubeck to Trieste, behind which we had no knowledge of what was happening. All we knew was that puppet governments were being set up about which we were not consulted, and at which we were not allowed to peep.

The situation, said Churchill, was incomprehensible and intolerable. He objected to Britain being treated 'as if they were of no account in the afterwar world'. Their determination not to see this happen had moved them to postpone the demobilisation of the RAF – an attempt at a veiled warning of the fact that Britain, weak in many ways, possessed a potent strategic bomber force. He went on:

> They were perfectly willing to meet the Russians and to talk in the friendliest way, but it must be on terms of equality, but the Russians seemed to close down upon every place they had occupied and to shut it off from the rest of the world. This could not be allowed. Why could not the Russians content themselves with the Curzon Line and let us have a look at what was happening west of it?

Clark Kerr noted that Gusev listened to all this 'with a stunned expression on his large face'.[322]

As these remarks to the ambassador show, Churchill was cogitating at this time how Britain's mobilised military power could be exploited as an influence in Anglo-Soviet relations. This caused him to instruct the military planners to consider the scenario of war with the USSR in order to obtain a better settlement for Poland – the paper they produced was strangely codenamed Operation Unthinkable, despite the fact that the Chiefs of Staff and their Policy Planning Staff had been thinking actively of such an eventuality (albeit in ten to fifteen years' time) for over a year. They were deeply pessimistic of the likely prospects, and Churchill ordered an alternative assessment of British defensive prospects if the Soviets gained control of the continent.[323]

Before the conference a settlement was reached on Poland. Hopkins went to Moscow while Davies was in London, and persuaded Stalin to invite Mikołajczyk and a few other non-Lublin Poles to Moscow. Churchill had misgivings that this really was no advance, since no representative government was to be set up, especially when sixteen leaders of the AK were still in prison in Moscow, having been arrested in April after being lured with promises of negotiations. Repeated pleas to release them were of no avail, even when Hopkins did so personally in Moscow. Truman was very keen to recognise the new Polish Provisional Government, which included Mikołajczyk and three others from outside the Lublin group. Eden wanted conditions attached, but Churchill was anxious to fall in with American wishes and the Polish Government was recognised on 5 July.[324]

Churchill went to Potsdam extremely concerned. As he had told Brooke and the other Chiefs of Staff on 11 June 'he had never in his life been more worried by the European situation than he was at present'.[325] However, at the first meeting both Stalin and Churchill were friendly. Eden was more worried about Soviet acquisitions than Churchill, it seemed to Cadogan. Eden pleaded with Churchill not to give way to Stalin. Cadogan remarked however, that Stalin 'knows exactly how to manage Churchill'.[326] The conversation between the two on 17 July reproduced the joviality of the final meeting in August 1942: Stalin joked that he had taken to smoking cigars and Churchill remarked that the news would shake the world. The Foreign Office note of the meeting on 18 July commented that it was informal and genuinely friendly. It was typical of the tone of frank friendliness that they had evolved in their personal interactions that Churchill could support Soviet claims to access through the Straits, by describing it as a giant with its nostrils pinched, and at the same time speak of his anxiety about the Soviet Union rolling westwards. Stalin for his part stated he was against Sovietisation, and that any parties except Fascist ones could participate in elections, which was a shift from the line recently taken over Poland, when he had said that the only people who could join the government were those who had actively shown friendship to the USSR.[327] Eden noted in his diary;

> But he is under Stalin's spell again. He kept repeating 'I like that man'. I am full of admiration of Stalin's handling of him. I told him I was, hoping it would move him. It did a little.[328]

These eyewitness accounts contradict somewhat the common wisdom about Potsdam, which sees Truman and Churchill presenting a new, tough, united front. This underestimates how Churchill was still attracted to maintaining influence with Stalin through personal interactions, and indeed Stalin's ability to play his part in such interactions. Churchill's earlier calls for holding on to territory occupied by Anglo-American forces can be seen as an attempt to seize bargaining chips for diplomatic purposes, rather than preparations for confrontation. Calling the prime minister's method 'jocular bluntness', Moran recollected Churchill saying

> We must listen to these Russians. They mobilised twelve million men and nearly half of them were killed or are missing ... If they want to be a sea power, why not?[329]

Stalin, however, let the mask slip, for a little later, Churchill was complaining:

> The Russians are being very difficult. They talk about the same things as we do, freedom, justice and that sort of thing, but prominent people are removed and not seen again. We are not even allowed to enter Vienna.[330]

For three days Churchill felt Truman's firmness had done the trick by producing the kind of hard bargaining atmosphere that had produced the arrangements at the Tolstoy conference, but then was not so sure. On 21 July there was a big wrangle over the Polish western frontier, which the Soviets wanted to be on the line Oder-Western Neisse, and the Anglo-Americans regarded as settled at Yalta on the Eastern Neisse. The Western Allies were worried about the treatment of the Germans in those areas and not reassured by Stalin's claim that they had all fled before the Red Army and that there would be no need for transfers of population when the area became Polish. The Western Allies were also worried, because these regions, and the Soviet zone, used to feed the western industrial part of Germany which was now the British, French and American zones and wanted to ensure provision of food for the Germans who would now be under their control. Soviet demands for reparations from the British and American zones as well as from their own would have made that task even more difficult, had they been satisfied.

The feeling of impotence that Churchill had been experiencing intermittently since Tehran, and the awareness of the vast potential of Soviet power, dropped away suddenly the following day. The reason was the successful test of the atom bomb in the New Mexican desert. Based on the result of one test, with no regard to the problems of delivery and of the Soviets quickly getting the bomb, Churchill became almost wildly optimistic to General Brooke. Brooke recalled Churchill as seeing himself 'as the sole possessor of the bombs and capable of dumping them where he wished, thus all powerful and capable of dictating to Stalin!'[331] Before the Soviets could get the bomb the British and Americans, as the only nations with principles, must fix things up.

The Potsdam Conference is often depicted as more confrontational than Tehran or Yalta, and this is usually ascribed to Truman's personality, together with the knowledge that he and Churchill had of the successful atom bomb test. The meeting on 24 July is taken as typical. Churchill and Truman told Stalin that the Soviets could not introduce their form of government into liberated countries and then expect the US to recognise it. This, said Truman, was his view today and would be his view tomorrow. Churchill added that in one country Allied representatives were restricted and shut in: it really amounted to internment. Stalin retorted that the prime minister was indulging in fairy-tales. Churchill at once replied that it was one way of conducting a debate, to represent what the other side said as just a fairy tale. Stalin saw that for once the Soviets were getting nowhere and said that their points of view were so different that discussion should be adjourned for private talks.[332] The atmosphere was certainly different to that at Tehran and Yalta. There Stalin had been at pains to get Roosevelt's backing, and the President had things he wanted of Stalin, so he would declare without a word to Churchill that a particular Soviet case was reasonable and would have his support. At Potsdam, Truman was more inclined to state US interests in a take-it-or-leave-it manner that was anathema to the arch-bargainer Roosevelt. Churchill welcomed the straightforwardness in contrast to Roosevelt's playing of his cards close to his chest and his willingness to suddenly make a gesture with no coordination with his ally. Truman, somewhat awe-struck by Churchill, treated him with more respect.[333]

However, despite the more direct language used by all the participants, it was still a functioning, working conference where deals were struck on some issues, and other matters, on which a solution was elusive, were deferred for later discussion by the foreign ministers. Churchill's personal relations with Stalin were cordial, very much in the vein of the Tolstoy meetings.[334] Churchill may well have hoped, as he later claimed, that this, along with the firmness of the American president and the new power of the atom bomb would enable him when he returned for the second half of the Conference, after the announcement of the British general election result, to settle favourably the many unresolved points, such as the precise form of the Italian peace terms, the disposal of the German navy, the immediate future of Austria, and the Polish occupation of the lands between the Eastern and Western Neisse. However, neither Eden nor Churchill was to return to Potsdam. As it was, for all the hard bargaining, the alliance remained operational after Potsdam, with the Council of Foreign Ministers established with the explicit purpose of keeping it functioning into the post-war period.

Conclusion: Churchill and Stalin

The Churchill-Stalin relationship underwent many fluctuations during the war, but there were certain constants. If Churchill's dislike of Bolshevism never wavered, his regard for Stalin's abilities as a warlord and realist, and his gratitude for the colossal sacrifices made by the Soviet peoples, were entirely genuine. At times they led him to see the future more hopefully than at others. He could see the cold self-interest which dictated Soviet policy, and which activated Stalin, but he did not consistently view the USSR as an expansionist imperialist power. With Stalin as its leader – a sagacious, realistic man who could be trusted – the Soviet Union need not necessarily be a threat to the Western democracies or the British Empire, so long as they were united and strong and firm in their resolve to face up to the Soviets and keep them in check. This was the important point; for Churchill – to him the USSR was a 'bully' but like all bullies, could be restrained by firm treatment. This was the real message behind his 'Iron Curtain' speech at Fulton, Missouri in 1946 – the democracies must not let their guard slip just because Hitler was beaten, because if they did the Soviet Union was waiting, poised to slip into the resultant vacuum.

Moreover, Churchill seems to have developed a liking for the Soviet leader, or at least for the construct of Stalin that he had created. Moran, Eden, and Harriman all felt this. From these witnesses it is obvious that Churchill retained his friendly feeling and even trust of Stalin to the end of the war. It was not constant – between meetings it quickly developed into irritation at Soviet behaviour, and his loathing for Bolshevism and his geopolitical awareness of Soviet/Russian power came out again. Once he had met Stalin again, as Eden put it, he came 'under Stalin's spell'. Stalin's harsh tone in his correspondence tended to aggravate Churchill – though as with their meetings in person, a few choice positive phrases from Stalin could usually revive for him the seductive vision of the warrior alliance.

Most probably Churchill was agreeably surprised when he first met Stalin in August 1942. Their correspondence had before this been infrequent and often veering more to the adversarial in tone, in comparison to that with Roosevelt before Churchill met the American leader. Churchill had been at pains to give the American all the benefit of the doubt: unlike with Stalin, he needed to draw Roosevelt into actions he was reluctant to take, whereas with Stalin, the main thing Britain wanted, Soviet belligerence, was a given from June 1941 and Churchill showed less concern than did many in his government that Soviet morale and will to resist were at risk. Stalin's humour and hospitality when they finally met must have come as a surprise, and according to Harriman, Churchill came back from his first Moscow meeting 'all for Joe'. So though it goes somewhat counter to the Churchill 'myth', it does seem that Churchill developed a liking for Stalin and that this affected his appreciation of the possibility of good relations with the USSR every time he had personal contact with the Soviet leader. At other times his dislike of Bolshevism and his distrust of it got the better of him, though he would still maintain you could trust Stalin if you could get his word on anything. He was consistent in distinguishing between Stalin and the 'communist leaders' he sometimes spoke about – a viewpoint that had a history for him going back at least to 1936.

By contrast, Stalin identified Churchill as more unequivocally part of a school of British opinion than he actually was, oversignifying Churchill's concerns not to completely eradicate the German state. Where Churchill had come to trust Stalin as a man of his word, and to build much on his belief that he was in effect a realist and a moderate in contrast to other Soviet leaders, Stalin never really trusted Churchill. Setting aside Stalin's own personal pathology, looking objectively at their interactions in the war, it has to be said that Stalin had some cause. Of the two, Churchill was the one who tended to promise more and deliver less. His strategy of obscuring British inactivity, or incapability, by flowery phrasing and promises of a belligerent future – rich Churchillian fighting talk – while it had some value in lubricating face-to-face interactions, meant that there were many promises broken or long deferred. The frank aspect of their correspondence – arguably at times (when they were eschewing 'guff') much more direct and explicit than that of either of them with Roosevelt – bespoke the quality of their relationship, and possibly softened some of the consequences of Churchill's broken promises, but still left Stalin with the sure knowledge that he could not take Churchill's word.

Churchill's emotional inconsistencies also meant that he was hard to predict in ideological terms. All that said, the traditional view that Stalin coldly manipulated his relations with his Big Three partners does not hold up under analysis. Stalin enjoyed his personal interactions with his fellow leaders, and the mutual cordiality was not all forced.[335] Stalin sought to manage and influence Churchill by a mixture of charm and bullying – or at least direct and forceful criticism. Stalin was long notorious in Soviet domestic politics for his *grubost* ('rudeness') – it was a central characteristic of many of his personal interactions. An example of how Stalin could not help being rude is in the exchange of telegrams in January 1944. Churchill sent a long message complaining about how insulted he felt by the *Pravda* story suggesting the British were making illicit peace feelers in Romania. Churchill said that even when Britain was alone, and did not know what side the USSR was on, he never considered a peace, when he could quite easily have done so, at Soviet expense. Stalin made a fist at mollifying him by saying that actually he would never have made a separate peace, but did it in a way that made it sound almost like an accusation that Churchill was now lying.[336] Some of his reactions – for instance in his October 1942 complaints to Maisky – also suggest Stalin may have felt in retrospect that Churchill had manipulated him at their personal meetings, and got the better of him. On the other hand, his very frankness in correspondence as much as bullying suggests a confidence in the robustness of their relationship. Indeed, Stalin on a number of times in his telegrams said that his idea of correspondence between allies was that they should say what they thought without fear of giving offence.[337] With that in mind, we might conclude that while the levels of trust in the relationship were asymmetrical, it was a mutually beneficial one, and one that each protagonist devoted much effort to maintaining, whatever the ideological gulf that existed between them. The frank directness, which was often sharp, also gives the correspondence a tone of intimacy and honesty that is somewhat surprising, given the character and background of the two protagonists. Churchill underlined at the start of their first discussion the realism that he saw as possible for them to maintain at the heart of their relationship. He said that he 'came here to talk about real things. We are going to talk to one another as friends.' Perhaps with Roosevelt, the friendliness and frankness were taken as a given and so did not need to be overtly expressed, but it is a characteristic of the Stalin-Churchill exchanges that they had an element of this harsh frankness, alongside the adulatory sentiments, that was seldom present (or considered advisable) with the American leader.[338]

Interestingly, despite the onset of the Cold War, the personal cordiality between Churchill and Stalin remained. In spite of his 'Iron Curtain' rhetoric in the address at Fulton, Missouri, Churchill continued to distinguish between Stalin and the actions of the Soviet state. Stalin responded to the Fulton speech with an attack on Churchill for the 'racism' inherent in his emphasis on the Anglo-American peoples, but was also prepared to maintain cordial personal exchanges on odd occasions. It is possible that he shared just a little of Churchill's nostalgic 'comrade-in-arms' feeling about their relationship.[339] For all that Stalin regarded Churchill as a 'dangerous bourgeois statesman', he seems, like Churchill, to have relished their wartime exchanges. They were sometimes elliptical and dressed in hyperbole, sometimes remarkably blunt and undiplomatically frank, but it is clear from the documents on both sides that it was a special – even unique – relationship.

Chapter 3

Allying with the Devil: Forging the Grand Alliance, 1941–1942

Hitler's invasion of the Soviet Union began just before dawn on 22 June 1941 with an attack across a 1,000-mile front by 180 divisions. Code-named Operation Barbarossa, the goal of the German blitzkrieg was to rapidly destroy the Red Army and occupy European Russia west of a line running from Archangel (Arkhangelsk) in the north to Astrakhan in the south. The 3-million strong invasion force was organised in three massed army groups: Army Group North attacked from East Prussia and fought its way along the Baltic coast towards Leningrad, Army Group Centre advanced towards Minsk, Smolensk and Moscow, and Army Group South headed for Kiev, the Ukrainian capital.

In little more than a week Minsk had fallen to the Germans, who executed a massive encirclement operation west of the city that trapped hundreds of thousands of Soviet military personnel. The same fate befell half a million Soviet soldiers at Kiev in September. Leningrad escaped capture but was surrounded and besieged by the Germans – a three-year ordeal that cost a million civilian lives. By early November the Wehrmacht was at the gates of Moscow and the Red Army had lost a stunning 200 divisions in battle. But to everyone's surprise – not least Hitler's – while the Soviet system buckled, it did not break.

There is a story – dating from Khrushchev's secret speech to the 20th Congress of the Soviet Communist Party in 1956 – that Stalin was so shocked by the initial success of the German invasion he suffered a nervous collapse. When Stalin's Foreign Commissar, Vyacheslav Molotov, was asked about this episode, he recalled: 'I wouldn't say he lost his head. He suffered, but he didn't show any signs of this. Undoubtedly, he had his rough moments. It's nonsense to say he didn't suffer.'[1] While the witness testimony is contradictory, the documentary evidence shows that Stalin may have been shaken by events but he remained in command of both himself and the situation. During the early days of the war he had many meetings and issued numerous orders. In early July he did disappear to his *dacha* for 36 hours or so but emerged to deliver a masterly speech on Soviet radio. If Stalin did have a breakdown it was short-lived and he staged a miraculous recovery.

What shook Stalin was not so much the German invasion – which was not unexpected – but the catastrophic failure of Soviet defences, particularly the collapse of the Red Army's Western Front and the rapidity with which Belorussia and its capital, Minsk, fell to the Wehrmacht. He feared, too, a switching of alliances in which Britain – led since May 1940 by the anti-Communist conservative

Winston Churchill – would realign with Nazi Germany and form an anti-Bolshevik alliance. Stalin was reassured on that score by a telegram from his ambassador in London, Ivan Maisky, on 22 June that Foreign Secretary Anthony Eden had told him there would be no change in British policy, nor would Britain slacken its military efforts.[2]

Even before the German invasion Churchill had said that 'if Hitler invaded Hell, I would at least make a favourable reference to the Devil in the House of Commons'.[3] True to his word, on the evening of 22 June Churchill broadcast his support for the USSR in the struggle against Nazi Germany. In his first-ever radio speech, on 3 July, Stalin highlighted Churchill's declaration of support and emphasised that the Soviet war against Germany would be fought in alliance with other states and peoples.

The Churchill-Stalin correspondence started with Churchill's message of 7 July (**Document 1**) which was delivered personally to Stalin by Stafford Cripps, the British ambassador in Moscow. Stalin raised with Cripps the need for a political agreement between the Soviet Union and Great Britain in which the two states would pledge mutual military aid and guarantee they would not sign a separate peace with Germany.[4] It was Cripps' report on this discussion that prompted Churchill's second message to Stalin on 9 July (**Document 2**) and on 12 July an Anglo-Soviet agreement on joint military action against Germany was signed.

An early example of military cooperation was the British and Soviet occupation of Iran in August 1941. The aim of the operation was to oust a pro-German government in Tehran in order to secure supply lines across Persia for delivery of Western aid to the USSR – a conduit of crucial importance later in the war.

In his first message to Churchill (**Document 3**), on 18 July, Stalin raised a matter that was to become a running sore in his relations with the British PM: the need for a second front to draw Wehrmacht forces away from Russia. Stalin suggested second fronts in northern France and the Arctic but a large-scale landing on the French coast was his priority. Churchill responded that while Britain would undertake any feasible military operation it would not court disaster (**Documents 8–10**). While Stalin was desperate for any help, no matter how risky, Churchill intended to conserve his forces in the event the Red Army was beaten by the Germans. In Churchill's mind, too, was the memory of huge British losses in France during the First World War. He was also a great believer in air power as a war-winning weapon and hoped the destruction of Germany's industry and infrastructure would precipitate the country's internal collapse.

Military supplies were of more immediate importance to Stalin than the opening of a second front, and he welcomed Churchill and Roosevelt's proposal (**Document 7**) to convene a conference in Moscow to discuss the allocation of joint resources to the various theatres of military action. The United States had yet to enter the war but in December 1940 Roosevelt had declared the US to be the 'arsenal of democracy' and in March 1941 Congress passed the Lend-Lease legislation which authorised large-scale aid to Britain. Roosevelt announced the extension of Lend-Lease to the USSR shortly after the German attack and at the end of July he sent his trusted confidant, Harry Hopkins, to Moscow for face-to-face discussions with Stalin.

Hopkins came to Moscow highly recommended. 'You can trust him absolutely. He is your friend and our friend', Churchill messaged Stalin (**Document 6**). Hopkins was not a well man and Stalin was impressed by his courage in under-taking the arduous journey to Moscow. As Averell Harriman recalled, apart from Churchill and Roosevelt, Hopkins was the only foreigner to whom Stalin ever showed any personal warmth.[5]

Hopkins' visit was followed by the Moscow supplies conference at the end of September, which resulted in a detailed (and secret) agreement on extensive Western supplies to the Soviet Union. During the course of what Churchill later called the Grand Alliance, Britain, the United States, Canada, Australia and other Western Allies supplied the Soviet Union with about 10 per cent of its total economic needs, including food for a third of its population.[6]

Churchill was represented at the conference by Lord Beaverbrook, his Minister of Aircraft Production, and Roosevelt by Harriman, who was his Lend-Lease coordinator in London. Beaverbrook and Harriman had two meetings with Stalin. Most of their talk was about supplies but at the second meeting, on 30 September, Stalin said he thought the 12 July agreement should be turned into an Anglo-Soviet treaty of alliance covering the post-war period as well as the war. Beaverbrook agreed and promised to raise the matter with Churchill and other members of the War Cabinet.[7] Harriman was impressed by Stalin's comments about peace but noted that Beaverbrook didn't ask Stalin what he had in mind.[8]

The supplies conference concluded with a grand dinner in the Catherine the Great room in the Kremlin attended by over a hundred people, including Stalin, who told Beaverbrook and Harriman that the war should be won by the armies of the three countries meeting.[9] According to Captain H.H. Balfour, a member of the British delegation, Stalin

> talked a lot about Churchill. He thought that Chamberlain had been a disaster for England and for Russia. He explained plausibly how he had come to sign the Russo-German pact in 1939. He thought that Chamberlain and the Conservative Party ... fundamentally disliked and distrusted the Russians. He would not send a Cabinet Minister to Russia in 1939. He saw war coming, and Russia must know where she stood. If he could not get an alliance with England, then he must not be left alone – isolated – only to be the victim of the victors when the war was over. Therefore, he had to make his pact with Germany. However, this was purely defensive, and he had made clear to Hitler that never at any time would he be a party to fighting Britain alongside Germany.[10]

Stalin followed up his suggestion to Harriman and Beaverbrook in a message to Churchill on 8 November (**Document 12**) urging clarity on war aims and the post-war organisation of the peace. In response Churchill sent his Foreign Secretary, Anthony Eden, to Moscow.

Eden's trip to the Soviet Union in December 1941 was the first official visit by a British Foreign Secretary, though as Minister of State for Foreign Affairs (i.e. deputy FM) Eden had travelled to Moscow to meet Stalin in March 1935.

Eden arrived in the Soviet capital on 15 December in the company of Maisky, who acted as interpreter at his talks with Stalin and Molotov. Next day, at his first meeting with Stalin, Eden faced an unexpected proposal from Stalin: that Britain and the Soviet Union should sign not just a pact on mutual military aid during the war but a general agreement on the settlement of post-war problems. The details of the settlement were set out in a secret protocol on the reorganisation of European borders after the war: Europe's pre-war territorial-political status quo would be largely restored but Hitler's allies would lose some territory and his enemies gain some. Germany itself would be weakened by disarmament and dismemberment as well as territorial losses. Post-war security would be further enhanced by a military alliance of democratic states (**Document 15**).

Just a few weeks earlier Moscow had been on the verge of falling to the Germans, now Stalin proposed to pre-empt any Versailles-type peace conference by a settlement in advance with the British of the most important political and territorial issues. The context of Stalin's radical proposal was that in early December the Red Army had launched a successful counter-offensive in front of Moscow. That counter-attack was now developing into a broad-front strategic offensive to reverse Operation Barbarossa and drive the Germans out of the USSR. Stalin evidently expected the war to be over sooner rather than later and wanted to negotiate post-war changes from a position of strength.

Another factor in Stalin's calculations was the Americans' entry into the war following the Japanese attack on Pearl Harbor on 7 December 1941 and Hitler's declaration of war on the US a few days later. It was not clear at this stage how much attention the US would pay to Europe compared to the Far East but Washington was opposed to the old-style type of great-power agreement proposed by Stalin to Eden and it was imperative for the Soviets to concoct a deal with the British before American influence was brought to bear.

Eden was not opposed in principle to such a deal but said one couldn't be agreed without consultation with his colleagues in London, with the member states of the British Commonwealth, and, most important, with the Americans. As the documents on his conversations with Stalin show, Eden took the same line in response to what emerged as Stalin's priority in the talks – British recognition of the USSR's borders at the time of the German attack on Russia, including territory the Soviets had occupied or extracted from Poland, Romania, Finland and the Baltic States during the period of the Nazi-Soviet Pact. Stalin pressed Eden hard on this matter and was more than a little frustrated by his obdurate resistance to recognising extant Soviet borders, pointing out that during the First World War Britain was willing to grant Tsarist Russia much more territory, including control of Constantinople and the Black Sea Straits.

Eden left Moscow on 22 December 1941 with no agreement having been reached. In London the Cabinet was divided about whether or not to recognise the USSR's 1941 borders in an Anglo-Soviet treaty. On 9 March 1942 Churchill messaged Stalin that he had urged Roosevelt to approve the signature of an agreement on Soviet borders (**Document 19**). The Americans were not for turning, however, and formal British proposals to the Soviets contained no such proviso. During discussions with Maisky in London Eden suggested that Molotov should travel to Britain to sign an Anglo-Soviet agreement.[11] Stalin took up this suggestion in a message to Churchill on 22 April (**Document 21**), noting also that Roosevelt had invited Molotov to the United States to discuss the question of a second front.

Molotov flew to Scotland, arriving on 20 May.[12] After travelling south by train, he stayed at Chequers, the British government's country retreat north of London. He was not overly impressed by his accommodation, complaining later about its lack of a shower and comparing it unfavourably with the White House, where he stayed on the Washington leg of his trip. According to Churchill – not always the most reliable of witnesses – Molotov slept with a revolver beside his bed, but he still thought very highly of the Foreign Commissar's skills as a diplomat, comparing him to the great realpolitik statesmen of the nineteenth century: 'in the conduct of foreign affairs, Mazarin, Talleyrand and Metternich would welcome him to their company'.

Molotov's mission was to continue the Anglo-Soviet treaty negotiations, in particular the sticking point about the USSR's western borders, and, most importantly, to lobby for a second front. As in Moscow, Maisky acted as interpreter for the Soviet side. At his first meeting with Churchill, on 22 May, Molotov made it clear that for the Soviets the most important issue was the second front. He argued repeatedly that the second front was primarily a political question – of Allied commitment to the common cause – and warned his British hosts that the balance of forces on the Soviet-German front favoured Hitler, and the Red Army might not be able to hold out. It was imperative that substantial German forces be diverted to contest a second front in the West. But Churchill was unmoved, insisting that Britain would do what could be done but would not undertake any risky military adventures (**Document 22**).

After two days of discussions Molotov reported to Stalin: 'while he is showing me particular personal attention – lunch, dinner, a long personal conversation till late at night at Chequers – Churchill is behaving with obvious lack of sympathy towards us concerning the substance of the two main questions ... All the recent conversations give me the impression that Churchill is waiting for new events on our front and is not in a hurry to agree with us at the moment.'[13]

Later that day Molotov met Eden, who gave him the draft of a twenty-year treaty of mutual assistance. Since the document did not include any commitments about the USSR's borders or the organisation of the post-war peace, Molotov cabled Stalin that it was an 'empty declaration' and should be rejected. No one was closer to Stalin than Molotov and he must have been surprised by Stalin's response, which broke with what had hitherto been Moscow's unyielding policy: 'We have received the draft treaty Eden handed you. We do not consider it an empty declaration but regard it as an important document. It lacks the question of the security of frontiers, but this not too bad perhaps, for it gives us a free hand.

The question of frontiers, or to be more exact, of guarantees for the security of our frontiers at one or another section of our country, will be decided by force.'[14]

Stalin's about-turn may be explained by reference to events on the battlefield. A Red Army operation to retake Kharkov, the Ukraine's second-largest city, had just failed abysmally. Soviet losses were huge and the prospects for rolling back the German advance much diminished. Stalin's new priority was to solidify the alliance with Britain and, if possible, to secure a second front.

Molotov signed the Anglo-Soviet treaty of alliance on 26 May 1942. It provided for a twenty-year mutual assistance pact against Germany and pledged 'close and friendly collaboration after the reestablishment of peace for the organisation of security and economic prosperity in Europe'.

In Washington Molotov's arguments in favour of a second front received a more sympathetic response from Roosevelt than from Churchill. In mid-1942, however, there were very few American troops in Britain, which meant that the last word on this matter would be Churchill's. But Molotov did manage to get the Americans to agree a communique which stated that 'full understanding was reached with regard to the urgent task of creating a Second Front in Europe in 1942'. The threat of a second front was better than nothing and it would at least keep the Germans guessing about Allied intentions.

Molotov left Washington on 5 June and flew to London, determined to get Churchill to agree the communique, too. At his first meeting with Churchill, on 9 June, Molotov reiterated the argument that delaying a second front until 1943 would not make the operation any easier since it would give the Germans time to strengthen their defences. Molotov cited Roosevelt's support for this view but Churchill made it clear that the most the British had in mind for 1942 was a small-scale landing in Europe of six to ten divisions (**Document 30**). Churchill agreed to the text of the communique but as Molotov said in a summary assessment to Stalin on 10 June: 'The British Government is not undertaking any obligations to open the second front this year, but is saying, and with reservation at that, that it is preparing a trial landing.'[15]

After Molotov's visit Churchill was emollient in praise of the Soviet war effort (**Document 32**) but unforthcoming about the second front. Stalin's political and intelligence sources in Britain and the United States kept him abreast of Anglo-American discussions about the second front so he had no illusions about the prospects for its launch in 1942. This must have been at the back of his mind when he responded to a long message from Churchill on 18 July explaining the cancellation of convoys to Northern Russia by not just berating that decision but by raising the issue of the second front, whose delay until 1943, said Stalin, could not be tolerated (**Document 33**).

By this time the Germans had launched Operation Blue – a thrust into southern Russia designed to capture Stalingrad and occupy the Soviet oilfields at Baku on the far side of the Caucasus. The operation had already achieved considerable success and once again the Red Army was in full retreat. On 28 July Stalin issued Order 227. Its rallying call was 'Not a step back! This must now be our chief slogan. It is necessary to defend to the last drop of blood every position, every metre of Soviet territory, to cling to every shred of Soviet earth and defend it to the utmost.'

Churchill responded to Stalin's complaints about the convoys and the second front by suggesting a meeting between the two of them, a proposal that Stalin accepted. The scene was set for Churchill's first visit to Moscow, a trip into the ogre's den, as his wife Clementine put it.

Before Churchill's arrival in Moscow Stalin was briefed by Maisky. The purpose of Churchill's trip, Maisky reported on 7 August, was threefold. First, to pacify public agitation in Britain for a second front. Second, to discuss Allied strategy to defeat Germany. Third, to convince Stalin that a second front in Europe was impossible at the present time. Churchill feared a Nazi victory, counselled Maisky, and was looking for ways to support the Soviet Union short of a second front. In conclusion, Stalin's ambassador urged his boss to concentrate on demands for supplies rather than a second front.[16]

Documents 1–33

1. Churchill to Stalin, 7 July 1941

We are all very glad the Russian armies are offering such strong, courageous and steadfast resistance to the completely unprovoked and merciless invasion of the Nazis. The bravery and tenacity of the Soviet soldiers and people has evoked general admiration. We will do everything to help you that time, geography and our growing resources allow. The longer the war lasts the more help we can give. British air forces are day and night making big raids on all German-occupied territories and all of Germany that is within our reach ... We hope to force Hitler to return some of his air power to the west and gradually take some of the strain off your country. Besides this, at my request the Admiralty has prepared a serious operation in the Arctic, which they will mount in the near future, after which I hope contact will be established between the British and Russian Navies ...

We welcome the arrival of a Russian Military Mission with the aim of agreeing future plans.

We have only got to go on fighting with all our strength in order to beat the life out of these villains.

2. Churchill to Stalin, 9 July 1941

Immediately on receiving Sir Stafford Cripps' report of his talk with you and the terms of a proposed Anglo-Soviet declaration under two heads, namely,

(1) mutual aid without limits to extent or character, and

(2) a commitment that neither country will conclude a separate peace,

I convened the British War Cabinet, including Mr Fraser, Prime Minister of the Dominion of New Zealand, who is in London just now. You will understand that it will be necessary to ask for the views of the Dominions – Canada, Australia, and South Africa. At the same time, I would like to assure you that we are wholly in favour of the proposal for an Anglo-Soviet declaration. We think it should be signed as soon as we have had responses from the Dominions and publicised immediately thereafter.

3. Stalin to Churchill, 18 July 1941

Allow me to thank you for both your personal messages.

Your messages have initiated agreement between our two Governments. Now, as you with every justification put it, the Soviet Union and Great Britain have become fighting allies in the struggle against Hitlerite Germany. I have no doubt our two countries have sufficient strength to defeat our common enemy, all the difficulties notwithstanding.

Perhaps it would be useful to inform you that the position of Soviet troops at the front remains strained. The results of Hitler's unexpected violation of the non-aggression pact and the sudden attack on the Soviet Union has placed German troops at an advantage and are affecting the position of the Soviet armies ... It seems to me, furthermore, that the military position of the Soviet Union, as well as that of Great Britain, would improve significantly if a front was established against Hitler in the west (northern France) and the north (the Arctic).

A front in northern France would not only draw Hitler's forces from the east, it would make impossible the invasion of Britain by Hitler. Establishment of this front would be popular both with the British army and with the population of southern England. I am aware of the difficulty of establishing such a front, but it seems to me, difficulties notwithstanding, it should be established, not only for the sake of our common cause, but also in Britain's own interest. The best time to open this front is now, when Hitler's forces have been switched to the east and he has not yet been able to consolidate the positions he has occupied in the east.

It would be easier still to open a front in the north. This would call for action only by British naval and air forces, without landing troops or artillery. Soviet land, naval and air forces could take part in the operation. We would be glad if Great Britain could send a light division or more of Norwegian volunteers, who could be moved to northern Norway for insurgent action against the Germans.

4. Churchill to Stalin, 20 July 1941

I am very glad to receive your message and to learn from many sources of the valiant fight and many vigorous counter-attacks with which the Russian armies are defending their native soil. I understand fully the military advantage you have gained by forcing the enemy to deploy and engage on forward western fronts, thus weakening the force of his initial blows.

Anything sensible and effective that we can do to help you will be done. I ask you, however, to bear in mind the limitations imposed upon us by our resources and geographical position. From the first day of the German attack upon Russia, we have examined the possibilities of attacking occupied France and the Low Countries. The Chiefs of Staff do not see any possibility of doing anything on a scale that could be of any help to you. In France alone the Germans have forty divisions, and for more than a year the whole coast has been fortified with typical German zeal and bristles with cannon, wire, pill-boxes and beach mines. The only part where we could have even temporary air superiority and air fighter protection is from Dunkirk to Boulogne. Here there are a mass of fortifications, with scores of heavy guns commanding the sea approaches, many of which can fire right across the Straits. There is less than five hours of darkness, and even in this period the whole area is illuminated by searchlights. To attempt a landing in force would be to encounter a bloody defeat, and small raids would only lead to failure, doing far more harm than good to both of us. It would all be over without their having to move, or before they could move, a single unit from your fronts.

You must remember that we have been fighting completely alone for more than a year, and that, although our resources are growing, and will grow fast from now on, our forces are at the utmost strain both at home and in the Middle East by land and air, and also that the battle of the Atlantic, on which our life depends, and the movements of our convoys in the face of the U-boat and Focke-Wulf blockade, strain our naval forces, great though they be, to the utmost limit. It is, however, to the north that we must look for any speedy help that we can give. For the past three weeks the Naval Staff have been preparing an operation by sea-borne aircraft upon German shipping in northern Norway and Finland, hoping thereby to destroy the enemy's power to transport troops by sea to attack your Arctic flank …

There is no Norwegian Light Division in existence, and it would be impossible to land troops, either British or Russian, on German-occupied territory in perpetual daylight without having first obtained reasonable fighter air cover. We had bitter experiences at Namsos last year, and in Crete this year, of trying such enterprises. We are also studying, as a further development, basing some British fighter air squadrons on Murmansk … Do not hesitate to suggest anything else that occurs to you, and we will also be searching earnestly for other ways of striking at the common foe.

5. Churchill to Stalin, 25 July 1941

I am very glad to inform you that the War Cabinet has decided to send to Russia as soon as possible two hundred Tomahawk fighter aeroplanes, despite the fact that this will seriously deplete our fighter resources. One hundred and forty of these will be sent from here to Archangel, and sixty from our supplies in the United States of America … From two to three million pairs of ankle boots should shortly be available in this country for shipment. We are also arranging to provide this year large quantities of rubber, tin, wool and woollen clothes, jute, lead and shellac. All your other requirements for raw materials are receiving careful consideration …

We are watching with admiration and emotion the magnificent struggle of your armies. Our information shows the heavy losses and alarm of the enemy. Our air attacks on Germany will continue with increasing strength.

6. Churchill to Stalin, 28 July 1941

… Harry Hopkins has been with me these days. Last week he asked the President to let him go to Moscow. I must tell you that there is a flame in this man for democracy and to beat Hitler. A little while ago, when I asked him for a quarter of a million rifles, they came at once. He is the closest personal representative of the President. The President has now sent him full instructions, and he leaves my house tonight to go to you. You will be advised of his arrival through the proper channels. You can trust him absolutely; he is your friend and our friend. He will help you to plan for the future victory and for the long-term supply of Russia. You can also talk to him freely about policy, strategy and Japan.

The grand resistance of the Russian armies in defence of their soil unites us all. A terrible winter of bombing lies before Germany. No one has yet had what they are going to get ...

7. Churchill and Roosevelt to Stalin, 14 August 1941

We have taken the opportunity afforded by the consideration of the report of Mr Harry Hopkins on his return from Moscow to consult together as to how best our two countries can help your country in the splendid defence that you are putting up against the Nazi attack. We are at the moment cooperating to provide you with the very maximum of supplies that you most urgently need. Already many shiploads have left our shores and more will leave in the immediate future.

We must now turn our minds to the consideration of a more long-term policy, since there is still a long and hard path to be traversed before there can be won that complete victory without which our efforts and sacrifices would be wasted.

The war goes on upon many fronts and before it is over further fighting fronts may develop. Our resources, though immense, are limited and it must become a question of where and when those resources can best be used to further to the greatest extent our common effort. This applies equally to manufactured war supplies and to raw materials.

The needs and demands of your and our armed services can only be determined in the light of the full knowledge of the many facts which must be taken into consideration in the decisions that we take. In order that all of us may be in a position to arrive at speedy decisions as to the apportionment of our joint resources, we suggest that we prepare a meeting, which should be held in Moscow, to which we would send high representatives who could discuss these matters directly with you. If this conference appeals to you, we want you to know that pending the decisions of that conference we will continue to send supplies and material as rapidly as possible.

We realise fully how vitally important to the defeat of Hitlerism is the brave and steadfast resistance of the Soviet Union, and we feel therefore that we must not in any circumstances fail to act quickly and immediately in this matter of planning the programme for the future allocation of our joint resources.

8. Stalin to Churchill, 3 September 1941

... The relative stabilisation of the front achieved some three weeks ago has been upset recently by the arrival of 30–34 fresh German infantry divisions and enormous numbers of tanks and aircraft to the Eastern Front, and also by the activisation of 20 Finnish and 26 Romanian divisions. The Germans look on the threat in the west as a bluff, so they are moving all their forces from west to east with impunity, knowing there is no second front in the west nor is there likely to be one. They think it perfectly possible that they will be able to beat their enemies one at a time, first the Russians and then the British.

As a result, we have lost more than half of Ukraine and, what is more, the enemy is now at the gates of Leningrad ...

Here it is pertinent to ask what is the way out of this more than unfavourable situation.

I think the only way is to open a second front this year somewhere in the Balkans or in France, one that would divert 30–40 German divisions from the Eastern Front, and simultaneously to supply the Soviet Union with 30,000 tons of aluminium by the beginning of October and a minimum monthly aid of 400 aeroplanes and 500 tanks (of small or medium size).

Without these two kinds of aid the Soviet Union may be defeated or will be weakened to such an extent that it will lose for a long time the ability to help its allies by active operations in the struggle against Hitlerism.

I realise this message will cause Your Excellency some vexation. But what can I do? Experience has taught me to face up to reality, no matter how unpleasant it may be, and not to shrink from telling the truth, no matter how unpleasant.

The matter of Iran came off well indeed. Joint operations by British and Soviet troops settled the issue. And so it will be in the future wherever our forces operate jointly. But Iran is merely an episode. It is not in Iran that the outcome of the war will be decided.

The Soviet Union, like Britain, does not want war with Japan. The Soviet Union does not deem it possible to violate treaties, including its treaty of neutrality with Japan. But should Japan violate that treaty and attack the Soviet Union, she will be properly rebuffed by Soviet troops.

In conclusion, allow me to thank you for the admiration you have expressed for the operations of Soviet troops, who are waging a bloody war against Hitler's robber hordes for our common liberation cause.

9. Churchill to Stalin, 6 September 1941

1. I reply at once in the spirit of your message. Although we should shrink from no exertion, there is in fact no possibility of any British action in the west, except air action, which would draw German forces from the east before the winter sets in. There is no chance whatever of a second front in the Balkans without the help of Turkey. I will, if Your Excellency desires, give all the reasons which have led our Chiefs of Staff to these conclusions. They have already been discussed with your Ambassador in conference today with the Foreign Secretary and the Chiefs of Staff. Action, however well-meant, leading only to costly fiascos would be no help to anyone but Hitler.

2. The information at my disposal gives me the impression that the culminating violence of the German invasion is already over and that winter will give your heroic armies a breathing-space. This however is a personal opinion.

3. About supplies. We are well aware of the grievous losses which Russian industry has sustained, and every effort has been and will be made by us to help you. I am cabling President Roosevelt to expedite the arrival here in London of Mr Harriman's mission, and we shall try even before the Moscow Conference to

tell you the numbers of aircraft and tanks we can jointly promise to send each month, together with supplies of rubber, aluminium, cloth, etc ...

5. We are ready to make joint plans with you now. Whether British armies will be strong enough to invade the mainland of Europe during 1942 depends on unforeseeable events. It may be possible however to assist you in the extreme north when there is more darkness. We are hoping to raise our armies in the Middle East to a strength of three-quarters of a million before the end of the year, and thereafter to a million by summer 1942. Once the German-Italian forces in Libya have been destroyed all these forces will be available to come into the line on your southern flank, and it is hoped to encourage Turkey to maintain at the least honourable neutrality. Meanwhile we shall continue to batter Germany from the air with increasing severity and keep the seas open and ourselves alive.

6. In your first paragraph you used the word 'sell'. We had not viewed the matter in such terms and have never thought of payment. Any assistance we can give you would better be upon the same basis of comradeship as the American Lend-Lease Bill, of which no formal account is kept in money. We are willing to put any pressure upon Finland in our power, including immediate notification that we will declare war should they continue beyond the old frontiers. We are asking the United States to take all possible steps to influence Finland.

10. Stalin to Churchill, 13 September 1941
In my last message I set forth the views of the government of the USSR on the opening of a second front as the chief means of promoting our common cause. In reply to your message, where you again stress the impossibility of opening a second front at the present moment, I can only repeat that its absence is playing into the hands of our common enemies.

I have no doubt the English Government wants the Soviet Union to win and is searching for ways to attain that goal. If at the moment the opening of a second front in the west seems unfeasible to the English Government, then perhaps some other means could be found of rendering the Soviet Union active military aid against the common enemy. It seems to me that England could safely land 25–30 divisions at Archangel or ship them to the southern areas of the USSR via Iran for military cooperation with the Soviet troops on Soviet soil in the same way as was done during the last war in France. That would be a great help. I think that help of this kind would be a severe blow to Hitler's aggression.

Please accept my thanks for the promise of monthly British aid in aluminium, aircraft and tanks.

I can only be glad that England sees this aid not as selling and buying aircraft, aluminium and tanks, but as comradely cooperation.

It is my hope that the English Government will have not a few opportunities of satisfying itself that the Soviet Government knows how to appreciate help from its ally ...

11. Stalin to Churchill, 3 October 1941

... The arrival of the British and American missions in Moscow and particularly the fact that they were led by Lord Beaverbrook and Mr Harriman, had a most favourable effect. As for Lord Beaverbrook, he did his utmost to expedite consideration and, possibly, solution, of the most pressing problems discussed at the Moscow Tripartite Conference and to make them quick and effective. I can say the same for Mr Harriman. I wish therefore to convey to you and Mr Roosevelt the sincere gratitude of the Soviet Government for sending such authoritative representatives to Moscow.

Arising from a number of unfavourable circumstances on our front and the resulting evacuation of a further group of enterprises, to say nothing of the fact that a number of issues have been put off until final consideration and settlement in London and Washington, I have to admit that our present requirements in military supplies, transcend the decisions agreed at the conference. Nevertheless, the Moscow Conference did a great deal of important work. I hope the British and American Governments will do all they can to increase the monthly quotas and also to seize the slightest opportunity to accelerate the planned deliveries right now, since the Hitlerites will use the pre-winter months to exert the utmost pressure on the USSR.

... As regards the prospects of our common struggle against the bandits' lair of Hitlerites, who have entrenched themselves in the heart of Europe, I am confident that despite difficulties we shall secure the defeat of Hitler in the interest of our freedom-loving peoples.

12. Stalin to Churchill, 8 November 1941

... I agree with you that we need clarity, which at the moment is lacking in relations between the USSR and Great Britain. The unclarity is due to two circumstances: first, there is no definite understanding between our two countries concerning war aims and plans for the post-war organisation of peace; secondly, there is no treaty between the USSR and Great Britain on mutual military aid in Europe against Hitler. Until understanding is reached on these two main points, not only will there be no clarity in Anglo-Soviet relations, but, if we are to speak frankly, there will be no mutual trust. To be sure, the agreement on military supplies to the Soviet Union is of great positive significance, but that does not settle the issue, nor does it fully cover the question of relations between our two countries.

13. Churchill to Stalin, 21 November 1941

Many thanks for your message just received. At the very beginning of the war I began a personal correspondence with President Roosevelt which has led to a very solid understanding being established between us and has often helped in getting things done quickly. My only desire is to work on equal terms of comradeship and confidence with you.

... I notice that you wish also to discuss the post-war organisation of peace. Our intention is to fight the war in alliance with you and in constant consultation with you, to the utmost of our strength and however long it lasts, and when the war is won, as I am sure it will be, we expect that Soviet Russia, Great Britain and the USA will meet at the council table of victory as the three principal partners and as the agencies by which Nazism will have been destroyed. Naturally the first object will be to prevent Germany, and particularly Prussia, from breaking out upon us for a third time. The fact that Russia is a communist state and that Britain and the USA are not and do not intend to be is no obstacle to our making a good plan for our mutual safety and rightful interests …

It may well be that your defence of Moscow and Leningrad, as well as the splendid resistance to the invader along the whole Russian front, will inflict mortal injuries upon the internal structure of the Nazi regime. But we must not count upon such good fortune but simply keep on striking at them to the utmost with might and main.

14. Stalin to Churchill, 23 November 1941

Thank you for your message.

I sincerely welcome the desire, expressed in your message, to collaborate with me through personal correspondence on a basis of friendship and trust, and I hope it will contribute in many respects to the success of our common cause …

I fully support your proposal to send your Foreign Secretary, Mr Eden, to the USSR in the near future. Discussion and approval of an agreement on joint operations by the Soviet and British troops on our front and the speedy execution of that task would be of great positive significance. It is quite true that the discussion and adoption of a plan for the post-war organisation of peace should be designed to keep Germany, above all Prussia, from again breaking the peace and again plunging nations into a bloodbath.

I also agree that the different state structures of the USSR on the one hand, and of Great Britain and the USA, on the other, should not and cannot be an obstacle to a favourable solution of the fundamental problems of safeguarding our mutual security and rightful interests. I hope that reticence or doubts on this score, if any, will be dispelled by the talks with Mr Eden …

15. Eden-Stalin meeting in Moscow, 16 December 1941

Present: Eden, Cripps, Stalin, Molotov, Maisky (acting as interpreter)

After the exchanging of greetings, with Eden expressing his pleasure at again being in Moscow and meeting Stalin, **Stalin** proposed to Eden two draft treaties – one on mutual military assistance and one the resolution of post-war problems. Upon glancing at the texts **Eden** said while he did not have any objections in principle to this kind of treaty, he would like, of course, to study the proposed texts more carefully and, perhaps, introduce some minor amendments.

Stalin and **Molotov** did not object to Eden's plan.

Then **Stalin** said that in his opinion it would be desirable to attach to the second treaty a secret protocol which would outline a general scheme for the reorganisation of European frontiers after the war. This scheme envisaged:

1. Poland. The western frontier of Poland should encompass East Prussia and the Corridor, while the German population of these regions should be evacuated to

Germany. The eastern frontier of Poland, i.e. frontier with the USSR, should go along the River Nemen, while Tilsit should be in the hands of Lithuania, which is part of the USSR. Further south this frontier should approximate the Curzon Line, which could be modified in certain places.

2. Czechoslovakia must be restored to its old borders, including the Sudetenland. The latter region, in view of its strategic importance, can in no event remain in the hands of Germany. Moreover, the territory of Czechoslovakia should be enlarged in the south at the expense of Hungary, which must pay the appropriate penalty for its behaviour during the war.

3. Yugoslavia should be restored to its old frontiers and somewhat expanded at the expense of Italy (Trieste, Fiume, islands in the Adriatic Sea, etc.).

4. Albania could be reconstituted as an independent state, with its independence guaranteed by other powers.

5. Turkey can get the Dodecanese, the Turkish-populated area in Bulgaria south of Burgas and, perhaps, some territories in Syria as compensation for observing neutrality. It would also be appropriate to give Turkey some islands in the Aegean Sea which block access to the sea from its major ports, such as Smyrna. On this point **Eden** noted that the Dodecanese had long been claimed by Greece because the islands were populated by Greeks, but he recognised the necessity to discuss different ways of settling this question. On his part, **Stalin** added that the detachment of the Burgas region from Bulgaria would be punishment for Bulgaria's behaviour during the war. Bulgaria ought to endure a small territorial loss at the Yugoslav frontier as well. In Comrade Stalin's opinion it is enough for Bulgaria to have one sea port, such as Varna.

6. Greece should be restored to its old frontiers. The same should be done in relation to all other countries occupied by Germany.

7. France. On the question of the future of France, **Stalin** asked Eden what he thought about this question? It is clear that Petain and company are completely hopeless people who counted on a German victory. At any rate, what is the possible future of France? Can one now express certain intentions in relation to this matter or is it better to ignore the problem? **Eden** replied that he fully agreed with Stalin's estimation of Petain and company. As to the future of France, it seems to him that France will go through a very long period of demoralisation and depression before it can become a great power again. It is not excluded that this will never happen and that France will pass to the position of a second-rate European power, like Spain. **Stalin** expressed the view that if France remained in a state of prolonged prostration after this war, in the interests of Britain's security it would be advisable for it to have military and naval bases on the French coast at such points, for example Boulogne, Dunkirk, etc. Similarly, it would be advisable for Belgium and Holland to have an open military alliance with Great Britain and for the latter to have the right to keep its military, air and naval bases in their territories as well. This would be important not only from the point of view of the security interests of Great Britain, but also as a guarantee of the independence of

Belgium and Holland. The Soviet Union would be prepared to support such English claims. Also, the Soviet Union would not object if England had naval bases in Norway or Denmark, as long as some other powers were guaranteed access to and from the Baltic Sea. Eden thanked Stalin for his promise to support Great Britain in acquiring naval and other bases in the countries mentioned.

8. Germany. In relation to Germany **Stalin** said that it is absolutely essential to weaken Germany, in the first place by the detachment of the Rhineland with its industrial area from the rest of Prussia. The future destiny of the Rhineland – as an independent state, protectorate, etc. – can be discussed later. Most important is the separation. Austria should be reconstituted as an independent state. Possibly, the same could be done for Bavaria.

9. The Soviet Union considers it essential to restore its frontiers as they were in 1941, on the eve of the German attack on the USSR. This includes the Soviet-Finnish frontier established by the Soviet-Finnish peace treaty of 1940, the Baltic republics, Bessarabia and Northern Bukovina. As for the Soviet border with Poland, it might, as has been said, in general and as a whole, follow the Curzon Line, with Tilsit being incorporated into the Lithuanian Republic. Moreover, the Soviet Union, which returned Petsamo to Finland in 1940 as a gift, considers it necessary to take it back in view of the position taken by Finland in the present war. Further, the Soviet Union would like Romania to have a military alliance with the USSR, the latter having the right to military, air and naval bases on Romanian territory. The size of Romania itself should be somewhat expanded in the west at the expense of Hungary within the area where up to 1,500,000 Romanians now live. This would also be an additional punishment of Hungary for its role in the war. In the north, the Soviet Union would like to have similar relations with Finland, i.e. Finland should have a military alliance with the USSR, the latter having the right to military, air and naval bases on Finnish territory.

Setting forth all this, **Stalin** noted that this scheme should be the basis of a secret protocol attached to the treaty on post-war problems. Further, Stalin touched upon two more questions of the post-war order. Firstly, he expressed the view that Germany must pay damages to countries (Great Britain, the USSR, Poland, and others) it had damaged. Secondly, in the future, reconstructed Europe, it is desirable, in the interests of maintaining peace and order, to establish a military alliance of democratic States, which would be headed by a council or other central organ having international military forces at its disposal. The Soviet Union would also not object to the establishment of one or another state federations in Europe. Stalin asked Eden to express his opinion on all the questions that had been broached.

Eden began with the texts of the public treaties and in this connection submitted to Stalin his draft of an agreement. He thought that the text of the future treaties might be to a certain extent combine the Soviet text with the British text, especially since they coincided on a number of points.

Concerning the problems of post-war Europe, Eden said he was very much obliged to Stalin for such a detailed and frank an exposition of what he thought about this matter. Personally, he agreed with the views expressed by Stalin. He believes that in post-war Europe the responsibility for its reconstruction and maintenance of law and order will rest mostly with our two states, together, of course, with the United States, in so far as the latter is generally ready to collaborate in this matter. In relation to the future Germany, he can assure Stalin that the British people are determined to do everything in their power to prevent a repetition of German aggression. How to do this needs careful consideration and discussion. It seems to Eden that in all circumstances and conditions the strictest military control over Germany will be needed and that England, the Soviet Union and the United States (should the latter so wish) should organise such control. On the question of breaking up Germany the British Government has taken no decisions but it does not object to it in principle. To Eden it seems it is desirable that the breaking up of Germany should be done, if possible, by stimulating separatist movements in Germany. However, the British Government is prepared to discuss other ways of implementing this policy. The British Government stands for the independence of Austria under all circumstances. It is prepared to examine the question of the independence of Bavaria and the independence of the Rhineland. He must state, however, that the British Government has not yet examined seriously either the problem of the future of Germany or the problems of post-war Europe in general. In this it is far behind the Soviet Government. Hence, he can only express his own opinion as an individual minister. Upon returning home, however, he will report the entire issue to the Cabinet, which will discuss it, and after which discussion the matter may be continued through Maisky in London or Cripps in Moscow. Concerning reparations, the British Government maintains that money reparations are worthless. The experience of the last war shows that money reparations result only in various financial and economic problems and cause more harm to the victors than to the defeated. Restitution of the material assets that Germany destroyed or captured (commodities, machinery, etc.) is quite another matter.

Stalin remarked that the Soviet Union also thinks money reparations are of little use and that Germany ought to make restitution in kind. In the interests of the occupied or damaged countries it would be best to deprive Germany and Italy of high-technology machine-tools

Eden fully agreed with Stalin and said he saw no grounds for not demanding that Germany restore to the Soviet Union the machine-tools, machinery, factories etc. it had destroyed.

Passing on to the more general question of the scheme for post-war reconstruction Eden added that even before the USSR's involvement in the war, Roosevelt had sent a message to Churchill asking the British Government to refrain from secret obligations concerning post-war reconstruction without preliminary consultations with him. Of course, this does not exclude the possibility of discussions between Britain and the USSR on the question of the basis of future peace. However, in the interests of a more successful and smooth restructuring of post-war Europe it would be very important to keep in close contact with the United States at all times.

Stalin objected, saying there was a number of questions related solely to the interests of the security of our two countries. These questions, it would seem, we could discuss quite independently.

Eden partly agreed with this, but continued to insist, nonetheless, that the participation of the United States in matters of world order is imperative.

Stalin agreed with this last statement.

Eden expressed his gratitude to Stalin for his positive attitude to the question of the federalisation of small European states. Eden believed the future confederation of Poland and Czechoslovakia should be considered as a positive fact. It would be desirable for the Balkan countries to establish some form of federative union as well. In this way it would be easier for these countries to preserve and maintain their economic and political independence.

Eden then returned to the question of the treaties and asked Stalin, how best to deal with the three documents we have (two Soviet and one English)? Should they not be combined in some way?

Stalin replied that the text proposed by Eden much resembled a declaration. The Soviet Government, on the contrary, was proposing two agreements. A declaration is algebra, agreements are simple, practical arithmetic. We want arithmetic, not algebra. As Eden laughed at this point somewhat ambiguously, Stalin added that he should not conclude from his words that he disrespects algebra. Algebra is a good science and he fully respects it, but now, in the present concrete circumstances, we prefer arithmetic. Hitler boasts at every step of the treaties he has concluded. Therefore, it would be more expedient not to confine ourselves to declarations but to conclude genuine treaties. Stalin then asked what to do with the secret protocol proposed by him?

Eden answered that he cannot sign such a document without preliminary consultation with his colleagues. Besides, the British Government has not yet properly studied the problems raised by Stalin.

Stalin then said he did not insist on immediate adoption of those of his proposals that concern the change of frontiers outside the USSR, but he presumed the question of the USSR's western frontier could be resolved immediately.

Eden objected that he could not give an answer to this question now. This question, like all other questions concerning changes of frontiers that have taken place during the war, have so far been postponed by the British Government until a peace conference. The British Government has declared more than once that it does not consider it possible to recognise new frontiers immediately before the end of the war. Such was the British Government's policy over the past two years. Moreover, the British Government has promised to consult the US Government on all such questions. Finally, according to the Constitution of the British Empire, the British Government must consult with the Dominions as well. He will, therefore be able to give an answer to the question of the Soviet western frontier only in London through Maisky, after he has communicated with the afore-mentioned bodies.

Eden believed this method was more correct, not only from the purely legal, but also from the political point of view.

Stalin inquired whether the resolution of the question of the recognition of the Soviet western frontier would be facilitated if this question were settled in London not as a treaty issue but in an exchange of notes?

Eden answered that, technically, this might somewhat facilitate a desirable settlement of this issue, but all the same, it was essential for the British Government to consult with the United States and the Dominions before making a proper decision.

Stalin remarked that he was not objecting to informing the United States of our negotiations on this question. On the contrary, he would be glad if the United States participated in the recognition of the 1941 Soviet western frontier.

Eden responded that he doubted the US Government was prepared to do so at present. In his opinion, it would be better if upon his return to England he first informed the Prime Minister and then communicated his point of view to us.

Stalin replied that he wanted to stress his desire to come to terms with Britain on this matter and to have a united front with it.

Eden confirmed that he, too, would like very much to have a united front with the Soviet Union in this and in many other fields, nevertheless he was in a very difficult position at the moment. The question of frontiers has not been studied and has not been decided upon by the British Government. He illustrated this point with an example. On the question of the future of Poland he, personally, fully agreed that East Prussia should be within the Polish Republic. He had no grounds to assume that Churchill would be against this. Nonetheless, he could not speak for the Premier at the moment simply because he has never discussed this subject with him.

Stalin said that he understood Eden's position entirely, but he must forcefully stress that the military goals of the USSR and Britain must be identical, since only then can our alliance be strong. If we have different military goals, there will be no alliance.

Eden expressed agreement with this position and added that his aim was to reconcile the military goals of the two countries. He assumed there may be certain differences between the USSR and Britain on some points, but he had no doubt that basically our military goals were similar and that a united front in this field was entirely possible. Nonetheless, since the question of frontiers had not been discussed and decided upon by the Cabinet, he did not consider it possible to take upon himself binding obligations here in Moscow. Eden asked Stalin if he had talked with the Poles about the question of the future frontiers of Poland?

Stalin replied that he had not spoken about it but would do so if necessary. In any case, he believed Poland should be given all lands up to the Oder, and let the rest be Prussia, or to be more exact, not Prussia but the state of Berlin.

Eden expressed doubts about the expediency of splitting Germany into parts if there was no precondition for this in the form of separatist movements among the German people. Otherwise, an irredentist movement might arise in the near future to reunite the whole country.

Stalin objected that precisely such reasoning had led us to this war. Did Eden want a new assault from Germany?

Somewhat confused, **Eden** tried to defend himself by pointing out that such matters should not be oversimplified.

He added that he had been authorised by the Premier to acquaint Stalin with Britain's military situation and to submit data on the strength and disposition of its military forces ...

Following Eden's account, **Stalin** said that in the opinion of the Soviet military command rather large German air forces (up to 1,500 planes) had been sent to Japan, and that it was those German and not Japanese planes that had delivered such bitter blows to the British fleet in the Far East. To corroborate this Stalin pointed out that the amount of German aviation had decreased recently on our front, while German aircraft production averages 2,000 to 2,500 per month. Where then have the German airplanes gone? Besides, we well know from our own experience what kind of pilots the Japanese are. We observed them in China. It can be said for certain that the latest events in Malaya are not the work of the Japanese.

Eden was greatly interested in Stalin's information and started asking him how the Germans managed to transfer their air forces to the Far East?

Stalin replied that most probably it was done through South America, and possibly through Spain and Portugal as well.

Eden expressed his great thanks to Stalin for this information and said that on his part he would try to make a proper check through English channels. Eden then said that on leaving Britain he had had 10 air squadrons 'in his pocket', which he had intended to offer for the Soviet front, as soon as operations in Libya permitted. However, he has just received a message that the British Government has been pressed to send these 10 squadrons to Singapore.

Stalin replied that he quite understood the British Government's position and did not object to the redirection of the 10 squadrons.

Eden expressed his regrets at such a turn of affairs, but **Stalin** reassured him again that he fully understood the current situation as we, on our front, had also come through difficult periods more than once. Stalin inquired whether the latest events would affect the delivery of tanks to the USSR?

Eden replied that as far as England is concerned they would not. However, Eden has some fears concerning the USA. If the Americans curtail their supplies, then the English in the Middle East, for instance, will find themselves in a very difficult situation because there they operate with American planes while the Hurricanes made in Britain go to the USSR.

Stalin then asked what Eden would like to know about our military situation?

Eden answered that he would be interested to have an idea about our general plan of operations during the winter and next spring.

Stalin remarked that Soviet war policy had been reduced to a policy of fighting retreat. We have defended every point, every region, trying gradually to tire and wear out the German forces. Now we are at a turning point. The German army is tired. Its commanders had hoped to finish the war before winter and did not make necessary preparations for a winter campaign. The German army is badly dressed, poorly fed, and demoralised. It is beginning to feel the strain. Meanwhile, the USSR has prepared large reinforcements and put them into action in recent weeks. This has brought about a fundamental change on the front and led to the events we witnessed over the past weeks. The Germans are trying to dig in but they are hardly likely to build solid fortifications. Our troops are breaking through their fortifications. Our counter-attacks have gradually developed into counter-offensives. We intend to follow a similar policy throughout the winter. The Germans will probably attempt to muster new units and launch them at the Eastern Front so as to arrest our advance. We don't know when this will happen but we think no earlier than in two months. We shall try to use this time as best as possible. It is hard to know how far we shall advance in the course of our attack but, in any event, that will be our strategy until spring. We now have a measure of superiority in the air, although not very significant. The Germans still have great superiority in tanks, and we badly need tanks, especially the Valentines which are quite suited to winter operations. The Matilda tanks, on the other hand, are fit for summer operations, but not winter, as their engines are not powerful enough for winter conditions. We are advancing and will continue to advance on all fronts. In the final analysis, the German army is not that strong. Its reputation is highly exaggerated.

Eden thanked Stalin for the information, stressing its great importance and interest for the British Government. Then Eden broached the question of Turkey and asked if anything could be done to tie Turkey closer to the allies?

Stalin replied that the best way to achieve such a result would be to promise it the Dodecanese.

Eden reiterated the Greek claim to the Dodecanese, but Stalin replied there are Turks in Greece as well and that, in any case, it might be possible to offer the Turks and the Greeks an exchange of islands.

Eden admitted that Stalin's thinking was entirely correct but noted that some time ago, when the British intended capturing the Dodecanese, they had attempted to negotiate with the Greeks and the Turks about the islands' future. These discussions had not led to any positive results. Nonetheless, Eden believed that an attempt could be made to follow the line suggested by Stalin. Eden then asked if any changes in the Turkish attitude to Germany had been observed recently?

Stalin replied that though the Turks fear the Germans greatly, they do not like them either.

Eden inquired about Stalin's opinion on the question of whether the Turks would let German troops march through their territory?

Stalin said he doubted it.

Eden agreed with Stalin.

In conclusion Eden suggested that Maisky and Cadogan … should meet in the morning and on the basis of the three available documents compose a draft text of the two treaties that Stalin had in mind.

This proposal was accepted. The meeting [which had begun at 19.00] concluded at about 20.30.

16. Eden-Stalin meeting in Moscow, 17 December 1941

Present: Stalin, Eden, Molotov, Cripps, Cadogan and Maisky (acting as interpreter)

After the opening of the meeting **Eden** began with the question of whether Stalin had seen the results of the morning's work on the texts of the agreements? Eden meant the texts of the agreements prepared in the morning and finalised by Maisky and Cadogan.

Stalin said that the results were certainly interesting, but that he was much more interested in the question of the USSR's future frontiers. Had Eden not received a reply to this question from the British Government?

Eden replied that he had not and had not even tried as the Prime Minister was at sea and he had no possibility of communicating with him about the question raised by Stalin. In London, there was nobody with sufficient authority to answer this question in the name of the British Government. Eden could only repeat what he said yesterday, namely, that on his return to London he would place the question of the USSR western frontiers before the Government and consult with the United States on the same question. Further communications on this matter would have to be conducted through normal diplomatic channels.

Stalin objected that the question of Soviet frontiers (irrespective of the general question of frontiers in Central and Western Europe) was of exceptional importance. The Soviet Government was especially interested in it because, in particular, it was precisely the question of the Baltic States and Finland that had been the stumbling-block in the negotiations in 1939 with Chamberlain's Government about a pact of mutual assistance.

Eden replied that he had not been a member of Chamberlain's Government and did not know all the details of those negotiations. He fully understood, however, the exceptional importance of the western frontier for the Soviet Union and would do everything possible to settle this question in favour of the USSR. However, he begged not to be asked to do the impossible. Here in Moscow at the moment he is unable officially to recognise the Soviet western frontier as it was in 1941.

Stalin then asked if a special decision of the British Government was required to settle the question of the Baltic States? This question was axiomatic. The USSR is waging a fierce struggle against Hitlerite Germany. It is making heavy sacrifices, losing hundreds of thousands of people in common struggle alongside Great Britain, our ally. It is bearing the brunt of the war on its shoulders. In such circumstances, is a decision of the British Government required to recognise the USSR's western frontier? Is not this question axiomatic?

Eden remarked that as far as the British Government is concerned, the legal position is that the three Baltic States do not at present exist. They do not have diplomatic status. The Baltic envoys who continue to stay in London keep their position only as matter of courtesy. The British Government neither conducts negotiations with them, nor exchanges notes, documents, etc. However, he cannot fulfil Stalin's wish and officially recognise the 1941 frontier. He again repeated the argument he put forward at the previous meeting.

Stalin said in that case it will be very difficult to conclude the treaties being discussed.

Eden returned once again to his argument and recalled that the British Prime Minister had long ago declared publicly that England could not recognise any changes of frontiers in Europe that had taken place during the war.

Stalin objected that yesterday he had raised the question of British recognition of the USSR's frontiers as they were in 1941. Our troops may occupy the Baltic States again in the near future. In that event, will Great Britain refuse us recognition of these frontiers?

Eden repeated, with slight variations, the motivation for refusal stated above.

Stalin then asked, where might such a formulation of the question lead England? Perhaps tomorrow England will declare that it does not recognise the Ukraine as part of the USSR.

Eden replied that there was an obvious misunderstanding here. Only changes of frontiers that have taken place during the war were not recognised by Britain. The Ukraine had been part of the USSR before the war. Therefore, the Premier's declaration did not relate to the Ukraine.

Stalin replied that the position taken by Eden did not differ essentially from the position of Chamberlain's Government on the question of the Baltic States. He was greatly surprised by this commitment and, if it really was the case, it would obviously be very difficult to agree and conclude the treaties.

Eden expressed regret at this and again returned to his argument, this time emphasising the necessity for preliminary consultations with America on the question of the USSR's western frontier. In conclusion he pointed out the difference, in his view, between the state of affairs in 1939 and in 1941. At that time the British Government recognised the Baltic countries as independent states. Now it does not recognise their independent existence and, therefore, the actual situation has radically changed.

Stalin noted that a highly ridiculous situation had come about.

Eden agreed that the situation might indeed seem ridiculous, but he did not consider this question an important political problem. The Baltic States have ceased to exist. Actually, they are part of the Soviet Union. Did Stalin wish the British Government to recognise the Baltic States as part of the USSR *de jure*?

Stalin replied we are now in the thick of the greatest war in history and you are carried away with subtle formulas concerning *de jure* and *de facto*. This is untimely. In compliance with the Soviet Constitution, the three Baltic States are part of the USSR. This was the result of plebiscites in which the great majority of the population voted for joining the Soviet Union. If the USSR retains the three Baltic States in its Constitution, will the British Government object?

Eden replied that of course the British Government cannot have any objections to this.

Then **Stalin** said that if this is so, some form of words should be found to phrase this position.

Eden repeated his former argument, adding only that the Atlantic Charter did not countenance a change of a state's status without the consent of its population.

And in this particular case the provision in the Atlantic Charter might be considered applicable.

Stalin reacted that if Eden did not change his position, the signature of the treaties would have to be postponed.

Eden replied that the question of whether to sign or not to sign a treaty depended on the Soviet Government. He, however, did not think that there were sufficient grounds to forgo signature of the treaties, even if the question of the western frontier of the USSR could not be satisfactorily resolved at the moment. The treaties might actually facilitate recognition of the 1941 Soviet frontiers by Great Britain and the United States.

Stalin responded that the whole war between the USSR and Germany started because of the USSR's western frontier including, in particular, the Baltic States. He would like to know whether England, our ally, was ready to support us in the restoration of these frontiers.

Eden again returned to his argument and recalled that during the Soviet-Polish negotiations preceding the signature of the treaty of 30 July he had similarly refused to recognise the Polish frontiers that Sikorski insisted on.

Stalin stressed that we are bound by the clauses of our Constitution. Eden replied that he is not bound by the clauses of the [Soviet] Constitution but is bound by the British Premier's declarations on the question of frontiers, as well as by his promise to Roosevelt not to make any commitments in this sphere without first consulting the United States. Besides, the entire question of the western frontier of the USSR arose before him today in a somewhat unexpected form. When he left London he did not know that official recognition of the Soviet western frontier as it was in 1941 would be required of him.

Stalin again returned to the absurdity of the present situation. If Soviet troops were to occupy the three Baltic States tomorrow, perhaps Britain will object to this occupation at the peace conference? The best thing in the present situation is to postpone signature of the treaties.

Eden replied that if Soviet troops occupied the Baltic States tomorrow, it would give him much pleasure.

Stalin responded in that case he really could not understand the position taken by the British Government. Presumably, one ally must support another ally. If someone came to him and said it was necessary to separate the Irish Free State from the British Empire, he would just send him packing. If Great Britain wished to have air and naval bases in Belgium and Holland he would give full support. That is the way an ally should behave. If England did not find it possible to take such a stand, then it would be better to postpone signature of the treaties and hold to the pact of mutual assistance which was concluded between the two countries in July.

Eden remarked that not to sign the treaties would cause great disappointment in England and the Dominions. After all, the treaties contain nothing that would weaken the USSR's position in its demand for recognition of the 1941 frontiers.

Stalin objected that public opinion existed not only in Britain but in the USSR as well. If our public opinion heard this discussion it would be horrified, and it would not do him and Molotov much good if they signed the treaties without recognition of the 1941 frontiers.

Once again **Eden** tried to defend his position by referring to the element of surprise. He claimed not to have been warned that in Moscow he would be asked for recognition of the western frontier of the USSR.

Stalin objected that Eden had been notified through Maisky that the Soviet Government wished to conclude two treaties – one on mutual military assistance and the other on the post-war organisation of peace and security, including the question of European states' frontiers. Stalin did not insist on the recognition of all European frontiers in the form he had set out yesterday since he understood that it was a complicated and new question for the British Government. However, Soviet frontiers were quite another matter. Stalin again expressed his surprise at the attitude of England, our ally, in relation this question.

In reply **Eden** appealed to his record as an advocate of British-Soviet rapprochement. No one in Great Britain had done as much as him to achieve this goal. However, we must understand that any minister's possibilities are limited. If now, having no powers to do so, he was to recognise the USSR's western frontier of 1941, what would the Dominions say, Canada, for example, which is sending hundreds of thousands of soldiers to help Britain? Should a minister do such a thing he would not last as a minister more than 24 hours after his return to England.

Stalin responded that he certainly did not want to demand the impossible from Eden. He well understood the limits of his authority, and he did not address him, but the British Government through him. An unwitting impression has been created that the Atlantic Charter was directed not against those striving for global supremacy but against the USSR.

Eden began resolutely dispute such an inference, arguing that the question of Soviet frontiers was not in contradiction to the Atlantic Charter. He had no power to recognise the Soviet western frontier immediately, for reasons already given. It requires only time and a little delay.

Stalin remarked that when England gave her promises to America we were not yet allies. At that time the British and French Governments were going to render assistance to Finland in the war against the Soviet Union. Now the situation had changed radically. Proof of this fact is that England is now at war with Finland.

Eden remarked that Britain had done this to satisfy a request from the USSR.

Stalin responded that, in any event, the entire situation today differed sharply from the earlier one, yet it looks as if the USSR has to ask Britain for a favour.

Eden started to protest against Stalin's last remark, stressing that the treaties in question rested on the basis of complete equality and reciprocity.

Molotov expressed surprise at Eden's persistent defence of his position. We are talking about common military goals, common struggle, but in one of the most important military goals, our western frontier, we cannot get support from Great Britain. Is this really normal?

Eden responded that, as People's Commissar for Foreign Affairs, Molotov should understand his, Eden's, position very well: he cannot commit his

Government without the proper instructions. Eden said he was confident that if the Prime Minister were here with him, even the two of them could not recognise the USSR's western frontier officially without consulting the Dominions and the United States. There are other difficulties. How, for instance, could one agree to fixing the Polish-Soviet frontier without saying a word to the Poles?

Stalin replied that he was in no way insisting on the immediate settling of the Polish frontier. He hoped an agreement on this question would be reached later, in negotiations between Poland and Britain. As Eden already knew, he was ready to make the Curzon Line the basis of the Soviet-Polish frontier. He was more interested now in getting recognition of Soviet frontiers with Finland, the Baltic States and Romania. It was very important for us to know whether we shall have to fight with Britain over our western frontiers at the peace conference.

Eden expressed the hope that such a thing certainly would not happen. The British Government quite understood the need to arrive at an agreement on frontiers prior to a peace conference, but, all the same, it was necessary to discuss this question in the proper bodies, with the proper people. He was not happy at having to persist in his unwillingness to give immediate official recognition of the USSR's western frontier, but Stalin must understand his position.

Stalin acknowledged that he understood the position, but at the same time again expressed surprise at the British Government's stand on this question.

Molotov voiced the opinion that since the question of the USSR's western frontier was the outstanding question for us, it would be better to postpone signature of the treaties for now.

Eden again asserted that this was a question to be decided by the Soviet Government. He would be really sorry if the signature did not take place. It would have a bad effect on public opinion in allied countries. It would be used by the Germans, who would eventually find out what happened in Moscow.

Stalin proposed putting off discussion of this question until the next day, so as to give both sides time to think it over and perhaps arrive at some conclusions that would enable them to reach agreement. Stalin's proposal was accepted.

Then Stalin touched on the situation in the Far East, expressing the opinion that Japan might have some initial success there, but that she must suffer collapse within a few months.

Eden replied that Stalin's words raised his spirits immensely, as he held his judgements in great respect.

Stalin then asked Eden whether he thought – if his expectations with regard to Japan were realised and if our troops succeed in pressing the Germans in the west – conditions would be ripe for opening a second front in Europe, in the Balkans for example?

Eden replied that he was prepared to discuss this question. General Nye [Vice-CIGS], who he had brought with him, was in the waiting-room and might take part in this discussion to good advantage. One of the reasons the British Government was mounting operations in Libya was precisely in order to prepare the grounds for offensive operations in Europe. Then Eden asked Stalin if he really believed that Japan would collapse in, say, the next six months?

Stalin replied that he really thought so, because Japanese forces were worn out and could not hold out for long. If, in addition, the Japanese dared break neutrality and attack the USSR, the end of Japan will come even sooner.

Eden expressed his doubts that the Japanese would risk such an attack. They would be mad to do so.

Stalin, however, again said that such a possibility could not be ruled out.

The meeting [which began at 24.00] closed at about 02.00.

17. Eden-Stalin meeting in Moscow, 18 December 1941

Present: Molotov, Cripps, Cadogan and Maisky (acting as interpreter)

Stalin presented to Eden a new draft of the treaty on the post-war organisation of peace and security … and expressed the opinion that it seemed to him that the formula found for Article 4 might satisfy both parties.

Eden said that he too had drawn up some compromise proposals, but first he would like to discuss Stalin's new draft.

As it took some time to translate and type Article 4 of Stalin's draft, the meeting turned to discussion of the military treaty.

Stalin asked Eden why we should not conclude the treaties in due form right now? Why was Eden suggesting instead only an agreement? Great Britain has, for instance, a treaty of mutual assistance concluded in due form with Turkey. Is the USSR inferior to Turkey? If the British Government sees some obstacles to the conclusion of a formal treaty with the USSR, it would be better if we were told about it openly.

Eden objected that Stalin's suspicion that the British Government did not wish to conclude a formal treaty with the USSR was unfounded. Eden was proposing an agreement and not a treaty on purely juridical grounds. A formal treaty can only be concluded in the name of the King, who is the King of not only Great Britain but also of the Dominions, and the Emperor of India. The conclusion of such a treaty demands not only the consent of the British Government, but also of the Dominion governments. Eden has the authority to speak for the British Government, but not for the Dominion governments. That is why he is proposing an agreement whose legal force in the eyes of the British is no less than the force of a treaty. If, however, Stalin prefers a treaty, he suggests the following: sign an agreement in Moscow and then, on his arrival in London, consult with the Dominions and make the agreement into treaty which would be ratified. Such a procedure was possible.

Stalin agreed to this proposal of Eden's. He then passed on to the next issue and pointed out that if we did not want the military agreement to remain only on paper, it was necessary to back it up with practical actions. We have already raised the question of a second front, but the British Government objected on various grounds. Then we made another suggestion – the sending of British troops to the Soviet front. If the British Government considered this proposal barely realisable at the moment, we were ready to withdraw it and make a new, third suggestion: a joint Anglo-Soviet operation in the north, in the Petsamo region and in northern

Norway. The USSR could provide land forces for the operation, while England might help with naval and air forces. As a result, Petsamo would be occupied and a centre of resistance to German aggression established in northern Norway. Norwegian volunteers might be sent there afterwards. There were not many German troops in that area, and they were mostly Austrians. Stalin was interested in Eden's opinion of a northern operation.

Eden replied that England did not have enough forces at the present time to send reinforcements to the Soviet southern front. As for a northern operation, he found it highly desirable and practicable. He was willing to start negotiations immediately, during his stay in Moscow, and engage General Nye in discussion of this question. Eden wanted to know, however, approximately when the operation would be launched.

Stalin said the northern operation might be launched in a month or perhaps six weeks.

Eden promised to consider this question without delay.

The conversation then turned to the question of dispatching British troops to the USSR at a later stage, and Eden asked Stalin to which sector of the front he would find it advisable to send the English troops.

Stalin replied that if English troops were transferred by the northern route, he would be prepared to send them to the Leningrad front, somewhere on the border with Estonia. He could, of course, give them a spot on the Finnish front, but he believed the British would probably want to avoid armed actions against Finland. If British troops come from the south they could participate in operations on the Ukrainian front.

Eden replied that until the end of the Libyan campaign, including the advance to Tripoli, England would hardly be capable of sending any troops to the USSR. Besides, in deciding this question, one more circumstance should be taken into consideration, namely, that the dispatch of British troops by the northern or southern route would inevitably affect the delivery of essential military supplies to the USSR. Eden thought it uneconomical from the military point of view to send troops to the USSR at the expense of equipment. Moreover, the English did not have suitable troops for winter operations. Nonetheless, if Stalin thought it desirable, he was ready to raise the issue with the Prime Minister.

To this **Stalin** remarked that he would not insist on the sending English troops to the USSR if the British Government considered it impossible.

Just then the English text with the new wording of Article 4 given by Stalin arrived and the meeting turned to a discussion of the second treaty – on the post-war organisation of peace and security.

Eden proposed introducing the following words into Article 1 of Stalin's draft: 'Both Contracting Parties undertake to consult jointly on the provisions of the peace treaty, including the question of frontiers'.

This proposal was accepted by **Stalin** with an amendment that both Parties will not 'consult jointly' but will 'act by mutual agreement in working out the terms' of a local treaty, etc. Eden agreed to the proposed modification.

Eden then proposed a new text for the first part of Article 4 which read: 'Both Contracting Parties undertake to work together for the reconstruction of Europe after the war with full regard to the interests of each Party'. Mention of 'acquisitions' and non-interference in the internal affairs of other nations was removed.

Stalin objected that he could not agree to this formulation. On the contrary, he considered it necessary to preserve mention of 'acquisitions', specifically as 'territorial acquisitions', as well as mention of non-interference in the internal affairs of other nations. The latter was especially necessary, as many people abroad were saying that the USSR intended 'to Bolshevise Europe'.

Eden agreed with Stalin. He refused, however, to accept the wording of Article 4 in Stalin's draft which he saw as recognition of the 1941 Soviet frontiers, if in a slightly veiled form. Eden further proposed submitting a letter simultaneously with the signature of the treaty in which he would take upon himself the obligation to arrange a discussion on future Soviet frontiers between the Governments of the USA, Great Britain and the USSR. Eden submitted a draft of the letter to Stalin …

Stalin agreed with the text of the letter on condition that mention of the USSR frontiers be removed.

Eden did not object to the deletion. A stalemate occurred with Article 4, however. Eden rejected Stalin's formula, while Stalin said that Eden's formula was unacceptable. **Eden** tried to defend his position, saying that the intention of his mission in Moscow was to produce and publish a 'Moscow Charter', which to a certain extent, would counterbalance the 'Atlantic Charter'. Now he saw this cannot be done. He would ask Stalin to accept his wording of Article 4 with a supplementary letter, the draft of which he had just handed him.

Stalin responded that this was not enough. Stalin also expressed his surprise at Eden's unwillingness to acknowledge the need to restore our old frontiers, the frontiers of 1941, although at the previous meeting he had been ready to acknowledge an increase in the territories of Yugoslavia, Poland, Greece, and other allied states. Meanwhile, the restoration of the old frontiers was absolutely necessary. The best example was Leningrad. If the British Government did not agree to this, an impression would be created that maybe it would not object to dismemberment of the USSR.

Eden began to protest strongly against this suspicion. The point is that, due to reasons already cited, the British Government was refusing to recognise any new frontiers emerging in the course of the war – be it the frontiers of Yugoslavia, Greece, or even Great Britain itself. Eden said he very much regretted that he had to insist on his point of view, but he had no alternative: the issue could not be resolved without consultation with the USA and the Dominions.

Molotov remarked that, in view of the forthcoming meeting of Churchill and Roosevelt, resolution of the question of frontiers might now be easier.

Stalin emphasised the immense sacrifices made of the Soviet people in the struggle against Germany. This struggle was being waged not in the interests of the King of Prussia, but in order to secure our own frontiers.

To substantiate his own position **Eden** advanced the following argument: how could he explain the recognition of our 1941 frontier to, say, the Poles?

To clarify matters, **Cripps** raised the question of which frontiers did Article 4 of Stalin's draft refer? Are these the 1941 frontiers?

Stalin confirmed that the wording meant the 1941 frontier.

Eden said that implementation of Stalin's demand would signify the recognition of the Polish frontier as it was in 1941.

Stalin responded that the agreement might not apply to the Polish frontier. He would be ready to submit a special letter on this matter to Eden simultaneously with the signature of the treaty.

Eden tried to defend his position by noting the letter would be of a secret nature and if Eden was asked a question about the Polish-Soviet frontier in Parliament or any other place, he would be unable to reference it.

Stalin replied that he would send a copy of his letter to Eden to General Sikorski and would even be ready to publish it.

However, **Eden** continued to resist acceptance of Stalin's wording of Article 4.

On his part, **Stalin** said that in view of the British Government's unclear attitude on the question of Soviet frontiers, as revealed in yesterday's meeting, the Soviet Government had to insist on including a clause on the recognition of Soviet frontiers in the treaty on the post-war organisation of peace and security.

Molotov remarked that we intend to sign a treaty of alliance with the English, but it is necessary to know what we are fighting for.

Eden replied that we are fighting to beat Hitler. He refused to make any concessions as to the wording of Article 4.

Stalin expressed regret and said that in this case the signature of the treaty cannot take place.

Eden replied that, anxious as he was about it, he had to conclude that signature cannot indeed take place. The situation was now clear to him, he is aware of the difficulties they had discussed, and on his return to London he would take steps to remove these difficulties. But at the moment he did not see any other way out except to postpone the treaty.

Stalin remarked that Eden should have communicated with the Prime Minister on this question. At the time of Chamberlain's Government Churchill had sharply attacked the failure of the negotiations for a mutual assistance pact because of the Baltic States. Stalin did not think that the Prime Minister would object to signing a treaty on the basis of the proposed draft.

Eden responded that he was absolutely confident that the Prime Minister would take the same position as his. Stalin's demands meant in essence the immediate recognition of part of the future peace treaty. The time had not yet come for this. Besides, it was technically very difficult to communicate with the Prime Minister just now. Eden could only suggest that the present situation should be thought about once again and final words spoken tomorrow.

The meeting [which had begun at 19.00] ended at 21.00.

18. Eden-Stalin Meeting in Moscow, 20 December 1941

Present: Molotov, Cripps, Cadogan and Maisky (acting as interpreter)

Eden began by reporting that he had received a reply from the War Cabinet to his telegram to London about the difficulties that had arisen, which he would like to bring to Stalin's attention. Eden then read the text of this reply which, in all essentials, confirmed the line he had taken. He then said he was prepared to sign the first treaty, on military assistance, as well as the first version of the second treaty on the post-war organisation of peace and security proposed by Stalin, together with the letter he had spoken about earlier. As a last resort, he would be willing to sign just the first treaty. If Stalin agreed with the method proposed by him he was ready upon his return to Britain to raise the question of recognising the 1941 Soviet western frontier with the British Government, the Dominions, and the government of the United States.

Stalin replied that the two treaties were closely linked and it would be difficult to separate them. Also, he did not like the idea of turning an agreement into a treaty, a possibility discussed by Eden yesterday. The agreement would be published and turning it into a treaty would occasion various undesirable interpretations and rumours. Therefore, it would be better to postpone the signature of the agreements for the two or three weeks needed by Eden to consult with all interested parties.

Eden remarked that he found it necessary to explain that from a legal point of view the British Government did not distinguish between an agreement and a treaty. Both are binding.

Stalin replied that in this case there were even more grounds for signing treaties rather than agreements.

Eden stated that, as he had already said, he had no objection to concluding treaties. He then began a lengthy argument to the effect that it would be a pity to throw away two agreements that might be signed so easily to the good of both parties. If nothing came of these treaties, the effect on Anglo-Soviet relations would be negative. Eden did not understand why the Soviet Government refused to conclude treaties that in no way weaken the Soviet position on the question of frontiers, which, on the contrary were an important step on the way to recognition of the 1941 Soviet frontiers. In view of the above considerations, Eden asked Stalin to sign the treaties under negotiation.

Stalin objected that, in his opinion, irrespective of whether the treaties were signed, Anglo-Soviet relations should improve, for the war had compelled the two countries to draw closer and closer together. The war also compels different countries to discard their various prejudices and biased views. In the light of these considerations, the non-signing of the treaties should not be seen as too tragic. If these treaties are signed in London in two- or three-weeks' time, it will change nothing. In the meantime, our relations will be based on the July [1941] treaty of mutual assistance. Stalin continued that he might have been ready to sign both treaties, perhaps with minor editorial amendments, had we not debated the question of frontiers. The discussion had revealed something unexpected. He recalled that England had an alliance with Tsarist Russia when it comprised Finland,

Bessarabia and more than half of Poland. Not a single statesman in Britain had then thought of protesting against the alliance on the grounds that these territories were part of the Russian Empire. Now, however, the question of the Finnish frontier and the Baltic republics seems to be a stumbling-block. Stalin pointed out that he had proposed attaching protocols to the treaties, but the British side was against it, and he had discarded the protocols. He had also dropped his request for opening a second front. The position in relation to a northern operation in the Petsamo area was also unclear. In view of all these concessions, Stalin thought he had the right to request some compensation in the form of recognition of the 1941 western frontier.

Eden responded to Stalin's remarks with the statement that he was very happy about the prospects for improvements in Anglo-Soviet relations. He was especially pleased because in his recent message to the Prime Minister, Stalin had spoken of the absence of good relations and the necessity to improve relations (NB: the text which follows has not been edited by Maisky) by concluding treaties of military assistance and the post-war organisation of peace and security. It was precisely to improve relations by concluding the said treaties that Eden had come from London to Moscow. If, however, Stalin thought that improvement would happen automatically, without the treaties, then Eden wondered why he had undertaken such a long and arduous journey.

Eden then touched again on the question of frontiers and reiterated his well-known argument as to why he was unable now to sign a treaty that would officially recognise the 1941 Soviet western frontier. In connection with Stalin's statement that he had dropped his insistence on opening a second front, Eden cited a number of messages he had just received on the military situation in Hong Kong and the Malay peninsula. The situation was very serious and, of course, it would be of the utmost importance to the British Government if the USSR could put pressure on Japan in order to divert its forces from the south. Nonetheless, the British Government was not making such a request because it well understood the difficulty the USSR would have in satisfying such a request at present. The Soviet Government must also understand the difficulty facing England in satisfying requests to create a second front in Europe that the USSR has addressed to Great Britain in recent months. In relation to Petsamo the position is quite clear here: the British side was ready to take part in this operation and it would be good if General Nye might talk about this seriously with [the Soviet military].

Stalin replied that in his message to the Prime Minister, mentioned by Eden, it was only said that Anglo-Soviet relations were uncertain and the reason for this uncertainty was the absence of bilateral treaties on military goals and the organisation of peace after the war. Stalin added that clarity on these points would facilitate improvement in relations. On the other hand, continued uncertainty might produce a negative effect on relations and create obstacles to mutual trust. In that message he had not raised the question of sending someone from England to Moscow. What he wanted was to define and clarify relations, which could be done either in London or Moscow. Mr Churchill, however, suggested sending

Eden to Moscow, and he could not but treat this proposal with full consideration. In the light of the above, Eden had no grounds for reproaching the Soviet Government that he had to make a long journey to no purpose.

Eden responded to Stalin by saying that he was reproaching no one, but simply expressing his disappointment.

Stalin replied that he was also disappointed – at the impossibility of reaching agreement. He was, however, somewhat surprised at the dependence of English policies on the US Government. It had seemed to him that Britain had great freedom of movement in its relations with other countries. The cause of the difficulty in reaching an agreement lay, perhaps, in his underestimating the role America plays in the British Government. He was in no way hurt by the fact that England had not been able to establish a second front or dispatch troops to the USSR. He had sent his message to Churchill on 8 November, when the situation was much better for Britain than it is now, while the position on the Soviet front was much worse than today. The situation had changed since then, and this change should be taken into consideration. He did not mean to ask for the impossible and therefore did not insist on sending English troops to the Soviet front. If the British Government was prepared to take part in operations at Petsamo, he could not but welcome this and was ready to arrange a meeting for General Nye with Chief of the Soviet General Staff, Marshal Shaposhnikov.

And then, over the telephone, Stalin arranged with the Marshal that Shaposhnikov and Nye would meet today at 11.00pm.

Eden remarked that Anglo-Soviet relations were more important than the treaties. Therefore, he did not intend to insist any longer on their signature, and on his return to London would try to do his best to settle the difficulties that had arisen.

Stalin thanked Eden for this promise and expressed his belief that further improvement in Anglo-Soviet relations was not too far away. For his part, was ready to promote such improvement.

Eden then raised the question of the Far East. In view of the gravity of the situation there, he asked Stalin to say whether and when England might expect help against Japan. He understood that such help was hardly thinkable at the moment. But how would things look in the spring, for instance?

Stalin replied that if the USSR declared war on Japan, it would have to wage a real, serious war by land, sea and air. It would not be like declarations of war on Japan by Belgium or Greece. Consequently, the Soviet Government had to make a careful estimate of its possibilities and forces. At present the USSR was not ready for war with Japan. A considerable number of our Far Eastern troops have recently been transferred to the Western Front. New troops are being assembled in the Far East, but no less than four months would be required before the USSR was properly prepared in these regions. He thought it would be far better if Japan attacked the USSR. This would create a more favourable political and psychological atmosphere in our country. Warfare of a defensive nature would be more popular and would create monolithic unity among the Soviet people. The best illustration of this was the Soviet war against the Hitlerite aggression. He thought that an attack by Japan on the USSR was possible and even probable, if the Germans started to lose at the front. Then Hitler would use all possible means to draw Japan into war against the USSR.

Eden expressed his fear that the Japanese in Eastern Asia might use purely Hitlerite tactics, beating their enemies one by one: first finishing off England and then attacking the USSR.

Stalin objected that Britain was not fighting Japan alone. It was fighting alongside China, the Dutch East Indies and the United States.

Eden responded that so far England had been bearing the brunt of the attack on the Malay Peninsula, where its allies could not help.

Stalin was interested to know whether China could help Britain?

Eden reported that General Wavell [British Commander-in-Chief in India] should arrive in Chungking today. The Chinese Government had promised assistance to England, but it lacked arms for an offensive, and England could not help with this at present.

Stalin asked what Eden thought of China's position? Was it actually going to wage war?

Eden replied that the Chinese Government had declared its readiness for war.

Stalin objected that the Chinese Government was actually doing nothing at the moment. He added that he would be prepared to resume talks with England on the subject of the Far Eastern situation in the spring. It's possible, of course, that the Japanese will attack the USSR earlier, and in this case the position would be clear.

Eden thanked Stalin for his willingness to return to the Far Eastern question in a few months and added that if the USSR were to go to war with Japan, it could help England considerably with its submarines. England did not have any submarines in the Far East. The Dutch Government has about fifteen. In addition, it has a number of light cruisers. This is not enough. For the first time in its history England was having to endure the unpleasant and unaccustomed position of waging war without naval supremacy.

Stalin remarked that submarines can be built quickly and easily. If you begin now, Britain and America could achieve within six months a great advantage over the Japanese in this type of armament.

Eden responded that while this might be so, it was necessary to survive for the next six months. For now, the situation remains highly dangerous. He further reported that the telegram he received today said the British Government has decided to continue the offensive campaign in Libya, notwithstanding events in the Far East. For the next weeks and months the Far East will evidently have to rely on its own resources.

Stalin expressed the view that the British Government's decision was quite reasonable. Italy was the weakest link in the Axis chain. If this link is broken the whole Axis will collapse. It was a pity England had not attacked Italy in 1939 or even earlier. Had it done so then, it would now be master of the Mediterranean.

Eden said: 'We succumbed to blackmail'.

Stalin asked whether democratic illusions had perhaps played a significant role?

Eden replied that illusions had played a part, as well as the great overestimation of Italy's might. Here Eden reported that yesterday British ships had an indecisive encounter (because of darkness) with an Italian convoy carrying reinforcements from Italy to Libya. Four merchant ships were escorted by battleships, cruisers and destroyers. In all probability, German troops were being transported to Libya.

Stalin remarked that the Italians were fighting badly on our front. The Germans treat them like Negroes, and often shoot them. Italy will soon be fed up with its alliance with Germany. The Libyan campaign must be completed and it would be good if the English reached Bizerta. That would be nothing immoral or in violation of democratic principles. Temporary occupation of strategic points or territories during a war was quite admissible and reasonable. Maybe Vernon Bartlett [British journalist and MP] would be disappointed and object to such actions, but that doesn't matter at all.

Eden stated he agreed completely with Stalin. Anything that helped the democratic struggle was moral. The British had fired on the French fleet at Oran.

Stalin agreed it was the right thing to do. War has its logic and during a war one should not be ashamed to occupy the necessary strategic points.

Eden said that in the past two days the English had captured the Portuguese island of Timor.

Stalin exclaimed: 'Very good! Had not you done so, the Japanese would have.'

Eden reported that the Libyan campaign was developing successfully and that the English had already captured 10,000 prisoners, including 4,000 Germans.

Stalin remarked that the Germans were not surrendering to us, except for the odd unit. In Klin we proposed they should capitulate and promised to spare their lives, but our proposal was rejected. We had no choice but to destroy the Germans. The same thing happened in Kalinin.

Eden thanked Stalin for his permission to visit Klin. He had seen a number of German prisoners and was struck by their appearance and clothing. Their clothes were absolutely unfit for Russian winter conditions.

Stalin with irony noted that in October Hitler had boasted of being prepared for a winter campaign.

Eden remarked that according to the prisoners all German soldiers wore the same clothing.

Stalin responded that there was one exception and that was the SS troops, who were better equipped. But there were few such troops left.

The conversation then turned to discussion of the drafts of the communique proposed by Stalin and Eden. The text proposed by Stalin was accepted unanimously.

The meeting [which had begun at 19.00] finished at 20.30.

19. Churchill to Stalin, 9 March 1942

I have sent a message to President Roosevelt urging him to approve our signing an agreement with you about the frontiers of Russia at the end of the war ...

20. Stalin to Churchill, 14 March 1942

Thank you very much for your message ... concerning the frontiers of the USSR – I think we still need to exchange views on the text of an appropriate treaty ...

21. Stalin to Churchill, 22 April 1942

... A few days ago the Soviet Government received from Mr Eden the drafts of two treaties between the USSR and Britain which substantially depart on certain points from the texts of treaties discussed during Mr Eden's stay in Moscow. As this circumstance involves fresh differences which are hard to iron out by correspondence, the Soviet Government has resolved, despite the difficulties, to send V.M. Molotov to London for personal talks with a view to settling the issues holding up the signing of the treaties. This is all the more essential as the question of a second front in Europe, raised by Mr Roosevelt, the US President, in his latest message to me, in which he invited V.M. Molotov to go to Washington to discuss the matter, calls for a preliminary exchange of views between representatives of our two governments.

22. Molotov-Churchill Meeting in London, 21 May 1942

Present: Attlee, Eden, Cadogan, Sargent, Maisky, Firebrace and Pavlov (interpreters)

Churchill welcomed Molotov and his advisors and expressed his satisfaction at Molotov's arrival in London. He asked Molotov how the flight went.

Molotov thanked him and replied the flight had been a safe one.

Churchill expressed his regrets about the fatal crash of the English plane in which staff of the military attaché in the Soviet embassy in London had been killed.

Molotov replied that it was a very sad fact, but accidents in aviation were always possible.

Molotov said that he would like to say a few words concerning his visit to London. He was empowered by the government to conduct negotiations with the British Government and to convey the opinion of the Soviet Government on two fundamental questions. Afterwards he would visit the United States of America to discuss the second question.

The first question concerned the two treaties, the protocol, and the letter on the Polish question, the drafts of which were discussed during the December talks in Moscow between Eden, Stalin and himself.

The second question was the opening of a second front in the west.

Molotov said that to begin with he would like to set forth the opinion of the Soviet Government on the first question, namely the treaties dealing with collaboration between England and the USSR during the war and in the post-war period. We did not manage to conclude these issues last December. Without dwelling on the substance of the treaties, he expressed the hope and desire of the Soviet Government to conclude this work in the coming days. Molotov said he was ready to start discussing the details and the substance of these treaties as soon as Churchill and Eden were ready to do so.

Molotov pointed out that while he recognised the importance of the first question and was ready to give it all the necessary attention, he had to say that the Soviet Government considers the question of the second front in the west as especially important. The initiative for raising the question of a second front did not come from the Soviet Government. The question was put forward for discussion most urgently by President Roosevelt. In a message to Stalin, Roosevelt stated that in view of the impossibility of arranging a meeting with him in the immediate future, he thought it desirable that Molotov should visit America. As the Soviet Government had no doubt that the question of a second front concerned the USSR and Great Britain the Soviet Government agreed to his visit to the USA, while at the same time recognising that Molotov had to discuss this question with Churchill and Eden in London before leaving for the USA. Molotov recalled that it was eleven months today, almost a year, since the beginning of an extremely hard Soviet-German war, which underlined the importance of the question raised by Roosevelt. We acknowledge the importance of this question not only from the point of view of the USSR, but also of England and America. He realised that the question of a second front was a military one. For this reason, he was accompanied by Major-General Isaev, who had good knowledge of the details of this question. But he would like to stress that the question of a second front was in the first instance a political question and it seemed to him that consideration of this question, in England as well as in the USA, should be of that character.

Molotov apologised for such a long preamble on the purpose of his visit. He thought now one could turn to the substance of the above issues or to issues that might be raised by the English Government. Which issues were to be discussed first he would leave to the Prime Minister to decide.

Churchill said that the English Government was glad that Molotov wanted to discuss the question of a second front both in England and the USA. But he would like to agree with Molotov about the publicity on his stay in England. Churchill asked Molotov if he did not think it advisable to publicise his visit to England? He thought it highly improbable that Molotov's stay in England would pass unnoticed. The English Government could prohibit publication of information on Molotov's visit in the British press, but there were many neutral embassies in London and they might inform their governments about his visit. Besides, the fact of his coming could become known in the USA where there was no press censorship.

Molotov replied that the Soviet Government requests the governments of the USA and England not to publish any reports of his visit until he had returned to Moscow. In this regard we adhere to the same method that was used during Eden's visit to Moscow. Molotov reiterated the Soviet Government's request to the English Government to refrain from publicity concerning his visit to London until he had returned to Moscow. Molotov pointed out that, of course, a leak of information about his arrival was possible, including to Germany, but it was quite another matter if such information were corroborated by the British and Soviet

Governments. Molotov asked the British Government to do everything in its power to prevent publicity about his visit.

Churchill replied that of course the English Government would do everything possible to fulfil the request of the Soviet Government.

Molotov proposed beginning discussion of issues that interest both parties.

Churchill said he would like to propose starting with a general discussion of the drafts of the treaties and then continue with discussion of the treaties tonight, during Molotov's meeting with Eden.

Regarding discussion of a second front, Churchill suggested they should limit themselves to general remarks on this matter during this conversation and meet tomorrow morning for a more detailed consideration of the matter at a session he and the British Chiefs of Staffs would attend. He would be glad if Molotov invited Soviet generals to attend the session.

Molotov did not object to Churchill's proposal but stressed again that the question of a second front was above all a political question, not a military one.

Churchill proposed starting a general discussion of the drafts of the treaties.

Molotov said that the Soviet Government was familiar with the drafts of the British Government, and the British Government knew the drafts of the Soviet Government. The draft of the treaty submitted by Eden through our ambassador in London differed significantly from the draft of the treaty discussed last December in Moscow. The latter English draft even contained completely new articles. As our drafts of the treaties, as well as of the additional protocol, were known to the British Government, he would appreciate a brief explanation as to why the English Government was unable to accept the Soviet proposals?

Churchill in his reply said that the Soviet drafts ran into great political difficulties in England because they contradicted the principles of the Atlantic declaration. He knew, too, that Roosevelt disapproved of the drafts under discussion. Therefore, he thought that the conclusion of these treaties would cause great concern to public opinion both in England and America, which would harm our common efforts. Churchill stressed that the English Government wanted very much to collaborate with the USSR, not only during the war but in the interests of the security of the USSR and England in the post-war period as well, with the aim of eliminating Nazism and preventing war. The English Government's wish to demonstrate this fact was so great that it was ready to sign a treaty with the Soviet Union on the basis of the last English proposals. The English Government had to report on its actions to Parliament and secure the support of a majority in the Parliament and among English public opinion. Unless this condition was fulfilled, the conclusion of the treaties would serve no purpose and could harm Anglo-Soviet relations. In conclusion Churchill proposed that the question of the Anglo-Soviet treaties be discussed with Eden in detail.

Molotov stated that it was precisely the purpose of his trip to London to discuss all matters relating to our treaties, and he was prepared to do this in compliance with Churchill's suggestions. The Soviet Government considered it a duty to discuss both the treaty of military alliance and the treaty on post-war collaboration first of all with the British Government, with which it had raised these issues, hoping to find a common language and come to an agreement. Molotov said he had no doubt both parties would take the opinion of the US Government into consideration, but he had to say that the talks should deal with treaties acceptable not only to English public opinion but to Soviet public opinion as well. If we can't sign treaties that are acceptable to both Soviet and English public opinion, we shall have to postpone the resolution of this question. It was possible to live without the treaties for some time, but it would be better, of course if they were concluded.

Molotov said he must convey the Soviet Government's frank opinion on the matter of the treaties. Now, when a year of the Soviet-German war is nearing its end, the matter of the treaties had become more serious than in the past year from the point of view of Soviet sentiment and public opinion. Our country has had to live through many difficulties and make many sacrifices. He felt sure that nobody in the USSR would agree to treaties that lacked the minimum provisions to justify Soviet sacrifices in the Soviet-German war, or that lacked minimum provisions for future Soviet security. In our drafts of the treaties we have limited ourselves to such minimum provisions, which would be understandable to Soviet public opinion, and it would be difficult for us to go any further.

Molotov added that the Soviet drafts did not contradict the Atlantic declaration. But when we are told that the opinion of the former governments of Lithuania, Latvia and Estonia, which have long lost the ground under their feet, should be taken into consideration, he felt constrained to say that such a demand had no basis. Regarding Poland, he should say that the Soviet Government hoped and was ready to come to an amicable agreement on the most complex issue, namely the Soviet-Polish frontier, past and present difficulties in Soviet-Polish relations notwithstanding. We are ready to do this with our minimum interests in mind. He hoped that the Soviet Government's point of view would be fully understood by the British Government.

Molotov said he would like to add a few words about the question of the minimum provisions to be included in the Anglo-Soviet agreement. For us, the minimum provision is the restoration of the Soviet frontiers violated by Hitler in the war against the USSR. We cannot make concessions in this matter. After the sacrifices that have been made nobody in the USSR would approve of the Soviet Government if it gave up the demand to restore that which had been violated by Hitler. On the other hand, because this arduous war was thrust upon us the restoration of violated frontiers is not enough. We want to ensure that Soviet security north-west and south-west of its frontiers should have minimal guarantees for the future. Treaties that lack these minimum provisions will be received negatively in the USSR and will not be approved. It would be good if we can manage to agree with the British Government within this framework. If this is not possible, it would be better to postpone signing the treaties.

Concerning the most delicate issue, that of the Soviet-Polish frontier, the Soviet Government states that it would do everything to agree with the Polish Government amicably and on the basis of reciprocity. All the rest can be settled without difficulty.

Churchill in his reply pointed out that there were two drafts of the treaties. The difference between these drafts could be discussed with Eden in the evening. Just now he wants Molotov to have confidence in the British Government's goals. The British Government was sure that it was possible to win the war and that after the war the British, Soviet, and US Governments would have full responsibility for the peace settlement. The British Government wished to work together with the USSR in the interests of both countries. But it was impossible to sign documents that accentuate the differences between the USSR and Great Britain. The goal of British policy was friendship with the USSR. If that goal was achieved, all the rest would follow.

Coming to the question of a second front, Churchill said he would like to note the following. Both Great Britain and the USA were prepared to invade the European continent with their largest forces. At present, the English Government was examining the question of establishing a second front in Europe, as well as rousing the populations living under the Nazi tyranny and liberating these peoples. The English Government would do everything to achieve this goal. The questions to be discussed in connection with this were of a technical and tactical nature: problems of transportation, shipping, landing craft, the enemy's air defences, etc. All these matters were now being examined by British military specialists. He would like to report that last August he had discussed these matters during his meeting with Roosevelt and had asked him to take measures to build the required number of landing craft. He also asked Roosevelt about this during his meeting with him in January of this year. England is also working for the solution of this problem and preparing for the invasion with maximum energy. We are ready to take a serious risk if there is a well-grounded hope for the success of our operations.

Churchill said that at tomorrow's meeting Molotov will be briefed on the British Government's physical possibilities. A second front will be established in Western Europe as soon as adequate conditions for invasion were formed. At present, however, the British Government is limited in its possibilities.

Molotov in his reply to Churchill said he shared his opinion that friendship between our countries derived from historical conditions and met the profound interests of both states. Since our countries have found a common language, matters of interest to them will become clear, and the friendship will produce results after the war as well. Regarding the second front, Molotov said he understood the considerations set out by Churchill, but he hoped the question could be resolved shortly and positively.

Churchill stated that he understood the urgency of the question of a second front. It was clear to all that the difficulties of an invasion might grow. But he would like Molotov to acquaint himself with the possibilities of realising the desire of both Governments at the present time.

Churchill asked if Molotov agreed to hold a meeting of Soviet and British generals in order to discuss the possibilities of organising a second front now?

Molotov said he did not object to the meeting, but he would like first to clarify the political aspect of the question of a second front. He said that however

important the military aspect of this question, it had an especially political character and must be resolved not only from the military but, above all, from the
political point of view.

23. Molotov-Churchill Meeting in London, 22 May 1942
Present: Maisky, Sobolev, Isaev, Kharlamov, Eden, Attlee, Cadogan, Pound,
Nye, Portal, Ismay, Hollis, Firebrace and Pavlov (interpreters)
Opening the meeting, **Churchill** said that yesterday Molotov had expressed the
view that the question of the second front was not only a military-technological,
but also a political question. He asked Molotov to set out the Soviet Government's views on the second front.

Molotov said that the question of the second front in Western Europe was
not new. It had been raised ten months ago. Recently it had been put forward on
Roosevelt's initiative, who requested Comrade Stalin in April to send him,
Molotov, to Washington for negotiations about the second front. Roosevelt also
asked for a general to be sent with Molotov. This invitation had been accepted
by the Soviet Government. Although the initiative had in this case come from
the USA and Roosevelt, the Soviet Government felt that initially the problem of
the organisation of the second front might fall mainly on Britain. Therefore, the
Soviet Government thought it necessary to discuss these questions with the
British Government and to clarify current English thinking about this question
before his visit to the United States. We must consider this question as allies and
as the states most interested in this matter. The Soviet Government considers the
question of the second front crucial and urgent. It is desirable that the English
Government should treat this question in the same way. Molotov stated that there
was no need to dwell on the great extent of the Soviet-German Front and on how
active and tense this front has been for many months. There was no need to prove
to both the military and non-military men that the next weeks and months will be
especially hard and fraught with danger for the USSR, and of consequence for our
allies. When our troops were beating the German Hitlerite army this winter, they
were at the same time preparing for the events of spring and summer 1942. We
experienced great pressure in the winter, conducting offensive operations in difficult conditions, but we believed this would be the best preparation for the defeat
of the Hitlerite army of plunderers. But Hitler is not going to surrender. He can
be finished off only by force and stubborn struggle. The main burden of the
struggle and of crushing the Hitlerite forces is being shouldered by our army. It
is proud of this honour. Especially difficult will be the next weeks and months
because the Hitlerite army will make a desperate attempt to strike at the Red
Army. This determines today's formulation of the question of the second front.
The present company knows that on both sides of the Soviet-German front
are great military forces equipped with great quantities of weapons. Britain and
the USA have played and are now playing their honourable role in supplying
the USSR with arms. But now the problem is more acute than at any time in the
Soviet-German war and the issue is not only an increase of supplies but the crucial
and urgent matter of opening a second front. He could not say how the British

Government saw the question of the second front because he doesn't know. But he wants to look truth in face, to see the facts as they are. We regard the facts in the following way: the two sides oppose each other with millions of troops and have partially begun decisive summer operations. We do not know the exact balance of forces but consider it probable, and proceed from the assumption, that the enemy's forces outnumber our forces, which explains the difficult situation of our armies at present. In any event, we think that now – after eleven hard months' of war with Germany, after Hitler, using violence, oppression and coercion, has grabbed almost the whole of Europe and managed to recruit into his army immense hordes of soldiers from countries allied with Germany – we should not close our eyes to the possibility that the advantage lies with our implacable enemy.

The purpose of his visit was to find out how the British Government viewed the prospects in 1942 for drawing off a certain number of German troops from the USSR, where the Germans evidently have superior forces at present. It should be remembered that Hitler can amass the forces and resources of the peoples he has oppressed and enslaved, who inhabit the greater part of Europe. The danger of the situation that has formed on our front of the struggle with Germany cannot be ignored.

Speaking concretely, the proposal he has to make is the following: could the allies of the Soviet Union, in the first instance Britain, draw from our front at least 40 German divisions in summer and autumn 1942 and tie them up fighting a battle in Western Europe? If this could be done, the destruction of Hitler could be achieved in 1942; at any rate, Hitler's defeat could be predetermined this year. Could the allies do that? We would like to know the British Government's answer to this question.

Churchill says that in all previous wars naval superiority had given the nation which enjoyed it great advantages, namely the possibility of landing troops on the enemy's coast at its own discretion because the enemy cannot be ready every-where to meet an invasion from the sea. The use of aviation has radically changed the situation. For instance, in France and Holland the enemy could transfer air forces to any threatened spots on the coast in a few hours. Bitter experience has shown that a landing operation in the face of enemy air power is not a sen-sible military move. An inevitable consequence is that we have been deprived of the possibility of using a significant part of the coast for an assault landing. There-fore, we have had to study our possibilities at those points on the coast where the superiority of our fighter aircraft would give air supremacy. Our possibilities have turned out to be limited to the Pas de Calais, the tip of the Cherbourg peninsula and part of the Brest region. The question of landing in one of these places this year is under study and preparations are being made with maximum energy. Our plans are built on the assumption that landing attacking forces will provoke air battles, and that if they continue for a week or ten days, they will end in the virtual destruction of air power on the continent. When this is achieved, and air resis-tance is liquidated, troops could be landed at other points under the cover of our superior naval forces. Of decisive significance for the realisation of our plans and preparations is availability of special landing craft, necessary for the initial landing on the enemy's rather strongly protected coast. Unfortunately, our resources in relation to these special craft are quite limited. Last August, at the meeting in the Atlantic, he, Churchill, persuaded President Roosevelt of the urgent necessity for the USA to build the greatest possible number of tank-landing and other such vessels. Later, in January of this year, the President agreed the USA should put more effort into building these ships. On our part, for more than a year we have been producing as many vessels as we could, bearing in mind the requirements of the navy and the merchant fleet, which have suffered great losses.

In April President Roosevelt sent Mr Hopkins and General Marshall [Chief of Staff of the US Army] to London with the proposal that the USA together with Great Britain should in the shortest possible time relieve the struggle being waged by Russia. We agreed to this proposal at once, and this issue is now being jointly studied. However, the USA cannot be expected to have the necessary military forces earlier than the end of 1942 or that we shall have the great quantities of badly-needed landing craft. By 1 August we will have only 383 units and by 1 September only 566. In 1943 we will have many more vessels to deploy and we will be able to land on the enemy's coast at five or six points, anywhere from Nordkap to Bayonne. However, the British Government is determined to examine what can be done this year to aid to the valiant Russian armies that have taken on the greater part of Germany's military power, which has already wounded them so deeply.

However, it is necessary to bear in mind two points: firstly, even with the best will and effort, no operation we could launch in 1942, even a successful one, would draw a significant part of the enemy's land forces from the Eastern Front. In the air the situation is different; in various theatres of war we are already tying up one-half of the fighter strength and one-third of the bomber strength of the German air force. If the planned air battles over the continent prove successful, the Germans will be faced with the choice of either the destruction of their fighter planes in the west or transferring part of their air force from the east.

The second point refers to Mr Molotov's suggestion that our objective should be to draw off at least 40 German divisions from Russia. It should be noted that 11 Axis divisions are now in action against us in Libya, including 3 German divisions; in Norway, there is an equivalent of 8 German divisions, and 25 divisions are in France and Holland. That is 44 divisions in all.

But we are not satisfied with this and if some effort could be made or a reasonable and feasible plan devised to ease the burden on Russia this year, we would not hesitate to implement it. It is clear that if for the sake of action we launched some operation which ended in disaster and allowed the enemy to triumph over us, it would do no good for Russia, or the Allies as a whole. To sum up, we and the USA will do everything that is physically possible to meet the wishes of the Russian Government and people in this matter.

Molotov said that if he could he would like to put some questions.

He asked if Roosevelt shared Churchill's view on the second front, since in his statement he had referred to the government of the USA?

Churchill replied that the American Government shared the desire and the determination of the English Government to invade the European continent with as much force as they could as soon as they could. The English Government intends to mount this operation in 1943, when England and the USA have amassed a million to a million and a half American and English troops. The English Government was preparing to land great numbers of assault troops, using many vessels. But if a landing was possible in 1942, America would not be able to take an active part in it because of lack of troops and landing craft.

Molotov asked Churchill if he had correctly understood that the views of the American and English Governments concerning the establishment of the second front did not differ?

Churchill replied that there was no difference in the two governments' views on this issue. Both the Americans and the English were studying the question of opening the second front and so far no decision had been made about the date.

Molotov asked what percentage of English troops had taken part in active military operations in Europe and Africa, if you took any of the most demanding months of the war in 1942.

Churchill replied that at present there was an equivalent of 40 divisions on the British Isles, of which 20 were actively mobile. These divisions were not engaged in combat operations. If they were, England would not have the manpower to defend its islands. He should say that 50,000 troops had been leaving the British Isles monthly to fight in the Middle and Far East. In April and March Great Britain had 16 divisions in the Middle East between Persia and Libya and 7 divisions in India. English losses in the war with the Japanese amounted to 4–5 divisions.

Molotov said the Soviet Government did not doubt the British Government wanted the Soviet army to achieve success in summer 1942. The Allies want the same as we do. Still, he would like to ask Churchill the British Government's estimation of the Red Army's prospects in the summer battles. Irrespective of whether the British Government found these prospects favourable or unfavourable, or simply unclear, he would ask Churchill to express his frank opinion.

Churchill replied that he did not know the reserves or resources of the Red Army. A year has passed since the beginning of the Soviet-German war. Many military experts in other countries, including Germany, had thought the Soviet Union would be soon defeated. Contrary to these expectations Hitler sustained a series of defeats, especially in the winter. The battles on the Soviet-German Front have been and continue to be waged under conditions in which the Red Army is gaining the initiative. On the basis of information from its intelligence services the English Government does not see a concentration of large German forces for a big offensive. The English Government observes only that the German offensive fixed for May has been postponed until the middle of June. This is of considerable importance. The English Government believes that Hitler's advance this year will be weaker than it was last year. But we are not quite sure of this. To repeat, he did not know the resources of the Soviet armies and is not asking his guests about them.

Molotov said that the Soviet Government and the great people of the USSR believed in our strength. But we must take into consideration the possibility of serious danger. In this connection he would like to ask Churchill what the position of Great Britain would be if the USSR failed to withstand the pressure in the coming battles of 1942, which Hitler will certainly try to raise to the maximum. Molotov said that if Churchill could answer this question, he would like to communicate it to his Government.

Churchill said that if the Russians suffered defeat or Soviet military power were seriously undermined by the Germans, Hitler, in all probability, would shift as many of his troops and aircraft as possible to the west, with the aim of invading Great Britain. He might also strike at the Caucasus and Persia through Baku. This would put us in most serious danger and we would in no way feel sure that we had enough forces to counter this blow. Therefore, our safety depends on the Soviet Army's resistance. Nonetheless, if, contrary to expectations, the Soviet Army were defeated and the worst came to the worst, we will fight and hope with the assistance of the United States to gain overwhelming air superiority, which in the next 18 months or two years will make possible a devastating attack on German cities and industry. We will, moreover, maintain the blockade and land more and more troops on the continent. Finally, the might of Britain and the United States will prevail. The fact cannot be ignored that for a year after the fall of France, Britain opposed Hitler's victorious legions alone, and with poorly armed troops. Such a continuation of the war would be tragedy for humanity, and we sincerely hope for a Russian victory and are eager to take our share in crushing the demonic forces. He wanted Mr Molotov to understand the cherished desire of the British nation and army to join battle against the enemy as soon as possible and thus help the courageous struggle of the Russian army and people.

In conclusion, Churchill asked Molotov to take into consideration the difficulty of an invasion from the sea. After France was knocked out of the war, we in Great Britain were almost defenceless – we only had a few poorly armed divisions, less than 100 tanks and less than 200 cannons. Yet Hitler did not make any attempt to invade because he was incapable of gaining air supremacy. Now we face the same difficulty.

Finishing he proposed that General Isaev [administrative head of the Soviet General Staff] and Admiral Kharlamov [chief of the Soviet military mission to Britain] should meet with Lieutenant-General Nye [Vice Chief of the Imperial General Staff] and Vice-Admiral Lord Mountbatten [British Chief of Combined Operations] today, and the latter would explain in detail what special means of transportation were needed for the landings.

Molotov asked with a touch of irony, 'But what, in fact, are the prospects for such a military meeting?'

Churchill, faltering momentarily, again suggested arranging such a meeting.

Molotov agreed with this.

He thanked Churchill for his reply. He repeated that we firmly believe in our strength. We have already done a lot to finish Hitler off and will do more to defeat him utterly. We believe in our strength and in the strength of our allies.

Churchill said that the British Government sincerely wished to begin action as soon as possible on as wide a front as possible to help the USSR in its arduous struggle.

24. Molotov-Churchill Meeting at Chequers, 22 May 1942

Churchill and Eden arrived at Chequers on the evening of 22 May. After dinner, at about 10pm, Churchill and Eden invited Molotov and Maisky to a separate room where, as it happens, there was a large revolving globe of the earth, and a three-hour conversation took place. Maisky interpreted.

1. The military situation. **Churchill**'s report on the military situation took up the lion's share of the time. Much of the report was already known from the press, but there were also things of a secret nature. The Premier delivered his lecture (his report indeed resembled a lecture) standing near the globe, with a cigar between his teeth and sipping a glass of whisky ...

2. The Treaties. After Churchill completed his 'lecture' on the military situation, the conversation turned to the question of the treaties. Churchill once again detailed the motives which caused him to be cautious about the inclusion of the question of frontiers in the text of the treaty. My main aim, said Churchill, is to establish close collaboration between the USSR, Great Britain and the USA now and after the war. From this point of view, we should strive to remove all those points that might separate these powers and, conversely, to emphasise those points that can unite them. The question of frontiers, in Churchill's opinion, is undoubtedly among the points that create misunderstanding and disagreement between the United States on the one hand, and England and the USSR on the other. Therefore, Churchill considered it more profitable from the point of view of the common cause to avoid all those points that might cause American mis-understanding and disagreement over the Anglo-Soviet treaties. After this intro-duction Churchill gave the floor to **Eden**, who informed us that he had developed a draft of a new treaty (one, not two) which, in his opinion, could extricate us from the difficulties that had arisen. This new treaty contains no controversial points but provides a sound plan for collaboration between the USSR and Great Britain now and after the war. The new treaty stipulates not only mutual military aid between the two powers, but also reciprocal aid after the war for a term of twenty years. Eden promised to supply the text of the new treaty tomorrow, 23 May. In conclusion, Eden added that he hoped very much that Molotov would be ready to accept this new draft as the basis of negotiation. **Molotov** replied that he could not give any judgement without seeing the text of the new treaty. He thought, however, that it would be far better to complete what two parties have been working since last December rather start a new discussion. **Eden** did not agree with this and made it clear that if Molotov insisted on the conclusion of the old treaty, its signature would have to be postponed until Molotov's return from America.

3. Bombing operations. At one point in Churchill's report on the military situ-ation, **Molotov** interrupted him to ask if it was possible for Soviet bombers

bombing Berlin to fly on to England – instead of going straight back to the USSR – to have a break, refuel, take on a fresh load of bombs and then start on a return flight of London-Berlin-USSR? **Churchill** responded to this idea positively and said: 'Yes, of course it would be very good'.

4. **Molotov** also asked Churchill if he would agree to provide the Soviet military with the English instrument mounted on planes which determines the exact distance and position of an enemy plane? Churchill, pointing out that Britain is already providing us with a very important military appliance for anti-aircraft defence, flatly refused to give us this instrument, saying that the English did not allow its use outside the country to ensure the Germans did not capture it. Churchill also refused to do this in exchange for a Soviet military secret of interest to England, saying that he could not bargain in such a matter.

Some other issues were touched upon during the conversation (for instance, a court case in Ankara), but this happened incidentally, and without special discussion.

25. Churchill to Stalin, 23 May 1942
We have greatly enjoyed receiving Mr Molotov in London and I have had fruitful conversations with him on both military and political affairs. We have given him a full and true account of our plans and resources. As regards the treaty, he will explain to you the difficulties, which are mainly that we cannot go back on our previous undertakings to Poland and have to take account of our own and American opinion.

I am sure it would be of the greatest value to the common cause if Molotov could come back this way from America. We can then continue our discussions, which I hope will lead to the development of close military cooperation between our three countries. Moreover, I shall then be able to give him the latest development of our own military plans.

Finally, I hope that political discussions might also then be carried a stage further. For all these reasons I greatly hope you will agree that M. Molotov should pay us a further visit on his way home to you.

26. Stalin to Churchill, 24 May 1942
… Both Vyacheslav Molotov and myself think it advisable for him to stop in London on his way back from the USA to complete discussions with British Government representatives on matters of interest to our two countries.

27. Molotov-Churchill Meeting in London, 25 May 1942
The conversation took place at 10 Downing Street – the Prime Minister's city residence. Only four people were present: Churchill, Eden, Molotov, and Maisky (interpreting). The conversation started at 10.00pm and finished after 1.00am. The Premier behaved as he had during the conversation on the 22nd – he never stopped smoking his cigar and sipping a glass of whisky.

1. The conversation began with **Churchill** asking Molotov about the situation on the Soviet front and our views of military prospects for the summer. Churchill was also interested in military production in the USSR. Talking about the Soviet

front, Churchill asked to see the map of the front made by the British General Staff on the basis of information received.

Molotov briefed Churchill about the situation on the Soviet front, pointed out several inaccuracies on the English map and gave him some data on Soviet military production (mostly planes). In general **Churchill** was satisfied with the information, but made an obvious gesture of surprise, mixed with a touch of disbelief, when Molotov said that according to our estimates the Germans might have approximately the same numbers of troops as the USSR on the Soviet front this year, perhaps even a few more. For his part, Churchill expressed the opinion that the military situation in general was improving from the Allies' point of view, and said he was confident about the inevitability of an Allied victory ... Even now the Allies have a great preponderance over the Axis in aircraft production. This preponderance will grow with time and victory was assured. In this regard Churchill noted that shortly, as soon as the weather improved, England would start gigantic bombing raids on Germany, with a thousand bombers at a time. In this connection Churchill remarked that he was going to visit the USA again in the near future. The main reason for his trip was that although aircraft production was increasing rapidly in the USA, US deliveries to Britain were becoming more and more difficult, because the Americans were refusing to let their aircraft go abroad on the pretext that they were building up their own air force. Churchill's visit will be aimed at getting more planes from the USA, now, this summer and in the autumn. **Molotov** then put before Churchill the urgent question of larger deliveries of fighters and Valentine tanks to the USSR, referring to the special message he had received from Stalin today. **Churchill** promised to deal with this problem immediately and to give a reply. Emphasising England's adherence to the pledges made in the Moscow Protocol, the Premier pointed out, however, that great difficulties had recently emerged with the convoys. In this regard he said it would be highly desirable to organise a joint Anglo-Soviet operation in northern Norway and Finland to clear these areas of Germans. Should this be achieved, supply shipments from Britain to the USSR would become easier and safer. Churchill promised to prepare a draft for such an operation in a few days. Churchill also proposed to convey daily to our embassy in London military information received from the front and asked for a specialist to be appointed for this purpose.

2. The conversation also touched upon the draft of the new treaty, which **Eden** had spoken about on the evening of 22nd May. As the text of the treaty was largely approved by both sides on the afternoon of the 25th, Eden presented a draft of some amendments to the treaty, which were agreed after a brief exchange of opinion.

Eden also produced the draft of his statement to the Turkish Ambassador concerning the forthcoming conclusion of the treaty, which he intends to announce on the afternoon of the 26th.

The 'protocol' of that meeting with Churchill (on the morning of 22 May), where the question of the second front was discussed, was also handed out.

3. **Molotov** handed Churchill Stalin's message, in which Stalin gave his consent to Molotov's second visit on his way back from America. Churchill and Eden were very pleased, and the Premier made it clear that he would like very much to meet Stalin. Molotov seconded the Premier's intention and said that a meeting would undoubtedly be very useful and interesting, and that Stalin would be glad to see Churchill. Churchill became animated and exclaimed: 'So, we shall clear the north of Norway and arrange our meeting on the conquered territory, perhaps a meeting of three – together with President Roosevelt'.

P.S. The record is rather brief, it does not reflect many characteristic details of the conversation (Churchill's questions about Comrade Stalin's methods of work, etc.), which it is impossible to recreate because, naturally enough, at the time of this unofficial conversation, no note was taken. V.M.

28. Churchill to Stalin, 27 May 1942
We are most grateful to you for meeting our difficulties with the Treaty as you have done. I am sure the reward in the United States will be solid and that our three Great Powers will now be able to march together united through whatever has to come.

It has been a great pleasure to meet Mister Molotov and we have done a great deal towards beating down the barriers between our two countries. I am very glad he is coming back this way for there will be more good work to be done.

… Now that we have bound ourselves to be allies and friends for twenty years I take the occasion to send you my sincere good wishes and to assure you of the confidence which I feel that victory will be ours.

29. Stalin to Churchill, 28 May 1942
I am very grateful to you for the friendly feelings and good wishes occasioned by the signing of our new treaty.

I am certain this treaty will be of great importance in the further strengthening of the friendly relations between the Soviet Union and Great Britain, as well as between our two countries and the United States, and that it will ensure close cooperation by our three countries after victory.

I also hope that your meeting with Molotov on his way back from the United States will make it possible to complete the work left unfinished.

… Please accept my sincere good wishes and the expression of firm confidence in our common and complete victory.

30. Molotov-Churchill Meeting in London, 9 June 1942
Present: Attlee, Eden, Cadogan, Maisky, Sobolev, Firebrace and Pavlov (interpreters)

Churchill greeted Molotov and expressed his satisfaction at Molotov's safe return to London.

Molotov thanked Churchill and said he would like to report on his conversations in Washington … as well as to obtain information from Churchill on the questions of interest to him.

Molotov reported that he understood the British-Soviet treaty had been received positively; in particular, Roosevelt had been glad that the treaty did not mention frontiers.

a) On the main question, the question of the second front, he could say the following. The text of the joint Soviet-American communique, which says full understanding was reached regarding the urgent task of creating a second front in Europe in 1942, will be published after his return to Moscow. Molotov said he would also like to speak about the merits of the second front. For both he and his government the main issue was opening a second front this year, in the summer or in the autumn. He had several conversations with Roosevelt about the second front. Roosevelt had listened to him with great attention. Admiral King and General Marshall had taken part in the conversation when second front issues were discussed.

He found Roosevelt completely sympathetic to the idea of opening the second front in 1942. General Marshall was of the same opinion. True, Roosevelt had stated that the question of the second front should be discussed and resolved together with the British Government, because the establishment of the second front depended more on Britain than on the USA. At any rate, Roosevelt had declared that he would do everything possible to create a second front in 1942. He agreed with Molotov that delaying the second front until 1943 did not mean that it would be easier to open it in 1943 rather than in 1942, because if the USSR fails to withstand Hitler's attack – which cannot be completely excluded – then in 1943 our front will cease to be the serious force it is in 1942, when it is engaging the greater part of Hitler's forces. Hitler will be able to move to the Caucasus on the way to Baku and, consequently, strengthen himself significantly. Preparatory measures for 1943 are certainly important, but more difficult conditions may form for the second front in the event of our front weakening and Hitler's strengthening. Roosevelt agreed this fact should be taken into consideration and acknowledged that it was necessary to accelerate the establishment of the second front in 1942.

Molotov added that in his view the issue of creating a second front in 1942 had not been made sufficiently clear. It had been put to him that if the Soviet Government agreed to reduce its requests for the supplies that England and the USA had undertaken to deliver, it would make easier the task of opening the second front in 1942. Roosevelt had provided some figures to corroborate this proposal ... Roosevelt stated that if the Soviet Government reduced its demands ... the opening of the second front in 1942 would be facilitated ... Molotov said that while in Washington he was unable to give Roosevelt a reply ... The Soviet Government's reply to Roosevelt's proposal, just received by Molotov, said that if the British Government consider it possible to organise a second front in 1942, the Soviet Government would agree to reduce somewhat its requests for ... deliveries to the USSR ...

Molotov then said he would like to add to his information the following remark by Roosevelt, who had asked him whether it would be sufficient to land on the continent 6–10 divisions protected by air power, German aviation having been massacred already. Roosevelt stated that one could start with a landing of 6–10 divisions because it was easier to provide the shipping for such a landing. He said that it might be possible to risk a second Dunkirk and sacrifice 100,000–120,000 troops in order to begin the second front. He, Molotov, had replied that 6–10 divisions were by no means enough to establish a second front and again stressed that to relieve the Red Army at least forty German divisions need to be drawn off from our front and engaged in battle. Nonetheless, he considered it necessary to convey Roosevelt's idea to the British Government. He hoped that, as Churchill had promised, he would now get from him some clarification on the question of the second front. Molotov remarked in passing that although he welcomed the British air raids on Cologne and Essen, these operations were not a second front.

Churchill retorted that he would never go for a new Dunkirk and the useless loss of 100,000–120,000 troops, no matter who recommended him to do so.

Molotov said he had communicated Roosevelt's statement only for information and hoped the British Government would now give him a more definite and clear answer concerning the creation of a second front in 1942 since the Soviet Government still considers the second front absolutely necessary. Churchill had promised to give a more detailed explanation on this issue when he returned from the USA to London.

b) Molotov then came to Roosevelt's statements concerning post-war matters. Roosevelt had elaborated the idea that safeguarding peace after the war represented a problem that we should start working on right away. He put forward the idea that to safeguard peace after the war, it is necessary not only to disarm aggressive countries such as Germany, Japan, etc., but also to disarm other countries, for instance France, Romania and Poland, and to keep armed forces only in the USA, the USSR, Britain, and perhaps China, if it was able to create a centralised government. Roosevelt said it should be something like an international police force, without which, as this war has shown, it will be impossible to preserve lasting peace.

Molotov said that, for his part, he could add that the Soviet Government fully supports this idea of Roosevelt's and finds it appropriate.

Churchill retorted by asking Molotov: 'So, if we follow Roosevelt's idea, France will not have armed forces, while Franco's Spain will? Sweden will have an army, while Norway will not? Is that so? It's simply not practicable.'

Molotov replied that according to Roosevelt, only the USA, England, the USSR and perhaps China should keep their armed forces. All other states must be disarmed. He had reported this to Churchill as part of the information about his conversations with Roosevelt.

Molotov then said Roosevelt had expressed the idea that some mandated territories, in the Pacific, for instance, the Dutch Indies and the territories of Indochina, should not to belong to individual states, but ought to be placed under the trusteeship of three or four Great Powers.

Churchill retorted: 'What will the Dutch have to say about that?'

Molotov said that so far no concrete proposals had been made on this matter, just a general suggestion voiced by Roosevelt; it seems the idea of trusteeship came from Chiang Kai-shek.

Eden retorted that the territories mentioned by Molotov do not belong to Chiang Kai-shek and he cannot do what he likes with them.

Churchill said he did not agree with this plan of Roosevelt's. If these proposals made by Roosevelt were brought up for public discussion it would be a complete disaster.

Molotov asked Churchill if he meant both the question of organising a police force and the question of trusteeship.

Churchill replied that, in any event, all nations could take part in the organisation of a police force.

c) Continuing to inform Churchill about his talks in Washington, **Molotov** said that he was coming to the last question, namely military supplies to the USSR in the second year, that is from 1 July 1942 to 1 July 1943. He had received from Roosevelt a draft Protocol on supplies to the USSR by both the British and US Governments. He had already cited the figures for supplies to the USSR, as Roosevelt calculated them, but had not yet studied the draft Protocol in detail, though his attention had been drawn to a note in the Protocol to the effect that supplies from Great Britain would come within the framework of the Moscow Protocol. This he did not quite understand. He had not discussed the issue with Roosevelt and would like an explanation from Churchill as to whether this note was correct since he remembered Beaverbrook making an official statement to Maisky agreeing to increase delivery of tanks and planes to the USSR after 1 July 1942. The draft Protocol did not reflect that statement. Molotov said that it seems necessary to consider the validity of this statement by Beaverbrook. Molotov said he would like an answer from the British Government as to whether deliveries of planes and tanks, especially of the Valentine type, could be increased.

In reply **Churchill** stated he was much obliged to Molotov for the information about what the Roosevelt had said in Washington. He would say that when Roosevelt talks about the foundations of the post-war period it showed how important it was to win the war as soon as possible, rather than share out the fruits of a victory that has yet be won. Obviously, all these matters would be resolved at the peace conference. Of course, the English Government was firmly resolved to make it impossible for Germany to harm the world again. Germany must be disarmed and kept disarmed. In this connection the question of Germany's borders must be examined. But it would be a mistake to decide now what should happen to countries involved in the war, also the neutral states. He would certainly contact Roosevelt about this matter. He believed he could persuade Roosevelt to postpone settlement of these issues until we have won the war.

Churchill then passed to the question of supplies. He said the Memorandum, not the Protocol, as Molotov had called it, submitted by Roosevelt contained everything the English Government could do at present. It was absolutely correct that Beaverbrook had agreed to increase British deliveries by 50 per cent at the end of June, and by another 50 per cent at the end of the year. However, there is a proviso in the Moscow Protocol that the question of supplies to the Soviet Union may be reconsidered if new circumstances arise. A new situation has arisen. Japan has attacked Britain. Great Britain had to respond to this attack, which has affected supplies to other theatres of war. Instead of strengthening the Levant and the Caspian areas, the English Government has had to send a considerable number of tanks and planes to the Japanese front, including Australia. The English Government has had to do everything it can to rebuff the Japanese. Besides the new circumstances of the Japanese attack, to defend Australia the Americans have withdrawn a considerable number of planes and tanks to build up their own army and aviation. At present, virtually all US supplies intended for Britain are being sent to the USSR. The English Government has readily agreed to this and would do more if it could.

Molotov said it should be recalled that Beaverbrook had made his statement in March, that is, after the Japanese attack.

Churchill said there was one more factor acting against Great Britain, namely, the Americans' building up their own aviation and army for later operations. Because of this the Americans have cut their supplies to England. For example, according to the agreement reached between Portal and Arnold during Churchill's visit to America in January 1942, Great Britain was to receive 5,000 combat planes between January 1942 and April 1943. Roosevelt had given Britain only 1,000 planes so far. The British Government had been counting on 5,000 planes, for which it had trained the requisite personnel and counted on using these new English air units in forthcoming battles. But these planes were now lost to England because as a result of the war with Japan the USA was building up its own military. But, Churchill said, these difficulties would be overcome during the course of 1942.

Churchill then came to what he called the most important question, that of the second front. Churchill said it was very important the Soviet Government should know the state of play. He had received a message that Roosevelt would be sending him proposals about the second front. He had yet to receive these proposals.

Actually, said Churchill, preparations were underway to attempt a landing of six divisions in France in the autumn. The shipping needed would be withdrawn from naval transport. New landing facilities were being built and all kinds of preparations being made for this operation. But whether this operation would be carried out depended on the situation at the time. The problem of the shipping needed to invade the continent could not be resolved by way of withdrawing large sea-going ships from the navy, i.e. ships being used at present in convoys destined for the USSR. An invasion of the continent largely depended on the availability of special landing craft. That's why he didn't understand how Roosevelt's proposal to reduce supplies to the USSR could help resolve the problem of a landing. Churchill said that as soon as he had received Roosevelt's proposals, he would give them his immediate consideration. He again declared that all-out preparations were being made to carry out a landing in the autumn, but this could not be taken as the final decision. The launching of this operation would depend on the situation at the time. Churchill said he would gladly discuss details with Soviet military specialists and give them thorough explanations, show them the difficulties involved and the physical limits on carrying through an operation of such scope this year.

Churchill added that the English Government was also examining the feasibility of landing operations in the Far North in the area of Petsamo. If this was of interest to the Soviet Government, the English Government was prepared to discuss it with them. Such an operation would require sending English fighter aircraft to Murmansk beforehand, in order to secure airfields captured from the sea. After the German airfields are occupied, bomber aircraft could be sent to the Petsamo area. This was a technical question, and its details can be discussed with Soviet commanders. Churchill stated that these operations were scheduled for 1942, but the British and American Governments intended to invade the continent in 1943 with 40 to 50 divisions. Should it be necessary, the number of divisions will be increased as far as possible. Colossal preparations were being made to achieve this goal. To Britain must come a million American troops. Airfields and camps were being built for them. In 1943, landings in six or more places on the coast would make it possible to move a great army onto the continent and to hold the ports needed for the supply of this army.

These issues made up the draft of an agreement presently being worked out with the Americans. He understood the danger that the Germans could be stronger in 1943 than in 1942. He would, therefore, like to give a detailed explanation of what the English could do in 1942. He was prepared to do this during these talks, but it would require a lot of time and if Molotov, understandably, intended leaving London as soon as possible – he was ready, if it suited, to prepare a written statement from the British Government as to what the Soviet government may and may not count on in 1942.

Molotov said it would be desirable to have such statement.

Churchill said the statement must be strictly confidential.

Molotov replied that this was a matter of course.

Churchill said that tomorrow he proposed to discuss technical questions related to the organisation of the second front in 1943. He would like to set out Britain's capabilities. Molotov might like to invite his generals to take part in the meeting. In addition, he would put on paper what the English can and cannot do.

Molotov agreed with Churchill's proposal and noted that as far as he understood, Churchill was against landing 6–10 divisions in Europe, fearing that such an operation could turn into a second Dunkirk. However, at the same time Churchill had said that such an operation was being prepared.

In his reply **Churchill** stated that if he thought 100,000–120,000 troops were going to be sacrificed and no success achieved, he would regard an attempt to carry through such an operation as folly. An operation ending like a second Dunkirk would be of no value either to the English or the Russians, and the Hitlerites would make it a laughing-stock. We cannot win the war by doing stupid things. The war will be won by successful operations. If there is little or no chance of success, he would never undertake an operation. He would rather resign as Prime Minister. Let someone else take responsibility for such an action. If an operation has a chance of success, he is ready to pay the price. He is ready to pay any cost for victory. Churchill said that landing 6–10 divisions would be a complex task. Such an operation required a lot of preparatory work and training of troops. It was much more difficult to order soldiers to land on the coast than leave the barracks. The troops must be trained to go ashore from boats and to master other skills. Lines of fuel supply across the Channel must be prepared. The troops will have to try to get to ports that might be mined. Once landed, the troops will have to fight on a short front, bearing in mind the need to protect it with English fighter aircraft. On the other hand, the enemy will have to deploy huge forces to counterattack the landing troops. But if this operation has a chance of success, it will be carried out, and it will make possible the preparation of a larger scale landing.

31. Molotov-Churchill Meeting in London, 10 June 1942
Present: Attlee, Eden, Cadogan, Maisky, Sobolev, Firebrace and Pavlov (interpreters)

Eden stated that the communique on Molotov's visit to London could be considered agreed. The text of the communique, with corrections by Molotov made in conversation with Cadogan today, had been agreed by the Prime Minister.

Churchill stated that he would like to make clear once again that the formulation in the communiqué regarding a second front in 1942 did not mean that the English government's hands were tied in relation to the date of the operation.

Molotov replied that he understood this.

Eden then asked how today's conversation between Molotov and Sikorski [Prime Minister of the Polish Government-in-Exile] had gone. He would like to know whether during the conversations all the questions that concerned Sikorski had been settled.

Molotov said that Sikorski had raised a series of questions that would have to be worked on in Moscow. Resolving all these questions in the course of one conversation was impossible.

Churchill said that Poles had asked about the evacuation of several thousand Polish children from the USSR. He would like to know the Soviet Government's attitude to this request from the Poles.

Molotov replied that the Soviet government has only just finished the evacuation of Polish citizens. Now the Poles are again raising the question of evacuation. Apart from the fact that it might disturb the Polish population, a second evacuation would create problems for the Soviet government since it would have been easier to resolve this problem in one go. As regards evacuation of the children of Polish citizens, that would also be awkward. If these children were removed from the USSR it would create an impression among the Polish population that the Soviet government was unable to look after them. That would not correspond to reality: the Soviet government can care for 150 million of its own citizens and is certainly able to do the same for 50,000 Polish children. Instead of a concrete discussion about how to improve the situation of these children within the USSR, as proposed by the Soviet government, the Poles are insisting on their evacuation.

Churchill stated that if the USSR had Poles fit for military service that the Soviet government was unable to equip, the British government was willing to take them. The fact is that England has a population of only 44 million, not 150 million and it needs more people.

Molotov repeated that we don't want to carry out one evacuation after another. Molotov added that difficulties notwithstanding, we will gradually repair relations with the Poles.

Churchill stated that the English Government attached great importance to the restoration of a strong, independent Poland as a member of the European family of nations. The English Government would like relations between Poland and the USSR to improve. He had always refused to discuss Poland's frontiers with the Poles since he believed this question would become clearer when Germany had been defeated and had to be punished.

Molotov replied that we are not against the rebirth of a strong and independent Poland, about which Stalin had already talked to General Sikorski.

Churchill then communicated to Molotov that according to information received by the English government the Japanese had strengthened their forces by one division in Manchuria and now had 24 divisions concentrated there.

Molotov said that because of his absence from Moscow, he had no recent information about this issue.

Churchill handed Molotov a memorandum and explained that it set out what the English Government could do to relieve the military position of the USSR in 1942. Churchill asked that the memorandum be translated for Molotov and then asked if the Soviet Government was interested in a joint operation in the Kirkenes region?

Molotov replied that the Soviet Government was highly interested in this operation in the north, but not as a substitute for a second front in Europe.

Churchill said that he would like to drink with him a farewell glass of champagne. Proposing a toast in Molotov's honour, he said the English Government viewed Molotov's two visits to London with great satisfaction. He would like to express his deep appreciation to Molotov for undertaking the risk of two journeys to Great Britain and two visits to London. As a result of this visit we have established personal relations based on trust, friendship and comradeship. These relations will last. We will do everything to be good allies of the Russians. We are confident of the future, of our common victory. Whatever happens we will be together with you, sharing adversity. Our energy will not slacken until complete victory is won and until the working people of the whole world are free from the danger and horror of unprovoked Nazi and Fascist aggression. We will go on to the end and when we get to the end we will make sure it actually is the end. We are very grateful to Premier Stalin for sending this memorable mission to London. We trust that the publication of the treaty and communique will increase the alarm of our enemies and encourage and stimulate our friends, as well as freedom-loving and progressive-minded people throughout the world.

Answering the toast Molotov stated: 'I thank the Prime Minister for his cordial speech about my visit to London and the negotiations we have conducted. I was carrying out instructions from the Soviet Government when I raised questions of interest to our country and I believe I have fully expressed the opinion of the Soviet Government about what needs to be done to better and more quickly secure our common victory. I received Comrade Stalin's personal instructions on this question, which is of paramount importance to our country. I am satisfied that the leaders of the English Government, above all Mr Churchill, have sincere and friendly feelings towards the USSR and are ready to do what is necessary to relieve the position of our country. I leave reassured and with hope for the future. I hope the treaty and the unwritten agreement we have reached will during and after the war be of lasting and great benefit to our nations and to all nations striving to secure a free and prosperous life. I am sincerely grateful to Mr Churchill for the attentiveness and hospitality he has shown me in England. I am also thankful to Eden for his active participation in what we have done during my stay in London. I raise this glass to the health of the Prime Minister of Great Britain, Mr Churchill.'

PS. This last conversation with Churchill was preceded by another that took place at his flat together with Attlee and Eden. A note of that conversation was not taken. It was basically devoted to questions (in connection with the opening of a second front in 1942) covered in the enclosed *aide-memoir*.

32. Churchill to Stalin, 21 June 1942

As the Soviet Union enters the second year of the war I, as Prime Minister of Great Britain, which in a few months' time will enter its fourth year of the war, send to you, the leader of the great allied Soviet peoples, a renewed expression of our admiration for the triumphant defensive struggle of your armed forces, guerrilla bands and civilian workers during the past year, and of our firm conviction that those achievements will be equalled and surpassed in the coming months. The fighting alliance of our two countries and of our other allies, to whom there have now been joined the vast resources of the United States of America, will surely bring our enemies to their knees. You can count on us to assist you by every means in our power.

During the year which has passed since Hitler fell upon your country without warning, friendly relations between our two countries and peoples have progressively strengthened. We are thinking not only of the present but of the future and of our treaty of alliance and cooperation in the war against Hitlerite Germany, signed during Mr Molotov's recent visit to this country, which has been welcomed as sincerely by the British people as by the Soviet people. That treaty is a pledge that we shall confound our enemies and, when the war is over, build a sure peace for all freedom-loving peoples.

33. Stalin to Churchill, 23 July 1942

I have received your message of July 18.

I gather from the message, first, that the British Government refuses to go on supplying the Soviet Union with war materials by the northern route and, secondly, that despite the agreed Anglo-Soviet Communique on the adoption of urgent measures to open a second front in 1942, the British Government is putting off the operation until 1943.

... The British Admiralty's order to the PQ17 convoy to abandon the supply ships and return to Britain, and to the supply ships to disperse and make for Soviet harbours singly, without escort, is, in the view of our experts, puzzling and inexplicable. Of course, I do not think regular convoys to northern Soviet ports are possible without risk or loss. But then no major task can be carried out in wartime without risk or losses. You know, of course, that the Soviet Union is suffering far greater losses. In any case, I never imagined that the British Government would deny us delivery of war materials at the very moment when the Soviet Union is badly in need of them in view of the grave situation on the Soviet-German front ...

As to the second point, namely, that of opening a second front in Europe, I fear the matter is not being treated with the seriousness it deserves. In view of the situation on the Soviet-German front, I state most emphatically that the Soviet Government cannot accept the postponement of the second front in Europe until 1943.

I hope you will not take it amiss that I have seen fit to give you my frank and honest opinion, and that of my colleagues, on the points raised in your message.

Chapter 4

Into the Ogre's Den: Churchill in Moscow, August 1942

Churchill and his entourage arrived in Moscow via Cairo and Tehran on 12 August 1942. He was accompanied, at the American's own request, by Averell Harriman who thought it a good idea for him to observe Churchill's talks with Stalin on Roosevelt's behalf. On the way over, Harriman recalled, 'there was no discussion of what would be the strategy of our talks . . . For Churchill this trip was sort of going into the unknown and he didn't want to make any commitments.'[1]

Within three hours of their arrival in Moscow they had a meeting with Stalin in his Kremlin office (**Document 34**). The meeting went better than might have been expected given that Churchill told Stalin there would be no major second front in 1942 and that a small-scale landing in northern France was too risky. Stalin was not happy about this news and told Churchill to take risks, to blood his troops and not to be afraid of the Germans. According to the British report of the meeting Churchill responded that 'war was war but not folly and it would be folly to invite a disaster which would help nobody'. According to the same report Stalin got glummer and more restless as the conversation progressed but the atmosphere improved considerably when the talked turned to British bombing of German cities and industry and Churchill said that he 'hoped to shatter almost every dwelling in almost every German city'.[2]

Churchill then told Stalin about Operation Torch – the Anglo-American invasion of French North Africa planned for October–November 1942. To illustrate the value of the operation Churchill drew for Stalin a picture of a crocodile and said that rather than attacking the hard snout of the beast in northern France the aim was to attack its soft underbelly in the Mediterranean. Stalin already knew about Torch from his own sources but affected great support and interest in the operation.

According to Harriman both he and Churchill were delighted with how the meeting went. The elation did not last. At their second meeting on 13 August, Stalin gave Churchill a memorandum (**Document 35**) highly critical of the decision to postpone the second front until 1943. 'The argument that followed', recalled Harriman, 'was rude on Stalin's part and hot but circumspect on the PM's.'[3] The conversation was so heated and florid that Dunlop, the British embassy's translator, found it difficult to keep up. As Harriman commented in his memoirs: 'Dunlop tried to recapture what the Prime Minister had said. But he stumbled over his notes. It was a difficult task at the best of time to find appropriate Russian words for Churchillian English . . . Stalin . . . intervened, smiling broadly. "Your words are of no importance", he said to Churchill. "What is important is your spirit".[4]

According to the British report of the second meeting Stalin again accused his ally of being frightened of the Germans: 'He felt that if the British Army had been fighting the Germans as much as the Russian Army, it would not be so frightened of them. The Russians, and indeed the RAF, had shown that it was possible to beat the Germans. The British infantry could do the same provided they acted at the same time as the Russians.'[5] This comment was not recorded by the Russian interpreter, Vladimir Pavlov (**Document 37**). But neither report gives as negative impression of the meeting as Harriman does, who reports 'that night and the next day the PM was sunk'.[6]

Harriman was more sanguine than Churchill because he thought Stalin was repeating a pattern he and Beaverbrook had experienced the year before – a soft approach at the first meeting followed by hardball negotiating tactics in the second. He fully expected Stalin to revert to a friendlier tone at the next meeting.

Churchill was disgruntled by his second talk with Stalin but nonetheless accepted a dinner invitation from the Soviet dictator and promised to consider staying a little longer in Moscow. At dinner Stalin continued to niggle Churchill about the second front. In his toast to intelligence officers Stalin pointedly referred to British over-estimation of Turkish forces at Gallipoli during the First World War, which led to a premature withdrawal from the peninsular (**Document 38**). The point would not have been lost on Churchill who at the time was the political head of the Royal Navy and one of the architects of the Gallipoli operation.

Critical of the British military in private conversation with Harriman, Stalin was publicly respectful towards the Prime Minister, walking him to the door when Churchill left the party. On his way back Stalin met Harriman and told him that 'he had to pay the respect to Churchill because of his superior years, 4 years older than himself'. Harriman flattered that the age gap must be more but 'Stalin crossed his heart' and said 'yes, that is my age'. Another illuminating snippet from Harriman's notes on the dinner is this exchange:

> **Churchill** to **Stalin**: 'You know, I was not friendly to you after the last war.'
> **Stalin**: 'I know but you were always honest about your opposition. I prefer an honest opponent to a treacherous man who pretends to be friendly – like Lloyd George.'
> **Churchill**: 'Will you ever forgive me?'
> **Stalin**: 'It is not a matter for me to forgive. It is for God to forgive.'[7]

According to Harriman, Stalin referenced God quite a lot during this period.[8]

Harriman was absent from Churchill's third conversation with Stalin, on 15 August (**Document 39**). For this meeting Churchill had a new interpreter, Major A.H. Birse, a replacement for the unfortunate Dunlop, who was said to be sick. Born to Scottish parents in St Petersburg in 1889, Birse was brought up in Russia and was as fluent in Russian as he was in English. Interpreters are notorious for their professional rivalry and jealousy but Birse is universally recognised as one of the very best and he served for the rest of war as Churchill's interpreter at meetings with Stalin.

Stalin's interpreter was Vladimir Pavlov who translated Stalin's words into English while Birse interpreted Churchill's English into Russian. At first Birse found Stalin's Russian difficult to follow because of his Georgian accent: 'It was as if a native of the remote Highlands of Scotland were speaking English. His Russian was perfectly correct, simple and with no flourishes, but it sounded foreign until one's ear got used to it.'[9]

As both interpreters' reports show,[10] the meeting went well and Stalin and Churchill agreed that it had been good to get to know each other. Indeed, the conversation went so well that Stalin invited Churchill to a private dinner in his Kremlin apartment. Pavlov recalled that when Churchill accepted the invitation 'Stalin's face brightened. He showed the way and soon the guests entered a dining room with a table set for four people. Somehow the conversation began with talk about daughters. Churchill said his daughter Sarah had red hair. Stalin remarked that his daughter, Svetlana, had red hair, too, and called for her. He presented her to Churchill who gave her a little present.'[11]

Neither Pavlov nor Birse took notes during the conversation so each had to reconstruct what was said from memory. Birse's report is more detailed than Pavlov's (which is translated here as **Document 40**). According to Birse, towards the end of the conversation the talk turned to the pre-war period:

> The Prime Minister said that early in 1938, before Prague and Munich, he had a plan for a League of the three Great Democracies: Great Britain, the United States and the USSR which between them could lead the world. There were no antagonistic interests between them. Stalin agreed and said that he had always hoped for something of that nature, only under Mr Chamberlain's Government such a plan would have been impossible. He recalled the visit to Moscow of the British Delegations in 1939 ... M. Stalin had the impression that the talks were insincere and only for the purpose of intimidating Hitler, with whom the Western Powers would later come to terms.

Birse concluded his report by noting that 'the whole atmosphere was most cordial and friendly'.[12]

Churchill was in a good mood the next day. He met Harriman at the airport, who noted that Churchill 'had been up all night dining with Stalin. He was much pleased – taken into the family, seen his daughter and drink, food and jokes. PM has been all for Uncle Joe ever since.'[13]

On the flight back from Moscow General Wavell composed a 'Ballade of the Second Front':

> Prince of the Kremlin, here's a fond farewell,
> I've had to deal with many worse than you,
> You took it, though you hated it like hell,
> No Second Front in 1942.[14]

Stalin took it, but not for very long. After Churchill left Moscow, Molotov wrote to Maisky that while the formal negotiations 'were not entirely smooth', they had been 'followed by an extensive conversation in Comrade Stalin's personal residence, making for a close personal rapport with the guest ... Even though Churchill failed to come up with a satisfactory response on the main question [of the second front], the results can nevertheless be regarded as satisfactory.'[15]

But Stalin's attitude soured as the growing crisis at Stalingrad magnified the impact of the absence of a second front in France. His growing impatience with his Western allies came to a head in replies in early October to written questions submitted by Henry Cassidy, Associated Press correspondent in Moscow. Answering Cassidy's questions about the second front Stalin complained about the ineffectiveness of Western aid to the USSR, a situation that could only be resolved by Britain and the United States fulfilling their obligations. Stalin returned to the question of the second front in November in his speech on the 25th anniversary of the Bolshevik Revolution when he told his audience that its absence explained the Germans' current military success in Russia. Had the second front been launched 'the German-fascist army would already have been on the verge of disaster'.

These tensions about the second front coincided with another inter-Allied controversy. The Soviets had been invited by the British and Americans to participate in a war crimes commission but before they could reply London had announced a plan that would postpone punishment of war criminals until after the war. The Soviets responded by demanding that Rudolf Hess, Hitler's deputy – languishing in prison since his dramatic flight to Britain in May 1941 to broker an Anglo-German peace – should be put on trial during the war. This war crimes controversy was to the backdrop to an extraordinary telegram from Stalin to Maisky on 19 October 1942:

> All of us in Moscow have formed the impression that Churchill is intent on the defeat of the USSR in order to then come to terms with ... Hitler ... at our expense. Without such a supposition it is difficult to explain Churchill's conduct on the question of the Second Front in Europe, on the question of arms supplies to the USSR, which are progressively reducing, despite the growth in production in England, on the question of Hess, whom Churchill seems to be holding in reserve, on the question of the systematic bombing of Berlin by the English in September, which Churchill proclaimed he would do in Moscow and which he did not fulfil one iota, despite the fact that he could undoubtedly do it.[16]

Maisky replied to Stalin on 23 October, pointing out that a German victory over the USSR would hardly be welcomed by Churchill since it would leave Hitler dominating not only Europe but Africa and the greater part of Asia, too. There were British advocates of the defeat of the USSR and of a deal with Hitler but they did not enjoy great influence at present. Maisky ascribed Churchill's faults to the fact that he wanted an 'easy war'. Supplies were being reduced because of the demands of Torch. Churchill didn't bomb Berlin because he feared retaliation against London. Hess was not tried because the Germans might retaliate by taking repressive measures against British POWs. Besides, concluded Maisky, Churchill thought the war would last a long time and Hess might prove to be useful one day.[17]

Stalin responded to Maisky on 28 October:

> I still think that as a proponent of an easy war Churchill is easily influenced by those pursing the defeat of the Soviet Union, since the defeat of our country and a compromise with Germany at the expense of the Soviet Union is the easiest form of war between England and Germany.
>
> Of course, the English will later understand that without the Russian front and with France out of action they, the English, are doomed to destruction. But when will they understand this? We will see …
>
> Churchill told us in Moscow that by spring 1943 about a million Anglo-American troops would have opened a second front in Europe. But Churchill belongs, it seems, among those leaders who easily make promises in order to forget them or break them. He also promised in Moscow to bomb Berlin intensively in September–October. However, he has not fulfilled his promise and has not even tried to inform Moscow of the motives for non-fulfilment. Well, from now on we will know what kind of allies we are dealing with.
>
> I have little faith in Operation 'Torch'. If, contrary to expectations, the operation finishes successfully, one could reconcile oneself to the fact that aircraft are being taken away from us for the sake of the operation.[18]

Stalin was undoubtedly feeling the strain of the battle of Stalingrad but even now the Red Army was preparing a great counter-offensive that would encircle and entrap the Germans fighting in the city. Launched on 19 November, Operation Uranus transformed the strategic situation on the Soviet-German front. Hitler's defeat was now inevitable and the main victor in the war as a whole would be Stalin and the Soviet Union. While Stalin still needed Western aid and the opening of a second front remained urgent, his power relations with Churchill and Roosevelt had changed dramatically. Roosevelt and particularly Churchill now became suitors of Stalin in the triangular relations of the Big Three. Before Stalingrad Churchill and Roosevelt had resisted discussing the future peace, but now Stalin's Western allies were increasingly anxious to settle a number of post-war questions. Stalin was happy to play ball. He favoured a peacetime Grand Alliance with Britain and the United States, not least because he saw the need for a long-term strategy to contain Germany, fearing a repeat of the revival of German power that occurred after the First World War. To avoid what he called a halfway-house peace like the Versailles Treaty – which had antagonised the Germans without keeping them down – Stalin wanted a punitive peace that would permanently weaken Germany, a goal that could only be achieved and sustained in collaboration with Churchill and Roosevelt.

Documents 34–40

34. Churchill-Stalin Meeting in Moscow, 12 August 1942

Present: Harriman, Molotov, Voroshilov, Kerr and interpreters Pavlov and Dunlop

Churchill stated that the plane with Brooke [CIGS], Wavell [Commander-in-Chief India], Tedder [Middle East Air Chief] and Cadogan [Permanent Under-Secretary of State for Foreign Affairs] had to return to Tehran because of a break-down and they will arrive in Moscow tomorrow. But he, Churchill, can begin military negotiations in general outline and then discuss all questions in detail with the English and Soviet military.

Stalin asked how the trip went. **Churchill** replied that the trip was very pleasant and he is not at all tired.

Stalin asked how matters stand in Cairo. **Churchill** replied that he will report about it in a strictly classified manner, as it is not yet published. He, Churchill, considers it necessary to replace Auchinleck by Alexander, who had fought well in Burma. As well as this Churchill has made radical changes at the headquarters in the Middle East. He hopes that in the course of August or September the English will win the battle in Egypt. The English have at their disposal a significantly greater army, larger quantity of airplanes, tanks and artillery, and better communications than Rommel. But the Germans possess great art in using heavy tanks and anti-armour cannons. Churchill had discovered an atmosphere of fear about fighting the Germans. Nevertheless, we will start an offensive in August or September, using reinforcements from England and India. We hope that we will defeat the Germans where they are now. Churchill thinks that at the present moment there is no danger of the Germans taking Cairo or the Suez Canal. Churchill is grateful to Stalin for the 40 Bostons which he was kind enough to make available to the English government. Churchill is now organising a separate command for Persia and Iraq. We are trying to create a 10th Army to defend south of the Caspian. But first it is very important to win the battle in Egypt and destroy Rommel. In that event it would be possible to send large reinforcements to the Caspian. In battle one can hope for success but it cannot be guaranteed.

Stalin said that our affairs at the front are going badly. The enemy is trying to get to Baku and reach Stalingrad. It was difficult to credit the Germans' assembly of so many troops and tanks from all over Europe. At the moment on our front is List, with forces from the Balkans, a lot of Italians and Hungarians and not a few Romanians. We were not successful in stopping the advance. As a counter-measure we undertook a diversion at Rzhev and Viazma. There our progress is not too bad. The operation's aim is to force the enemy to regroup its forces.

Churchill asked Stalin if he thinks Hitler has at his disposal an extra army to advance to Moscow from the west and from Voronezh. **Stalin** replies that he can't say. The front is big. Hitler can take about twenty divisions and concentrate force at any place. One doesn't need to have extra reserves; one needs about twenty infantry and 2–3 tank divisions. Here, in Moscow, our situation is sounder, but there is no guarantee against the unexpected.

Churchill states that he came here to talk about real things. We are going to talk to one another as friends. Churchill hopes that Stalin will speak sincerely about what he considers useful to do at present time.

Stalin said that he is prepared to do this.

Churchill said that he had told Molotov when he visited London that the English are trying to find the resources for an effective diversion in the form of an offensive on German positions in France. But Churchill also said and presented Molotov with a memorandum that he couldn't promise it for this year. After the Americans and the English studied this question thoroughly they came to the conclusion that they were not in a position to carry out operations in September, which is the last month of favourable weather for an operation that aims to attract enemy infantry divisions from the Russian front. But, as Stalin knows, England and the USA are getting ready for large operations in 1943. To this end a million American soldiers are coming to England in 1943. Hence the American expeditionary force will by spring 1943 consist of 27 divisions, to which English will add 21 divisions, half of them tank divisions. Until now only 2.5 American divisions have arrived in England, but large transportations of forces are expected in September, October, November, etc. I am well aware that in 1942 the number of available divisions is not going to be of any help to Russia, and that when these forces are ready in 1943 it's possible the Germans will have larger forces to counter the English and Americans than at present.

As to the question of an attack on French coast I would like to present some thoughts. We have landing craft to transport six divisions to land on a fortified coast. If the landing was successful we would need to support the operation with shipping that England and USA do not possess. We studied in detail two operations, which we could undertake in September with our negligible forces. Two regions were considered. Firstly, an operation in the Pas-de-Calais region somewhere between Dunkirk and Dieppe. This operation would aim to draw the enemy's air forces in France, which are quite strong, into very intense battles. We do not have enough forces to penetrate deeply into French territory in order to help the USSR. An operation on the Pas-de-Calais has the big advantage that we have air superiority in this region and undertaking it will cause rather intense battles with the enemy. On the other hand, the enemy is aware of this, and there is no doubt they could concentrate in this sector more significant forces than we could transport there this year. Because of high tides in the Dover Strait all landing operations are rather difficult. The one advantage that could be derived from this landing operation is the air force battles. But it seems certain that this gain would be at the cost of the destruction of the expeditionary force and the enemy would rejoice at such a catastrophe. Furthermore, to carry out the attack on the Pas-de-Calais this year, we would need to interrupt the big preparations for 1943, divert key people and use up most of our landing craft. For this reason we didn't think it made sense to attack the Pas-de-Calais this year.

Stalin said that it would be possible to land at Cherbourg, occupy the islands in the Channel and from these islands supply the forces operating on the peninsula.

Churchill replied that it would be impossible to do this, since the English fighter air forces cannot at that long distance secure control of the Cherbourg peninsula. Churchill is prepared for the English military to discuss this question in detail with Marshal Voroshilov. Churchill asks Stalin if the latter wishes for this discussion to take place.

Stalin replied that he is not against such a discussion, but he would like to ask Churchill if he understands correctly that there will be no second front this year and that the English government is also declining an operation to land 6–8 divisions on the French coast this year.

Churchill asks Stalin what he means by the second front.

Stalin replies that he understands the second front to be an invasion of Europe by large-scale forces this year.

Churchill said that the English are not able to open the second front in Europe this year, but they think a second front could be created in a different location. With regard to landing 6–8 divisions on the French coast this year, the English government thinks this operation would do more harm than good and would have a negative impact on preparations for a large-scale operation in 1943. Churchill is afraid that this will be unpleasant news for Stalin, but he can reassure him that if the English and Americans knew that throwing away 150,000–200,000 people would help their ally by drawing significant forces from the Russian front they wouldn't hesitate because of the losses. However, if this operation didn't result in the withdrawal of any forces, it would damage the prospect for operations next year and, consequently, would be a big mistake. Churchill asks Harriman for his opinion. Harriman says that he supports Churchill's arguments and doesn't have anything to add.

Stalin said that he looks at the war differently. He thinks that those who don't want to take risks will never win the war. The memorandum given to Molotov in London mentioned that the English expected to land 6–10 divisions on the coast of France this year. If we knew earlier that they wouldn't be able to do this we could have given them three corps for a landing from the air. For example, in Dorogobuzh there were 2,500 people landed amongst Germans. They fought brilliantly and, when it was no longer necessary, they boarded the planes and left. To become real soldiers, troops need to be thrown into the flames and shot at. Until forces are tested in battle nobody can say what they are worth. It is a perfect opportunity to test forces in battle. In England's place he would act differently. There is no need to be afraid of Germans.

Churchill irritably noted that they are not afraid of the Germans and asks Stalin, did he ask himself why Hitler didn't invade England in 1940, when England had barely 20,000 troops, 200 machine guns, and 50 tanks at the time when Hitler had all sorts of barges, parachute forces etc. If Hitler had invaded England at that time then Churchill wouldn't be in Moscow now.

Stalin replied that the landing in England would have been met by the population's resistance, whereas a landing in France would be met by the French population with sympathy.

Churchill said that exactly because of that it is all the more important not to make the French rise as it would result in many futile deaths.

Stalin said that if the English cannot land he doesn't insist or demand it. However, he cannot agree with the arguments presented by Churchill.

Churchill said that he thanks Stalin for his observations, but hopes that Stalin will allow the English and Soviet military to discuss the statements he has presented today.

Stalin said that these questions must be resolved by politicians, not the military who are merely consultants.

Churchill expressed his agreement with Stalin's statement and notes that in England the military are consultants too.

Churchill says further that a second front in Europe is not the only second front. In the opinion of the English and American governments there are other military operations that could be undertaken, which would be more useful for the common good. We don't think France is the only place a second front could be created. The Americans and English have decided to undertake another operation and Churchill has been authorised by Roosevelt to tell the Russian government about this operation under condition of full confidentiality. This operation can only be kept secret under the screen of the other operation. It has to be conducted under the command of an American supreme commander, who has already been appointed their representative in England. The operation is named 'Torch' and involves the capture of the Northern coast of French Africa. For this purpose, 250,000 troops will used, approximately comprising seven USA divisions and five English divisions. The troops will land in several places along the coast of Northern Africa up to Bizerte. The president has set 30 October as the latest date for the beginning of the operation. However, we propose to make every effort to start it at the beginning of October.

Stalin asked Churchill if de Gaulle [leader of the Free French] is informed about this operation.

Churchill answered that de Gaulle is not informed about this operation, the same as he wasn't informed about the Madagascar operation. The fact is that de Gaulle and the people surrounding him talk too much and he didn't want to inform de Gaulle about Anglo-American plans. Churchill says that capture of the French coast would make it possible to clear the Mediterranean Sea, obtain bases for the bombardment of Italy – Hitler's weakest ally – and it would also open up additional ways to invade continental Europe next year. Besides, Churchill thinks this operation would favourably affect the positions of Spain and Turkey.

Stalin said that from a military point of view he quite understands an operation to capture the northern African coast. In his opinion, it has four advantages. As a result of this operation lines of communications through the Mediterranean Sea would be opened and the Allies would get bases to bombard Italy and they would have got behind Rommel's army and closed the route to Dakar. However, he thinks that politically this operation is not sufficiently justified. He is interested in the question of will there be a declaration at the beginning of the Anglo-American operation against Northern Africa. He thinks the operation would be more usefully conducted with the participation of de Gaulle or other French generals.

Churchill said the American government has many agents in Northern Africa. It calculates that landing Anglo-American forces on the Northern African coast under the American flag will be met with weak resistance from the French population and perhaps cooperation even. Besides, he thinks, this operation could be presented as the beginning of the liberation of France, thus preventing its representation as the encroachment of Anglo-American imperialism. Churchill also considers that as a result of this operation the Germans will put serious demands to Vichy, and the Vichy government will either fail or run away. In his opinion, it would be highly desirable to pit the Germans against the Vichy government.

Stalin states that he quite understands the operation from the military point of view and says: 'May God helps its realization'.

Churchill said that he will report Stalin's opinion to Roosevelt. Then Churchill would like to move to the following question, which concerns aid to the southern flank of the Russian front by help from the English air force to defend the Caucasus and the Caspian Sea. However, at the present time, Churchill cannot make a definite proposal to provide to USSR with 15 or more English squadrons, as the English have to see first how the operation in Egypt unfolds.

Stalin replied that we would be grateful for help from the air force, as we suffer from the lack of aviation in this region.

At the conclusion of the talk Churchill said that an operation to capture the North Africa coast is so obvious the press might talk about it. It is important, therefore, to pretend we are going to move in another direction, that we are going to strike at Pas-de-Calais. Nothing should be said about the fact that we are not going to attack the enemy at the French coast this year. Another cover for Operation 'Torch' could be to pretend to the enemy that we are going to attack Norway this year. Actually, there are a few arctic divisions being prepared in England, which the enemy can't but notice and think about the possibility of a Norway attack this year.

35. Stalin to Churchill, 13 August 1942
Memorandum

As a result of the exchange of views in Moscow on August 12 I have established that Mr Churchill, the British Prime Minister, considers it impossible to open a second front in Europe in 1942.

As is well-known, the decision to organise a second front in Europe in 1942 was reached at the time of Molotov's visit to London and found expression in the agreed Anglo-Soviet communique released on 12 June.

It will be recalled further that the organisation of a second front in Europe was designed to divert German forces from the Eastern Front to the west, to set up in the west a major centre of resistance to the German-Fascist forces and thereby ease the position of the Soviet troops on the Soviet-German front in 1942.

Needless to say, the Soviet High Command, in planning its summer and autumn operations, counted on a second front being opened in Europe in 1942.

It will be readily understood that the British Government's refusal to open a second front in Europe in 1942 delivers a mortal blow to Soviet public opinion, which had hoped the second front would be opened, complicates the position of the Red Army at the front, and undermines the plans of the Soviet High Command.

I say nothing of the fact that the difficulties arising for the Red Army as a result of the refusal to open a second front in 1942 are bound to impair the military position of Britain and other allies

I and my colleagues believe that the year 1942 offers the most favourable conditions for a second front in Europe as nearly all German forces, including their best troops, are tied down on the Eastern Front, while only negligible forces, and the poorest, too, are left in Europe. It is not known whether 1943 will offer as favourable conditions for opening a second front as 1942. We think, therefore, that it is possible and necessary to open a second front in Europe in 1942. Unfortunately, I did not succeed in convincing the British Prime Minister of this, while Mr Harriman, the US President's representative at the Moscow talks, fully supported the Prime Minister.

36. Churchill to Stalin, 14 August 1942
AIDE-MEMOIRE
In reply to Premier Stalin's memorandum of 13 August the Prime Minister of Great Britain states:

1. The best second front in 1942, and the only large-scale operation possible from the Atlantic, is 'Torch'. If this can be effected in October it will give more aid to Russia than any other plan. It also prepares the way for 1943 and has the four advantages mentioned by Premier Stalin in the conversation on 12 August. The British and United States Governments have made up their minds about this and all preparations are proceeding with the utmost speed.

2. Compared with 'Torch', the attack with six or eight Anglo-American divisions on the Cherbourg Peninsula and the Channel Islands would be a hazardous and futile operation. The Germans have enough troops in the west to block us in this narrow peninsula with fortified lines and would concentrate all their air forces in the west upon it. In the opinion of all the British Naval, Military and Air authorities the operation could only end in disaster. Even if the lodgement was made, it would not bring a single division back from Russia. It would also be far more of a running sore for us than for the enemy and would use up wastefully and wantonly the key men and landing craft required for real action in 1943. This is our settled view. The Chief of the Imperial General Staff will go into details with Russian Commanders to any extent that may be desired.

3. No promise has been broken by Great Britain or the United States. I point to paragraph 5 of my Aide-Memoire given to Mr Molotov on the 10th June, 1942, which distinctly says: 'We can, therefore, give no promise.' This Aide-Memoire followed upon lengthy conversations, in which the very small chance of such a

plan being adopted was made abundantly clear. Several of these conversations are on record.

4. However, all the talk about an Anglo-American invasion of France this year has misled the enemy and has held large air forces and considerable military forces on the French Channel coast. It would be injurious to all common interests, especially Russian interests, if any public controversy arose in which it would be necessary for the British Government to unfold to the nation the crushing argument which they conceive themselves to possess against 'Sledgehammer'. Widespread discouragement would be caused to the Russian armies who have been buoyed up on this subject, and the enemy would be free to withdraw further forces from the west. The wisest course is to use 'Sledgehammer' as a blind for 'Torch', and proclaim 'Torch', when it begins, as the second front. This is what we ourselves mean to do.

5. We cannot admit that the conversations with Mr Molotov about the second front, safeguarded as they were by reservations both oral and written, formed any ground for altering the strategic plans of the Russian High Command.

6. We reaffirm our resolve to aid our Russian allies by all possible means.

37. Churchill-Stalin Meeting in Moscow, 13 August 1942
Also present: Harriman, Molotov, Brooke, Cadogan, Wavell, Jacob, Tedder, and interpreters Pavlov and Dunlop.

Stalin stated that he has summarised the results of yesterday's meeting in a memorandum.

Churchill, familiarising himself with the memorandum, said that he will send a written reply. We, he continues, looked at these questions day after day over several months and the conclusions we came to were the best aid that we can provide to our Russian allies. The English and Soviet military can discuss in detail every point of our statements and explain the position. These decisions were taken together with the Americans and are final. We hope we can show that our proposals will be the best help to our Russian allies. We would be glad to touch upon the positive as well as negative side of the question at the special meeting between the English and Soviet military with maps and statistical information, which could be put to that meeting in a greater volume than here. However, Churchill would like to point out that they greatly desire to help the Russian army at the present time and in the course of next few months. An undertaking which gave the Germans reason to celebrate and cause losses to us, will not help the Russian army. He hopes that we can consider this stage of discussions finalised with the exception of the viewing these questions from a military point of view.

Churchill asked Harriman if he has anything to add to this statement. **Harriman** replied that these proposals resulted from a serious analysis that concluded a few weeks ago. Decisions were made with the President's agreement. The President is fully resolved to use more resources at a time when it would be most advantageous for the cause of the United Nations. The decisions were made on the basis of a policy of best use of the resources at his disposal. The President is ready to make any sacrifice if there is sufficient chance of success. The Anglo-American proposals should not be viewed as the absence of help at this critical moment in the battles being fought by the Soviet army.

Stalin answered that he considers the projected operations in North Africa correct from a military point of view. The difference between us is that English and Americans view the Russian front as secondary, whereas we considered it paramount. From a military point of view Operation 'Torch' is the correct operation, yet it is not substantiated politically. This can be done. Churchill talked about our military discussing some issues. He, Stalin, doesn't see what they can discuss. He is in favour of more communication between our military. As for the operation in North Africa, we have no direct relation to it. Hence, he doesn't see what issues of common interest there are to discuss. As for material help from England and USA, we are grateful for and value this help. But in this connection he has to say the following. There were so many plans made, there were escorts for convoys determined, but then all were cancelled, so now we are getting very little from the English and Americans. He is not complaining but he would like all that was promised to be sent. For example, it was planned to send 4.4 million tons of supplies, yet it was cancelled. His dissatisfaction lies in not that we are given little, but in that we are not given what was promised. He is grateful for what has been done with regard to supplying the USSR and we value this. But if promises are made they have to be fulfilled. Now it is proposed to discuss a new supply program. This interferes with our plans. This is the basis of my dissatisfaction and not the fact that we are getting so few supplies. As for our front, Churchill considers it to be secondary, whereas we consider it primary, and that's why the Allies are giving their divisions to other places. There can be disagreements between allies, there's nothing tragic in that. Stalin expresses his gratitude to England and America for the supplies.

Churchill said that the English and Americans have supplies for 100 steamships. The question is how to get them to USSR. Churchill says that with regard to the promise of supplies he has to say that he did everything that was humanly possible to keep his promises. He has to recall that they promised to get supplies for USSR as far as the dispatch ports. In this regard they fulfilled their duties. Hitler was responsible for the disruption of the plans mentioned by Stalin.

Stalin said that the disruption is not Hitler's fault. The fact is that we are getting just the leftovers from England and America. These leftovers are sent to USSR when there's a surplus. If there's no surplus there are no dispatches.

Churchill replied that he cannot accept this statement.

Harriman said that the fulfilment of the supplies agreement with the USSR is, in accordance with the President's directive, carried out as a priority, therefore he also cannot agree with Stalin's statement.

Stalin said that the issue lies in an estimate of our front's significance, which we consider as the main front, where a majority of the enemy's forces are concentrated.

Churchill said in an anxious tone that they are envious of their Russian ally's glory. We would like to assure our Russian ally that we want to participate in this tough struggle. If our Russian ally does not trust us, – he continues – then we have to let events persuade them otherwise. He doesn't see any point in protesting in this regard.

Stalin said that he is not protesting. We are losing 10,000 people every day. We have 280 enemy divisions against us. However, we do not cry.

Churchill replied that he entirely agrees with what Stalin said. We admire the Russian troops' courage and we mourn their losses. We hope to prove in the course of the war that the English and Americans are not delaying their actions and are not devoid of courage, that they are ready to give blood when there is a chance of success. However, oceans, seas and transport are not factors they can be blamed for.

Stalin said that he would like to invite Churchill and Harriman for dinner tomorrow at 8–8:30.

Churchill thanked him. He would like to establish friendly relations with Stalin. His heart is aching for the burden that Russia has to bear. But he would like to recall that England was on its own against the enemy for a year. Now there are two great allies on the side of England – the USA and Russia. Ahead lies certain victory. We have the strength and possibility to shape the world's future. Churchill wants the hand of friendship from his Russian allies. If it would help Russia, he is ready to sacrifice 100,000 British soldiers in a landing on the French coast. He, Churchill, wants Stalin to believe in England's loyalty, sincerity and determination to fight.

Stalin said there can be disagreements between the allies – the result of differing views on military issues. He thinks the main precondition of a coastal landing is domination of the air. If the English have air supremacy it is possible to shoot up artillery and trench-mortar forces on the French coast. Stalin thinks this can be done, Churchill thinks it can't. War teaches and perhaps Churchill or Stalin will give up their opinions. This is a different estimation of the situation, morals have nothing to do with it. If there was no air supremacy, he wouldn't have posed the question about the second front in Europe. The Germans lack aviation in the west. With domination of air space he is sure that it is possible to establish a bridgehead on the coast. Churchill thinks it is impossible. However, Stalin looks at the matter differently. Stalin asks if he can pose few questions to Churchill. **Churchill** expresses agreement.

Stalin said that from bases in northern Norway the Germans are attacking convoys from the USSR. In this regard he would like to learn Churchill's opinion about the possibility of destroying the Germans in northern Norway, for example, by an ambush. Soviet and English aviation could take part in this operation. The convoys' routes are set. There's no space to manoeuvre. The Germans have a small fleet and it has to be destroyed, rather than disband the convoys. Stalin then says that English departments often ask us to show them new models of weapons. We are not against this, if it is useful. But Stalin would like to know if an agreement could be reached that the English will show us new models of their armaments.

Churchill replied that there's one class of British inventions the English government would not like to disclose. There are devices on British planes that if they were captured by Germans would facilitate the destruction of English bombers over Germany. Churchill says because of the struggle of the Soviet army the English government feels indebted and doesn't consider it has the right to ask for demonstrations of new inventions. As for the suggestion of an agreement, Churchill welcomed the idea and thinks the matter should be discussed further.

Stalin said that the Germans, on capturing territory, build first and second lines of fortification, using wood, stone, and cement. These fortifications cannot withstand our new rocket mortar. We now have a 132mm rocket mortar to use against infantry. This mortar is simple in design and is not unlike rockets for airplanes. In a few seconds the mortar fires 36 projectiles. It is possible to fire three volleys of 36 projectiles that cover two hectares, where nothing will be left alive. He points out that these trench-mortars are especially useful against the Germans, who are fond of counterattacks. If the English military so wish, we could show them these mortars in action.

Churchill expressed his gratitude for this offer. Churchill says further that the talks have been simple and sincere. It was possible to speak about one's difficulties, as well as what could be done for the common good. Churchill hopes that these talks will result in closer collaboration between our countries. Soviet and English military representatives could meet to discuss the details of what was discussed between him and Stalin. On the other hand, there were political and diplomatic matters. These issues could be discussed by Molotov and Cadogan. There was also the question of publicizing Churchill's visit, of using it to maximum effect so as to cause the greatest annoyance to the enemy.

Stalin said that we were thinking to annoy the Germans with an Anglo-Soviet communique. A promise that cannot be fulfilled. Stalin would like to state in the communique something that could be fulfilled, not to make empty promises and not to repeat the same mistake.

Churchill replied that, on the other hand, the enemy cannot be allowed to think that there are disagreements between the allies and that he can feel safe in the west. In any case, Churchill would suggest that Molotov and Cadogan discuss the text of a communiqué.

Stalin agreed.

Churchill said that they gratefully accept Stalin's dinner invitation for tomorrow, knowing about the famed Soviet hospitality. They're planning to fly out on Saturday morning so as to cross the Caspian Sea early.

In conclusion, Churchill would like to thank Stalin for making his stay in Moscow comfortable.

Harriman joined Churchill in these thanks.

Stalin said that it is our duty. In conclusion **Churchill** said that he would like to ask Stalin one question which he is very interested in. He says that while not insisting on the revealing of plans for the movement of military forces and reserves, they would very much like to know Soviet plans for defending the Caucasus. This question interests the English government because, as he mentioned yesterday, it is trying to create an army and air force in Iran and Iraq. If it is possible to get this information he would be very grateful, as it has significance for their own plans in the Near East.

Stalin said that he is ready to satisfy this request and then presents plans for the defence of the Caucasus on a relief map.

Churchill thanked Stalin for the information.

38. Dinner in Honour of Churchill and Harriman, 14 August 1942

Molotov proposed a toast to Churchill. In response Churchill thanked Molotov and asked his colleagues, friends and comrades to drink to the health of that outstanding warrior and Head of State, Stalin.

Then Molotov raised a toast to **Harriman** who thanked Molotov and said that last October he had been in Moscow as a representative of a neutral country, whereas now he was happy to be here as an ally. Harriman raised a toast to the great leader of the Soviet army and people, Stalin. During the dinner **Molotov** also raised toasts to Roosevelt, Brooke, the British and American armies and navies, Standley and Kerr, Cadogan, Wavell, Tedder, Faymonville, Miles and others. Kerr, Standley [US ambassador], Cadogan, Wavell, Tedder, Faymonville [US Military Attaché] and Miles responded with toasts.

Then **Stalin** spoke. He said that everyone present praised the Red Army. Of course, the Red Army had successes and setbacks. But don't forget that no army was invincible and the Red Army could suffer defeats. It had its advantages and disadvantages. The Red Army had suffered substantial blows. Never in history had such a great number of forces invaded Russia as at present. Two fronts had existed in the [last] world war. The English were in France and the Balkans had not been seized by the Germans. Now the situation was different. Men of all ages were being mobilised in Poland. Polish divisions were attacking us at the front. Against us we have Italians, Romanians, Hungarians, Finns and volunteers from Spain and Slovakia. All united against Russia. There had never been a time when the whole of Europe had attacked Russia and if the Red Army could bear the blow and continue to fight, it was worthy of praise. One of the main organisers of the Red Army was Marshal Voroshilov and he, Stalin would like to raise a toast to Voroshilov.

Then Stalin raised a toast to the health of Marshal Shaposhnikov, one of the chief organisers of the Red Army and its general staff. Stalin raised a toast to General Voronov, Head of the Red Army artillery. After that toast Stalin said that in raising military toasts he might perhaps be behaving fractionally. But it had to be done and he begged the indulgence of his guests to raise a toast to General Novikov, the Air Force Chief. Making the next toast, Stalin said that it continued to be military and asked his guests to join him in a toast to Lieutenant-General Golovanov, Commander-in-Chief of Long-Range Aviation. After that, Stalin said that fractionalism was a dangerous disease. Yet he continued to be fractional and raised a toast to the health of Soviet tank troops and their leader, Lieutenant-General Federenko. When Stalin spoke next he said he felt he had exhausted military toasts but there was one military profession he had yet to mention. He had in mind military intelligence. He would like to drink to army, navy and air force intelligence officers. They were the eyes and ears of their country. For some reason people did not talk about intelligence officers. That was a crying shame. To intelligence officers, said Stalin, friends honourably and tirelessly serving their people. A little later Stalin said he would like to say a few words about the significance of intelligence. He had read and was continuing to read about the history of intelligence. Intelligence officers were good people who selflessly serve their state. Nobody envies their fate when they fall into enemy hands. From the history of military intelligence, he knew a single fact that with particular clarity demonstrated the special importance of military intelligence.

As everyone knows, during the last world war the English wanted to carry out an operation to occupy the Dardanelles. However, the allies retreated because they over-estimated the enemy. In reality, the Turks and the Germans were a hairsbreadth from defeat and had their bags packed. This was the result of poor intelligence by the English and would not have happened if they had good intelligence in the area.

39. Churchill-Stalin Meeting in Moscow, 15 August 1942

Churchill said that he didn't mean to trouble Stalin knowing how busy he is. On the other hand, he didn't want to leave Moscow without thanking Stalin for all the courtesy that had been shown to him. Churchill realised that what he had to say about the second front would be painful to hear for his Russian friends, for whom it would be a blow and a disappointment. Because of that Churchill thought it better to fly to the USSR. He considered it his duty. He believed also that his visit would better prove his sincerity than a telegraph communication through the ambassador. That's why Churchill asked to talk candidly. Churchill would like to say that he had no negative thoughts or feeling about what was said in the talks, even though he couldn't agree with what was said. He hoped he hadn't said anything that would stand between him and Stalin, as, apart from his basic task, he came to Moscow to reach the mutual understanding that he already had with Roosevelt, which would be advantageous in resolving all kinds of difficulties. Churchill thinks that Stalin feels that there was success in this regard. This is all that Churchill wanted to say for now.

Stalin said that if the question is about the value of Churchill's visit then he thinks that no matter what the result of the exchange of opinions has been, the meeting itself is of the great importance. He and Churchill had gotten to know and understand each other and if there were differences of opinion, that was in the nature of things, and there could be disagreements between allies. The fact that he and Churchill had met, got to know each other and prepared the basis for future agreements is of great importance. He, Stalin, was inclined to look at the matter more optimistically.

Churchill expressed his agreement. He said that he had thought about the American troops arriving in England. In this regard he has a document, which he doesn't have the right to leave, as the document belongs to Roosevelt. But Churchill would like to show this document to Stalin so that he could see the great effort to enlarge the allies' forces. The document shows the schedule of American troops' arrival in England up to 9th April 1943. The number of American troops in England by that date should be 1,049,400. Of course, there could be some delays.

Molotov asked how many American troops have arrived in England already.

Churchill replied, around 85,000.

Stalin said that Hitler could, in part, interfere with the plan to transport American soldiers to England

Churchill replied that in the course of the war England has transported about a million troops with virtually no losses. All troop convoys are well defended. Churchill does not think the enemy submarines can do much damage in this respect, though the activities of these submarines present the greatest danger to the transfer of American troops from the USA to England. Churchill believes there's a competition between the English bombers and the attacking submarines. However, the result of the war does not depend on this competition. Together with the Americans, he is ready to lose 600,000 tons of shipping by the end of 1943, but even after these losses the situation of the English and the Americans with regard to shipping will improve. But Churchill hopes that such big losses won't take place after the Americans organise a reliable convoy system, while the English will establish dominance of the air. Churchill declares that he was especially glad to hear such a quick assessment of the four advantages of Operation 'Torch', though he realises that this operation has no direct relation to the USSR.

Stalin asked if Churchill has hopes for the success of this operation.

Churchill replied that he does. In the event the operation is carried out successfully it will present big difficulties for Hitler and Vichy. Churchill is quite sure the operation will be successful because the coastal defensive forces will resist Allied forces weakly and may even greet our troops with friendship.

Stalin said that although the operation is not connected directly with Russia, its value is great because the success of the operation will be a blow against the Axis. In this connection Stalin would like to ask Churchill if the operation is needed to occupy France. He thinks that it wouldn't be bad in this regard.

Churchill replied that we are, of course. striving to enter Italy with a large army, and France, too, from both sides.

Stalin said that is good.

Churchill said that in October, when Operation 'Torch' is carried out, the Germans will need to decide what to do on the south coast of France. They could present demands to Vichy, which might be rejected by Petain's government. English planes will bomb Sicily and Italy and this will force the Germans to redeploy their air forces to protect those territories. At the same time Hitler won't be able to take troops and planes from the west coast of France as he will be waiting for an English attack on the French coast. To keep Hitler under pressure in expectation of attack in the Channel there will be a more serious raid on French coast than before, weather permitting. The raid will be a reconnaissance battle by 8,000 men and 50 tanks. These troops will spend a day and night on the French coast, will take prisoners and then return to England. Churchill would liken this operation to the act of dipping a finger into a hot bath to check the temperature. As the English intend to leave the French coast immediately, the French population will be advised to stay at home so that the Germans don't take revenge on them, as happened before. The aim of the operation is firstly, reconnaissance, and, secondly, giving the impression that an invasion of the continent can be expected. Churchill thinks that it is highly important not to give the Germans any reason to think here won't be a landing in Europe in 1942.

Stalin replied that Germans will say that the landing hasn't been successful.

Churchill remarked that Germans will say that, but the English will also have their say.

Stalin said that if Operation 'Torch' is successful everybody will understand what's happened.

Churchill asked Stalin if he had received from him the messages in relation to the results of the convoy to Malta.

Stalin replied affirmatively.

Churchill said that he has received further reports that two more tankers from the convoy had arrived to Malta. Two cruisers that were thought to be sunk had returned. Now the Malta garrison has enough provisions and ammunition till next year and that the battles in Egypt in September and Operation 'Torch' in October will be safeguarded.

Stalin said that he could pass on some experience from Black Sea operations when we supplied Sebastopol. Initially, we undertook systematic raids on German airfields near Sebastopol for 2–3 days, and only on the 4th day did ships with provisions – protected by aviation – enter the port of Sebastopol. The job was carried out with virtually no losses. Stalin asks how it was done in Malta. In his opinion, the essential matter is air action against enemy airfields. Is Churchill aware of the role of aviation and the details of the operations carried out by English, that, he, Stalin, is interested in?

Churchill replied that the difficulty with Malta is that it only has three aerodromes, whereas the enemy has substantial forces in Italy, three times bigger than the English forces based in Malta. The English have to use the airfields in Malta for fighter aircraft, not for the desired number of bombers. If the English win the battle in Egypt then the position should improve in this regard. We are bombing enemy airports but we are weaker than the Germans. The Germans have deployed 450 planes, whereas the English have a third of this number in the Malta region.

Stalin said that we use fighters as bombers, when each aircraft carries 200 to 250 kilograms of bombs.

Churchill asked Stalin whether he could tell him about the position on the front.

Stalin was ready to do so and says that the position of the front could be characterised briefly as follows. The Germans gathered their forces in the Ukraine region, where Kleist, List, Bock and their tank armies are active. The Germans broke through the front and one column headed for the Northern Caucasus, while another went east to Stalingrad and Voronezh. The front was penetrated but the Germans didn't have enough forces to exploit their success. The Germans intended to move from Voronezh to Ryazan and Yelets, around the Moscow front, but it didn't happen because they are lacking troops.

Churchill thanked Stalin for the information. He says further that he had warned the Soviet government about Germany's forthcoming attack on the USSR. His first message in this regard was quite brief and was based on events in Yugoslavia in spring 1941. On the same day that Paul [Prince Regent of Yugoslavia] signed the pact of neutrality with Germany, the Germans ordered three out of their five tank divisions in the Balkans to Krakow. Within ten days there was the coup in Yugoslavia and the three tank divisions returned to action against Yugoslavia. When Churchill learned about the movement of tank divisions from the Balkans to Krakow, he was sure that Germany would attack the USSR.

Stalin replied that we never had any doubts about this but he wanted six more months to prepare for the invasion.

In conclusion Churchill reported that according to the latest information, the German ambassador in Tokyo asked the Japanese to declare against the USSR, but Japan refused to do so.

Stalin thanked Churchill for this information.

40. Churchill-Stalin Conversation in Stalin's Kremlin apartment on the night of 15–16 August 1942

Present: Pavlov and Major Birse (interpreters), joined later by Molotov.

During the conversation there was an exchange of views on general matters of military strategy, particularly naval strategy. **Churchill** touched upon the subject of invading northern Norway, stating that he wishes and intends to carry out this operation, together with Soviet forces, in the winter of this year. He promised to discuss the plan with Stalin later.

Stalin replied that it would be good to carry out this operation and stated that he was ready to allocate two-three divisions to the operation. Stalin said that we were in urgent need of trucks for our front. He stated that he would be grateful if England could supply us with 20,000–25,000 trucks, instead of tanks even. We could receive just the chassis and make the bodies ourselves.

Churchill replied that he would try to satisfy this request but pointed to the fact that shortage of shipping makes it difficult to supply the USSR with trucks produced in England in large-enough quantities.

Then **Stalin** asked for help with supply of aluminium, shortage of which we would be experiencing until next year.

Churchill replied that he will investigate if this request could be satisfied, although England was short of aluminium, too.

Further in the conversation Churchill asked about kolkhozes and the fate of kulaks.

Stalin replied that collectivization got rid of poverty, as every member of a peasant family was able to earn the money and live independently. Stalin recounted that collectivization was necessary to introduce large machinery to agriculture, to raise its productivity. This was only possible in a large farm. As a result of collectivization crop yields had increased significantly, especially thanks to the introduction of high-quality seeds. As far the kulaks were concerned, some were relocated the northern regions of USSR where they got plots of land. The rest of the kulaks were killed by the peasants themselves – such was the hatred for the kulaks.

Churchill, having attentively listened to Stalin, noted that collectivization must have been quite a hard task.

Stalin replied that the collectivization was indeed a hard task that required several years.

Stalin told Churchill that very soon we are going to undertake an air raid on Berlin. Of course, being far away we can send only around 150 bombers. England is in better position, but there were rumours England had reached an agreement with Germany to mutually abstain from raids on London and Berlin.

Churchill somewhat irritably replied that there was no such agreement and that they intended to bomb Berlin as soon as the meteorological condition were favourable and the nights long enough. He said that we needed to coordinate the raids of English and Soviet planes to avoid any collisions.

Stalin replied that, of course, that needed to be done.

Talking about Germany, **Churchill** said that it was necessary to eradicate Prussian militarism and Nazism and to disarm Germany after the war.

Stalin replied that it was necessary to kill German military cadres. Besides that, it was necessary to weaken Germany by detaching the Ruhr region.

Stalin asked Churchill about the numbers of forces England had on its islands.

Churchill replied that the number of English divisions was approaching 40 but didn't give any clear answers to Stalin's further specific questions.

At the end of the conversation it was agreed to release a communique about the talks. At Churchill's insistence there was accepted a formulation about decisions concerning the war against Hitler's Germany and its allies in Europe. Churchill also proposed to add to the communique that 'both Governments are determined to carry on with all their power and energy until the complete destruction of Hitlerism and any similar tyranny has been achieved'.

This formulation was also accepted.

Chapter 5

The Rocky Road to Tehran

The issue of opening a second front in France continued to dominate Churchill's relations with Stalin, and it was not resolved until the Tehran Conference in November 1943. Having failed to secure a second front in 1942 Stalin pushed hard for one to happen in 1943, as Churchill and Roosevelt had promised. Stalin's suspicions were aroused by the dragging out of the Anglo-American invasion of North Africa and by decisions to expand operations to Sicily and Italy. It became increasingly apparent that operations in the Mediterranean would drain shipping and other resources necessary for a cross-Channel invasion of France. Finally, on 4 June, Churchill and Roosevelt informed Stalin that, for strategic reasons, a second front in France had been postponed until spring 1944. Stalin's response was angry but impotent and his subsequent recriminations with Churchill were pointless except as a guilt-tripping exercise to extract more material aid from the West.

The Allied rout of Axis forces in North Africa and the invasion of Sicily on 10 July precipitated a coup against Benito Mussolini and he was replaced at the end of the month by a government headed by the monarchist Marshal Pietro Badoglio, who had fallen out with the Fascist dictator in 1940. When Badoglio began armistice negotiations with the British and Americans, Stalin was keen to be involved and to participate in the occupation regime that would be established in Italy. In his message to Churchill and Roosevelt on 22 August he urged the establishment of a tripartite military-political commission (**Document 59**). Such a commission in the form of an Advisory Council for Italy was set up but it had very little power. Roosevelt, and especially Churchill, were determined to control Italy's occupation and insisted that Allied armies on the ground should run the show. Since the Soviets had no troops fighting in Italy (unless you counted the numerous communist partisan bands) they had no real say in the occupation. The Churchill-Roosevelt stance on Italy backfired in the long run since it established a precedent for occupation regimes established by the Red Army as it expanded into central and eastern Europe in 1944–5. When the Red Army invaded Bulgaria, Hungary and Romania, Stalin was able to cite the Italian model and to minimise Western influence in his zones of military occupation.

Another issue of importance for the future of the Grand Alliance was Soviet relations with the Polish Government-in-Exile in London, which were severed by Stalin in April 1943 following the discovery by the Germans of the mass graves of thousands of Polish POWs who had perished at the hands of the Soviets three years earlier.

When Hitler invaded Poland in September 1939 he did so knowing Stalin would remain neutral, not least because the Soviet-German non-aggression treaty included a secret protocol that allocated Poland's eastern territories – broadly Western Belorussia and Western Ukraine – to a Soviet sphere of influence. On 17 September the Soviets invaded Eastern Poland and subsequently 'Sovietised' and incorporated Western Belorussia and Western Ukraine into the USSR.

These territories were east of the so-called Curzon Line – the ethnographic frontier between Russia and Poland drawn up at the Paris Peace Conference in 1919 – but they had been occupied by the newly-created Polish state during the course of its war with Bolshevik Russia in 1919–20. Under the 1921 Treaty of Riga with Poland the Soviets acquiesced in these losses, but Stalin was never reconciled to them, not least because he wanted secure ethnic boundaries for the USSR. Having millions of Belorussians and Ukrainians on the other side of the Soviet border was potentially destabilising, a situation that had been exploited by Nazi propagandists before the war. Under no circumstances was Stalin going to relinquish these territories now that he had reoccupied them.

The complication was that after the German invasion of the USSR in June 1941, Stalin's erstwhile Polish enemies became his allies. In July 1941 the Soviet Union signed a treaty of alliance with the Polish Government-in-Exile and agreed to amnesty Polish citizens who had been detained in the USSR as result of the Red Army's invasion of eastern Poland. There were some 400,000 Polish prisoners or detainees in the USSR, most of whom were quickly released, many to serve in Polish armies raised on Soviet soil. But more than 20,000 Polish military officers and police officials were missing.

The Polish Government-in-Exile pressed the Soviets for an explanation as to the whereabouts of the missing POWs but Stalin stonewalled and said the prisoners must have escaped. In truth, they had been executed in March–April 1940. They were killed because they were seen as anti-Soviet and as a security threat. Important in this respect were Soviet fears in spring 1940 they could soon be involved in a war with Britain and France over Finland, which the USSR had attacked in December 1939 following the breakdown of negotiations about changes to the Soviet-Finnish frontier in the vicinity of Leningrad.

The onset of the so-called 'Winter War' prompted Anglo-French moves to aid the Finns, either by sending an expeditionary force to Finland or by bombing the Soviet oilfields at Baku. In truth, the British and French were seeking to exploit the Soviet-Finnish conflict for their own ends, notably using it as a pretext to seize control of neutral Sweden's iron ore fields – an essential resource of the German war machine. But neither the Swedes nor the Finns relished Scandinavia becoming a battleground of the wider European war. The same was true of the Soviets and having achieved his limited territorial goals Stalin authorised a peace treaty with Finland in March 1940. But by that time the mechanisms leading to the execution of the Polish POWs had been set in motion.[1]

When the Germans announced the discovery of the mass graves in the Katyn forest near Smolensk, Moscow responded by claiming it was a Nazi propaganda ploy and that the Germans themselves must have shot the Poles. The Polish

Government-in-Exile, however, supported the idea of an investigation by an independent medical commission. The Soviets were outraged and on 21 April Stalin fired off an indignant telegram to Churchill deploring what he character-ised as an anti-Soviet slander campaign by the London Poles (**Document 48**). Churchill did what he could to avert a break in Polish-Soviet relations, but to no avail.

While Churchill suspected the Soviets had killed the Polish POWs, his priority remained to maintain and, if possible, improve relations with Stalin, a task that was complicated enough given the postponement of the second front. Also, he and Roosevelt had been pressing Stalin for a meeting of the Big Three and the Katyn episode, though disturbing, was not important enough to deflect those efforts. A breakthrough came when Roosevelt sent Joseph Davies, a former American ambassador to the Soviet Union, to Moscow in May 1943 to lobby for a meeting between Stalin and the President. Stalin agreed in principle and the meeting was later broadened to include Churchill.

As part of the preparations for a Big Three summit in Tehran at the end of November it was agreed the American, British and Soviet foreign ministers would meet in Moscow in October 1943. The Moscow Foreign Minister's con-ference (19–30 October) was the first big Grand Alliance tripartite conference. The Soviet delegation was led by Molotov, the British by Eden and the Americans by Secretary of State Cordell Hull. While the Soviets tabled only one item for the agenda on 'measure to shorten the war against Germany and its allies in Europe', the British and Americans wanted to discuss a number of political questions as well.[2] The conference was held in the Spiridonovka Palace, the venue of the ill-fated Anglo-Soviet-French military negotiations of summer 1939. It was chaired by Molotov, who was praised by Eden and Hull for his deft handling of the proceedings.

Stalin did not attend the conference but was briefed extensively by Molotov and met privately with both Eden and Hull. He also hosted the closing confer-ence dinner. Stalin's priority was evident from his talk with Eden on 27 October when he predictably pressed the Foreign Secretary on the question of the second front, stressing that the Soviet Union would not be able to mount any more big offensives against the Germans if Hitler was not forced by a substantial threat from the west to divide his forces.[3]

At the conference the Western Powers reaffirmed their commitment to open a second front in France in spring 1944. Agreement was also reached on the need to persuade Turkey to enter the war against Germany and there was discussion of a Soviet proposal for Allied air bases in Sweden. Cordell Hull's priority was agree-ment on the establishment of a successor to the discredited League of Nations. A declaration to this effect was issued by the conference. At the Soviets' sugges-tion it was agreed to hold further trilateral discussions on the proposed new security organisation – talks which led eventually to the foundation of the United Nations in 1945. Another important decision was the adoption of a British pro-posal to establish a European Advisory Commission of three powers with the initial task of examining the armistice terms for Germany. The only specific agreement reached at the conference on the future of Germany was a declaration that Austria would be detached from the Reich and made an independent state again. But in the discussion of the German question it became plain that all three foreign ministers were broadly agreed on the need to disarm, demilitarise, denazify, democratise and dismember Germany. It was also agreed that the major Nazi leaders would be tried as war criminals. A communiqué issued at the end of the conference declared the three states' commitment to 'continue the present close collaboration and cooperation in the conduct of the war into the period following the end of hostilities' and concluded by noting 'the atmosphere of mutual confidence and understanding which characterised all the work of the Conference'.

Stalin's public verdict on the conference was delivered in his speech on the anniversary of the Revolution on 6 November 1943. In a section of the speech entitled 'The Consolidation of the Anti-Hitler Coalition and the Disintegration of the Fascist Bloc' Stalin said:

> The victory of the Allied countries over our common enemy approaches and, notwithstanding the efforts of the enemy, relations between the Allies and the military cooperation of their armies is not weakening but strength-ening and consolidating. In this regard the historic decisions of the Moscow Conference ... are eloquent testimony ... Now our united countries are fully resolved to carry out joint blows against the enemy which will lead to our final victory over them.[4]

Despite all the talk about the future of the Grand Alliance, Stalin's priority remained a second front in France to draw substantial German forces to the West and ease the Soviet path to victory on the Eastern Front. In his speech, Stalin noted the Allied military action in North Africa, the Mediterranean and Italy and the impact of the continuing air bombardment of German industry. He also went out of his way to praise Western supplies to the USSR, saying that these had greatly facilitated the success of the Soviet summer campaign. The sting in the tail was his observation that Allied military action in southern Europe was not the second front, which when it was opened would further strengthen the Allies' military cooperation and accelerate the victory over Nazi Germany.

As the Tehran Conference showed, the realisation of a second front in France remained Stalin's primary goal in his relations with Churchill and Roosevelt. 'The main issue being decided now is whether or not they will help us', Stalin is reported to have said on the way to Tehran.

Stalin's meeting with Churchill and Roosevelt took place in Tehran because the Soviet leader insisted on a venue that would enable him to remain in direct telephone and telegraphic contact with his General Staff in Moscow. Iran had been occupied by Britain and Soviet Union since August 1941. Their troops had been withdrawn from the Iranian capital but it remained full of Allied soldiers and the grounds of the Soviet embassy were considered a safe location for the conference. For security reasons Roosevelt stayed in the Soviet embassy with Stalin, while Churchill resided at the British Legation nearby.[5]

Stalin's first bilateral meeting at Tehran, on 28 November, was with Roosevelt. As this was their first ever meeting it was more a social call than anything else but they established a good rapport and there was a meeting of minds on many issues. Harriman reports that he went to see Churchill when he heard the PM was upset because Roosevelt had talked to Stalin before him but

> the Prime Minister was not in too bad a mood. He said that he was glad to obey orders. That he had a right to be the Chairman of the meeting because of his age; because his name began with C and because of the historic importance of the British Empire which he represented. He waived all these claims but he would insist on one thing, which was that he should be allowed to give a dinner party on the 30th [November] which was his 69th birthday to which he expected to invite a total of about 30 people.[6]

Still, much to Churchill's chagrin, the Roosevelt-Stalin axis dominated the summit's discussions. At the first plenary session of the Big Three later that day Stalin and Roosevelt ganged up on Churchill and insisted that Operation Overlord – the Allied invasion of northern France – should have absolute priority in Anglo-American military operations for 1944. Although he agreed in principle with Overlord, Churchill still doubted the wisdom of a cross-Channel invasion against the well-fortified French coast and instead favoured continuing to attack the 'soft underbelly' of the Axis in the Mediterranean.

Churchill and Stalin had an interesting and typical exchange at dinner that evening (**Document 64**). Lubricated by drink, Churchill waxed lyrical about the Big Three as the future guardians of world peace, while Stalin remained focused on the specifics of containing the revival of defeated Germany's power. Surprisingly, Stalin refused to be drawn on the Polish border even though Churchill and Eden's proposal to compensate Poland for territorial losses to the USSR by giving it German lands was also Soviet policy. But perhaps Stalin was circumspect because this was a dinner conversation and unlike Churchill he didn't like to make policy on the hoof.

Before the second plenary session, on 29 November, Stalin met Roosevelt again. The main topic of this conversation was Roosevelt's plans for a post-war international security organisation. Stalin knew the President's views since Roosevelt had already, in mid-1942, presented to Molotov his idea of the great powers constituting themselves as an international police force dedicated to maintaining peace. On hearing of Roosevelt's proposal, Stalin had cabled Molotov in Washington on 1 June 1942 that the President's 'considerations about peace protection after the war are absolutely sound. There is no doubt that it would be impossible to maintain peace without creating a united military force by Britain, the USA and the USSR capable of preventing aggression. Tell Roosevelt that ... [he] is absolutely right and that his position will be fully supported by the Soviet Government.'[7]

Stalin's conversation with Roosevelt was interrupted by a ceremony at which he was presented by Churchill with the 'Sword of Stalingrad' – a gift from King George VI in honour of the citizens of the heroic city that had stopped the

Germans dead in their tracks. As was usual on such occasions, a band played the Communist Internationale (still at this time the Soviet national anthem) and the British anthem, God Save the King. After the Soviet dictator and the British Prime Minister had exchanged pleasantries about Anglo-Soviet relations, Stalin took the sword from Churchill, kissed it, and handed it to Voroshilov, who nearly dropped it!

At the second plenary session the discussion on Operation Overlord continued and Stalin pressed Churchill on the date of the invasion of France, on the appointment of an Anglo-American supreme commander of the operation, and on the relationship between Overlord and other planned military actions by the Western Allies. The sharpness of the exchanges with Churchill during this session was summed up in Stalin's barb that he 'would like to know whether the English believe in Operation Overlord or simply speak of it to reassure the Russians'.[8]

According to Harriman's recollections, Stalin's interchange with Churchill at dinner that evening was much less friendly than it had been the night before. He needled Churchill about wanting a soft peace for Germany and said that at least 50,000 German officers should be liquidated. This was too much for Churchill: 'the British Parliament and people will not tolerate mass executions'. To break the tension Roosevelt jocularly suggested that only 40,000 officers should be killed; Churchill was not amused. But 'recognising that he had pushed Churchill too far, Stalin turned abruptly to praising the British. They had fought well in the war, he acknowledged, and he personally would like to see the British Empire expanded.'[9]

On the following day, 30 November, Churchill and Stalin had their one and only bilateral meeting at Tehran (**Document 65**).[10] At this meeting Churchill continued to doubt the feasibility of Overlord and refused to commit on the date the second front would be launched. Stalin insisted that since the Red Army was counting on an Allied invasion of northern France he had to know now if the operation would go ahead. If it did go ahead the Red Army would be able to mount a multi-pronged offensive to keep the Germans tied down in the East.

At the tripartite lunch that followed, Roosevelt announced that it had been agreed to launch Overlord in May 1944, together with a supporting invasion of southern France. With the decision on a second front finally nailed down, the conversation between Churchill and Stalin took an altogether friendlier turn. Churchill started the ball rolling by saying Russia had a right to warm-water ports and Stalin took the opportunity to raise the issue of Turkey's control of the Black Sea Straits and the need to revise the Straits regime in Russia's favour. Stalin also spoke of securing warm-water outlets in the Far East, including the Manchurian ports of Darien and Port Arthur, leased by Tsarist Russia in the nineteenth century but ceded to Japan following defeat in the Russo-Japanese war of 1904–5. Churchill responded by reiterating that 'Russia must have access to warm waters' and then continued that 'the direction of the world must be concentrated in the hands of those nations who are fully satisfied and have no pretensions ... our three nations are such countries. The main thing is that after we have agreed between ourselves we will be able to consider ourselves fully satisfied.'[11]

Churchill's birthday party at the British embassy went very well. Birse, the British interpreter, recalled that Stalin was initially anxious about how to use the array of different-sized knives and forks set before him but 'his fear, if he had any, of doing the wrong thing soon vanished, for the proceedings became increasingly friendly and jovial'.[12] The friendly exchanges continued the next day at lunch during a long plenary discussion of Churchill's pet project of persuading Turkey to enter the war on the side of the Allies. Stalin was sceptical but committed the Soviet Union to declare war on Bulgaria if Turkey's entry into the war precipitated a Bulgarian–Turkish conflict. Since Bulgaria was a traditional Russian ally this gratified Churchill greatly, and he thanked Stalin for making such a commitment. Discussing Finland, Churchill expressed sympathy and understanding of the USSR's security needs in relation to Leningrad but hoped the country would not be swallowed up by Russia after the war. Stalin replied that while he believed in an independent Finland there would have to be territorial adjustments in the Soviet Union's favour and that the Finns should pay reparations for war damages.[13] Churchill reminded Stalin of the Bolshevik slogan during the First World War – 'No annexations, no indemnities' – but the Soviet leader quipped, 'I already told you, I have become a conservative'.[14]

After lunch, at the formal plenary session, amicable agreement was soon reached about distribution of the Italian naval and merchant fleet, with Churchill and Roosevelt promising to deliver ships to Stalin as soon as they could. The next subject for discussion was a little trickier: Poland. Churchill and Roosevelt raised with Stalin the question of the re-establishment of Soviet relations with the Polish Government-in-Exile in London. Stalin was adamant that this would not happen while the Polish exiles continued to collaborate with the Germans. On the territorial question Stalin supported the idea of Poland being compensated at the expense of Germany but insisted that the eastern border must be that established in 1939, i.e. with the incorporation of Western Belorussia and Western Ukraine into the USSR. When Eden suggested that this meant the 'Molotov-Ribbentrop line', Stalin said that he could call it what he liked. Molotov intervened to say that they were talking about the 'Curzon Line' and there were no essential differences between the ethnographical frontier established by the British Foreign Secretary Lord Curzon and the Russo-Polish border proposed by the Soviets. Stalin did concede, however, that any area east of the Curzon Line with a majority of ethnic Poles could go to Poland.

The final topic discussed by the Big Three at Tehran was the dismemberment of Germany. The 'German question' was raised by Roosevelt, and Stalin asked him what he had in mind. 'The dismemberment of Germany', said Roosevelt. 'This is what we prefer', chipped in Stalin. During the war Stalin expressed a strong preference for the dismemberment of Germany – a fact that was embarrassing to the Soviets during the Cold War when they liked to trumpet their commitment to a united Germany. When they published their records of the Tehran, Yalta and Potsdam conferences the Soviets edited them to give the impression that Britain and the United States had made the running on dismemberment during the war.[15]

At the Tehran discussion Churchill said he, too, favoured the partition of Germany but when questioned by Stalin about his commitment to such a project the British leader explained that he thought Prussia had to be dealt with more severely than the rest of the country and that he favoured a Danubian confederation of Germany's southern provinces, mainly to head off future demands for German reunification. According to the British record of the discussion Stalin's view was that

> it was far better to break up and scatter the German tribes. Of course, they would want to unite, no matter how much they were split up. They would always want to reunite. In this he saw great danger, which would have to be neutralized by various economic measures and in the long run by force if necessary. That was the only way to keep the peace. But if we were to make a large combination with Germans in it, trouble was bound to come. We had to see to it that they were kept separate ... There were no measures to be taken which excluded a movement towards reunion. Germans would always want to reunite and take their revenge. It would be necessary to keep ourselves strong enough to beat them if they ever let loose another war.

Churchill asked if Stalin favoured a fragmented Europe of little states. Not Europe, only Germany, replied Stalin. Roosevelt said Germany had been safer when divided into 107 principalities but Churchill stuck to his view that five or six larger units was better. Stalin reiterated that 'Germany should at all costs be broken up so that she could not reunite' and proposed that the matter be referred to the tripartite European Advisory Commission, established by the Moscow conference to examine the terms of Germany's surrender and occupation.[16]

At the very end of the conference Churchill returned to the question of Poland's frontiers and tabled a formal proposal that they be constituted by the Curzon Line in the east and by the River Oder in the west. Stalin said: 'The Russians have no ice-free ports on the Baltic Sea. Therefore, the Russians need the ice-free ports of Königsberg and Memel ... The Russians need a lump of German territory. If the English agree to transfer to us this territory we will agree to the formula proposed by Churchill.' Churchill said he would study this very interesting proposal.[17]

On 7 December 1943 the fact that a Big Three meeting had taken place in Tehran was announced to the world and the famous picture of Churchill, Roosevelt and Stalin sitting in front of the conference building was published in the Allied press. A communiqué in the name of the three leaders stated that

> We express our determination that our nations shall work together in war and in the peace that will follow. As to war – our military staff have joined in our round table discussions, and we have concerted plans for the destruction of the German forces. We have reached complete agreement as to the scope and timing of operations to be undertaken from the east, west and south ...

And as to peace – we are sure that our concord will win an enduring peace ...
We came here with hope and determination. We leave here, friends in fact,
in spirit and in purpose.

After Tehran, Stalin's private office composed a document summarising Stalin's
discussions at the conference, a document that was hand-corrected by Stalin. In
relation to dismemberment the document stated:

Comrade Stalin declared that in relation to the aim of weakening Germany,
the Soviet government preferred to dismember it. Comrade Stalin positively
favoured Roosevelt's plan but without pre-determining the number of states
into which Germany is to be split. He came out against Churchill's plan to
create, after the division of Germany, a new, unsustainable state like the
Danubian Federation. Comrade Stalin spoke in favour of separate Austrian
and German states.[18]

Documents 41–65

41. Stalin to Churchill, 27 November 1942
... I fully share your view that it is highly important to promote our personal
relations.

I am grateful for the steps you are taking to send another large convoy to
Archangel. I realise this is particularly difficult for you at the moment, especially
in view of considerable operations by the British fleet in the Mediterranean.

I agree with you and President Roosevelt concerning the desirability of doing
everything to bring Turkey into the war on our side in the spring. That, without
a doubt, would mean a great deal for the speedy defeat of Hitler and his
accomplices ...

I have carefully read your communication saying that you and the Americans
are continuing preparations along your south-eastern and southern coasts in
order to keep the Germans pinned in the Pas de Calais, etc., and that you are
ready to take advantage of any favourable opportunity. That, I hope, does not
imply renunciation of your Moscow promise to open a second front in Western
Europe in the spring of 1943.

I accept President Roosevelt's and your suggestion that we call a conference of
representatives of our three Staffs in Moscow to make appropriate war plans for
1943. We are prepared to meet your representatives, and, the Americans, whenever you like ...

42. Churchill to Stalin, 3 December 1942
The President tells me he has proposed a meeting for us three in January somewhere in North Africa.

This is far better than the Iceland project we talked about in Moscow. You
could get to any point desired in three days, I in two, and the President in about
the same time as you. I earnestly hope you will agree. We must decide at the
earliest moment the best way of attacking Germany in Europe with all possible
force in 1943. This can only be settled between the heads of the governments and

states with their high expert authorities to hand. It is only by such a meeting that the full burden of the war can be shared according to capacity and opportunity.

43. Stalin to Churchill, 6 December 1942

... I welcome the idea of a meeting of the three heads of the Government of the three states to establish a common strategic line. To my great regret, however, I shall be unable to leave the Soviet Union. I must tell you that this is such a crucial moment that I cannot be away even for a single day ...

I await your reply to that part of my previous message concerning the opening of a second front in Western Europe in 1943 ...

44. Stalin to Churchill and Roosevelt, 30 January 1943

Your friendly joint message reached me on 27 January. Thank you for informing me of the Casablanca decisions about operations to be undertaken by the US and British armed forces in the first nine months of 1943. Assuming that your decisions on Germany are designed to defeat it by opening a second front in Europe in 1943, I should be grateful if you would inform me of the concrete operations planned and their timing.

As for the Soviet Union, I can assure you the Soviet armed forces will do all in their power to continue the offensive against Germany and its allies on the Soviet-German front. We expect to finish our winter campaign, circumstances permitting, in the first half of February. Our troops are tired, they are in need of rest and will hardly be able to carry on the offensive beyond that period.

45. Churchill to Stalin, 9 February 1943

Your message of 30 January. I have now consulted the President and the matter has been referred to the Staffs on both sides of the ocean. I am authorised to give the following joint reply:

(a) There are a quarter of a million Germans and Italians in Eastern Tunisia. We hope to destroy or expel these during April, if not earlier.

(b) When this is accomplished, we intend in July, or earlier if possible, to seize Sicily with the object of clearing the Mediterranean, prompting an Italian collapse with the consequent effect on Greece and Yugoslavia and wearing down of the German Air Force; this is to be closely followed by an operation in the Eastern Mediterranean, probably against the Dodecanese.

(c) This operation will involve all the shipping and landing craft, we can get together in the Mediterranean and all the troops we have trained in assault-landing, and will be of the order of 300,000–400,000 men. We shall press any advantage to the utmost once ports of entry and landing bases have been established.

(d) We are also pushing preparations to the limit of our resources for a cross-Channel operation in August, in which British and United States units would participate. Here again, shipping and assault-landing craft will be the limiting factors. If the, operation is delayed by the weather or other reasons, it will be prepared with stronger forces for September. The timing of this attack must, of course, depend upon the condition of German defensive positions on their side of the Channel.

(e) Both operations will be supported by very large United States and British air forces, and that across the Channel by the whole metropolitan Air Force of Great Britain. Together, these operations will strain to the very utmost the shipping resources of Great Britain and the United States ...

46. Stalin to Churchill, 16 February 1943

On 12 February I received your message on the forthcoming Anglo-American military operations.

Thanks for the additional information on the Casablanca decisions. At the same time, I cannot but make certain observations on with your message ...

It appears from your message that the date – February – which you had fixed earlier for completing the operations in Tunisia is now set back to April. There is no need to demonstrate at length the undesirability of this delay in operations against the Germans and Italians. It is now, when the Soviet troops are still keeping up their broad offensive, that action by the Anglo-American troops in North Africa is imperative. Simultaneous pressure on Hitler from our front and from yours in Tunisia would be of great positive significance for our common cause and would create most serious difficulties for Hitler and Mussolini. It would also expedite the operations you are planning in Sicily and the Eastern Mediterranean.

As to the opening of a second front in Europe, in particular in France, it is planned, judging by your communication, for August or September. It seems to me, however that the situation calls for shortening these time limits to the utmost and the opening of a second front in the west at a much earlier date. So that the enemy should not be given a chance to recover, it is very important that the blow from the west be delivered in spring or early summer, instead of being put off till the second half of the year.

According to reliable information at our disposal, since the end of December, when for some reason Anglo-American operations in Tunisia were suspended, the Germans have moved 27 divisions, including five tank divisions, to the Soviet-German front from France, Belgium, Holland and Germany. Thus, instead of the Soviet Union being aided by diverting German forces from the Soviet-German front, what we get is relief for Hitler, who, because of the let-up in Anglo-American operations in Tunisia, was able to move additional troops against the Russians.

All this says that the sooner we jointly exploit the Hitler camp's difficulties at the front, the more grounds we shall have for anticipating an early defeat for Hitler. Unless we take account of this and profit from the present moment to further our common interests, it may well be that, having gained a respite and rallied their forces, the Germans might recover. It is clear to everyone how undesirable it would be to allow this to occur ...

47. Stalin to Churchill, 15 March 1943

I received your reply to my message of 16 February.

It is evident from your communication that Anglo-American operations in North Africa are not being hastened, but are, in fact, being postponed till the end of April. And even this date is rather vague. Thus, at the height of our fighting against Hitler's troops in February and March, the Anglo-American offensive in North Africa, far from having been stepped up, has been called off, and the date fixed by yourself has been put back. Meanwhile Germany has succeeded in moving 36 divisions from the West, including six tank divisions, for use against Soviet troops. It is easy to understand the difficulties that this has created for the Soviet Army and the extent to which it has eased the German position on the Soviet-German front will be readily appreciated.

For all its importance 'Husky' can by no means replace a second front in France, but I fully welcome, of course, your intention to speed up the operation,

I still regard the opening of a second front in France as the important thing. You will recall that you thought it possible to open a second front as early as 1942 or this spring at the latest. There were serious reasons for this. Hence it should be obvious why I stressed in my previous message the need for striking in the west no later than this spring or early summer.

Soviet troops fought strenuously all winter and are continuing to do so, while Hitler is taking important measures to revive and reinforce his army for spring and summer operations against the USSR; it is therefore particularly essential for us that the blow from the west be delayed no longer, that it be delivered this spring or in early summer.

... I recognise the difficulties. Nevertheless, I need to give a most emphatic warning, in the interest of our common cause, of the grave danger of any further delay in opening a second front in France. For this reason the vagueness of your statements about the contemplated Anglo-American offensive across the Channel causes apprehension about which I cannot be silent.

48. Stalin to Churchill, 21 April 1943

The Soviet Government considers the recent behaviour of the Polish Government towards the USSR completely abnormal and contrary to all the rules and standards governing relations between two allied states.

The anti-Soviet slander campaign launched by the German fascists in connection with the Polish officers whom they themselves murdered in the Smolensk area, in German-occupied territory, was immediately seized upon by the Sikorski Government and is being fanned in every way by the Polish official press. Far from countering the infamous fascist slander against the USSR the Sikorski Government has not found it necessary even to address questions to the Soviet Government or to request information on the matter.

The Hitler authorities, having perpetrated a monstrous crime against the Polish officers, are now staging a farcical investigation, using for the purpose certain pro-fascist Polish elements picked by themselves in occupied Poland, where everything is under Hitler's heel and where no honest Pole can open his mouth.

Both the Sikorski and Hitler Governments have enlisted for the 'investigation' the aid of the International Red Cross, which, under a terror regime of gallows and wholesale extermination of the civil population, is forced to take part in an investigation farce directed by Hitler. It is obvious that this 'investigation', which, moreover, is being carried out behind the Soviet Government's back, cannot enjoy the confidence of anyone with a semblance of honesty.

The fact that an anti-Soviet campaign has been started simultaneously in the German and Polish press and follows identical lines is indubitable evidence of contact and collusion in this hostile campaign between Hitler – the Allies' enemy – and the Sikorski Government.

At a time when the peoples of the Soviet Union are shedding their blood in a grim struggle against Hitler's Germany and using all their strength to defeat the common foe of freedom-loving democratic countries, the Sikorski Government strikes a treacherous blow at the Soviet Union to help Hitler's tyranny.

These circumstances compel the Soviet Government to consider that the present Polish Government, having descended to collusion with the Hitler Government, has, in practice, severed its relations of alliance with the USSR and adopted a hostile attitude to the Soviet Union.

For these reasons the Soviet Government has decided to interrupt relations with that Government ...

49. Churchill to Stalin, 24 April 1943

Ambassador Maisky delivered your message to me last night.

1. We shall certainly oppose vigorously any 'investigation' by the International Red Cross or any other body in any territory under German authority. Such investigation would be a fraud, and its conclusions reached by terrorism. Mr Eden is seeing Sikorski today and will press him as strongly as possible to refrain from moral support for any investigation under Nazi auspices. We should never approve of any negotiations with the Germans or any sort of contact with them and we shall press this point upon our Polish allies.

2. I shall telegraph you later how Sikorski reacts to the above points. His position is one of great difficulty. Far from being pro-German or in league with them, he is in danger of being overthrown by Poles who consider that he has not stood up sufficiently for his people against the Soviets. If he goes we will only get somebody worse. I hope, therefore, that your decision to 'interrupt' relations is to be read as a final warning rather than a break and that it will not be made public, at any rate until every other plan has been tried. The public announcement of a break would do the greatest possible harm in the United States, where the Poles are numerous and influential ...

50. Stalin to Churchill, 25 April 1943

I have received your message concerning Polish affairs. Thank you for your sympathetic stand on this issue. I must tell you, however, that the matter of interrupting relations with the Polish Government has already been decided and that today V.M. Molotov delivered a Note to the Polish Government. All my colleagues insisted on this because the Polish official press did not for a minute cease its hostile campaign but is actually intensifying it day by day. I also had to take cognisance of Soviet public opinion, which is deeply outraged by the ingratitude and treachery of the Polish Government.

As to publishing the Soviet document on interrupting relations with the Polish Government, I fear that it is simply impossible to avoid doing so.

51. Churchill to Stalin, 25 April 1943

Mr Eden saw General Sikorski yesterday evening. Sikorski stated that far from synchronising his appeal to the Red Cross with that of the Germans his Government took the initiative without knowing what line the Germans would take. In fact, the Germans acted after hearing the Polish broadcast announcement. Sikorski also told Mr Eden that his Government had simultaneously approached Monsieur Bogomolov [Soviet ambassador to Allied governments-in-exile in London] on the subject. Sikorski emphasised that previously he had several times raised this question of the missing officers with the Soviet Government and once with you personally. On his instructions the Polish Minister of Information has reacted strongly against German propaganda in his broadcasts and this has brought an angry German reply. As a result of Mr Eden's strong representations Sikorski has undertaken not to press the request for the Red Cross investigation and will so inform the Red Cross authorities in Berne. He will also restrain the Polish press from polemics. In this connection I am examining the possibility of silencing those Polish newspapers in this country which attacked the Soviet Government and at the same time attacked Sikorski for trying to work with the Soviet Government.

In view of Sikorski's undertaking I would now urge you to abandon the idea of any interruption of relations.

I have reflected further on this matter and I am more than ever convinced that a break between the Soviet and Polish Governments can only assist our enemies. German propaganda has produced this story precisely in order to make a rift in the ranks of the United Nations and to lend some semblance of reality to its new attempts to persuade the world that the interests of Europe and the smaller nations are being defended by Germany against the great extra-European Powers, namely the Union of Soviet Socialist Republics, the United States and the British Empire

I know General Sikorski well and I am convinced that no contacts or understanding could exist between him or his government and our common enemy, against whom he has led the Poles in bitter and uncompromising resistance. His appeal to the International Red Cross was clearly a mistake though I am convinced it was not made in collusion with the Germans ...

52. Churchill to Stalin, 30 April 1943

1. I cannot refrain from expressing my disappointment that you should have felt it necessary to take action in breaking off relations with the Poles without giving me time to inform you of the results of my approach to General Sikorski, about which I had telegraphed to you on 24 April. I had hoped that, in the spirit of our

treaty of last year, we should always consult each other about such important matters, more especially as they affect the combined strength of the United Nations.

2. Mr Eden and I have pointed out to the Polish Government that no resumption of friendly or working relations with the Soviets is possible while they make charges of an insulting character against the Soviet Government and thus seem to countenance the atrocious Nazi propaganda. Still more would it be impossible for any of us to tolerate inquiries by the International Red Cross held under Nazi auspices and dominated by Nazi terrorism. I am glad to tell you they have accepted our view and that they want to work loyally with you. Their request now is to have dependents of the Polish army in Iran and the fighting Poles in the Soviet Union sent to join the Polish forces already allowed to go to Iran. This is surely a matter which admits of patient discussion. We think the request is reasonable if made in the right way and at the right time and I am pretty sure that the President thinks so, too. We hope earnestly that remembering the difficulties in which we have all been plunged by the brutal Nazi aggression, you will consider this matter in a spirit of collaboration.

3. The Cabinet here is determined to have proper discipline in the Polish press in Great Britain. The miserable rags attacking Sikorski can say things which German broadcasts repeat open-mouthed to the world to our joint detriment. This must be stopped and it will be stopped.

4. So far this business has been Goebbels' triumph. He is now busy suggesting the USSR will set up a Polish Government on Russian soil and deal only with them. We should not, of course, be able to recognise such a government and would continue our relations with Sikorski, who is by far the most helpful man you or we are likely to find for the purposes of the common cause. I expect this will also be the American view.

5. Personally, I think they have had a shock and that after whatever interval is thought convenient the relationship established on 30 July 1941, should be restored. No one will dislike this less than Hitler and it makes sense for us to do what he doesn't like.

6. We owe it to our armies now engaged, and presently to be more heavily engaged, to maintain good conditions behind the fronts. I and my colleagues look steadily to the ever-closer cooperation and understanding of the USSSR, the United States and the British Commonwealth and Empire, not only in the deepening war struggle, but after the war. What other hope can there be for this tortured world?

53. Stalin to Churchill, 4 May 1943

In sending my message of 21 April on interrupting relations with the Polish Government, I was guided by the fact that the notorious anti-Soviet press campaign, launched by the Poles as early as 15 April and aggravated first by the statement of the Polish Ministry of National Defence and later by the Polish Government's declaration of 17 April, had not encountered any opposition in London. Moreover, the Soviet Government had not been forewarned of the anti-Soviet campaign prepared by the Poles, although it is hard to imagine the British Government was not informed of the projected campaign. I think that from the point of view of the spirit of our treaty it would have been only natural to dissuade one ally from striking a blow at another, particularly if the blow directly helped the common enemy. That, at any rate, is how I see the duty of an ally. Nevertheless, I thought it necessary to inform you of the Soviet Government's view of Polish-Soviet relations. Since the Poles continued their anti-Soviet smear campaign without any opposition in London, the patience of the Soviet Government could not have been expected to be infinite.

You tell me that you will enforce proper discipline in the Polish press. I thank you for that, but I doubt if it will be so easy to impose discipline on the present Polish Government, its following of pro-Hitler boosters and its fanatical press. Your statement that the Polish Government wants to work loyally with the Soviet Government notwithstanding, I doubt it will keep its word. The Polish Government is surrounded by such a vast pro-Hitler following, and Sikorski so intimidated by them, there is no certainty at all of his being able to remain loyal in relations with the Soviet Union, even granting he actually wants to be loyal.

As to the rumours, circulated by the Hitlerites, that a new Polish Government is being formed in the USSR, these fabrications hardly need refuting. Our Ambassador has already told you so. This does not rule out Great Britain, and the USSR and the USA taking measures to improve the composition of the present Polish Government in terms of consolidating the Allied united front against Hitler. The sooner this is done, the better. Upon his return from the USA Mr Eden told Maisky that President Roosevelt's supporters in the USA thought the present Polish Government had no prospects for the future and doubted whether it had any chance of returning to Poland and assuming power, although they would like to retain Sikorski. It seems to me that the Americans are not so very far from the truth as regards the prospects of the present Polish Government ...

54. Churchill to Stalin, 12 May 1943

I am much obliged to you for your message about the Polish affair.

The Poles did not tell us what they were going to do and so we could not warn them against the peril of the course they proposed to take.

The Polish press, and all other foreign language publications, will in the future be controlled.

I agree the composition of the Polish Government could be improved, though there would be a great difficulty in finding better substitutes. Like you, I think that Sikorski and some others should in any event be retained in the government. If Sikorski were to reconstruct his government under foreign pressure he would probably be repudiated and thrown out and we would not get anyone so good in his place. Therefore, he probably cannot make changes immediately, but I will take every opportunity to urge him to do so as soon as possible. I will discuss this with President Roosevelt ...

55. Stalin to Churchill and Roosevelt, 11 June 1943

Your message informing me of certain decisions on strategic matters adopted by you ... reached me on 4 June. Thank you for the information.

It is apparent from your communication that these decisions run counter to those reached by you ... earlier this year concerning the date for opening a second front in Western Europe.

You will remember, of course, that in the message of 26 January ... you informed me of the decision to divert considerable German ground and air forces from the Russian front and to bring Germany to her knees in 1943.

After this, on 12 February, Mr Churchill communicated ... the specified time of the Anglo-American operation in Tunisia and the Mediterranean, as well as on the west coast of Europe. The communication said that Great Britain and the United States were vigorously preparing to cross the Channel in August 1943 and that if the operation were hindered by weather or other causes, then it would be prepared with an eye to being carried out in greater force in September 1943.

Now, in May 1943, you ... have decided to postpone the Anglo-American invasion of Western Europe until the spring of 1944. The opening of the second front in Western Europe, previously postponed from 1942 till 1943, is now being put off again, this time until the spring of 1944.

Your decision creates exceptional difficulties for the Soviet Union, which has been fighting the main forces of Germany and her satellites for the past two years with all its strength, and leaves the Soviet Army almost alone fighting for its allies as well as its own country against an enemy that is still very strong and dangerous.

Need I say what a painful and negative impression this new postponement of the second front and the abandonment of our Army, which has sacrificed so much, and without serious support from the Anglo-American armies, is having in the Soviet Union ...?

As for the Soviet Government, it cannot subscribe to a decision that was taken without its participation and without any attempt at a joint discussion of such a critical matter, and which may gravely affect the subsequent course of the war.

56. Churchill to Stalin, 19 June 1943

1. I received a copy of your telegram of 11 June to the President. I quite understand your disappointment but I am sure we are doing not only the right thing but the only thing that is physically possible in the circumstances. It would be no help to Russia if we threw away a hundred thousand men in a disastrous cross-Channel attack such as would, in my opinion, certainly occur if we tried under present conditions and with forces too weak to exploit any success that might be gained at very heavy cost. In my view and that of all my expert military advisers we should, even if we got ashore, be driven off as the Germans already have forces in France superior to any we could put there this year and can reinforce far more quickly across the main lateral railways of Europe than we could do over the beaches or through any of the destroyed Channel ports we might seize. I cannot see how a great British defeat and slaughter would aid the Soviet armies. It might, however, cause the utmost ill-feeling here if it were thought it had been incurred

against the advice of our military experts and under pressure from you. You will remember that I have always made it clear in my telegrams to you that I would never authorise any cross-Channel attack which I believed would lead to only useless massacre.

2. The best way for us to help you is by winning battles, not by losing them. This we have done in Tunisia, where the long arm of British and United States sea power has reached across the Atlantic and ten thousand miles around the Cape and helped us to annihilate great Axis land and air forces. The threat immediately resulting to the whole Axis defensive system in the Mediterranean has already forced the Germans to reinforce Italy, the Mediterranean islands, the Balkans and Southern France with land and air forces. It is my earnest and sober hope that we can knock Italy out of the war this year and by doing so we shall draw far more Germans off your front than by any other means open. The attack that is now not far off will absorb the capacities of every port under our control in the Mediterranean from Gibraltar to Port Said inclusive. After Italy has been forced out of the war the Germans will have to occupy the Riviera, make a new front either on the Alps or the Po and above all provide for the replacement of 32 Italian divisions now in the Balkans. The moment for inviting Turkey to participate in the war actively or passively will then arrive. The bombing of the Romanian oilfields can be carried through on a decisive scale. Already we are holding in the west and south of Europe the larger part of the German Air Forces and our superiority will increase continually ... No one has paid more tribute than I have to the immense contribution of the Soviet Government to the common victory and I thank you also for the recognition which you have lately given to the exertions of your two Western Allies. It is my firm belief that we shall present you before the end of the year with results which will give you substantial relief and satisfaction ...

4. At the end of your message you complain that Russia has not been consulted in our recent decisions. I fully understand the reasons which prevented you from meeting the President and me at Khartoum whither we would have gone in January and I am sure you were right not to relinquish even for a week the direction of your immense and victorious campaign. Nevertheless, the need and advantage of a meeting are very great. I can only say that I will go at any risk to any place that you and the President may agree upon ...

57. Stalin to Churchill, 24 June 1943

... I fully realise the complexity of organising an Anglo-American invasion of Western Europe, in particular of transferring troops across the Channel ...

From your messages this year and last I was sure you and the President were fully aware of the difficulties of organising such an operation and were preparing the invasion accordingly, with due regard to the difficulties and with all necessary forces and means. Last year you told me that a large-scale invasion of Europe by Anglo-American troops would be carried out in 1943 ...

At the beginning of this year you told me, on your own behalf and on behalf of the President, of decisions concerning an Anglo-American invasion of Western

Europe intended to 'divert strong German land and air forces from the Russian front'. You had set yourself the task of bringing Germany to her knees as early as 1943 and named September as the latest date for the invasion ...

In February, when you wrote to me about those plans and the date for invading Western Europe, the difficulties of that operation were greater than they are now. Since then the Germans have suffered more than one defeat: they were pushed back by our troops in the south, where they suffered appreciable loss; they were beaten in North Africa and expelled by Anglo-American troops; in submarine warfare, too, the Germans found themselves in a more difficult position than earlier, while Anglo-American superiority increased substantially; it is also known that the Americans and British have won air superiority in Europe and that their navies and mercantile marines have grown in power.

Hence the conditions for opening a second front in Western Europe during 1943, far from deteriorating, have, indeed, greatly improved.

That being so, the Soviet Government could not have imagined the British and US governments would change the decision to invade Western Europe, which they adopted earlier this year. On the contrary, the Soviet Government had every reason to believe the Anglo-American decision would be implemented, that the necessary preparations were underway and that the second front in Western Europe would, at long last, be opened in 1943 ...

So when you now declare: 'I cannot see how a great British defeat and slaughter would aid the Soviet armies', is it not clear that such a statement in relation to the Soviet Union is utterly groundless and directly contradicts your previous responsible decisions ... concerning extensive and energetic measures by the British and Americans to organise an invasion this year, measures on which the complete success of the operation would depend?

... It goes without saying that the Soviet Government cannot accept this disregard of vital Soviet interests in the war against the common enemy.

You write that you quite understand my disappointment. 1 must say that the point is not the disappointment of the Soviet Government, but the preservation of trust in its Allies, which is being severely tested. One should not forget that it is a question of saving millions of lives in the occupied areas of Western Europe and Russia and of reducing the colossal sacrifices of Soviet armies, compared with which the losses of the Anglo-American armies are not great.

58. Churchill to Stalin, 27 June 1943

1. I am sorry to receive your message of the 24th. I have at all times been sincere in my relations with you: at every stage the information I have given you as to our future intentions has been based upon the written conclusions of the British and American Staffs. Although until 22 June 1941 we British were left alone to face to the worse that Nazi Germany could do to us, I immediately began aiding Soviet Russia to the best of our limited means from the moment that it was attacked by Hitler. I am satisfied that I have done everything in human power to help you. Therefore, the reproaches which you now cast upon your western Allies leave me unmoved ...

2. The views of our Staffs, which I have shared at every stage, have been continually modified by the course of events. In the first place, although all shipping has been fully occupied, it has not been possible to transport the American army to Britain according to the programme proposed in June 1942. Whereas it was then hoped that 27 American divisions would be in Great Britain by April 1943, in fact there is now, in June 1943, only one and by August there will only be five. This is due to the demands of the war against Japan, the shipping shortage, and above all the expansion of the campaign in North Africa, into which powerful Nazi forces were drawn. Moreover, the landing craft which in January of this year we proposed to make available for a cross-Channel attack, have either not to date all been built or have been drawn into the great operation impending in the Mediterranean. The enemy's uncertainty as to where the blow will fall and what its weight will be has already, in the opinion of my trusted advisers, led to the delaying of Hitler's third offensive in Russia, for which it seemed great preparations were in existence six weeks ago. It may even be that you will not be heavily attacked this summer. If that is so, it would vindicate decisively what you once called the 'military correctness' [literally in Russian 'military expediency'] of our Mediterranean strategy. However, in these matters we must await the unfolding of events ...

59. Stalin to Churchill and Roosevelt, 22 August 1943

... I think the time is ripe for us to set up a military-political Commission of the representatives of the three countries – the USA, Great Britain and the USSSR – for consideration of problems related to negotiations with the various Governments deserting falling Germany. To date it has been like this: the USA and Britain reach agreement between themselves while the USSR is informed of the deal between the two powers as a third party looking passively on. I must say that this situation cannot be tolerated any longer. I propose setting up this commission and making Sicily its seat for the time being ...

60. Stalin to Churchill and Roosevelt, 24 August 1943

... I fully share your opinion, and that of Mr Roosevelt, concerning the importance of a meeting between the three of us. At the same time, I earnestly request you to appreciate my position at a time when our armies are exerting themselves to the utmost against the main forces of Hitler and when Hitler – far from having withdrawn a single division from our front – has already transferred, and keeps transferring, new divisions to the Soviet-German front. At a moment like this I cannot, in the opinion of all my colleagues, leave the front without injury to our military operations to go to so distant a point as Fairbanks, even though, had the situation on our front been different, Fairbanks would doubtless have been a perfectly suitable place for our meeting, as I indeed thought before.

As to a meeting between representatives of our states, and perhaps representatives in charge of foreign affairs, I share your view of the advisability of such a meeting in the near future. However, the meeting should not be purely exploratory but should have a practical-preparatory character so that after this conference our Governments can take specific decisions and thus avoid delay in resolving urgent matters.

Hence I think I must revert to my proposal for fixing beforehand the range of problems to be discussed by the representatives of the three states and the drafting of proposals they will discuss and submit to our Governments for final decision ...

61. Stalin to Churchill, 8 September 1943

1. ... I think the most pressing problem is that of the military-political commission ... After receiving your previous messages, I expected the matter of setting up the tripartite military-political commission to be settled positively and without delay. But the solution of this very urgent problem has been delayed. ...

2. Your proposed date for the meeting of representatives of the three governments – early October – suits me. I suggest that it be held in Moscow. The thing now is for us to agree beforehand on the range of problems and the proposals concerning the problems which interest our governments. I still think this is essential for the success of the meeting, which should draft agreements for subsequent decision by the governments ...

3. About the personal meeting of the heads of the three governments – I have informed the President that I, too, am anxious for it to be held as early as possible, that the date suggested by him – November or December – suits me, but that it would be advisable to hold it in a country where all three are represented, for example Iran. I made the reservation that the actual date would have to be specified later, with due regard to the situation on the Soviet-German front, where more than 500 divisions are engaged on both sides and where supervision of the Supreme Command of the USSR is required almost daily ...

62. Stalin to Churchill and Roosevelt, 12 September 1943

1. The question of the military-political commission can be regarded as settled. We have appointed as the Soviet Ambassador A. Y. Vyshinsky, Deputy Chairman of the Council of People's Commissars and Deputy People's Commissar for Foreign Affairs, whom you know. A. Y. Bogomolov, the Soviet Ambassador to the Allied Governments in London, has been appointed his deputy ...

2. Concerning the meeting of our three representatives I suggest that we consider it agreed that Moscow be the place, and the date, October 4, as suggested by the President.

I still believe that for the conference to be a success it is essential to know in advance the proposals of the English and American Governments. I do not, however, suggest any limitations as far as the agenda is concerned.

3. As regards the meeting of the three heads of the governments, I have no objection to Tehran, which, I think, is a more suitable place than Egypt where the Soviet Union still has no representation.

63. Churchill to Stalin, 25 September 1943

I have been thinking about the meeting of the heads of governments in Tehran. Good arrangements must be made for security in this somewhat loosely-controlled area. Accordingly, I suggest for your consideration that I make preparations at Cairo in regard to accommodation, security, etc., which are bound to be noticed in spite of all willing efforts to keep them secret. Then perhaps only two or three days before our meeting we should throw a British and a Russian brigade round a suitable area in Tehran, including the airfield, and keep this area absolutely closed until we have finished our talks. We would not tell the Iranian Government nor make any arrangements for our accommodation until this moment comes. We should, of course, control absolutely all outgoing messages. Thus we will screen out the world press, and also any unpleasant people who might not be as fond of us as they ought.

2. I suggest also that in all future correspondence on this subject we use the expression 'Cairo Three' instead of Tehran ... also that the code name for the operation should be 'Eureka' which I believe is ancient Greek. Let me know if you have other thoughts and we can then put them to the President. I have not yet said anything to him about this matter.

64. Churchill-Stalin After-Dinner Conversation at Tehran, 28 November 1943

The Prime Minister pointed out that this was a historical meeting, and that so much depended on the friendship of the three Heads of Government and the decisions reached at this Conference.

Marshal Stalin suggested that they should first consider the worst that might happen. He thought that Germany had every possibility of recovering from this war and might start on a new war within a comparatively short time. He was afraid of German nationalism. This was a possibility and allowances must be made for it. After Versailles peace seemed assured, but Germany recovered very quickly. We must, therefore, establish a strong body to prevent Germany starting a new war. He was convinced she would recover.

The Prime Minister asked how soon.

Marshal Stalin thought it might be within fifteen to twenty years.

The Prime Minister thought that the world must be made safe for at least fifty years. If it was only for fifteen to twenty years then we would have betrayed our soldiers.

Marshal Stalin thought that we should consider the economic side of the question. The Germans were an able people, very industrious and cultured and they would recover quickly.

The Prime Minister said that certain measures would have to be taken. He would forbid all aviation, civil and military, and he would forbid the General Staff system.

Marshal Stalin asked whether he would also forbid the existence of watchmakers' and furniture factories which could easily be turned into factories for making parts of shells and into aircraft factories. The Germans had produced toy rifles ... used for teaching hundreds of thousands of men how to shoot.

The Prime Minister said nothing was final. The world rolled on. We had now learnt something. Our duty was to make the world safe for at least fifty years

(a) by disarmament, (b) by preventing rearmament, (c) by supervision of German factories, (d) by forbidding all aviation, and (e) by territorial changes of a far-reaching character.

Marshal Stalin thought that was correct, but Germany would work through common countries.

The Prime Minister said that it all came back to a question of whether Great Britain and the United States and the USSR kept a close friendship and super-vised Germany in their mutual interest. He said they should not be afraid to give orders as soon as they saw any danger.

Marshal Stalin said there had been control after the last war, but it had failed.

The Prime Minister said people were inexperienced. The last war was not to the same extent a national war and Russia was not a party at the peace conference. It was different this time. He had a feeling that Prussia should be isolated, that Bavaria, Austria and Hungary might form a broad, peaceful cow-like confeder-ation. He thought Prussia should be dealt with more severely than the other parts of the Reich, so that the latter would not want to go into Prussia.

Marshal Stalin thought all his was very good but insufficient.

The Prime Minister said that Russia would have her army. Great Britain and the United States navies and air forces. In addition, all three Powers would have their other forces, all strongly armed, and they must not assume any obligation to disarm. They were the trustees for the peace of the world. If they failed, there would perhaps be 100 years of chaos. If they were strong they would carry out their trusteeship.

Marshal Stalin said he would think it over.

The Prime Minister said that there was more than merely keeping the peace. The three powers should guide the future of the world. He was not a Communist and he did not want to enforce any principles on other nations. But he asked for freedom and for the right of all nations to develop as they liked. He said that they must keep friends in order to ensure happy homes in all countries.

Marshal Stalin asked what was to happen to Germany.

The Prime Minister replied that he was not against toilers in Germany, but only against the leaders and against dangerous combinations.

Marshal Stalin said there were many toilers in German divisions, who fought under orders. When he asked German prisoners who came from the labour class why they fought for Hitler, they replied that they were executing orders. He shot such prisoners.

The Prime Minister suggested that they should discuss the Polish question.

Marshal Stalin agreed and invited the Prime Minister to begin.

The Prime Minister said we had declared war on account of Poland. Poland was therefore important to us. Nothing was more important than the security of the Russian western frontier. His country, and he personally, were the leading powers of Europe. But he had given no pledges about frontiers. He wanted heart-to-heart talks with the Russians about this. When the Marshal felt like telling us what he thought about it the matter could be discussed and they could reach

To Marshal & Premier Stalin, who at the head of the Russian Armies & of the Soviet Government broke the main strength of the German military machine and helped all the United Nations to open paths to Peace Justice & Freedom.

From his friend

Winston S. Churchill, September 1944

Signed photograph presented by Churchill to Stalin, September 1944.

Stalin in his Marshal's uniform.

People's Commissar for Foreign Affairs, Vyacheslav Molotov.

Averell Harriman, American Ambassador in Moscow, 1943–5.

British Foreign Secretary, Anthony Eden.

Ivan Maisky, Soviet Ambassador to Great Britain, 1932–43.

Churchill and Stalin in Moscow, August 1942.

Presentation of King George VI's Sword of Stalingrad to Stalin at the Tehran conference.

The Sword of Stalingrad is shown to the seated Roosevelt at the Tehran conference.

...alin talking to Sarah Churchill at the Tehran conference. Churchill's daughter was also one of ...ree Western women at Yalta, the other two being Averell Harriman's daughter, Kathleen, and ...oosevelt's daughter, Anna Boettiger.

...urchill, Molotov and Field Marshal Alan Brooke in Moscow, October 1944.

Churchill, Stalin and Soviet interpreter Vladimir Pavlov at the Yalta conference.

Stalin, Roosevelt and Churchill at the Yalta conference.

...en and Molotov at the Potsdam conference.

...alin at the Potsdam conference.

Churchill, Truman and Stalin at the Potsdam conference.

Stalin, Truman and Churchill at the Potsdam conference.

some agreement, and the Marshal should tell him what was necessary for the defence of the western frontiers of Russia.

Marshal Stalin said he did not feel the need to ask himself how to act. So far his heart did not feel stimulated. [He meant that the Prime Minister should become more precise.]

The Prime Minister said that after this war in Europe, which might end in 1944, the Soviet Union would be overwhelmingly strong and Russia would have a great responsibility for hundreds of years in any decision she took with regard to Poland. Personally, he thought Poland might move westward like soldiers taking two steps left close. If Poland trod on some German toes, that could not be helped, but there must be a strong Poland. This instrument was needed in the orchestra of Europe.

Marshal Stalin said that the Polish people had their culture and their language, which must exist. They could not be extirpated.

The Prime Minister agreed and asked if we were to draw frontier lines.

Marshal Stalin said Yes.

The Prime Minister said he had no power from Parliament, nor he believed had the President, to define any frontier lines. He suggested that they might now, in Tehran, see if the three Heads of Government, working in agreement, could form some sort of policy which might be pressed upon the Poles and which we could recommend to the Poles, and advise them to accept.

Marshal Stalin said we could have a look.

The Prime Minister said we should be lucky if we could.

Marshal Stalin asked whether it would be without Polish participation.

The Prime Minister replied in the affirmative and said that this was all informally between themselves and they could go to the Poles later.

Marshal Stalin agreed.

Mr Eden said he had been much struck by what the Marshal had said that afternoon to the effect that the Poles could go as far west as the Oder. He saw hope in that and was much encouraged.

Marshal Stalin asked whether we thought he was going to swallow Poland up.

Mr Eden said he did not know how much the Russians were going to eat. How much would they leave undigested?

Marshal Stalin said the Russians did not want anything belonging to other people, although they might have a bite at Germany.

Mr Eden said what Poland lost in the east she might gain in the west.

Marshal Stalin said possibly they might, but he did not know.

The Prime Minister demonstrated with the help of three matches his idea of Poland moving westwards, which pleased Marshal Stalin.

65. Churchill-Stalin Meeting at Tehran, 30 November 1943, 12.40

Churchill said that first of all he would like to point out that he is half-American, from his mother's side.

Stalin said that he had heard about this.

Churchill continued that he loves Americans, so what he is going to say should not be understood as putting the Americans down. He, Churchill, is completely loyal to the Americans but there are things which are better discussed one-to-one. Firstly, Churchill wants Marshal Stalin to understand that the quantity of British forces in the Mediterranean is significantly larger than that of America. He believes that in the region of Mediterranean Sea there are 3–4 times more English forces than American. Churchill says he wants Stalin to understand why he is so interested in the Mediterranean area – because he doesn't want this huge British army to remain idle. Churchill wants English forces to be active in the war at all times.

There are 13 or 14 Anglo-American divisions and 9 or 10 German divisions in Italy. Two armies are stationed in Italy: the 5th American Army, half of it consisting of British forces, and the 8th Army, all British. Churchill states that he says this to get Stalin to understand why he attaches such significance to the Mediterranean theatre. At present the situation is such that there must be a choice made between operation 'Overlord' and Mediterranean operations. But this is not all. The Americans want the English to carry out a landing operation in the Bay of Bengal in March next year. He, Churchill, is not especially positive towards this operation. Of course, it would be another matter if the English had enough landing craft in the Mediterranean to share with the Bengal operation, then he could accomplish what he wanted in the Mediterranean and carry out operation 'Overlord' in time. Thus the issue is not only the choice between the Mediterranean operation and 'Overlord', but between the Bengali operation and the date of 'Overlord'. Churchill wanted to say this all now because Marshal Stalin wouldn't have understood this from the previous conversations when the Americans were present.

Churchill said that he thinks, however, there is a way to resolve this issue and that there will be enough resources for all the operations. The Americans are insisting on carrying out 'Overlord' in the established timeframe, and the victim has been operations in the Mediterranean for the past two months. The English army was particularly disappointed with the withdrawal of seven divisions from the Mediterranean. The English have already sent three experienced divisions to take part in 'Overlord' and in the near future the Americans will also send four divisions. These actions explain why the English and Americans were unable to make full use of Italy's bankruptcy.

Churchill continues that the English are at the same time getting ready for 'Overlord'.

Then Churchill moved to the question of commanders. He said he fully agrees the appointment of the Commanders is of vital importance. Until August 1943 the English thought that 'Overlord' would be led by an English officer, but at the Quebec meeting the president asked for an examination of another proposal – an American officer to command 'Overlord', while an English officer would command Mediterranean operations. Churchill says he agreed to this because when 'Overlord' begins the Americans will have the superior number of forces, a number that will continue to grow. Equally, in the Mediterranean there are more

British forces and the English are more interested in operations in this area. Churchill accepted Roosevelt's proposal, therefore, and now it remains only to appoint the commander.

Stalin asked if that means an English Commander will be appointed in place of Eisenhower [Allied Commander-in-Chief in the Mediterranean].

Churchill replied affirmatively and said that as soon as the Americans appoint their Commander, he will appoint a British Commander for the Mediterranean. The delay in appointing a Commander by the Americans is due to internal issues in relation to high-ranking individuals in the USA. Churchill hopes though that the 'Overlord' commander will be appointed before participants leave this conference. Churchill also says that it looks like it will be possible to set the date of this operation before leaving.

Churchill says further that he wants to move to the question of landing vessels. It is a narrow space. The English and Americans have plenty of forces in the Mediterranean even after redeploying seven divisions. In May 1944 there will be a large Anglo-American army in the United Kingdom. The argument between the English and Americans comes down to landing craft.

When Marshal Stalin made his historical declaration that after the defeat of Germany Russia will join the struggle against Japan, Churchill immediately supposed the Americans would be able to get landing craft from either the Mediterranean or the Pacific to supply 'Overlord'. The issue is that the Americans are very sensitive about the situation in the Pacific, but now there are great prospects for the war against Japan after defeat of Germany, it would be advantageous to defeat Germany quickly even if it meant cutting landing craft in the Pacific.

Churchill says he wants to explain to Marshal Stalin the issues being debated by the English and the Americans. Churchill says that Marshal Stalin might be thinking that he, Churchill, pays too little attention to the 'Overlord' operation. This is not the case. The crux of the matter is that Churchill thinks he can get the necessary resources for the Mediterranean while at the same time keeping to the start date of operation 'Overlord'. He hoped to get this from the Americans in Cairo but, unfortunately, General Chiang Kai-shek was present and Chinese matters took up all the time. Nevertheless, Churchill is sure that it is possible to find enough landing craft for all operations.

Further, Churchill says that he would like to say few words about operation 'Overlord'. The English will be ready on the set date. By that time the English will have 16 divisions which together with corps forces, communications, air defence etc, will constitute some 500,000 people. These are the best British forces, including experienced divisions, brought from Mediterranean. Besides this, the British fleet will give necessary support. Finally, there will be ready 4,000 first-line planes from the British air force. In addition, the transfer of American forces has already begun. Up to now the Americans were transferring mostly air forces and supplies, but in the next 4–5 months 150,000 people will be transferred monthly, amounting approximately to 600,000–800,000 people by May 1944. The damage being done to German submarines will allow these transfers.

Churchill says that he is very positive about a landing in southern France when the time for 'Overlord' comes, maybe a bit earlier or maybe a bit later. He will have enough forces in Italy for this operation, while at the same time keeping the Germans in check. From the 22–23 Mediterranean divisions a sufficient number will be deployed to France, while the other divisions hold the front in Italy.

Churchill says that he would like to talk about the coming battles in Italy. On the eastern front, south of Rome, the 15th Army group consisting of the 5th and 8th Armies are under the command of General Alexander. At the moment there are 500,000 people in allied Armies in Italy, i.e. 13–14 Anglo-American divisions, against 9–10 German divisions, but it's raining in Italy, rivers are flooding and many bridges have been washed away. Nevertheless, the English propose to start an offensive against the Germans in December. Montgomery's army will deploy on the western coastline of Italy, to the north of the current front line, to carry out an outflanking manoeuvre.

Stalin asked if this manoeuvre would bypass Rome.

Churchill replied affirmatively. He explained that at the same time as pressure was being put on German positions on the south-western part of the front, on the western coast of Italy, north of the present front line, there will be a large landing in the Tiber region. This operation will conclude with the entrapment of all active German forces in this region. It will be a miniature Stalingrad. If this operation is successful, it would be not only the defeat, but the destruction of the Germans' forces. The Germans are already in a difficult position because they can't supply their army sufficiently due to the destruction of communication lines by the English and Americans. This is the importance of the operation in Italy, not the capture of Rome. The successful conclusion of this operation will allow Anglo-American forces to move north and approach the Apennines.

Churchill says he is against a plan to go to the wide part of Italy. He wants to create a front in the narrow part. There one can contain the Germans and transfer free troops to the landing in southern France.

Churchill asks if Stalin has any questions about what he has said and perhaps other questions.

Stalin said that must tell Churchill that the Red Army is counting on the carrying out of the landing operation in northern France. He is afraid that if this operation is not carried out in May then it won't happen at all, as the weather will deteriorate and it wouldn't be possible to supply the troops sufficiently. If this operation in not going to happen he has to warn that it will be a big disappointment and will create a bad atmosphere. He fears that the absence of this operation could cause very bad feelings of isolation. This is why he wants to know if operation 'Overlord' will happen or not. If it happens, that will be very good, if not, then he wants to know about it beforehand so that he can prevent the mood which the absence of the operation could cause. It is *the* most important question.

Churchill replied that the operation will, of course, happen, but on the condition that the enemy does not have more troops than the English and Americans. If, for instance, Germans could deploy 30 or 40 divisions to France then he, Churchill, doesn't think the landing could be successful. He is not worried about the actual landing but about what would happen after 30–40 days. But if Russian armies are going to engage German troops on their fronts, then the English and Americans could draw them into Italy and perhaps, to Yugoslavia, and if Turkey joins the war then Churchill supposes it will be a success. In those circumstances the Germans wouldn't have enough forces to transfer to the west.

Stalin said that only when the landing in northern France happens will the Red Army start its offensive. If it was confirmed that the operation was going to happen in May or June, the Russians could prepare not one but several attacks on the enemy. Stalin says that spring is the best time. March and April are usually quiet at the front so the troops can have some rest. It would be feasible to supply ammunition and by the time of landing in northern France it would be possible to launch a strike at the Germans so they wouldn't be able to transfer any troops to France. At the moment though the Germans are moving their troops to the Eastern front and will continue to do so. The Germans fear our movement towards Germany's frontier, they realise that we are not separated by the Channel or the sea. From the east it is possible to go right up to Germany. At the same time the Germans know that in the west the Channel protects them and that one needs to cross France to get close to Germany. The Germans won't transfer their troops to the west, especially if the Red Army advances, and it will advance if it receives help from its allies in the form of operation 'Overlord'.

Stalin say that he would still like to know from Churchill the date for the beginning of 'Overlord'.

Churchill replied that he can't say now as it will be discussed at breakfast with the President. Churchill says further that he would like to give Marshal Stalin a map which illustrates the position in Yugoslavia. Perhaps Marshal Stalin would like to compare the map with his own data.

(Churchill presents Stalin with a map of Yugoslavia. The conversation lasted an hour.)

Chapter 6

Crossing the Frontier: Poland and the Warsaw Uprising

The wartime politics of the Grand Alliance were dominated by two issues. First, the second front, which was resolved at Tehran when Churchill's objections to an invasion of northern France were finally overcome. When the invasion was launched in June 1944 Stalin was gushing in his praise (**Documents 74–7**). On 13 June he told *Pravda* that the D-Day landings in Normandy were a 'brilliant success for our allies . . . in the breadth of its conception, its giant dimensions and the mastery of its performance, there is nothing like it in the history of warfare'.

The second issue – Poland's borders and its political future – was more intractable. The Polish Government-in-Exile in London was anti-communist and anti-Soviet and adamant that Western Belorussia and Western Ukraine should return to Poland. In Italy a Polish army led by General Władysław Anders fought alongside the British and Americans. The bulk of Anders' army was made up of freed Polish prisoners in the USSR who had been evacuated from the Soviet Union in 1942. Within Poland, the exile government's military wing, the *Armiya Kraiowa* (AK: Home Army) was a formidable force with some 40,000 underground soldiers in Warsaw alone.

Stalin was determined to hold on to Western Belorussia and Western Ukraine and to establish a post-war Polish government friendly to the Soviet Union. Communism was weak in Poland but it was not negligible and the Red Army contained units of a pro-Soviet Polish People's army led by General Zygmunt Berling. But Stalin's main card was the fact that Poland would be conquered, liberated and occupied by the Red Army.

Churchill recognised both the realities of the situation and the justice of Soviet territorial claims. But, as he never tired of telling Stalin, Britain had gone to war against Germany to defend Poland's national independence and territorial integrity and there were powerful voices in British politics supporting the Polish Government-in-Exile. Like Churchill, Roosevelt was sympathetic to Stalin's point of view but his hands were tied by a constituency of millions of Polish-American voters in the United States. Not until he won his fourth presidential election in November 1944 could Roosevelt freely and openly bargain with Stalin about Poland.

In January 1944 the London Poles issued a statement noting reports that the Red Army had crossed into Poland – into Western Belorussia and Western Ukraine – and asserted their governmental rights in the liberated territories.[1] On 11 January Moscow issued its reply to the Polish statement, declaring that both territories had joined the USSR of their own free will in 1939. The Soviet statement added that the USSR stood for a strong and independent Poland, one bounded by the Curzon Line in the east and in the west by 'ancient Polish lands' reacquired from Germany. Additionally, the Soviet Union was willing to transfer to Poland any areas in Western Belorussia and Western Ukraine with a majority Polish population.[2]

The Soviets' protestations that they favoured a strong and independent Polish state were not new. There had been many such public statements, including by Stalin himself, and the restoration of an independent Poland after the war was the governing assumption of Soviet internal discussions on its post-war future. Nor was Moscow's insistence that Western Belorussia and Western Ukraine rightly belonged to the USSR at all surprising. But the public commitment to compensate Poland territorially at Germany's expense was a new development, although in private the Soviets had expressed support for such a move on many occasions. While the statement was critical of the Polish Government-in-Exile, it left open the possibility of a reconstruction of relations between it and the Soviet Union, and Moscow's promise to negotiate the ethnic details of the Curzon Line was a definite gesture of conciliation. From Stalin's point of view this was a moderate and positive statement on the Polish question and was presented as such to the American and British ambassadors in Moscow. When Molotov asked Harriman what he thought of the statement the ambassador replied that 'as a statement of the Soviet position of the Polish question it was most friendly in tone'.[3]

On 15 January the London Poles replied to the Soviets, reasserting their rights in relation to Western Belorussia and Western Ukraine and reiterating their desire to cooperate with the USSR in the struggle against Germany. This was not acceptable to the Soviets, who issued a rebuttal statement two days later emphasising that the key issue for them was recognition of the Curzon Line as the Polish–Soviet frontier.[4] In presenting a preview of this statement to the British and American ambassadors Molotov signalled a hardening of the Soviet position: Moscow was willing to negotiate with the London Poles, but only if their government was reconstructed and the anti-Soviet elements were excluded. At a further meeting with Harriman and Clark Kerr, the British ambassador, on 18 January Molotov clarified that the reconstructed Polish government he had in mind would include Poles living in Britain, the United States and the Soviet Union as well as those active in anti-German resistance in Poland.[5]

Acceptance of the Curzon Line and reconstruction of the Government-in-Exile – these were the constant themes of the Soviet position on the Polish question, repeatedly stated by Stalin and Molotov in their meetings with the two ambassadors and by Stalin in his correspondence with Churchill and Roosevelt. Stalin made no effort to hide his exasperation that the London Poles refused to negotiate on these terms. 'Again the Poles. Is that the most important question?' Stalin impatiently asked Harriman when he came to see him on 3 March 1944.[6] Churchill's efforts to broker a deal acceptable to both sides Stalin dismissed as a waste of time, even accusing the British Prime Minister of making threats to force the Soviets to settle the Polish question on terms unfavourable to the USSR

(**Document 73**). At a meeting with Clark Kerr on 29 February Stalin snorted and sniggered at the British compromise solution and reiterated that he wanted a reconstructed Polish Government-in-Exile and acceptance of the Curzon Line. 'This dreary and exasperating conversation lasted for well over an hour. No argument was of any avail', reported the British ambassador.[7]

The one positive constant in Stalin's and Molotov's statements on the Polish question was that they were prepared to contemplate a reconstructed government that included the exiled Poles' Prime Minister, Stanisław Mikołajczyk. As leader of the Polish Peasant Party, the largest political party in pre-war Poland, Mikołajczyk was an important bridge to the formation of a broad-based government in liberated Poland. Stalin resisted pressure from Polish communist circles to establish a provisional government for Poland based on a purely left-wing alliance. Although highly desirable, a leftist government would not be strong enough to rule effectively over a Polish population that remained staunchly nationalist, notwithstanding the wartime political gains made by the communists and their socialist allies. Stalin's decision to establish a Polish Committee of National Liberation (PCNL) in July 1944 was motivated, at least in part, by the need for an organisation that could be entrusted with the administration of Polish territories liberated by the Red Army. This was how he presented the decision to Churchill and Roosevelt on 23 July. But while Stalin said that he did not consider the PCNL to be 'a Polish Government', he noted that it could become 'the core of a Polish Provisional Government made up of democratic forces'. The door was open to a reconstructed government including Mikołajczyk, but the threat to bypass him remained. In the same message Stalin said that he would not refuse to see the Polish leader if he came to Moscow, as Churchill and Roosevelt had been suggesting (**Document 78**).

Stalin's conciliatory approach to the Polish question was encouraged by Oscar Lange, a Polish-American Marxist economist, who in January 1944 suggested the formula of a reconstructed Polish government based on the London Poles, pro-Soviet Poles in Moscow and Poland, and independent Polish political figures from the Polish émigré communities of Britain and the United States. In spring 1944 Lange travelled to Moscow with the pro-Soviet Polish-American Catholic priest Stanislaw Orlemanski to discuss with Stalin the way forward. Stalin's conversations with these two intermediaries were highly significant for what they revealed of his strategic thinking about Polish–Soviet relations. Stalin wanted a friendly Poland with a left-leaning government that included his communist allies, but he also wanted a united country that was strong enough to participate in a long-term alliance of Slavic states against the future German threat. As Stalin told Father Orlemanski on 28 April 1944:

> Germany will be able to renew itself in some 15 years. That is why we must think not only about how to end this war ... but also about what would happen in 20 years, when Germany revives itself. This is why an alliance between Russia and Poland is absolutely necessary in order not to let the Germans become an aggressor once again.[8]

In his talk with Lange on 17 May Stalin again emphasised that the USSR needed a strong Poland in order to be able to deal with German aggression in the future. Stalin also made clear his opposition to a 'half-hearted' punitive peace like the Versailles treaty. If that happened again there would be another war in 15 years' time. Germany had to be kept weak for 50 years, Stalin told Lange, and since he was talking to a Marxist economist he took the opportunity to make the point that capitalist Britain and the United States would support the destruction of German and Japanese industry because this would eliminate two of their trade competitors.[9]

This was the background to Mikołajczyk's visit to Moscow in August 1944 to discuss a Soviet-Polish agreement that would restore diplomatic relations between Moscow and the London Poles, which had been severed by Stalin because of the Katyn affair. But as Mikołajczyk arrived in Moscow the AK rose in revolt in Warsaw. The uprising was prompted by the success of Operation Bagration – the Soviet offensive to liberate Belorussia from German occupation. During the course of this hugely successful operation – which was timed to coincide with D-Day – the Red Army advanced to the outskirts of Warsaw.

Soviet attacks on Warsaw were spearheaded by Berling's 20,000-strong Polish army and Stalin and his generals expected to capture the Polish capital by early August. However, German forces rallied on the eastern bank of the Vistula and halted the Red Army's advance. The leaders of the AK had calculated the Red Army would soon arrive in Warsaw and moved to seize key buildings, occupy strategic locations and engage the Germans. It expected to be fighting the Germans for no more than a few days. Its aim was to liberate Poland's capital before the Soviets captured it, thus strengthening the hand of Polish nationalists in negotiations about the country's future.

German success in preventing the Red Army from capturing Warsaw upset everyone's calculations. The AK now faced a prolonged battle it could not hope to win and for the Soviets the problem was how to respond to the uprising while regrouping for another assault on Warsaw. Having unexpectedly found themselves with the time and capacity to crush the uprising, the Germans did so with the utmost brutality. The 50,000 troops tasked with this mission were a multinational force, including many Russian deserters and collaborators. But it took some time to flush out the insurgents and the AK did not finally surrender until 2 October. In two months of ferocious fighting 200,000 citizens of Warsaw were killed and a quarter of the city destroyed. When the battle was over the Germans razed to the ground what remained of Warsaw and expelled the city's 800,000 civilian survivors

Stalin's first meeting with Mikołajczyk was on 3 August. Mikołajczyk raised three questions: joint action in the struggle against the Germans; the agreement the Soviets had reached with the left-wing PCNL about the administration of liberated Polish territory; and the Polish–Soviet border issue. Mikołajczyk mentioned that an uprising in Warsaw had broken out and that he would like to be able to go to the Polish capital very soon to form a government that would combine the parties of the London Poles and those of the Polish communists. Stalin replied that the questions he had raised were of great political and practical importance but that Mikołajczyk had to negotiate those issues with the PCNL with a view to forming a united provisional government – a point that the Soviet leader repeatedly came back to in the ensuing conversation. When Mikołajczyk spoke of the military role of the AK in Poland Stalin pointed out that its units were very weak and lacked guns, let alone artillery, tanks and planes. When Mikołajczyk suggested that the AK should be armed, Stalin replied that the most effective aid to the Soviet campaign to liberate Poland would be the formation of a unified government.

When the conversation turned to the border issue Stalin restated the Soviet position that the Polish border should run along the Curzon Line in the east and the Oder River in the west; Poland would get Danzig but Königsberg would go to the Soviet Union. Responding to Polish claims to Lvov in Western Ukraine and Vilnius in Lithuania, Stalin said that 'according to Leninist ideology, all peoples were equal' and that he 'did not want to offend the Lithuanians, the Ukrainians or the Poles'. He went on to point out that the greatest territorial losses would be suffered by the Soviet Union, which was giving up that part of Poland that had once belonged to the Russian empire. At the end of the talk Mikołajczyk asked Stalin how he envisaged the frontier issue being resolved. Stalin's answer – that it would be negotiated with a united Polish government – was yet another signal that he was prepared to work with Mikołajczyk.[10]

The next day the British ambassador in Moscow sent Eden a very positive report of the Mikołajczyk–Stalin meeting: 'Although from time to time the talk was lively and direct, the atmosphere throughout was friendly ... There were no recriminations from the Russian side ... The Poles were impressed by the great "wisdom" and apparent willingness of Stalin and his readiness to listen. They felt that he in his turn was impressed and even surprised by the simplicity and liberalism of Mikołajczyk.'[11]

Mikołajczyk's talks with the PCNL leaders were less successful, the sticking points being the Polish Premier's insistence that his exile government should form the basis of a new provisional government and that the communist-led partisans should be assimilated into the AK. While Mikołajczyk was talking to the PCNL, Churchill and Stalin exchanged messages about aid to the Warsaw uprising. On 4 August Churchill told Stalin the British intended to drop 60 tons of equipment and ammunition in the south-west section of the city. In his reply to Churchill the next day Stalin doubted the AK would be able to take Warsaw, because it was defended by four German divisions.

On 8 August Stalin wrote to Churchill about his talk with Mikołajczyk: 'He has inadequate information about the situation in Poland. At the same time I had the impression that Mikołajczyk is not against ways being found to unite the Poles.' Although the talks between the PCNL and Mikołajczyk had not been successful they had been useful, Stalin told Churchill, because they had provided an opportunity for an exchange of views. This was the first stage in the development of relations between the PCNL and Mikołajczyk and 'let us hope that things will improve', Stalin concluded.

In Mikołajczyk's second talk with Stalin on 9 August the Polish Premier raised the question of Soviet aid to the Warsaw uprising. Stalin responded that he did not consider the uprising a 'realistic affair when the insurgents had no guns whereas the Germans in the Praga area alone had three tank divisions, not to speak of infantry. The Germans will simply kill all the Poles.' Stalin explained that the Red Army had advanced to within a few kilometres of Warsaw but the Germans then brought up reinforcements. The Red Army would continue its attack and capture Warsaw, said Stalin, but it would take time. He was willing to supply the insurgents with munitions but worried about the supplies falling into German hands and asked Mikołajczyk if there were safe places to drop guns. After being reassured that there were such areas Stalin promised to give the necessary orders and to pursue all possibilities. Towards the end of the conversation Stalin once again aired his fears of a German revival after the war and emphasised the need for a Polish–Soviet alliance to meet this threat.[12]

Mikołajczyk left Moscow the next day. According to Harriman, he departed the Soviet capital

> much more hopeful of the possibility of a settlement than when he arrived. He was impressed by his cordial reception and his frank discussions with Stalin and Molotov. At the meeting last night Stalin agreed to undertake to drop arms in Warsaw ... Stalin told him that he had expected to take Warsaw on August 6 but that because the Germans had brought in four new Panzer divisions and two other divisions to hold the bridgehead [on the east bank of the Vistula], the taking of the city had been delayed but he was confident that the new difficulties could be overcome.[13]

All these signs of a potentially amicable development of Polish–Soviet relations were shattered by the onset of intense inter-Allied acrimony about aid to the Warsaw uprising. The British had begun airlifting supplies to the Warsaw insurgents in early August, using their bases in Italy. On 13 August the Americans decided to drop supplies, using planes flying from Britain, but that required landing on Soviet airfields for refuelling before returning home. On 14 August Harriman forwarded to Molotov the request for landing and refuelling facilities. The response, a letter from Deputy Foreign Commissar Andrey Vyshinsky the next day, shocked British and American sensibilities. The Soviets would not co-operate with American air drops to Warsaw, announced Vyshinsky, because 'the outbreak in Warsaw into which the Warsaw population has been drawn is purely the work of adventurers and the Soviet Government cannot lend its hand to it'. In a face-to-face meeting with Harriman and Clark Kerr later that day Vyshinsky was equally obdurate, pointing out that the Soviets had sent a liaison officer to the rebels in Warsaw but he had been killed.[14] The next day Vyshinsky clarified the Soviet position: they would not cooperate with Anglo-American air drops but they would not object to them.[15]

This negative turn in the Soviet attitude to the Warsaw uprising seems to have been provoked by Western press reports that the AK's action had been coordinated with the Red Army, which was now refusing to aid the insurgents. On 12 August the Soviet press agency, Tass, issued an angry denial and blamed the London Poles for the tragedy that was unfolding in Warsaw. On 16 August Stalin wrote to Churchill pointing out that after seeing Mikołajczyk he had ordered supply drops to Warsaw but the liaison officer parachuted into the city had been captured and killed by the Germans:

> Further, having familiarised myself more closely with the Warsaw affair, I have concluded that the Warsaw action is a reckless and terrible adventure, which is taking a heavy toll of the population. This would not have been the case had Soviet headquarters been informed beforehand about the Warsaw action and had the Poles maintained contact with them. **[Document 82]**

Stalin refused to see Harriman and Clark Kerr on 17 August. Instead he deputed Molotov to convey his intransigent position that there would be no Soviet supplies to the Warsaw insurgents. Harriman was angered by these exchanges with the Soviets and reported to Washington that 'my recent conversations with Vyshinsky and particularly with Molotov tonight lead me to the opinion that these men are bloated with power and expect that they can force their will on us and all countries'.[16]

In retrospect, Harriman took a more dispassionate view of these events. 'I was convinced and still am that Stalin expected to cross the Vistula and take Warsaw', he told Elie Abel, 'and then was unable to do so and was unwilling to admit that he couldn't do so, which was one of the reasons everybody thought he double-crossed the Poles.' When Abel asked if he excluded political calculations from Stalin's thinking, Harriman replied:

> I think he would have crossed the Vistula without any thought of how it would affect the London Poles. He was thinking about the Red Army moving into Germany. And he wanted to cross and would have crossed if he hadn't been blocked. Now, not permitting us to reinforce these Poles, he didn't want to have anything to do with those people, directly or indirectly. He wanted it to be that they rose up on their own and they were disposed of by the Germans; it was not his responsibility. I'm satisfied that he thought that if he were to begin to send stuff in they would be his responsibility.

Harriman was also 'utterly convinced' that Stalin was 'delighted' to see the Poles rising in Warsaw killed off, pointing out that these same people were as dedicated to war with the Soviet Union as they had been in 1920.[17]

Harriman's speculation about Stalin's plans and expectations in relation to Warsaw have been borne out by documents from Soviet military archives. The Red Army intended to capture Warsaw and expected to do so quickly. When their first efforts failed the Soviets tried again. Not until the end of August was Operation Bagration halted and even then efforts to establish bridgeheads across the Vistula continued.[18]

On 20 August Churchill and Roosevelt appealed jointly to Stalin to drop supplies to Warsaw, if only to propitiate world opinion. Stalin replied on 22 August:

> Sooner or later the truth about the handful of power-seeking criminals who launched the Warsaw adventure will become clear ... From the military point of view a situation which keeps German attention riveted to Warsaw is highly unfavourable both to the Red Army and to the Poles. Nevertheless, Soviet troops, who of late have had to face renewed and strong German counter-attacks, are doing everything possible to smash the Hitlerite attacks and go over to a new large-scale offensive near Warsaw ... That will be the best and most effective help for the anti-Nazi Poles. [**Document 84**]

By September, however, the Soviets were beginning to worry about the public relations aspect of the affair. On 9 September the People's Commissariat for Foreign Affairs sent a memorandum to the British embassy proposing the establishment of an independent commission to investigate who was responsible for launching the uprising and why it had not been coordinated with the Soviet High Command. The memo also announced a change in policy on supplies to the insurgents, pointing out that the Soviets had already made several air drops but that each time the food and munitions had ended up in German hands. However, if the British and Americans insisted on such air drops the Soviets would co-operate and facilitate the operation.[19]

In mid-September the Soviets also began to step up their own air drops to Warsaw – a move which coincided with the renewal of the Soviet attack on the city. Between 14 September and 1 October the 1st Belorussian Front made 2,243 flights to Warsaw and dropped 156 mortars, 505 anti-tank guns, 2,667 sub-machine-guns and rifles, 3 million cartridges, 42,000 hand grenades, 500 kilos of medicines and 113 tons of food. This compared with British supplies during August and September of 1,344 pistols and revolvers, 3,855 machine pistols, 380 light machine guns, 237 bazookas, 13 mortars, 130 rifles, 14,000 hand grenades, 3,000 anti-tank grenades, 8.5 tons of plastic explosive, 4.5 million rounds of ammunition and 45 tons of food. Most of these supplies ended up in the hands of the Germans, although the Soviets claimed their low-level air drops were more accurate and effective than the high-altitude drops of the RAF.[20]

When Harriman and Clark Kerr saw Stalin together on 23 September the Soviet leader admitted that he had misjudged the motives of the Warsaw insurgents:

> He stated that it was now understood why the insurgency had started prematurely. The Germans had threatened to deport all the male population from Warsaw upon the approach of the Red Army. It thus became necessary for the men to rise up and fight – they had no other choice as they were faced with death either way.[21]

Heated though it was at the time, the controversy over aid to the Warsaw uprising proved to be a transient episode in the history of the Grand Alliance. By the end of September inter-Allied harmony had been restored and it was politics as usual. It was only in retrospect that the rising came to be seen as an important negative turning point in Soviet-Western relations and as an early harbinger of the Cold War. During the Cold War itself the blame game over the Warsaw uprising became one of the touchstones of East-West ideological polemics. Churchill and Roosevelt were blamed for appeasing Stalin and for not doing enough to aid the insurgents. Stalin was blamed for pausing the Red Army on the Vistula and for refusing to aid the uprising. The Soviets and their communist allies in post-war Poland accused the London Poles and the AK of recklessness and adventurism. Little was said about the main culprits – the Germans – but the Nazis massacred millions during the war and even Warsaw's suffering paled in comparison to the Holocaust.

Documents 66–86

66. Churchill to Stalin, 28 January 1944

1. Last Thursday accompanied by the Minister of Foreign Affairs and with the authority of the War Cabinet I met representatives of the Polish Government in London. I informed them that the security of Russian frontiers from the threat of German aggression was a matter of the highest importance to His Majesty's Government and that we would, of course, support the Soviet Union in all measures we considered necessary to achieve that goal. I noted that Russia had sustained two frightful invasions with immense slaughter and devastation at the hands of Germany, that the national independence and existence of Poland had been restored after the First World War, and that it was the policy of the great Allies to restore Poland once again after this war. I said that we had not gone to war for any particular frontier line but for the existence of a strong, free, independent Poland, which Marshal Stalin declared himself as supporting. Moreover, although Great Britain would have fought for years until something happened to Germany, the liberation of Poland from Germany's grip is being achieved mainly by the enormous sacrifices of the Russian armies. Therefore, the Allies had the right to ask that Poland to be guided to a large extent about the frontiers of the territory it would have.

2. I then said that I believed from what had passed at Tehran that the Soviet Government would be willing to agree to the easterly frontiers of Poland corresponding to the Curzon Line subject to the discussion of ethnographical considerations, and I advised them to accept the Curzon Line as a basis for discussion. I spoke of the compensations which Poland would receive in the north and in the west. In the north there would be East Prussia; but here I did not mention the point about Königsberg. In the west they would be secure and aided to occupy Germany up to the line of the Oder. I told them that having been liberated by Allied forces their task was to guard their frontiers against German aggression in an eastern direction. I said that to fulfil this task they would need a friendly Russia backing them and they would, I presumed, be supported by a guarantee of the three Great Powers against a new German attack. Great Britain would be willing to give such a guarantee if it was agreeable to its ally, Soviet Russia. I could not

forecast the action of the United States but it seemed the three Great Powers would stand together against all disturbers of the peace, at any rate until a long time after the war has ended. I made it clear the Polish Government would not be obliged to agree to the Curzon Line, as a basis of examination, except as part of an agreement which gave them good compensation in the north and the west ...

3. Finally, I said that if Russian policy unfolded in the sense I had described, I would urge the Polish Government to settle on that basis and His Majesty's Government would recommend the confirmation of such a settlement by a Peace Conference or conferences for the organisation of Europe following the destruction of Hitlerism and would support no territorial claims from Poland which went beyond it. If the Polish Ministers were satisfied that agreement could be reached along these lines, it would be their duty at the proper time not merely to acquiesce in it but to courageously recommend it to their people, even at the risk of being repudiated by extremists.

4. The Polish ministers were very far from rejecting the prospects thus unfolded but they asked for time to consider the matter with the rest of their colleagues, and as a result of this they have asked a number of questions, none of which seem to be in conflict with the general outline of my suggestions to them. In particular they wish to be assured that Poland would be free and independent in the new home assigned to her; that it would receive an effective guarantee against German revenge; that these Great Powers would also assist in expelling the Germans from the new territories transferred to Poland; and that Poles in regions incorporated into Soviet Russia who wished to do so would be assisted to depart for their new abodes. They also inquired what their position will be if a large part of Poland west of the Curzon Line is occupied by the advancing Soviet forces. Will they be allowed to go back and form a more broad-based government in accordance with popular wishes and be allowed to function administratively in the liberated areas in the same way as other governments whose countries have been overrun? In particular, they are deeply concerned about the relations between the Polish underground movement and the advancing Soviet forces, it being understood that their chief desire was to assist in driving out the Germans. This underground movement raises matters of great importance to our common war effort.

5. We also attach great importance to coordinating our actions in the different regions we hope to liberate. You know the policy we are following in Italy. There we have taken you fully into our councils, and we want to do the same in regard to France and other countries to whose liberation we look forward. We believe such uniformity of action is of great importance now and in the future, for the cause of the United Nations.

6. The earliest possible agreement in principle on the frontiers of the new Polish state is highly desirable to allow of a satisfactory arrangement regarding these two very important points.

7. While everyone will agree that Soviet Russia has the right to recognise or refuse recognition to any foreign government, do you not agree that to advocate

changes in the composition of a foreign government comes near to that inter-ference in internal sovereignty to which you and I have expressed ourselves opposed? I may mention that this view is strongly held by His Majesty's Gov-ernment.

8. I now report this conversation, which expresses the policy of His Majesty's Government at the present time upon this difficult question, to my friend and comrade Marshal Stalin. I earnestly hope these plans may be helpful. I had always hoped to postpone discussions of frontier questions until the end of the war when the victors would be round the table together. The dangers which have forced His Majesty's Government to depart from this principle are formidable and imminent. If, as we have reason to hope, the successful advance of the Soviet armies continues and a large part of Poland is cleared of the German invaders, a good relationship will be absolutely necessary between whatever forces can speak in the name of Poland and the Soviet Union. The creation in Warsaw of another Polish Government different from the one we have recognised up to the present, together with unrest in Poland, would raise for Great Britain and the United States an issue that would damage the close accord of the three Great Powers upon which the future of the world depends ...

67. Stalin to Churchill, 4 February 1944

Your message on the Polish question has reached me through Mr Kerr who arrived in Moscow a few days ago and with whom I had a useful talk.

I see you are giving a good deal of attention to the problem of Soviet-Polish relations. All of us greatly appreciate these efforts.

It seems to me that the very first question on which there must be complete clarity is that of the Soviet-Polish frontier. You are right, of course, in noting that on this point Poland should be guided by the Allies. As for the Soviet Govern-ment, it has already stated, openly and clearly, its views on the frontier question. We have stated that we do not consider the 1939 boundary final, and have agreed to the Curzon Line, thereby making very important concessions to the Poles. Yet the Polish Government has evaded our proposal for the Curzon Line and in its official statements continues to maintain that the frontier imposed upon us under the Riga Treaty is unalterable. From your letter I conclude that the Polish Government is prepared to recognise the Curzon Line, but, as we know, the Poles have not made such a statement anywhere.

I think the Polish Government should officially state in a declaration that the boundary line established by the Riga Treaty shall be revised and that the Curzon Line is the new boundary line between the USSR and Poland. It should state that officially, as the Soviet Government has done by declaring that the 1939 boundary line shall be revised and that the Soviet-Polish frontier should follow the Curzon Line.

As regards your statement to the Poles that Poland could considerably extend her frontiers in the west and north, we are in agreement, with, as you are aware, one amendment. I mentioned the amendment to you and the President in Tehran. We claim the transfer of the north-eastern part of East Prussia, including the port of Königsberg as an ice-free one, to the Soviet Union. It is the only German territory claimed by us. Unless this minimum claim of the Soviet Union is met, the Soviet Union's concession in recognising the Curzon Line loses all meaning, as I told you in Tehran.

Lastly, about the composition of the Polish Government. I think you realise that we cannot re-establish relations with the present Polish Government. Indeed, what would be the use of re-establishing relations with it when we are not at all certain that tomorrow we shall not be compelled to sever those relations again on account of another fascist provocation on its part, such as the 'Katyn affair'? ... That being so, no good can be expected unless the composition of the Polish Government is thoroughly improved. Excluding from it pro-fascist imperialist elements and the inclusion of democratic-minded people would, one hopes, create the proper conditions for the establishment of good Soviet-Polish relations, for resolving the problem of the Soviet-Polish frontier and, in general, for the rebirth of Poland as a strong, free and independent state. Those interested in improving the composition of the Polish Government along these lines are primarily the Poles themselves, the broad sections of the Polish people ...

68. Churchill to Stalin, 20 February 1944

... The Polish Government is prepared to declare that the Riga Line no longer corresponds to realities and with our participation are ready to discuss with the Soviet Government, as part of the general settlement, a new frontier between Poland and the Soviet Union together with the future frontiers of Poland in the north and west. However, since the compensations which Poland is to receive in the north and west cannot be stated openly or precisely at the present time the Polish Government clearly cannot make an immediate public declaration of their willingness to cede territory because such an arrangement ... would immediately be repudiated by a large part of their people abroad and by the underground movement in Poland ... It is evident, therefore, that the Polish-Soviet territorial settlement, which must be an integral part of the general territorial settlement of Europe, can only formally be agreed and ratified when the victorious powers are gathered round the table at the time of an armistice or peace ...

At the frontier negotiations ... the Polish Government, taking into consideration the mixed character of the population of Eastern Poland, would favour a frontier drawn with a view to assuring the highest degree of homogeneity on both sides, while reducing as much as possible the extent and hardship of an exchange of populations. Personally, I don't doubt ... these negotiations will inevitably lead to the conclusion you desire in regard to the future of the Polish-Soviet frontier ...

As regards the war with Germany, which they wish to prosecute with the utmost vigour, the Polish Government realises it is imperative to have a working agreement with the Soviet Government in view of the advance of the liberating armies onto Polish soil, from which these armies are driving the German invader ...

On 6 February I told the Polish Government for the first time that the Soviet Government wished to have the frontier in East Prussia to include, on the

Russian side, Königsberg. The information came as a shock to the Polish Government, who sees in such a decision a substantial reduction in the size and in the economic importance of the German territory to be incorporated in Poland by way of compensation. But I stated that, in the opinion of His Majesty's Government, this was a rightful claim on the part of Russia. Regarding, as I do, this war against German aggression as part of a thirty years' war from 1914 onwards, I reminded Mr Mikołajczyk of the fact that the soil of this part of East Prussia was dyed with Russian blood expended freely in the common cause ... Therefore, it seemed to me that the Russians had a historic and well-founded claim to this German territory.

As regards the composition of the Polish Government, the Polish Government cannot admit any right of foreign intervention. They can, however, assure the Russian Government that by the time they have entered into diplomatic relations with the Soviet Government they will include among themselves none but persons fully determined to cooperate with the Soviet Union. I am of the opinion that it will be much better for such changes to come about naturally and as a result of further Polish reflection on their interests as a whole. It might well be, in my view, that the moment for a resumption of these relations in a formal manner would await the reconstitution of a Polish Government at the time of the liberation of Warsaw when it would arise naturally from the circumstances attending that glorious event ...

I informed the Polish Ministers that should the agreement which has now been outlined in the various telegrams we have exchanged come to pass and all parties acted in its spirit, His Majesty's Government would support it at the Conference after the defeat of Hitler and would to the best of its ability guarantee that settlement in the years that followed.

69. Stalin to Churchill, 3 March 1944

... Having familiarised myself with the details of your conversations with the leaders of the Polish émigré Government, I have come more and more to the conclusion that such people are incapable of establishing normal relations with the USSR. Suffice it to say that far from being ready to recognise the Curzon Line, they claim both Lvov and Vilna. As regard designs to place certain Soviet territories under foreign control, we cannot agree to discuss such pretensions, even to raise such a question is insulting to the Soviet Union ...

70. Churchill to Stalin, 7 March 1944

1. I thank you for your message of 3 March about the Polish question.

2. I made it clear to the Poles that they would not get either Lvov or Vilna and references to these places as my message shows merely suggested a way in which Poles thought they could help the common cause in those areas. They were certainly not intended to be insulting either by the Poles or by me ...

3. Proposals I submitted to you make the occupation by Russia of the Curzon Line a *de facto* reality in the agreement with the Poles from the moment your armies reach it ...

4. Force can achieve much but force supported by the good will of the world can achieve more. I earnestly hope that you will not close the door finally to a working arrangement with the Poles which will help the common cause during the war and give you all you require at the peace ...

5. You spoke to Ambassador Clark Kerr of the danger of the Polish question making a rift between you and me. I shall try earnestly to prevent this. All my hopes for the future of the world are based upon the friendship and cooperation of the Western democracies and Soviet Russia.

71. Stalin to Churchill, 16 March 1944

... Notwithstanding that our correspondence is considered secret and personal, for some time past the contents of my messages to you have been getting into the British press and with serious distortions at that, distortions which I am not in a position to rebut. I consider this a breach of secrecy. This circumstance makes it difficult for me to speak my mind freely. I hope that you appreciate this point.

72. Churchill to Stalin, 21 March 1944

...

2. With regard to the Poles, I am not to blame in any way for revealing your secret correspondence. The information was given both to the American *Herald Tribune* correspondent and to the *London Times* correspondent by the Soviet Embassy in London. In the latter case, it was given personally by Ambassador Gusev.

3. Very soon I shall have to make a statement to the House of Commons about the Polish question. This will involve me saying that attempts to achieve an agreement between the Soviet and Polish Governments have broken down; that we continue to recognise the Polish Government, with whom we have been in continuous relations since the invasion of Poland in 1939; that we now consider all questions of territorial change must await the armistice or the peace conferences of the victorious Powers; and that in the meantime we can recognise no forced transfers of territory ...

5. Finally, allow me to express the sincere hope that our failure in relation to Poland will not have any effect upon our cooperation in other spheres where the maintenance of our common action is of the highest importance.

73. Stalin to Churchill, 23 March 1944

... Your messages and particularly Kerr's statement bristle with threats against the Soviet Union. I would like to call your attention to this because threats as a method are not only out of place in relations between Allies, but also harmful, for they may lead to contrary results.

The Soviet Union's efforts to uphold and implement the Curzon Line are referred to in one of your messages as a policy of force. This means that you are now trying to describe the Curzon Line as unlawful and the struggle for it as unjust. I totally disagree with you. Do not forget that at Tehran you, the President and myself were agreed that the Curzon Line was lawful. At that time you considered the Soviet Government's stand on the issue quite correct and said it would be mad for representatives of the Polish émigré Government to reject the Curzon Line. But now you maintain something to the contrary.

Does this mean that you no longer recognise what we agreed in Tehran and are ready to violate the Tehran agreement? I have no doubt that had you persevered in your Tehran stand the conflict with the Polish émigré Government could have been resolved. As for me and the Soviet Government, we still adhere to the Tehran standpoint, and we have no intention of going back on it, for we believe implementation of the Curzon Line to be evidence, not of a policy of force, but of a policy of re-establishing the Soviet Union's legitimate right to those territories, which even Curzon and the Supreme Council of the Allied Powers recognised as non-Polish in 1919.

You state in your message of 7 March that the problem of the Soviet-Polish frontier will have to be put off until the armistice conference is convened. I think there is a misunderstanding here. The Soviet Union is not waging nor does it intend to wage war against Poland. It has no conflict with the Polish people and considers itself an ally of Poland and the Polish people. That is why it is shedding its blood to free Poland from German oppression. It would be strange, therefore, to speak of an armistice between the USSR and Poland. But the Soviet Union is in conflict with the Polish émigré Government, which does not represent the interests of the Polish people or express their aspirations. It would be stranger still to identify Poland with the Polish émigré Government in London, a government isolated from Poland ...

In your message of 21 March you tell me of your intention to make a statement in the House of Commons to the effect that all territorial questions must await the armistice or peace conferences of the victorious Powers and that in the meantime you cannot recognise any forced territorial transfers. As I see it, you make the Soviet Union appear hostile to Poland, and deny the liberation nature of the war waged by the Soviet Union against German aggression ...

You are, of course, free to make any statement you like in the House of Commons – that is your business. But if you make such a statement I will think that you have committed an unjust and unfriendly act in relation to the Soviet Union.

In your message you express hope that the failure over the Polish question will not affect our cooperation in other spheres. As far as I am concerned, I stand and continue to stand for cooperation. But I fear that the method of threats and defamation, if continued, will not benefit our cooperation.

74. Stalin to Churchill, 9 June 1944

I have received your message of June 7 informing me of the successful development of 'Overlord'. We all salute you and the gallant British and American troops and fervently wish you further success.

Preparations for the summer offensive of the Soviet troops are nearing completion. Tomorrow, June 10, we begin the first round on the Leningrad front.

75. Stalin to Churchill, 11 June 1944

... It seems that the landing, conceived on a grandiose scale, has been crowned with success. I and my colleagues cannot but recognise that this is an enterprise unprecedented in military history as to scale, breadth of conception and masterly execution. As is known, Napoleon's plan for crossing the Channel failed disgracefully. Hitler the hysteric, who for two years had boasted that he would cross the Channel, did not venture even to try to carry out his threat. Only our Allies have succeeded in realising with honour the grandiose plan of forcing the Channel. History will record this as a feat of the highest order.

76. Churchill to Stalin, 12 July 1944

1. Some weeks ago it was suggested by Mr Eden to your Ambassador that the Soviet Government should take the lead in Romania and the British should do the same in Greece. This was only a working arrangement to avoid as much as possible the awful business of triangular telegrams which paralyses action. Mr Molotov then suggested very properly that I should inform the United States Government, which I did and always meant to, and after some discussion the President agreed to a three-month trial ... I would like to ask whether you agree to allow the plan to have its chance for three months. No one can say it affects the future of Europe or divides it into spheres. But we can ensure a policy in each theatre and we will all report to each other what we are doing. However, if you tell me it is hopeless I shall not take it amiss.

2. There is another matter I should like to put to you. Turkey is willing to immediately break off relations with the Axis Powers. I agree with you that she ought to declare war, but I fear that if we tell her to do so she will defend herself by asking both for aircraft to protect her towns, which we shall find it hard to spare or put there at the present moment, and also for joint military operations in Bulgaria and the Aegean for which we have not at present the means. And, besides all this she will demand once again all sorts of munitions, which we cannot spare because the stocks we had ready for her at the beginning of the year have been utilised elsewhere. It seems to me therefore wiser to take this breaking of relations with Germany as a first contribution. Then we can then push a few things in to help her against a vengeance attack from the air and out of this, while we are together, her entry into the war might come. The Turkish alliance in the last war was very dear to the Germans and the fact that Turkey had broken off relations would be a death knell to the German soul. This seems to be a pretty good time to strike such a knell ...

77. Stalin to Churchill, 15 July 1944

1. ... With regard to the question of Romania and Greece there is no need to repeat what you already know from correspondence between our Ambassador in London and Mr Eden. One thing is clear to me, that the American Government has certain doubts about this matter and it would be better to return to the issue when we get the American reply to our enquiry ...

2. The question of Turkey should be examined in the light of the facts with which the governments of Great Britain, the Soviet Union and the USA have been familiar since the negotiations with the Turkish Government at the end of last year. You will no doubt recall how insistently the Governments of our three countries proposed that Turkey should enter the war against Hitler Germany on the side of the Allies as early as November and December 1943. But nothing came of this. As you know, on the initiative of the Turkish Government we resumed negotiations with them last May and June, and twice made the same proposal that the three Allied Governments made at the end of last year. Nothing came of that either. As regards any half-measure by Turkey I do not at the moment see how it can benefit the Allies. In view of the evasive and vague attitude which the Turkish Government has assumed in relation to Germany, it is better to refrain from any further pressure and leave Turkey to itself. This means, of course, that having evaded fighting the Germans Turkey's claims to special rights in post-war affairs will also lapse.

78. Stalin to Churchill, 23 July 1944

... Events on our front are going forward at a very rapid pace. Lublin, one of Poland's major towns, was taken today by our troops, who continue their advance.

In this situation we find ourselves confronted with the practical problem of administration on Polish territory. We do not want to, nor shall we, set up our own administration on Polish soil, for we do not wish to interfere in Poland's internal affairs. That is for the Poles themselves to do. We have, therefore, seen fit to get in touch with the Polish Committee of National Liberation, recently set up by the National Council of Poland, which was formed in Warsaw at the end of last year, and consisting of representatives of democratic parties and groups, as you must have been informed by your Ambassador in Moscow. The Polish Committee of National Liberation intends to set up an administration on Polish territory, and I hope this happens. We have not found in Poland other forces capable of establishing a Polish administration ... I cannot consider the Polish Committee a Polish Government, but it may be that later on it will constitute the core of a Polish Provisional Government made up of democratic forces.

As for Mikołajczyk [Polish Prime Minister-in-Exile], I shall certainly not refuse to see him. It would be better, however, if he were to approach the Polish National Committee, who are favourably disposed towards him.

79. Churchill to Stalin, 27 July 1944

1. Mr Mikołajczyk and his colleagues have left. I am sure Mikołajczyk is most anxious to help unify all Poles upon the lines on which you, I and the President are, I believe, agreed. I believe that Poles who are friendly to Russia should join with the Poles who are friendly to Britain and the United States in order to establish a strong, free, independent Poland, a good neighbour of Russia, and an important barrier between your country and the possibility of future German aggression. We three will take good care there are no other barriers.

2. It would be a great pity, a disaster even, if the Western democracies find themselves recognising one Polish organ and you recognising another. It would lead to constant friction and might even hamper the great business which we have to do the wide world over. Please, therefore, receive these few sentences in the spirit in which they are sent, which is one of sincere friendship, and in the spirit of our twenty-years' alliance.

80. Stalin to Churchill, 28 July 1944

... Mikołajczyk and his companions will be given every help in Moscow.

You know our point of view on Poland, which is a neighbour of ours and relations with which are of special importance to the Soviet Union. We welcome the formation on the territory of Poland of the National Committee of the democratic forces. I think the creation of this Committee constitute a good beginning for the unification of those Poles who are friendly towards Great Britain, the USSR and the United States, and for overcoming the resistance of those Polish elements who are incapable of uniting with the democratic forces.

I realise the importance of the Polish question to the common cause of the Allies, and that is why I am willing to help all Poles and to mediate in achieving understanding among them. The Soviet troops have done, and are continuing to do, all in their power to accelerate the liberation of Poland from the German invaders and to help the Polish people restore freedom and prosperity for their country.

81. Stalin to Churchill, 8 August 1944

I wish to inform you of my meeting with Mikołajczyk, Grabski and Romer. My talk with Mikołajczyk convinced me that he has inadequate information about the situation in Poland. At the same time, I had the impression that Mikołajczyk is not against ways being found to unite the Poles.

As I do not think it possible to impose any decision on the Poles, I suggested to Mikołajczyk that he and his colleagues should meet and discuss their problems with representatives of the Polish Committee of National Liberation, first and foremost the matter of early unification of democratic forces on liberated Polish soil. Meetings have already taken place. I have been informed of them by both parties. The National Committee delegation suggested the 1921 Constitution as a basis for the Polish Government and expressed readiness if the Mikołajczyk group acceded to the proposal, to give it four portfolios, including that of Prime Minister for Mikołajczyk. However, Mikołajczyk could not bring himself to accept. Unfortunately, the meetings have not led to the desired results. But they have all the same been positive because they allowed Mikołajczyk and Morawski, as well as Bierut who had just arrived from Warsaw, to have a broad exchange of views, especially that the Polish National Committee and Mikołajczyk wish to work with each other and are anxious to seek practical possibilities in that direction. That can be considered as the first stage in relations between the Polish Committee and Mikołajczyk and his colleagues. Let us hope that things will improve.

82. Stalin to Churchill, 16 August 1944

After a talk with Mr Mikołajczyk I instructed the Red Army Command to drop munitions intensively into the Warsaw area. A liaison officer was parachuted, but headquarters report that he did not reach his objective as he was killed by the Germans.

Further, having familiarised myself more closely with the Warsaw affair, I have concluded that the Warsaw action is a reckless and terrible adventure, which is taking a heavy toll of the population. This would not have been the case had Soviet headquarters been informed beforehand about the Warsaw action and had the Poles maintained contact with them.

In this situation, Soviet headquarters has concluded that it must dissociate itself from the Warsaw adventure since they cannot assume either direct or indirect responsibility for it ...

83. Churchill and Roosevelt to Stalin, 20 August 1944

We are thinking about the reaction of world public opinion if anti-Nazis in Warsaw are in effect abandoned. We believe that all three of us should do the utmost to save as many of the patriots there as possible. We hope that you will drop essential supplies and munitions to the patriots of Warsaw or if you don't agree that you will agree to help our planes in doing it very quickly. We hope you will approve. Time is of the essence.

84. Stalin to Churchill and Roosevelt, 22 August 1944

The message from you and Mr Roosevelt about Warsaw has reached me. I wish to express my views.

Sooner or later the truth about the handful of power-seeking criminals who launched the Warsaw adventure will become clear to everyone. These people have abused the trust of the Warsawites, throwing many practically unarmed people against German guns, tanks and aircraft. The result is a situation in which every new day brings not the liberation of Warsaw by the Poles but the inhuman shooting of its inhabitants by the Hitlerites.

From the military point of view a situation which keeps German attention riveted to Warsaw is highly unfavourable both to the Red Army and to the Poles. Nevertheless, Soviet troops, who of late have had to face renewed and strong German counter-attacks, are doing everything possible to smash the Hitlerite attacks and go over to a new large-scale offensive near Warsaw. There can be no doubt that the Red Army will spare no effort to beat the Germans at Warsaw and liberate the city for the Poles. That will be the best and most effective help for the anti-Nazi Poles.

85. Churchill to Stalin, 27 September 1944

1. I was gratified to hear from Ambassador Sir A. Clark Kerr the praise which you gave to the British and American operations in France. We value very much such expressions from the leader of the heroic Russian armies. I shall use the occasion to repeat tomorrow in the House of Commons what I have said before, that the

Russian army tore the guts out of the German military machine and is at the present moment holding by far the larger portion of the enemy on its front.

2. I have just returned from long talks with the President and I can assure you of our intense conviction that on the agreement of our three nations, Britain, the United States and the Union of Soviet Socialist Republics, stand the hopes of the world. I was very sorry to learn that you had not been feeling well lately and that your doctors are against you taking long journeys by air. The President had the idea that the Hague would be a good place for us to meet. We have not occupied it yet but it is possible that even before Christmas the course of the war may alter the situation along the Baltic coast to such an extent that your journey would not be tiring or difficult. However, we have much hard fighting to do before any such plan can be made ...

4. I sincerely desire, and I know the President does too, that when the German army is beaten and destroyed, the Soviets will intervene in the Japanese war, as you promised at Tehran. The opening of a Russian military front against the Japanese would force them to burn and bleed, especially in the air, in a manner which would vastly accelerate their defeat. From all that I have learnt about the internal state of Japan and the sense of hopelessness weighing on their people, I believe it might well be that once the Nazis are shattered a triple summons to Japan to surrender from our three Great Powers might be decisive. Of course, we must thoroughly examine all these plans together. I would be glad to come to Moscow in October if I can get away from here. If I cannot, Eden would be very ready to take my place. Meanwhile I send you and Molotov my most sincere good wishes.

86. Stalin to Churchill, 30 September 1944

... I share your conviction that stable harmony between the three leading Powers is a sure guarantee of future peace and answers the best hopes of all peace-loving peoples. The continuation by our Governments of the policy that we achieved during this great war into the post-war period will, I believe, be the decisive thing.

Of course, I have a great desire to meet with you and the President. I attach great importance to it for our common cause. However, I have one reservation: my doctors advise me not to undertake long journeys. For a certain period I have to take account of this.

I wholeheartedly welcome your desire to come to Moscow in October. We have military and other issues of great importance to discuss. If anything keeps you from coming, we would, of course, be ready to meet Mr Eden.

Your information about the President's plans visit to Europe is of great interest to me. I feel sure, too, that he will win the election.

As regards Japan, our attitude remains the same as it was at Tehran.

I and Molotov send you our best wishes.

Chapter 7

With Bow against Bear: Churchill in Moscow, October 1944

Churchill's trip to Moscow in October 1944 is one of the most famous in diplomatic history. It was on this visit that Churchill offered Stalin the notorious 'percentages' deal dividing central and south-eastern Europe into British and Soviet spheres of influence. The existence of such a deal had long been rumoured but the full story – at any rate, Churchill's version of it – did not come out until the publication in 1954 of Vol. 6 of his memoir-history of the Second World War.

Churchill dined at the Kremlin his first night in Moscow and the percentages discussion took place after dinner. According to Churchill's celebrated account:

> The moment was apt for business, so I said [to Stalin], 'Let us settle about our affairs in the Balkans. Your armies are in Roumania and Bulgaria. We have interests, missions, and agents there. Don't let us get at cross-purposes in small ways. So far as Britain and Russia are concerned, how would it do for you to have ninety percent predominance in Roumania, for us to have ninety per cent of the say in Greece, and go fifty-fifty about Yugoslavia?' While this was being translated I wrote out on a half-sheet of paper:

Roumania	%
Russia	90
The others	10
Greece	
Great Britain	90
(in accord with USA.)	
Russia	10
Yugoslavia	50-50
Hungary	50-50
Bulgaria	
Russia	75
The others	25

> I pushed this across to Stalin, who had by then heard the translation. There was a slight pause. Then he took his blue pencil and made a large tick upon it, and passed it back to us. It was all settled in no more time than it takes to set down ... After this there was a long silence. The pencilled paper lay in the centre of the table. At length I said, 'Might it no be thought rather cynical if it seemed we had disposed of these issues so fateful to millions of

people, in such an offhand manner? Let us burn the paper'. 'No, you keep it', said Stalin.[1]

Even before he published this memoir of this meeting Churchill had told the story of the percentages deal to the Soviet ambassador in London, Jacob Malik, emphasising that Stalin had stuck to his side of the bargain and had not interfered in Greek affairs. The point of the story was the Soviet Union kept its agreements with other states. In the same conversation Churchill praised the recently-deceased dictator's sense of humour and recalled the great friendship and fun of his meetings with Stalin.[2]

Churchill liked to tell a good story but his main purpose in publicising the percentages agreement was to claim that it had saved Greece from communism. In 1956 he told the American journalist, C.L. Sulzberger: 'Stalin never broke his word to me. We agreed on the Balkans. I said he could have Rumania and Bulgaria; and he said we could have Greece ... He signed a slip of paper. And he never broke his word. We saved Greece that way. When we went in in 1944 Stalin didn't interfere.'[3]

In popular mythology, however, the Churchill-Stalin percentages agreement has gone down in history as an infamous encounter, as the occasion of a cynical Anglo-Soviet carve-up of the Balkans. During the 1950s and 1960s Churchill's story of the deal came to symbolise, for both Left and Right, the fate of post-war Europe; on the one hand, there was a leftist narrative of Stalin's betrayal of the revolution in Greece and, by extension, in Western Europe; on the other hand, a conservative parable of Churchill's sacrifice of Eastern European freedom on the altar of British strategic and imperial interests.

In the 1970s the British record of the 9 October meeting became available. But it made no mention of percentages, though the British ambassador's draft of the report did refer to 'a "naughty document" showing a list of Balkan countries and the proportion of interest in them of the Great Powers'.[4]

The Soviet report on the conversation (**Document 87**) does mention percentages although not in the same detail as Churchill's table. According to this account of the conversation Stalin was keen to amend the Bulgaria figure so that the Soviet Union was allocated a 90 per cent interest, the same as in the case of Romania.

Eden and Molotov discussed their bosses' deal at meetings held on 10 and 11 October. The upshot was an agreement to adjust the percentages in relation to Bulgaria and Hungary to 80-20 in the Soviet favour.[5] The other percentages remained as stated in Churchill's table. But what did these percentages mean? The closest that Molotov and Eden came to clarity was that the percentages related to degrees of influence on the Allied Control Commissions (ACCs) that were to run the military occupations of Bulgaria, Romania and Hungary, countries which had been or were about to be invaded by the Red Army. The Soviet model was the ACC for Italy controlled by the British and Americans: all three allies would be represented but the armies on the ground would run the show. The Soviets' lack of power in Italy would be applied to the British in

Bulgaria, Romania and Hungary, notwithstanding Eden's effort to extract a little more influence in the form of a percentage share. Even less clear was what Churchill's 50/50 in Yugoslavia meant since it was an Allied not an enemy state and there would be no occupation regime as such.

In truth, the only clear agreement to come out of the percentages discussion was that Stalin would not interfere with the British sphere of influence in Greece. Since the Red Army neither had nor intended a military presence in Greece there was not much that Stalin could do in that country. The Greek communists and the partisan movement they led were quite strong but Stalin was against any clashes with the British that would interfere with the struggle against Hitler. Not until the breakdown of the Grand Alliance after the war did Soviet policy in relation to Greece change from passivity to active support for the communist partisans in the Greek Civil War.[6]

After the 9 October meeting Churchill and Stalin never mentioned the percentages deal, except in passing. At the Potsdam Conference in July 1945 Churchill complained that he was not getting his 50 per cent share of influence in Yugoslavia, to which Stalin responded that the Soviet Union had no influence because Marshal Tito – the leader of the Yugoslav communists – was his own man. This was a somewhat disingenuous remark by Stalin: at that time Tito and the Yugoslav communists looked to Moscow for leadership and support and they were well-regarded by the Soviets because of their role in the powerful partisan movement that had liberated Yugoslavia from German occupation. But Stalin's comment did presage his split with Tito in the late 1940s over Yugoslav leadership ambitions in the Balkans. Like Churchill, Stalin ended up with no influence in Yugoslavia.

While the percentages deal amounted to little in practice, Churchill's willingness to negotiate such a wide-ranging deal and to demarcate vital interests must have been psychologically reassuring to Stalin. Of importance, too, were the tensions in Anglo-American relations revealed by Roosevelt's response to the British Premier's trip to Moscow. On the eve of Churchill's departure for the Soviet capital Roosevelt wrote to Stalin asking that Ambassador Harriman be allowed to observe proceedings, pointedly stating that 'in this global war there is literally no question, military or political, in which the United States is not interested. I am firmly convinced that the three of us, and only the three of us, can find the solution to the questions unresolved. In this sense, while appreciating Mr Churchill's desire for the meeting, I prefer to regard your forthcoming talks with the Prime Minister as preliminary to a meeting of the three of us.' It was a point that needed no labouring for Stalin. He knew where power lay in the western half of the Grand Alliance and he wrote back reassuring Roosevelt that the meeting was Churchill's idea and that he would report to him on its progress. But Stalin was a little peeved at Roosevelt's intervention, or pretended to be, and said so to Churchill at their first meeting, noting that the US President was demanding too many rights for himself and allowing too few to Britain and the Soviet Union which were, after all, bound together by a formal treaty of alliance whereas the USSR and the United States were not. Churchill defused the situation by joking that they would discuss the Dumbarton Oaks negotiations on the establishment of a successor to the League of Nations but not tell Roosevelt!

The primary purpose of Churchill's second trip to Moscow was to discuss Poland. By far the greater part of his and Stalin's time was taken up by the Polish question. This was the very first issue raised by Churchill at the meeting on 9 October, when he suggested that Mikołajczyk, who was in Cairo, should be invited to Moscow. The Polish leader was brought to Moscow and met Stalin and Churchill on 13 October, but the discussion got nowhere (**Document 89**). Stalin wanted Mikołajczyk to work with the Polish Committee of National Liberation (PCNL) to form a reconstructed Polish provisional government and to accept the Curzon Line as Poland's eastern border. The best Mikołajczyk could offer was the Curzon Line without Lvov, and that only as a demarcation line pending final negotiation of the Polish–Soviet frontier. This was unacceptable to Stalin, who emphasised that under no circumstances would he agree to the partition of Belorussia and Ukraine. Mikołajczyk then met the PCNL leader Bolesław Bierut, who offered him a quarter of the ministerial posts in a reconstructed Polish government, a figure that Stalin increased to one-third, including the position of Prime Minister. Churchill also met Bierut and was charmed by his intelligence, but it is doubtful that he believed Stalin's protestations that the Pole was not a communist. Stalin's growing impatience with Mikołajczyk was reflected in his comment to Churchill on 16 October that that he hadn't heard from the Pole 'one word of gratitude to the Red Army, which is liberating Poland . . . He thinks the Russians are in his service' (**Document 93**).

Churchill was exasperated by Mikołajczyk, too and told him: 'We are not going to wreck the peace of Europe because of quarrels between Poles. Unless you accept the frontier you are out of business forever. The Russians will sweep through your country and your people will be liquidated. You are on the verge of annihilation.'[7]

Mikołajczyk's hands were tied by the weight of opinion within his London Government-in-Exile, which was against the deal on offer. Personally, however, he was beginning to think it represented the best hope for an independent Poland. Indeed, after failing to persuade his colleagues of the merits of the Soviet terms when he returned to London from Moscow, he resigned as premier of the exile government at the end of November 1944.

The Polish logjam notwithstanding, Churchill's visit to Moscow went well socially as well as politically. For the first time Stalin agreed to dine at the British embassy. Lord Moran, Churchill's private physician recorded in his diary on 11 October that 'the dinner at the Embassy was rather tedious. People kept jumping up to propose toasts with turgid compliments . . . which all had to be translated.'[8] Other testimony suggests it was a rather splendid affair. At the end of the evening, in a private chat with Churchill, Stalin expressed scepticism about the Labour Party in relation to the coming British general election, placing them in the same category as the Mensheviks in Russia in 1917.[9] This was not a compliment; the Mensheviks were the Bolsheviks' mortal foes during the Russian Revolution.

The next evening Churchill and Stalin appeared together at the Bolshoi Ballet and were met with thunderous applause from the audience. An enthusiastic on-looker was Harriman's daughter, Kathleen, who accompanied her father on his mission to Moscow. She was thrilled to meet Stalin for the first time. Between acts she joined Churchill, Stalin, Molotov, her father and others for a sit-down dinner. 'Ave said that Stalin was exceptionally gay', she wrote to Churchill's daughter-in-law Pamela, 'he did have a good wit and looked as though he was enjoying his task as host to the P.M.' There were many toasts, including one to the 'Holy Trinity' – Churchill, Roosevelt and Stalin. Churchill 'must be the Holy Ghost he flies around so much', quipped Stalin.[10]

Churchill and Stalin's social intimacy was mirrored in their political discussions. At their meeting on 14 October (**Document 91**) Churchill told Stalin 'that the future of the world depends on friendship of the British and Americans with the Soviet Union. He will be frank and say to Marshal Stalin that small European countries are scared to death of Bolshevik revolution ... He remembers that in 1919–1920 the whole world feared world revolution.' Stalin replied that 'the world has nothing to fear now. The Soviet Union does not intend to stage Bolshevik revolutions in Europe.' I believe all that you say, responded Churchill.

Among the other topics discussed by Churchill and Stalin was the question of Turkey and the revision of the Montreux Convention on the control of the Black Sea Straits. This came up at the meeting on 9 October when Stalin told Churchill that 'under the Montreux Convention Turkey has all the rights to the Straits, while the Soviet Union has very few rights ... it was necessary to discuss the question of revising the Montreux Convention, which did not correspond to the current situation at all'. Churchill reiterated his support for warm-seas access for Russia but asked what exactly Stalin had in mind. Stalin was unable to say what specific changes to Montreux he wanted but he successfully pressed Churchill to agree that revision was necessary. According to the British record of this discussion Stalin also said:

> It was quite impossible for Russia to remain subject to Turkey, who could close the Straits and hamper Russian imports and exports and even her defence. What would Britain do if Spain or Egypt were given this right to close the Suez Canal, or what would the United States Government say if some South American Republic had the right to close the Panama Canal?[11]

There was one important discussion in Moscow that Churchill did not take a full part in – the question of the timing of Soviet entry into the Far Eastern war against Japan.

The United States began angling for Soviet involvement in the war against Japan in December 1941. Not surprisingly, Stalin, who had his hands full fighting Hitler, resisted these overtures. Stalin's policy was to stick to the terms of the Soviet–Japanese Neutrality Pact of April 1941 in the hope that Tokyo would do the same. Unlike Roosevelt in relation to Britain in 1940–1, Stalin made no declarations of political solidarity with the struggle of his Western Allies in the Far East. Soviet press coverage of the Pacific War was sympathetic to the

Western Allies but not particularly hostile to Japan. Even so, there could be little doubt that sooner or later the Soviet Union would involve itself in the war in the Far East. Soviet entry into the war would ensure a decisive and devastating defeat of Japan, would cement Stalin's relations with his Western Allies and would open the door to Soviet involvement in the Far Eastern peace settlement.

Stalin's road to war with Japan began in October 1943 at the Foreign Ministers' conference in Moscow when he told Hull and Harriman that the Soviet Union would enter the Far Eastern war as soon as Germany was defeated. This promise was firmed up by Stalin in his conversations with Churchill and Roosevelt at Tehran. After Tehran, Harriman raised the question of Soviet participation in the Far Eastern war on a number of occasions and his lobbying secured a decisive breakthrough during Churchill's October 1944 visit to Moscow.

Together with General Deane, the chief of the American military mission in Moscow, Harriman attended the military talk between Churchill and Stalin on 14 October (**Document 92**). That discussion focused on the European theatre but Deane gave a presentation on the war with Japan and was able to pose some questions to the Soviets: how soon after the defeat of Germany would the USSR enter the war against Japan; how long would it take for the Soviets to concentrate their forces in the Far East; and how much supplies could the Trans-Siberian railway carry to an American strategic air force in the Far East? Churchill complimented Deane on his daring: 'Young man, I admire your nerve in asking Stalin those last three questions. I have no idea that you will get an answer but there was certainly no harm in asking.'[12]

General Antonov replied to Deane's questions at a meeting the next day. It would take two-and-a-half to three months to concentrate sufficient Soviet forces, said Antonov. Stalin chipped in to say that it wasn't just a question of transporting forces to the Far East but of sufficient supplies to keep them going and on the supply side the Soviets would need American help. Asked by Harriman when the Soviet Union would enter the war against Japan, Stalin said three months after Germany's defeat.

On 16 October Stalin met Harriman and Deane again and gave them a list of supplies the Soviets would need if they were to participate in the Far Eastern war. Stalin also made it clear he would have political demands to make in relation to Soviet participation in the Far Eastern war since the Soviet people had to know what they were fighting for. These demands, it soon transpired, combined patriotic sensibilities with strategic interests. In the 1904–5 war with Japan, Tsarist Russia had suffered a humiliating defeat and been forced by the Treaty of Portsmouth to give up port facilities and territorial concessions in China and to concede to Japan the southern half of the island of Sakhalin. Basically, Stalin wanted to reverse the Treaty of Portsmouth and to make some additional gains, including occupation of the Kurils – a chain of islands that ran from the USSR's Kamchatka Peninsula to the northernmost tip of the Japanese home island of Hokkaido. The Kurils were the Far Eastern equivalent of Königsberg in Germany – a 'lump' of Japan in payment for the Soviet blood that would be spilled when the Red Army attacked Japanese forces in Manchuria.

On 17 October, at their final meeting before his departure from Moscow, Churchill and Stalin exchanged views on the future of Germany (**Document 95**). Once again Stalin expressed his fear of a revival of German power and made plain his preference for the dismemberment of the country. Asked by Churchill if he supported the formation of a federation of East European states to protect against German aggression, Stalin gave an interesting reply:

> For first 3–4 years after the war a nationalistic mood is going to prevail in Hungary, Czechoslovakia and Poland. The first wish of those nations will be to organise their own national life. These countries will object to the infringement of their rights by way of uniting them with other countries ... Hitler's regime engendered nationalistic sentiments to such an extent that Yugoslavia ... and other small nations, all want to have their autonomy. In the first years after the war one feeling will prevail over other sentiments – the desire to live a full national life without interference ... It is difficult to imagine that the Czechs and Hungarians, even the Czechs and the Poles, will find a common language. Unification is not possible at present but it is not excluded in the future.

Soviet opposition to federations or confederations of East European states was long-standing and was based on the fear that such associations would take an anti-Soviet character, even to the extent of reviving the cordon sanitaire around Bolshevik Russia established by the British and French after the First World War. Stalin's remarks also reflected his growing consciousness of ethnic issues and his preference for ethnic unification where possible. Hence his support for the return of Transylvania to Romania, a region inhabited mainly by Romanians, albeit with a significant Hungarian minority. In relation to the Soviet Union's own ethnic integrity this outlook led Stalin in 1945 to negotiate the transfer from Czechoslovakia to the USSR of sub-Carpathian Ukraine, a sparsely-populated region of no great economic or strategic importance.[13]

At the end of Churchill's trip a communiqué was issued that spoke of an open and sincere exchange of views and of progress in negotiations about the Polish question and about the formation of a united government for Yugoslavia. This was not much to show for an eleven-day visit by the British Prime Minister. On the other hand, the talks had been very friendly and there was none of the rancour that had punctuated Churchill and Stalin's previous discussions in Moscow in 1942 and at Tehran in 1943.

Upon his arrival in Moscow Churchill had given Stalin a photographic portrait of himself with a handwritten inscription: 'To Marshal & Premier Stalin, who as head of the Russian Armies & the Soviet Government broke the main strength of the German military machine and helped all the United Nations to open paths to Peace, Justice & Freedom. From his friend Winston S. Churchill.'[14] In return, as Churchill was leaving Moscow on 19 October Stalin presented him with a commemorative vase decorated with a picture entitled 'With Bow against Bear'.

Documents 87–97

87. Stalin-Churchill Meeting in Moscow, 9 October 1944, 22:00

Present: Molotov, Eden, Kerr, Birse and Pavlov (interpreters)

At the beginning of the conversation **Churchill** presented Stalin with an autographed portrait of himself.

Stalin accepted the portrait and thanked Churchill.

Starting the conversation **Churchill** declared that it was necessary to clarify a few questions and he came to Moscow because it is easier to do this in person than by correspondence. Personal conversations will enable us to ascertain what the two sides want and to resolve any issues. Personal conversations will spare both sides from telegraphic communication. The most difficult problem is that of Poland. Both sides will have to try and come to an agreement about a common policy in relation to Poland. Both sides are in possession of 'fighting cocks'.

Stalin noted that it would be difficult to manage without cocks. For example, they signal when it is time to get up.

Churchill agreed with this. He said that the question of the border between Poland and Soviet Union is already decided. One could look at the map once more.

Stalin said that if the question of the border on the basis of Curzon Line is decided, their task will be easier.

Churchill said that this is exactly the view of the British government.

Stalin said the Poles do not see it that way.

Churchill replied that when all the allies meet around the table at an armistice conference, it would be easier for Americans to resolve the issue, because in that case the President could take the decisions himself, whereas in the case of a peace conference the President would have to ask the Senate. He, Churchill, will support Russian claims for the frontier line that was shown to him at Teheran. This intention of Churchill's was supported by his cabinet. Churchill will declare that this frontier is just and necessary for the security and future of Russia. Churchill is sure the Americans will support him. If General Sosnkovsky protests it wouldn't be such a big deal as long as Great Britain and the United States consider the decision to be right. The English have been trying for months to get rid of General Sosnkovsky. As for General Bór, he will be taken care of by the Germans.

Stalin said that the Poles no longer have a commander.

Churchill replied they have one colourless person. He, Churchill, wanted to ask Marshal Stalin a question. Would Stalin consider it worthwhile for the English to bring Mikołajczyk, Romer and Grabski to Moscow? They are sitting in an airplane in Cairo. They could be delivered to Moscow in 36 hours. Should it be done? The English want to resolve this issue.

Stalin asked if the Poles have the power to resolve the question with the Polish Committee of National Liberation.

Churchill replied that he was sure the Poles from London would like to meet with the Polish Committee. But the British and Soviet sides could force them to agree here in Moscow.

Stalin said he has nothing against Mikołajczyk, Romer and Grabski coming to Moscow. Let's make another attempt. Mikołajczyk, Romer and Grabski will have to liaise with the Polish Committee of National Liberation. He, Stalin, asks Churchill to keep in mind that Polish Committee has an army, and not a bad army, it represents a serious force.

Churchill replied that in Italy a brave Polish corps is fighting on the allies' side. There are Polish troops in France, too. Polish forces have a lot of friends in England. The Poles are a brave and good people. The trouble is that they have foolish political leaders. The trouble is that when two Poles meet there is a dispute.

Stalin said that if a Pole is on his own he starts an argument with himself.

Churchill replied that we two have more chance to unite the Poles. The English can put pressure on their Poles, the Russians on theirs.

Stalin said let's both our sides try to do that.

Churchill announced that he would also like to touch upon questions with regard to truces with satellites forced by Germany to join the war, but which didn't excel during the war. Some of these satellites are not liked by the English, some by the Russians. He, Churchill, proposes that Eden and Molotov discuss these questions if Marshal Stalin agrees.

Stalin replied affirmatively.

Churchill said that the question of Hungary is very important and he hopes that Soviet troops will be in Budapest very soon.

Stalin said that is possible.

Churchill said here are two countries that interest England. Firstly, Greece. He, Churchill, is not bothered about Romania. Romania is mainly a Russian affair and the agreement with Romania proposed by the Soviet government was considered wholly reasonable by the British government and it testifies to the political wisdom of the Soviet government. Doubtless, this agreement will facilitate a general peace. However, as far as Greece is concerned, the British government has great interest in this country. The British government hopes that England will have the decisive voice in Greek affairs, the same as the Soviet Union has in Romania. Of course, in relation to both Greek and Romanian affairs, England and Soviet Union will remain in contact.

Stalin replied that he appreciates that Great Britain has suffered big losses because of German interdictions in the Mediterranean. He understands that if these routes are not secure Britain will suffer great damage. Greece is important to the security of these routes. He agrees that England should have the decisive voice in Greece.

Churchill replied that he has prepared a table. It would perhaps be better to state the thought expressed in this table in diplomatic language because the Americans, including the President, would be shocked by the division of Europe into the spheres of influence.

Stalin said that he would like to talk about Roosevelt. He, Stalin, got a message from Roosevelt in which he stated his wish that American ambassador Harriman attend meetings between Stalin and Churchill as an observer. Secondly, the

President asked that the decisions made at these meetings be of a preliminary character. He, Stalin, wanted to ask Churchill his opinion on the President's requests.

Churchill said he told Roosevelt that he welcomed Harriman's presence at the conversations with Marshal Stalin. However, Churchill would not like him to interfere in intimate conversations between Churchill and Stalin or between Eden and Molotov. In any case, Churchill will keep the President up to date. But he has to note that as an observer Harriman is not in the same position as them, Churchill and Stalin.

Stalin replied that he has to say that he sent a reply to Roosevelt where he said that he didn't know what issues would be discussed with Churchill. He had the impression from the President's message that the President was worried. He has to say that he didn't like the message because the President demands a lot of rights for himself and doesn't leave many for England and the Soviet Union, who are bound to each other by a treaty of mutual assistance. There is no such treaty between the USA and the Soviet Union. However, Stalin does not object to Harriman's presence at an official meeting, as opposed to a personal one, and he and Churchill will decide to which meetings Harriman will be invited to.

Churchill said that now he would like to discuss the Dumbarton Oaks conference. The President didn't want this question to be discussed in Moscow, especially now, and preferred it to be resolved at a meeting of all three of us. Of course, we have to keep in mind that the President is thinking about the elections which will take place in the United States.

Churchill said it would be fair to say that at first the English were inclined to accept the American point of view. But now the English see more fairness in proposals from the other side. Suppose China demanded the British Empire give up Hong Kong and if when this question was discussed Britain and China were asked leave the room while Russia and United States resolved the issue; Britain would not like it. On the other hand, if Argentina was in conflict with the United States, the US probably wouldn't like it if American representatives were asked to leave the meeting while China, Russia and Britain make decisions about Argentina. All this, says Churchill, is said not for the record. The sensible thing would be to wait for the meeting of the heads of all three governments. He hopes that Marshal Stalin will confirm when needed that this question wasn't discussed in Moscow.

Smiling, **Stalin** said that, of course, he will do that.

Churchill stated that he has prepared a pretty rough and ready document which shows the division of influence between the Soviet Union and Great Britain in Romania, Greece, Yugoslavia, Bulgaria. He came up with this table to show how English see this issue. The Americans would be startled by this document. But Marshal Stalin is a realist, and Churchill is not noted for his sentimentality, and Eden is completely depraved. He, Churchill, hadn't shown this document to the British Cabinet, though British Cabinet usually agrees with what Churchill and Eden propose. As for Parliament, the Cabinet has its majority there, though if this document was shown to the Parliament, they wouldn't understand anyway.

Stalin said that the 25 per cent envisaged for England in Bulgaria does not correspond to other the figures in the table. Stalin considered it necessary to correct it, namely 90 per cent for Soviet Union and 10 per cent for England in Bulgaria.

Churchill replied that the Bulgarians insulted the English greatly. During the last war they behaved very badly towards the English, having attacked Romania. During the current war Bulgarians have been very cruel towards the Yugoslavs and Greeks. After all that, Churchill can't let them sit at the same table as the allies.

Stalin said that of course Bulgaria has to be punished.

Eden stated that in Romania the English are spectators, but in Bulgaria they would like to be a bit more than just spectators.

Molotov asked if the Turkish issue is relevant here.

He, **Churchill**, hasn't touched upon the Turkish issue, all he wanted to do was to show what the English think. He is very glad the points of view of both sides are so close. He thinks that one more meeting could resolve this issue once and for all.

Stalin said that if Turkey is being discussed he has to say that according to the Montreux Convention Turkey has full rights on the Straits, whereas Soviet Union has few rights. According to the Montreux Convention the Soviet Union has the same rights as the Japanese Emperor. Stalin thinks that it is necessary to discuss revision of the Montreux Convention as it really doesn't correspond to the current state of affairs.

Churchill states that Turkey has lost its right to enter the war. It didn't join earlier because it was afraid of Germany as it doesn't have modern arms. Moreover, the Turks not only do not know how to use modern arms, they don't have enough ready troops.

Stalin remarked that in Phrakia [Thrace] the Turks have concentrated 26 divisions. It is not clear against whom they have concentrated those divisions.

Churchill stated the Turks were afraid of the Bulgarians, because the Germans gave the Bulgarians the arms they confiscated from the French. In the present war Turkey learnt to be afraid of Bulgaria. Looking to the future, he, Churchill, can say that the British policy doesn't entail cutting off Russia from the warm seas and the great world oceans. On the contrary, the British think that this goal is a component of Russian-British friendship. There is no Disraeli or Curzon policy anymore. What changes to the Montreux Convention does Marshal Stalin envisage?

Stalin replied that he cannot say what changes are required and or what could replace the Convention, but he feels the Convention does not correspond to the current situation and is pointed against Russia. He would like to ask Churchill if he agrees in principle that the Convention needs to be amended. Such a big country as the Soviet Union shouldn't be in fear of a small country like Turkey closing the Straits and put under threat its exports, imports and defence. He doesn't want to infringe Turkish sovereignty, but it is not possible to suffer such a situation when Turkey is choking Soviet trade and seafaring.

Churchill replied that in principle he shares this opinion of Stalin's but thinks that it would be better to fix this issue on paper a bit later, because Turkey could be alarmed and think we have demanded they cede Istanbul. Churchill's opinion is that Russia has to have an outlet to the Mediterranean for both military and trade vessels. We hope, he says, to work together with the Soviet Union on that question, but we would like to approach the issue carefully so as not to scare off Turkey. If the Soviet Union and England were sitting at a table drafting the armistice agreement and the Russians asked the English to agree that Russian military and trade vessels should have access to the Mediterranean, then he, Churchill, would say that Great Britain has no objection to this.

Stalin said that he is not pressing Churchill on this issue, but he wanted to warn him that this question is on the Soviet Union's agenda. He would like Churchill to acknowledge that raising this question is legitimate.

Churchill replied that he agreed not just in principle but considers the Soviet Union should take the initiative and declare its view that the Convention should be changed and tell the United States what it thinks about this question. For its part the British Government considers the Soviet Union's claims just in principle and morally founded.

Churchill stated that the Balkan campaign he mentioned will prevent any civil war there arising from ideological differences. He thinks the Allies cannot let Balkan peoples have a small civil war as they did after the Great War. Any discord in the Balkans must be quelled by the authority and power of the three great powers. We must, says Churchill, tell the Balkan peoples that issues will be resolved by the three powers and that they must be guided by the three great powers. While Britain will not impose a king on Yugoslavia, Greece or Italy, at the same time the British think that people should have the right to a plebiscite in peacetime. It doesn't matter what people choose – monarchy or another regime – they must have an opportunity to express their free will. He, Churchill, would like to ask Marshal Stalin if he would be against collaboration with a king if the king was chosen by the people.

Stalin said that he wouldn't.

Churchill said that the English are hoping that in northern Italy power will be exercised under the guidance of the Allied armies. The English do not value the Italian king, but they don't want a civil war there, either before or after Allied forces leave. We would like the Soviet government to put a brake on the activity of Italian communists, so that they don't disturb Italy and stir things up. Everything can be decided by the democratic process, but we do not want any turmoil in Italy, where Allied forces are situated, as these disturbances may lead to confrontation with the army. Roosevelt is well-disposed toward the Italians, though Churchill doesn't like them. The crux of the matter is that in the state of New York there are many Italian voters.

Stalin said he doesn't know that national situation in Italy and that it will be difficult for him to influence the Italian communists. Besides, there are no Soviet troops in Italy, unlike in Bulgaria where we can order to the communists to do this and that. But if, he, Stalin, started giving Ercoli [pseudonym of Palmiro Togliatti – leader of the Italian communists and a former Comintern official in Moscow] advice, Ercoli will tell me to go to hell, as I don't know the national situation in Italy. On the other hand, when Ercoli was in Moscow, we had conversations with him. Stalin can say that Ercoli is an intelligent person and won't undertake any adventures.

Churchill said let's hope the Italian communists don't upset the country.

Stalin said that the figures on Bulgaria need to be amended.

Churchill said that he doesn't give a damn about Bulgaria and maybe Eden and Molotov could discuss this issue.

Stalin agreed.

Churchill stated that there are a few more issues to be discussed. There should be a special discussion about the future of Germany. This question was only touched upon in Tehran. Harriman has to be present at the discussion about the future of Germany. Churchill was and is cautious about announcing severe punishment of Germany as it would make the Germans fight even harder. He would like to state that he stands for harsh treatment of Germany. In America there are two views on this question. The President is for harsh treatment of Germany. It would be best, of course, to defeat the Germans and then tell them what to do. It is necessary to decide if Eastern Prussia, the Saar and Ruhr are to be detached, to shatter the territory of Germany and to forbid the Germans to have arms.

Russian factories have suffered heavily in this war, as have the Belgian and the Dutch. He, Churchill, thinks the Germans have to compensate for this with machinery. The question arises: how to divide Germany. Perhaps, Eden, Molotov and Harriman could discuss this in detail and then present a full set of proposals to Stalin and Churchill.

Stalin agreed with this proposition and stated that in his opinion the Versailles Treaty was half-hearted. It gave birth to German revanchism but it didn't prevent Germany from having its revenge. Any restrictions on Germany will provoke a mood of revenge. The task is to prevent that revenge. For this purpose it is necessary to reduce heavy industry and all industries that could grow into military ones. If the allies don't take the opportunity for revenge there will be war with Germany every 25–30 years.

Churchill agreed with this, stating that those Germans who were part of fascist detachments, the Gestapo and the Hitler Youth, have to be sent to corrective labour camps, to show them that to build is much harder than to destroy. He can certainly say that there wouldn't be any support in England for the mass extermination of such individuals. They need to be reformed.

Stalin replied that nobody is suggesting mass extermination and that the best method of reform would be the prolonged occupation of Germany.

Churchill stated that Americans most likely do not intend to occupy Germany for a long time.

Stalin said that other Allied countries could be involved in the occupation, including France.

Churchill agreed.

Stalin stated that the armed forces of lesser allies might also be involved in occupation of Germany.

Churchill said that he would like troops of a united Poland involved in the occupation.

Stalin said the Poles would be quite eager to get involved in the occupation. The Poles should be given Eastern Prussia and Silesia, but Soviet Union will take the Königsberg region.

Churchill considered that fair but suggested Germans from these regions should be relocated to Germany. Now, after the Allies have exterminated around eight million Germans in Germany, there will be enough space for them.

Stalin agreed that Germans from Silesia and Eastern Prussia should be re-settled in Germany.

Churchill said that the last question is about the Anglo-American war against Japan. Secrecy is of the utmost importance here. It is telling that the Japanese still don't know the statement that Marshal Stalin made in Tehran. He, Churchill, has asked Roosevelt to inform him about American plans regarding war in the Pacific in 1945. Events are moving very fast and plans are changing quickly depending on the Americans' occupation of one island after another. Churchill knows that Roosevelt gave Harriman and General Deane [head of the American military mission in Moscow] a summary of American plans, which they should show us and discuss with Soviet generals.

Stalin stated that on the question of American plans there should have been a meeting between General Deane and the relevant Soviet military, but it didn't happen because the necessary detailed information from the Far East hadn't been received. He, Stalin, doesn't know the American plans. If the three sides could meet, that would be better.

Churchill stated that Harriman and Deane are to inform Stalin about these plans and can describe them in detail.

Stalin said that he is ready to discuss this question.

Churchill said that he hopes the plans will also be discussed with Marshal Brooke, a member of the combined chiefs of staff. Marshal Brooke is ready to discuss these plans but doesn't feel he has the right to criticise them.

88. Churchill and Stalin to Roosevelt, 10 October 1944

In an informal discussion we have taken a preliminary view of the situation as it affects us and have planned out the course of our meetings, social and others. We have invited Messrs Mikołajczyk, Romer and Grabski to come at once for further conversations with us and with the Polish National Committee. We have agreed not to refer in our discussions to Dumbarton Oaks issues, and that these shall be taken up when we three can meet together. We have to consider the best way of reaching an agreed policy about the Balkan countries, including Hungary and Turkey. We have arranged for Mr Harriman to sit in as an observer at all the meetings, where business of importance is to be transacted, and for General Deane to be present whenever military topics are raised. We have arranged for technical contacts between our high officers and General Deane on military aspects, and for any meetings which may be necessary later in our presence and that of the two Foreign Secretaries together with Mr Harriman. We shall keep you fully informed ourselves about the progress we make ...

89. Stalin-Churchill Meeting in Moscow with the representatives of the Polish Government in London, 13 October 1944, 17:00

Present: Molotov, Eden, Kerr, Harriman, Stevens, Mikołajczyk, Grabski, Romer, Mnishek, and Birse and Pavlov (interpreters)

Mikołajczyk thanked Marshal Stalin for the opportunity to come to Moscow and to be present at this meeting. He also thanked Churchill for not forgetting about the Poles. He would like to repeat briefly the content of the memorandum which was handed to Ambassador Lebedev in London some time ago. He would like to say few words about the composition of this memorandum. During his [earlier] visit to Moscow he learnt that the Soviet government had signed an agreement with the Polish Committee of National Liberation. He appreciates the prestige of the Soviet government that signed the agreement with the Polish Committee. On his return to London he decided to draw up a political programme which would be the basis for negotiations with the Soviet government. The memorandum concerns mutual relations between the two states and presents a programme to resolve internal Polish issues.

Molotov asked which memorandum is being talked about.

Mikołajczyk replied that he means the memorandum of 29 August and said that wants the whole Polish people to participate in establishing good relations with the Soviet government. The first paragraph of the memorandum talks about the reconstruction of the Polish government after the liberation of Warsaw.

Stalin said the text of the memorandum he had received talks about the reconstruction of the Polish government after the liberation of Poland

Mikołajczyk replied that he doesn't know how this mistake occurred. But even now Warsaw has not been captured.

Churchill said this misunderstanding should be noted and the discussion continued.

Mikołajczyk stated that he would like to form a new Polish government supported by the peasants', peoples' democratic, and workers' parties, as well as the Labour Party. The next paragraph of the memorandum states who is not to get into the government. Here it talks about representatives of Sanatsia and the fascist parties. Mikołajczyk thinks this represents the best basis for the unity of all the democratic parties. This new Polish government should name a President. Such a government will have diplomatic relations with the Soviet Union and then it would be possible to agree on the administration of liberated Polish territory and territories taken from Germany, also about the relationship between the Polish armed forces and the Red Army. The next paragraph of the memorandum notes the internal problems of Poland.

Churchill asked if the Polish government considered providing lines of communication to the Red Army in Poland during the German occupation.

Mikołajczyk replied that of course this was done. As he said in 1939 in Paris, there will democratic elections in Poland as soon as possible. The newly-elected parliament will devise a new constitution and elect a president on the basis of the new constitution. The next paragraph of the memorandum is about the alliance between Poland and the Soviet Union during and after the war. This alliance is based on the political and economic cooperation of the two countries and on the sovereignty and non-interference in internal affairs of the two countries. The most important thing is to exclude German interference in the affairs of Central Europe and prevent the possibility of German aggression in future. It goes without saying that Poland will rely on its alliance with Great Britain, will strive to conclude an alliance with Czechoslovakia and will maintain close friendly relations with the United States. Poland will collaborate in the restoration of peace and in the occupation of Germany. The next point of the memorandum deals with the border between the Soviet Union and Poland. We don't want Poland to have any less territory after the war. The Polish government wants the main centres of Polish cultural life in the east and the main regions of natural resources to belong to Poland. Poland lacks oil and raw materials. The question of the border should be decided in detail at the peace conference and be approved by the Polish government. As for the German territories, the Polish government would like to clear the Germans from them as it is impossible to live side by side with them. Next the memorandum expresses the desire to discuss the issue of citizenship and about Polish people removed to the Soviet Union, including those arrested. When an agreement on the eastern borders is signed, the Polish government would like to do an exchange of Ukrainian, Belorussian and Polish populations. The last paragraph of the memorandum concerns military issues. Since the Polish government doesn't want to establish a military government, a Commander-in-Chief with special rights is not stipulated. Instead it is proposed that the army will be under command of the government. The Polish government wants a Military Cabinet to deal with military issues. The first task is the continuation of the war. The next is cooperation between the Polish military and the Red Army. In the last, very important, paragraph it is stated that all Polish troops could join together to fight the Germans. He says that this memorandum had been sent to Poland and had been approved by existing Polish parties.

Stalin asked if these parties in Poland really exist and asks for a list of them.

Mikołajczyk said that these parties do exist in Poland. They are the Peasants' Party, Peoples' Democratic Party, the Socialist Party, and the Labour Party.

Stalin asked if this memorandum was approved at a congress of those parties and if it was reported in the media.

Mikołajczyk said that there was no congress of all parties called and the memorandum was approved by methods which should be very well known to Marshal Stalin after his underground work in Russia.

Stalin replied that he had never heard of a document being approved without calling a congress of parties. During illegal times in Russia, when parties were persecuted, even the Bolshevik party had six congresses, twelve conferences and 20–25 Central Committee meetings with Lenin. The party approved important documents at these conferences and conventions.

With regard to the memorandum Stalin said that in his view the memorandum has two major flaws. The first flaw is in that the memorandum ignores the existence of the Polish Committee of National Liberation. How can this fact be ignored? Mikołajczyk is aware of the huge work the Polish Committee has done. Not long ago in Poland a congress of the socialist party and Stronitstve Ludove (Peasants' Party) was called at which the practical work and line of the Polish Committee was approved. The Committee has an army. Mikołajczyk must know this. If one analyses the situation in Poland and if one analyses the ruling organs in Poland one would come to conclusion that either there is no government or there are two governments, which equates to having no government. He, Stalin, repeats that the main flaw of the memorandum is that the memorandum ignores the existence of the Polish Committee of National Liberation. The second is that it gives no answer to the question of the Curzon Line. If the Poles want to have relations with the Soviet Union without recognition of the Curzon Line such relations won't be established. What's good in the memorandum is the plan for relations between the Soviet Union and Poland after the liberation of Poland. But this plan represents only part of the general question, which mainly concerns the border between the Soviet Union and Poland. With regard to Polish internal issues, Stalin thinks the 1921 Constitution is better than the 1935 one. But this issue shouldn't become a stumbling-block between the Soviet Union and Poland. In the end its the business of the Poles to resolve these issues.

Churchill said that it seems to him that in Marshal Stalin's words there was a note of hope. He, Churchill, thinks the Polish government intends to reach an agreement with the Polish Committee of National Liberation. The memorandum does not present an obstacle to discussion. As for the border, Churchill has to say that Russia has suffered extensively in the war with Germany. Only its army has reached Poland and the British government considers the Curzon Line to be the only border between Poland and the Soviet Union in the east. He had told Polish representatives this in the last year. Of course, he knew at the time the Poles would get other territories in the west – part of Silesia and Eastern Prussia. Churchill thinks these territories in the west and in Prussia fully compensate the Poles. The Poles will get a long line of the seaboard, a good port at Danzig, and Silesia. It will be a great Poland, though in truth not like the one after the Versailles agreement, but it will be a good country for the Polish race. If Churchill was at the peace conference, he would use the same arguments, if trusted to by parliament and government.

Mikołajczyk said that Marshal Stalin was talking about the memorandum ignoring the existence of the Polish Committee. Partly that might be correct, but partly it might not. The efforts of the Polish government to organise an army, fleet and aviation have to be considered.

Stalin said that this he understands and accepts.

Mikołajczyk stated that the Polish government organised underground resistance in Poland. If Marshal Stalin recognises the Polish Committee then he ignores the Polish government in London.

Stalin replied that he does not ignore the Polish Government in London. He wants an agreement between the Polish Government and the Committee.

Mikołajczyk stated that the memorandum doesn't ignore the Committee as it suggests the formation of the government out of the five parties.

Stalin remarked that there is not one word about the Committee in the memorandum.

Mikołajczyk stated that in radio transmissions from Lublin those leaders working in liberated territories were not named, but there were telegrams which they signed. The Red Army was greeted, as well as the desire for a free and independent Poland.

Churchill stated that he doesn't understand why Mikołajczyk is saying this.

Stalin said that it seems Mikołajczyk denies the fact of the convening of the Peasants' Party congress.

Churchill said that there are more important issues to discuss than by whom, when and where those telegrams were sent.

Stalin said that's right.

Mikołajczyk states that both good and bad things are happening in the liberated territories of Poland.

Stalin remarks that it happens everywhere in the world.

Mikołajczyk remarks that it would have been better if they weren't receiving information about arrests. As for the Curzon Line he can't agree with either Marshal Stalin or with Churchill. He thinks the border question should be decided by the Polish people. It would be bad if, he, Mikołajczyk gave away 40 per cent of Polish territory and 5 million Poles

Stalin said there are not 5 million Poles there. These are Ukrainian and Belorussian territories.

Mikołajczyk states that Polish soldiers died for those territories, which they would like to return to, and he doesn't want to give them away.

Stalin said that a million and a half Ukrainians and Belorussians are fighting for these territories, and Mikołajczyk doesn't see it and wants to annex these territories. It is called imperialism.

Mikołajczyk said that he praises the bravery of Ukrainian soldiers. But what is to be done with the Poles; since autumn 1939 five million of whom have died fighting Germans or in concentration camps.

Churchill stated that the suffering of the Polish people is known to everybody. The concern now is how to end this suffering. To end the suffering it is important to form a new, united Polish government which is recognised by all the Allied powers.

Stalin said that's right.

Mikołajczyk said that if it he has to give away 40 per cent of the Polish territories then he needs a guarantee of Polish independence.

Stalin asked who is threatening Polish independence. Is it the Soviet Union?

Mikołajczyk says that he seeks independence for all Poles, so they can return to Poland.

Churchill stated that there could be a programme devised to resettle Polish people.

Stalin states that, of course, it is possible to do that and that resettlement is already taking place.

Mikołajczyk said that all governments have returned to the liberated territory of their countries except for the Polish government.

Churchill states that not all governments have returned to their countries. The aim of our negotiations, which have yet to concluded, is to discuss this question. He hopes Mikołajczyk accepts the fact that British government supports the Soviet Union in relation to the new eastern border. Whatever reservations Mikołajczyk has, this fact remains. Whatever Mikołajczyk says, it is the future of Europe that is being discussed. Marshal Stalin, as do his British and American allies, wants an independent Poland friendly to the Soviet Union.

Stalin said that all this is true. The Russians are not only saying so, they are doing so.

Churchill said that it is not acceptable for the Soviet Union to have an unfriendly neighbour. He supports demands of Russia not because it is strong but because it is right. He doesn't know which of the following proposals will be acceptable: Mikołajczyk could make a proposal that is acceptable to the Soviet Union but which would be rejected by his colleagues. On the other hand, he could say that the Polish government will make a practical decision in relation to the border for practical reasons and that it would have the right to appeal under peaceful adjudication.

Mikołajczyk stated that he would have preferred a demarcation line, but he thinks he is present at a discussion about the division of Poland.

Stalin stated that Mikołajczyk proposes to divide Ukraine and Belorussia. The Soviet government is against the division of Ukraine and Belorussia.

Mikołajczyk stated that as of now he has heard a declaration about the division of Poland but not of Germany.

Churchill stated that the division of Germany has been discussed in general terms. If a declaration about the division of Germany is made publicly it would reinforce the resistance of the Germans.

Churchill said that he appeals to Mikołajczyk to help the British government in the present matter. Britain joined the war because of Poland in spite of not being ready. The British government will consider its responsibilities fulfilled if there is a strong, independent Poland after the war. That will entail the Curzon Line and strengthening of the southern and northern borders. At this stage it would be bad for the Polish Government to separate from the British Government. That's why Churchill asks Mikołajczyk to make a brave move to safeguard peace for all of Europe.

Molotov states that he would like to add few words in relation to what was said at the Tehran conference. He would like to recall what Roosevelt said at Tehran. If he was wrong, others could correct him. He remembers well Roosevelt's statement that he was in full agreement with the Curzon Line as the border but that he considered it inadvisable to publicise this statement. Molotov thinks on this basis one could conclude that it is the opinion not only of England and the Soviet Union but the United States as well.

Mikołajczyk asked if he could learn how the question of Poland's western border was treated at Tehran.

Molotov replied that the view expressed was that the line of the Oder should be the western border of Poland. Molotov doesn't recollect if anybody was against that.

Churchill said that he supports this.

Eden said that he doesn't remember any objections. On the contrary, Poland could go as far west with its border as it wishes.

Churchill stated that Poland should be given Eastern Prussia to the west and south of Königsberg.

Stalin stated this is correct.

Churchill asked if the following formula would acceptable: a united Polish government accepts the Curzon Line as the eastern border of Poland *de facto*, reserving the right to discuss particular aspects at the peace conference.

Mikołajczyk stated he is not in a position to make such declarations.

Churchill stated that is not a declaration but a working formula. He doesn't want to make Mikołajczyk to say anything that would be rejected by his people, but the present suggestion is the best opportunity to form a united Polish state.

Mikołajczyk stated that he is being placed in a worse position than the Polish Committee, which hopes to get L'vov

Stalin stated that we are not trading Ukrainian lands and don't trade in other people's lands in general. He doesn't know what the Poles are thinking but they are not getting L'vov.

Churchill remarked that the Poles will get Danzig and territory of similar value.

Stalin said that the Poles will get those territories. The Russians think that not only Danzig will go to Poland but Stettin as well. The Russians sympathise and support this.

Churchill said that British government will also support this and asks the Poles to think seriously about the situation.

Stalin stated that to make everything clear he would like to say that the Soviet government can't accept the formula proposed by Churchill. The Soviet government can accept it with an amendment: that the Curzon Line will be the basis of the eastern border between the Soviet Union and Poland. The Soviet government can't have one border today and another one tomorrow. There are different systems in Poland and the Soviet Union. Advancing forward, the Red Army restores collective farms and Soviet power. If the border is questioned everything will have to be redone. In everything else he agrees with Churchill's proposals.

Churchill said that it follows that the Curzon Line is the basis of the border.

90. Stalin-Churchill Meeting in Moscow with representatives of the Polish Committee of National Liberation, 13 October 1944

Present: Molotov, Eden, Kerr, Harriman, Stevens, Bierut, Osóbka-Morawski, Rolya-Zhimerski, and Birse and Pavlov (interpreters)

At the beginning of the session **Molotov** reported briefly about the meeting with the representatives of the Polish government in London, which took place at 5pm today.

Stalin remarked that at this meeting the issue in question was a compromise between the Polish Committee of the National Liberation and the Polish government in London.

Churchill states that the English are very glad to meet representatives of the Lublin committee. Our aims and interests are to see a free Poland ruling itself. We are pretty upset by the differences between the Poles. Particularly regretful is that these differences are happening at the time when unity is required. We are here to achieve unity, which is possible thanks to the victories of Russia. We support our Russian ally on the Curzon Line. He hopes the Polish Committee will understand the position of the British Government. Britain joined the war because Germany attacked Poland. It was not the reason Britain entered the war, but it was a motive. The British government rallied the Poles and helped arm those Poles who escaped from France, also those who were evacuated to Persia. These Poles fought and the English value their contribution in Italy and in France. Britain gave refuge to the Polish Government, which followed General Sikorski's line. The British Government worked with the Polish Government and has faithfully maintained the ties created in those days, and everywhere in England the Poles left good memories. The British Government certainly cannot abandon people with whom they have been cooperating for five years. The same position, he hopes, is maintained by the United States. We are proud of our loyalty to our friends. He hopes the British get their due for their help in resurrecting Poland. Poland must be a strong country and friendly with Russia and other countries.

Bierut said that he would like to thank Churchill for the friendly words. He would like, on behalf of the reborn Polish state, to express his gratitude to Churchill for the friendly wishes towards the Polish people. The happiness of the Polish people is tied to the victory of the allies and he would like to do everything possible for a speedy victory. We consider the unification of the Polish people the main condition for a successful fight against the common enemy – Hitler. Krajowa Rada Narodowa put this slogan at the top from the very beginning of the struggle with the Germans. For three years Krajowa Rada Narodowa has deemed the unification of all the Polish people's forces to be not only a condition for victory over the German invaders but also the future of the Polish people. The future of the Polish nation lies with the democratic principles that unite all countries fighting the Germans. In Poland before the war there developed a tendency to violate democratic principles. Poland was a neighbour of the country which from 1933 announced the slogan of fighting democracy, and the influence of these tendencies took its toll on Poland. Expressive of the influence of those tendencies was the introduction in 1935 by the then new government of a new constitution. This constitution was forced upon the Polish people and was not approved by them. The Polish people struggled against this constitution because it deprived them of all their rights. In this regard the Polish government moved away from the democratic principles of all democratic countries, England included.

Churchill asked if it is correct that Sikorski, Mikołajczyk and others were against the 1935 constitution and that's why there were removed.

Bierut confirmed this and added that the Polish government in London is under the influence of anti-people elements. That is why the Polish Committee considers the first condition of true unity to be the renunciation of the 1935 constitution by Mikołajczyk and his colleagues. This opinion is shared by the great majority of the Polish population.

Churchill said he understands that this issue could be discussed among the Poles. The British government does not wish to interfere in purely Polish affairs. Churchill is confident this question can be discussed and hopefully resolved.

Stalin said that this issue should be resolved by the Poles themselves.

Churchill stated that Mikołajczyk has spoken out against the 1935 constitution and says that the 1921 constitution better meets the needs of the Polish people. Churchill hope that this stumbling block will be removed.

Bierut stated that Mikołajczyk's statements against the 1935 constitution notwithstanding, the Polish Committee has proof that all the legal and political actions of the Polish government in London are based on the 1935 constitution.

Churchill stated that the first task of the Poles is to help to get rid of the Germans.

Bierut replied that this is undoubtedly true, but the fact is that the emigre government is not willing to cooperate in fighting the Germans. The Polish emigre government was hoping to split the Allies, because it considered not only Germany but the Soviet Union to be an enemy of Poland. This position of the emigre Polish government made it necessary to organise those groups in the country, who for three years have fought the Germans independently from the policies of the emigre Polish government, and against those policies.

Churchill said that he hopes Bierut will understand that he, Churchill, is trying to remove difficulties. He doesn't think the question of the constitution cannot be resolved. If this is the only obstacle then it could be easily removed.

Bierut replied that this is not the only obstacle, though it is one of the major ones. The second, and the main difficulty with Mikołajczyk, concerns his relations with the Soviet Union, Poland's biggest neighbour. The Polish Committee thinks the Polish people want to have a friendly relationship with the Soviet Union.

Churchill stated that the future Polish government must maintain and strengthen friendly relations with the Soviet Union. Such is the thinking of the British government.

Bierut stated that because of that the Polish Committee concluded that the question of the border in the east has to be resolved not by war but in a friendly way, by means of a good neighbours' agreement. Poland cannot claim Ukrainian and Belorussian territories, which was a source of friction for 25 years and did not allow Poland the name of a democratic state. We would like to resolve this question by recognition of the Curzon Line as the border between the Polish and Ukrainian and Belorussian lands. We request support for the just aspirations of the Polish people and the return to the Polish people of territories annexed from Poland by Germany.

Churchill said that as far as Marshal Stalin and he is concerned, Bierut is knocking on an open door, as they have already agreed to this. The Polish Government doesn't agree with Marshal Stalin and Churchill, but he hopes they will agree. In so doing one more source of friction will be removed.

Bierut says that the Polish Committee held talks with Mikołajczyk on this question. A month ago during these talks Mikołajczyk was presented with the conditions for the unification of both parts of Polish political life. Amongst those conditions was the acceptance of the 1921 constitution, acknowledgement of the main provisions of the manifesto of the Polish Committee of the National Liberation, in which a question was posed with regard to the external policies of Poland, and those necessary reforms awaited by the Polish people, namely land reform, for which the Polish peasantry has been waiting for 200 years.

Churchill remarked that if the Polish peasantry was waiting for the reform for 200 years, then it could wait for a few more months while the Germans are being beaten. It is necessary to have territory in order to implement reforms.

Bierut said that it goes without saying the enemy has to be removed before the implementation of land reform, the problem is that reform has been promised by many governments. That is why the Polish people are asking the Polish Committee to implement reform, the people are demanding it. Mikołajczyk agreed in principle and promised to influence his colleagues towards reform. Mikołajczyk promised that he will go to London and consult them. But two months have passed and he hasn't kept his promise.

Churchill stated that land reform is just one point of the Mikołajczyk-led government programme. Churchill would like to ask if the Polish Committee would agree, if Mikołajczyk agrees, to implement reform in the course of freeing Polish lands from the enemy. Churchill thinks that while arms are still in use it is prudent to stall the reform.

Bierut says that during talks, Mikołajczyk agrees in words but in reality is not willing to work with the Polish Committee. He strives to organise officers of the Home Army against the Committee. They are conducting a brutal war against the Committee. Mikołajczyk hopes to succeed by fighting against the Committee.

Churchill stated that if civil war is being talked about, he is against anybody who starts it.

Bierut stated the Polish people want unity and reckons that if Mikołajczyk is prepared to unite then agreement can happen.

Churchill stated that it is necessary to achieve this. It is necessary to understand that it is bad for Poland and for all United Nations if the [Western] Allies recognise one Polish government and the Soviet Union another. Such a situation benefits only the Germans and is unpleasant for Allied countries. The task is to create a united Polish government acceptable to the three main Allies, so that the Allies can close ranks. Churchill thinks that Marshal Stalin will agree with him.

Stalin replied that he certainly agrees. He wants the Red Army's rear to be quiet and there to be no civil war. He, Stalin, would like to give some explanation with regard to land reform. Some think implementation of agrarian reform can wait several months and then, when all the territory is liberated, it can happen. This view is incorrect. What are the reports of Red Army political workers in Poland? What do peasants think about this question? We are told that some Polish landlords have gone with the Germans, while others remain. The land-lords are afraid to work the land as they are afraid the crop will be taken. Some of them do not have workers and workers don't go to work, thinking they are going to get the land. Thus a lot of land is not being worked. The peasants are asking why they are waiting for the lands promised to them. The issue of reform is becoming urgent. This is the situation according to reports of Red Army political workers. The peasants are not going to wait to be given the land, they are going to grab it for themselves and it will result in a fight. It would be better if the peasants are given the land at least of those landlords who left with the Germans.

Churchill asked what the peasants are demanding – collective farms or land ownership.

Stalin replied that there are no collective farms there. What's happening in Poland is similar to what was happening in France. The peasants want to take all the land into their possession.

Churchill said that it is a difficult question indeed, but for the sake of the war everything has to be done to maintain the working of the land with a view to the receipt of more production.

Stalin said that more production the better. But landlords located in London threaten terror to people implementing land reform.

Churchill remarks that if the peasants get the land it will be difficult for the landlords to take it back.

· **Osóbka-Morawski** notes that the primary difference between the Polish Committee and the Polish Government in London is that the Committee wants unity, but Mikołajczyk does not. The Committee indicated the principles on which it would like unity with Mikołajczyk, but he indicates no such principles. The Committee wants friendship with the Soviet Union but the soldiers of the Armia Krajowa are shooting the soldiers of the Red Army and Polish Army. The Committee mobilises but Mikołajczyk gives orders to ignore mobilisation.

Churchill stated that recently Morawski spoke in a negative tone about Poles who are fighting the Germans and are dying.

Morawski stated that the Committee wants to create an army, but Mikołajczyk struggles against the measures of the Committee in this regard. The Committee wants to rebuild factories, but Mikołajczyk is against. The Committee wants to restore schools, but Mikołajczyk is against.

Churchill stated that it is disappointing to hear it said that the Committee is all good and Mikołajczyk is all bad. Each side puts forward a claim against the other.

He, Churchill, is not here to listen to the complaints from one or another side, but to hear the words of reconciliation.

Osóbka-Morawski stated that he would like to say what the differences are between the Polish Committee and the Polish government. In the opinion of Mikołajczyk, General Bór(-Komorowski) and others are heroes, in the opinion of PCNL – they're not.

Churchill stated that Bór gained the sincere admiration of millions of people, not for his sensibleness, of course, but his bravery.

Stalin said that he disagrees with Churchill.

Churchill said that maybe Marshal Stalin knows more than Churchill, but he thinks the appointment of General Bór as a chief commander wasn't sensible.

Morawski states that the Polish Committee admires heroic fighters, but regard Bór and others differently, He would like to add that contrary to Mikołajczyk's statement, members of his own party not only don't support him, they are against him. This was established at party congresses, which Mikołajczyk attended. Mikołajczyk says that he is against Sanatsia but, in reality, is for it. As for land reform, it should be undertaken, otherwise the peasants will take the land themselves.

Stalin asked, don't the Poles consider it possible to achieve unity?

Bierut replied that they agree that is it but subject to the conditions he had voiced: acceptance of the 1921 constitution and immediate implementation of reforms.

Stalin asked if representatives of the Polish Committee will consider the possibility of a second meeting with Mikołajczyk.

Bierut replied that the Committee was calling all the time for unity with the London Poles, but didn't get any support from their side.

Stalin asked if the representatives of the Polish Committee are prepared to meet representatives of the Polish Government in London. To prevent a civil war, Molotov and Eden, with Harriman in attendance, would chair and run the meeting.

Bierut replied that he agrees.

91. Stalin-Churchill Meeting in Moscow, 14 October 1944, 16.30

Churchill stated that he had worked doggedly with the Poles all morning but didn't achieve much. The difficulty is that the Poles want the formal right to defend their cause at the peace conference. He, Churchill, had committed to paper everything he had conveyed to the Poles. The Polish were unhappy but they were not far from accepting it. Churchill showed Stalin a Russian translation of his proposal and said if anything that indicated a right to defend their cause at the peace conference could be added the Poles would immediately agree the text. He would like to know Marshal Stalin's impression of the document.

Stalin replied the document would be acceptable if the Curzon Line is the basis of the Polish-Soviet border.

Churchill stated that the Poles would be prepared to accept the document if it stipulates they agree with the Curzon Line under protest.

Stalin said that would not be acceptable.

Churchill stated that he can't guarantee the USA won't raise the Polish question at the peace conference. If agreement is not reached and it leaks, the Poles could make a big fuss and do a lot of harm to the President at the elections. That is why it would be better to keep this business secret for three weeks, including the document he just shown Marshal Stalin, until the elections are held in the USA.

Stalin asked if Churchill proposes to set aside the Polish question and thinks that Mikołajczyk ought to return to London, and Morawski and the others to Lublin.

Churchill replied that he thinks if the Polish question can't be resolved here in Moscow, it should be set aside for three weeks.

Excusing his candour, **Churchill** stated that if it is not possible to resolve the Polish question it won't be possible to reassure public opinion that the Lublin committee does not represent Russian will and necessity in the wake of the Red Army. Propaganda conducted by the Lublin Committee is a very effective weapon in the hands of the Polish Government in London in its campaign against the Lublin Committee. For example, Morawski berated participants in the Warsaw uprising. He has to say that these statement by Morawski do more harm than good.

Stalin noted that Morawski spoke against Bór and his masters, not the heroic population of Warsaw.

Churchill stated that there were very few communists in Poland before the war.

Stalin said that Polish people reason very simply. The Poles reckon the Red Army will liberate Poland and ask who among Polish leaders is a friend of the Red Army. The Poles can see that the Lublin committee is with the Red Army. They see that the English together with Americans are allied to the Red Army, and they ask why no representatives of the London Polish Government are with the Red Army. Polish peasants can't understand this. Mikołajczyk doesn't realise what great harm this fact does to him. As for the statement that PCNL expresses Russian will, it is incorrect as the Committee has the widespread support of the Polish people. Certainly, there are some conflicts within the Committee, but Churchill knows how capricious the Poles are.

Churchill asked that his frankness be forgiven, apologises and says that the British Government is acquainted with the biographies of the Lublin Poles. For example, it learnt that Bierut is a very capable and clever person, a communist who was imprisoned under Pilsudski but was later exchanged by the Soviet government.

Stalin said Bierut was a member of the Polish Communist party but left in 1937 or 1938. He met Bierut for the first time in Moscow recently. As to the fact of whether or not Bierut was exchanged, he would make enquiries.

Churchill stated that the British government fully sympathises with Stalin's wish for a Poland friendly to the Soviet Union.

Stalin replied that the Soviet Union needs not only a friendly, but a strong Poland. Stalin respects members of the PCNL for understanding that the Soviet

Union will not press Poles to assimilate with the Russians, as the Tsarist government did, and that the Soviet Union wants a strong and sovereign Poland. Mikołajczyk doesn't understand this, as he does not see the difference between the policy of the Tsarist and Soviet governments in relation to Poland.

Churchill stated that he is not sure if further efforts to reach agreement are needed. The fact of the matter is that if before the armistice the British government openly declared it had reached agreement with the Soviet Union in relation to the Polish border, it would be highly dangerous. But Churchill is upset that between England and the Soviet Union there should always be this unresolved Polish question, which causes a lot of trouble.

Stalin said that Mikołajczyk is influenced by the circles he moves in. The Poles in Mikołajczyk's circle are playing on the possibility of conflict among the Allies.

Churchill remarked that whether its conflict among the Allies or a critique of the Soviet Union, the Polish question is going to remain a seeping wound in relations between the Soviet Union and the Anglo-Saxon countries. The fact of the matter is that the Poles are afraid to declare formally they are renouncing their claims, though they know these claims are not going to be satisfied. He will make further efforts to try and convince the Poles to agree with the Soviet point of view and to look at the situation as a whole. The Poles must understand that if they agree they will have friendly relations with their largest neighbour, the Soviet Union. It would be silly to persist with the position in which the Poles find themselves at the moment. Churchill thinks that the future of the world depends on friendship of the British and Americans with the Soviet Union. He will be frank and say to Marshal Stalin that small European countries are scared to death of Bolshevik revolution. The explanation is that until the liquidation of the Comintern the Soviet Union declared that it intended to Sovietise the whole of Europe. He remembers that in 1919–1920 the whole world feared world revolution, although he was confident there would be no revolution in England.

Stalin replied that the world has nothing to fear now. The Soviet Union does not intend to stage Bolshevik revolutions in Europe. Churchill can look at the Romanian, Bulgarian and Yugoslavian examples.

Churchill replied that he believes all that Marshal Stalin says.

92. Military Discussion, 14 October 1944, 22.00
Present: Churchill, Stalin, Molotov Eden, Harriman, Deane, Page, Burrows, Jacob, Ismay, Brooke, Birse and Pavlov (interpreters)

Churchill asked Field Marshal Brooke [CIGS] to report on progress of operations on the Western front in Europe.

Brooke stated that the Allied advance would quicken after battles on the Seine and in Normandy. However, without ports it would be difficult for the Allies to supply its forces in Europe. Antwerp has huge significance for the Allies ...

Churchill ... The successful development of Allied operations depends, of course, on the Red Army holding down German forces in the east.

Stalin responded that the Germans cannot withdraw troops from the Eastern Front because there is no relief from active operations there.

Brooke then reported on operations in Northern Italy, pointing out that the Germans will withdraw across the Brenner Pass ... It goes without saying that if the Germans go into Switzerland they will be followed by the Allies.

Stalin remarked that Switzerland was not afraid and would use to its own advantage the Allies' flanking manoeuvres against the Germans. Switzerland looked after itself in this war, all the time helping the Germans.

Brooke stated that the Allies have prepared an amphibious landing on the Istria peninsula. The moment when the Allied armies should join up with the Russians is getting closer, he said.

Stalin remarked that the Soviet Command is not thinking about advancing to western Yugoslavia. It calculates that Allied forces will meet the Red Army in Austria.

... **General Deane** presented a report on the progress of operations in the Pacific ...

... **Antonov** [Deputy Chief of the Soviet General Staff] stated that ... Soviet forces are continuing operations on the Germans' flanks, on the left along the Baltic coast and on the right against Hungary. To invade Germany, Soviet troops must eliminate enemy forces in the Baltic area ... In Yugoslavia, Soviet troops are battling to liberate Belgrade in cooperation with the Yugoslavian People's Army. At first sight it seems that on the central part of the front there are no operations against the Germans. This is not so. On the central front attacks are unceasing and provide intelligence on enemy defences.

Churchill asked how many troops the Germans had on the Soviet-German front.

Stalin replied that there were 180 German division and 26 Hungarian divisions on the Soviet-German front.

Antonov said that Soviet forces had two main tasks: finishing operations in the Baltic area and forcing Hungary out of the war. When these operations are concluded Soviet troops stand ready to invade Germany ...

Brooke asked about the timing of the invasion of Germany.

Antonov replied that it was difficult to say as it depended on the liquidation of the enemy grouping in the Baltic area and on Hungary's exit from the war. Besides, military operations in the spring are difficult because of the rain and bad weather.

Churchill, Harriman, Brooke and Deane thanked Antonov for his report.

93. Stalin-Churchill Meeting in Moscow, 16 October 1944
Churchill stated that he had a terrible day with the Poles but worked a lot with them and has at last produced a draft agreement acceptable to them. Mikołajczyk knows he won't get L'vov and that he can't escape the Curzon Line but says that if he is unable to tell the Polish people they have the right to defend their cause at the peace conference, the Polish people are not going to accept him.

Stalin, having studied the document proposed by Churchill, said the statement that the Curzon Line is a demarcation line is not acceptable.

Churchill stated that he pressed the Poles hard, was rather rude with them, and this is the maximum that he could get out of them. He would like to ask Marshal Stalin whether in the event of an agreement about the border, it would it be acceptable to publish the agreement. He thinks that Mikołajczyk and Romer could meet Stalin for private talks with the aim of reaching agreement about a new Polish government. Mikołajczyk hopes that Marshal Stalin will see him and Romer. Then both Polish groups could meet, and Eden could stay in Moscow and assist in reaching agreement. He, Churchill, would like to separate from other topics the hotly discussed question of the border with the Soviet Union, which has acquired an international importance.

Stalin remarked that if the question of the border is solved then all other questions can be resolved. The proposed formulation of a demarcation line between the Soviet Union and Poland, is not acceptable, as it would mean that Soviet Union wouldn't have a permanent state border.

Churchill replied that in English there's little difference between a border and a demarcation line. He hopes that Marshal Stalin appreciates that in England, and perhaps in America, there will be a lot of people who will criticise him for acting on his own, without the US government, to tie the British Government to a formal and public agreement with the Soviet Government about the Curzon Line. Many will say that Churchill breached the Atlantic Charter. But he is ready to take that risk, not for the sake of Poland, of course. He is putting himself in a risky position but is ready to put his political career on line. He thinks that after the declaration is published, it will be of little consequence what Poles across the world say. But they would need to say something to denote their agreement in view of their relations with England and America. To make the proposed formulation acceptable to the Soviet Government Churchill will include words indicating the British Government agrees with and supports the Curzon Line as the basis of the border between Soviet Union and Poland. The crux of the matter according to Mikołajczyk is that if the Polish Government utters the word 'border' the Polish people will reject the idea. Then the Polish Government will lose all its value and there will be nobody to deal with. He asks Stalin to consider very seriously the consequences, which will be unpleasant for all. Not reaching agreement here, Mikołajczyk will return to London and might resign. Then, Churchill presumes, the Polish Government could veer to the right and though it would have less power, it would have a louder voice. All the efforts of the Allies would be rendered difficult by the loud noise the Polish Government is sure to produce. In Poland there could be civil war. He asks Stalin to consider the seeping wound, not in relations with Poland, but in relations with the English-speaking countries. This wound will open merely because of the words 'border' and 'demarcation line', at a time when he, Churchill, desires unity above all else. Perhaps Stalin could suggest another wording.

Stalin replied that he suggests saying the Curzon Line is recognised as the basis of the state border between Poland and Soviet Union. Further, in the paragraph about the creation of a new Polish government the existence of the Polish Committee of National Liberation can't be ignored. Therefore, it is desirable to formulate it as follows: 'Agreement has been reached that on territory liberated by Russian troops a Polish government of national unity will be immediately formed by an agreement (or an understanding) between the Polish government in London and the Polish Committee of National Liberation in Lublin.' Given that Mikołajczyk would be the head of the new Polish government, he would support this.

Churchill replied that he will to do everything possible but is not confident of success. However, he would like to ask Stalin, drawing on the suggestion that the wording on the border will be agreed with the Poles, does he think that both Polish groups should meet in the presence of the English and Soviet foreign ministers and Ambassador Harriman? Or should the Poles meet between themselves? In that case, however, the Poles are going to argue. Finally, one could bring the Poles together after they have met with Stalin separately. Churchill thinks the latter procedure has more chance of success.

Stalin replied that he could meet both groups of Poles and after that they could meet one another, without the foreign ministers and Harriman, whose presence could give the Poles the impression they are under pressure.

Churchill said that while in some cases he answers questions directly 'yes' or 'no', in others, when he is proposing this or that, he needs to consult the British Cabinet for final confirmation. In this case Churchill would like to propose a formulation, which has yet to be confirmed by the British Cabinet. He proposes to add to 'taking into account the above agreement, the Polish government accepts the Curzon Line as the demarcation line between Poland and USSR', the following words: 'while the Soviet and British governments agree that Curzon Line should be the border'. Churchill adds that it is necessary to bear in mind that the Soviet Union will, firstly, have its power, secondly, the consent of the English, and, thirdly, the Soviet Union will get, in the form of this wording, something that will be understood by everybody as the consent and submission of the Poles. Never has any border been so solidly established.

Stalin remarked that this wording will be read as recognition by the British and Soviet governments of the Curzon Line as the border, while the Polish Government does not tie itself to recognising the Curzon Line as the border.

Churchill said that Mikołajczyk is afraid of rejection by the Polish people if he agrees unequivocally to the Curzon Line as the border.

Stalin said that Mikołajczyk is not agreeing because he hopes the Polish Committee of National Liberation is not going to hold on to power in Poland. Mikołajczyk's statement that Polish people are going to reject him if he agrees to the Curzon Line as the border is just blackmail. The Polish Committee of National Liberation has said several times to the press and at meetings that for the sake of peace and friendship between Poland and Russia, the Curzon Line – which is approved by the governments of England, America and Soviet Union – is the only possible border between Poland and Soviet Union and that without recognition of the Curzon Line it is impossible to be friends with Russia. The Polish people didn't protest against these statements, on the contrary, they approved of them. This is a very good precedent, which makes all Mikołajczyk's fears contrived and not meaningful. As a result of assuming this position, Mikołajczyk is losing his authority among the Polish population, as Poles are asking why Mikołajczyk is not with the Red Army.

Churchill replied that some people are asking these questions, while others aren't. The British Government can judge the situation in Poland only on the basis of information they have gathered. Every week people who are going to and from England and the liberated areas of Poland are bringing information. He fears there could be uprisings and civil war in Poland, which will not only cost many Polish lives but also create difficulties in relations between the great nations. He would like to draw Stalin's attention to the fact that the statement of PCNL, cited by Stalin, about the Curzon Line being accepted by America does not correspond to reality. He had talks with Harriman and he doesn't think Molotov's statement at the meeting with the Poles about Roosevelt's position at Tehran on the border between Soviet Union and Poland was correct.

Stalin replied that Molotov gave an account of what Roosevelt stated at Tehran to me, too. Roosevelt agreed to the Curzon Line, including the handover of L'vov to the Soviet Union. The President indicated only that he didn't wish his position on Polish question to become public because it would hinder his election campaign.

Churchill said that he didn't know this but thinks that nothing would impede the President's election campaign more severely than no agreement with the Poles and news of the discussion of the present document. He would like to come back to the proposed document and draw Stalin's attention to the statement about the repatriation and resettlement of people from both countries, which attests to the settlement of the question of the border being of a permanent character. The Soviet Union will have the right to occupy all lands east of the Curzon Line and establish its own administration there. If it was possible to obtain Mikołajczyk's agreement there would be no unpleasantness from international public opinion.

Stalin said that he hadn't heard from Mikołajczyk one word of gratitude to the Red Army, which is liberating Poland. Mikołajczyk wants to finesse everyone. He thinks the Russians are in his service.

Churchill said that Stalin got as much gratitude from the Pole as he, Churchill, got from de Gaulle, i.e. very little. When, six weeks ago, Churchill went through Cairo, he wanted to see de Gaulle but de Gaulle didn't want to meet him, intentionally giving offence to Churchill.

Stalin asked what to do with the Poles now. Should they organise a meeting between the Lublin and London Poles? The Lublin Poles already want to go back.

Churchill stated that perhaps Stalin remembers the history of the Portsmouth Treaty. Witte was sent to negotiate with the Japanese under instruction from the Tsar not to sign any agreement with them. It was anticipated the Japanese would demand a big indemnity from Russia. Witte was to refuse the point about indemnities and not sign an agreement. But [Theodore] Roosevelt, the then President of United States, proposed that the negotiating parties move to other points of the agreement, leaving the question about indemnities unresolved. The participants proceeded to the discussion of further points and in the end the Japanese abandoned the indemnities demand. The agreement was signed and Witte was relieved of his post on his return to Russia. He, Churchill, will now return to trying to make bricks without straw, i.e. the hopeless job of trying to convince Mikołajczyk to accept Stalin's amendments.

Stalin said he thinks that sooner or later Mikołajczyk will accept the Curzon Line.

94. Churchill to Stalin, 17 October 1944

My dear Marshal Stalin,

We have had further conversations with Mikołajczyk, and we have made progress. I am more than ever convinced of his desire to reach an understanding with you and with the National Committee, despite the very real difficulties that confront him. Mikołajczyk is anxious to see you himself alone, in order to tell you what his plans now are and to receive your advice ...

I am looking forward to our conversation tonight on the question of the dismemberment of Germany. I think, as I feel you agreed yesterday, that we can clarify and focus our ideas with a precision which was certainly lacking at Tehran, when victory seemed so much more distant than now.

Finally let me tell you what a great pleasure it has been to me to find ourselves talking on the difficult and often unavoidably painful topics of state policy with so much ease and mutual understanding.

My daughter Sarah will be delighted with the charming token from Miss Stalin and will guard it among her most valued possessions.

I remain, with sincere respect and goodwill,

Your friend and war comrade, Winston Churchill

95. Stalin-Churchill Meeting in Moscow, 17 October 1944, 22.00

Molotov, Eden, Kerr, Birse and Pavlov (interpreters)

Churchill stated that very soon Soviet citizens freed by English forces in Western Europe would be sent from England to the Soviet Union. Most of these people were forcibly mobilised into the German army. Entire battalions were surrendering to the English.

Stalin remarked that there are traitors among these people, but we won't be too strict with them.

Churchill said that he feels entitled to ask about these people as they had surrendered to the English.

Stalin asked if Churchill is going to talk about the division of Germany.

Eden stated that British government hasn't reached any conclusion and hasn't discussed this question in Cabinet. It appears there are several ways to divide Germany. One of these is division of Germany into several states that have nothing common with previous German states. The difficulty with such a division is the absence of lines to determine the borders. The second possibility is the division of Germany on the basis of previous German states as a frame. The third possibility is establishment of permanent international control over the Ruhr,

Rhine and Saar regions after Russia and other allies have removed all equipment and machinery from German industry as compensation for damages suffered. To do this successfully it would be necessary to separate these regions from the rest of Germany. Personally, Eden thought it possible to discuss now this plan for division of Germany.

Molotov asked what 'international control' means.

Eden replied that this control will be political and economic and will be carried out by the Allies.

Stalin said it was a good plan. Heavy industry in Germany is the source of its strength.

Churchill said that, in his opinion, Prussia is the cause of evil. Prussia should be separated from Germany. Then he would like to divest Germany of control over the Ruhr and Saar regions. How this could be done can be discussed. In the first place, it is necessary to take from Germany a large amount of machinery, needed by other countries such as the Soviet Union, Belgium, Holland and France. Churchill knows that the western parts of Ukraine suffered greatly from the war and he supports reconstruction of these western regions of Soviet Union using equipment from German industry. He thinks this would be entirely just. But he thinks that some smaller allies should get their share of the disposed equipment from German industry. This removal will, of course, be followed by standstill in the Ruhr and Saar. In Quebec this plan was argued passionately by Morgenthau whose hatred of the Germans is indescribable. It seems the President supports Morgenthau and he asked why wouldn't England start producing goods for Europe in competition with other countries. Marshal Stalin will understand that England will come out of this war as the world's biggest debtor. Before Lend-Lease England spent all its foreign currency of 4 billion pounds on supplies. England has a mountain of sterling debt in different countries. After the war England has to increase its exports to be able to buy food. Hence the Russian interest in acquiring German equipment is, to an extent, in harmony with England's intention, to replace Germany as a supplier of goods for small countries in Europe. The interests of Soviet Union and England are heading in the same direction.

Stalin remarked that measures could be taken to recover the losses suffered by England. It needs to be thought about.

Churchill stated that he supports the Soviet Union getting the equipment from Germany. Churchill wouldn't like to entrust to the Germans highly developed chemical, metal and electrotechnical industries. He hasn't thought about how to divide Prussia, to isolate it and separate it from the two centres of heavy industry – the Ruhr and the Saar.

Stalin remarked that what remains of Prussia after the transfer of territory to Poland and the Soviet Union could become a separate state.

Churchill remarked that he hasn't made any decision in this regard but thinks that most of Prussia, namely Silesia, should go to Poland and the Königsberg region to the west and south of it to the Soviet Union. The Kiel canal should be neutralised, i.e. put under international control, also the Ruhr and Westphalia.

Stalin asked if a separate state should be created from the Ruhr and Westphalia?

Churchill replied that he hadn't thought about it, only about the destruction of German industry. He remembers very well the end of the last war. The Allies forbade Germany to have an air force, fleet and army and destroyed all German armaments. But the Allies didn't touch industry and this allowed Germany to revive.

Stalin remarked that it is not advisable to destroy all German tanks, to blow up the artillery and sink the ships, as this military equipment could be used in the war against Japan.

Churchill remarked that the Soviet Union can take whatever armaments it likes.

Stalin said the ships shouldn't be sunk as they will be of use to the English.

Churchill remarked that this war has shown that aviation is more important than a navy.

Stalin said that all the same a navy has a great significance. In his opinion, the greatest mistake Germany made was to try to conquer Europe without a strong enough navy.

Churchill agreed with this and said that England would welcome the existence of a powerful Russian fleet.

Stalin remarked that Soviet Union is a long way from this. It is easier to create an army than a navy.

Going back to what he said about the end of the last war, **Churchill** remarked that at the time a German industrialist – a Jew, [Walther] Rathenau – declared to the Germans after they had lost their fleet and army, that he would build factories that will give Germany enough arms. Rathenau added that if Germany built factories it could become a mighty state. But not one German leader until Hitler came along tried to develop manufacturing in Germany. The Allies shouldn't repeat this mistake as they do not want renewed German aggression.

Stalin said that we do not want this either.

That's why, said **Churchill**, he's talking about the industrial disarmament of Germany. That is what has to be done after the removal of equipment from Germany.

Stalin remarked that Germans should be divested of metal production. It's worth remembering that before the war Germany produced 40 million tons of crude iron a year i.e. more than England.

Churchill agreed with this.

Further conversation took place at the map.

Churchill and **Eden** presented a plan for the division of Germany into three states: Prussia, an international control zone consisting of the Ruhr, Westphalia and Saar regions, and an Austrian-Bavarian state incorporating the south German provinces.

Stalin approved the scheme and said that the division of Germany into three states is better than into five, as the President proposed in Tehran.

Churchill asked what the Russians would think about a plan to unite Poland, Czechoslovakia, Hungary and Austria into one group.

Stalin said that it needs to be thought about.

Churchill remarked that Europe is harmed by the existence of 10–15 different currencies and dozens of customs zones. It was impeding trade. Churchill would like to see Europe prosper and it was necessary to find some form of economic unity for European states, such as a Customs Union.

Stalin remarked that for the first 3–4 years after the war a nationalistic mood is going to prevail in Hungary, Czechoslovakia and Poland. The first wish of those nations will be to organise their own national life. These countries will object to the infringement of their rights by way of uniting them with other countries. Thus it is unlikely the peoples of Europe will agree to a customs union. Hitler's regime engendered nationalistic sentiments to such an extent that even in Yugoslavia not only the Croatians, but the Montenegrins, Slovenes, Serbs and other small nations, all want to have their autonomy. In the first years after the war one feeling will prevail over other sentiments – the desire to live a full national life without interference. After the last war a few unviable states were created, and they suffered bankruptcy because their creation had little basis. But it would be dangerous to rush to the other extreme and make small nations unite with each other. It is difficult to imagine Czechs and Hungarians, even the Czechs and the Poles, finding a common language. Unification is not possible at present but it is not excluded in the future.

Churchill thought that Germans should not have any aviation.

Stalin replied that Germans mustn't have any aviation – military or civil, and should be prohibited from having aviation colleges.

Churchill said that the Germans should not to be allowed to use German ships to navigate the seas and oceans.

Stalin replied that he agreed with Churchill.

Churchill remarked that he sees very little differences between him and Stalin.

Churchill asked if Stalin has any questions.

Stalin replied that he has one question for Churchill. He would like to ask Churchill to remember about the [Black Sea] Straits.

Churchill said that he accepted the validity of the Soviet Union's demands in relation to the Straits and he is ready to look at the issue when the Soviet side present its demands.

Churchill asked if there is any news about developments in Hungary.

Stalin replied that there is news that [Admiral] Horthy [Hungarian dictator] has been arrested. Stalin said that he heard the English consider 400 million dollars – the reparation sum to be taken from Hungary – to be too high. He would like to ask if Churchill will consider a sum of 300 million dollars, with 200 million going to Soviet Union and 100 million to other allies who suffered from Hungarian aggression.

Eden and **Churchill** replied that it seems to be acceptable to them but they don't know how it would be regarded by the Americans, who are very hardline on the reparations issue.

96. Stalin to Churchill, 19 October 1944

Dear Mr Churchill,

On the day of your departure from Moscow please accept from me two modest gifts as souvenirs of your stay in the Soviet capital: the vase 'Helmsman on a Boat' is for Mrs Churchill and the vase 'Hunter With Bow Against Bear' for yourself.

Once again, I wish you good health and good cheer.

97. Churchill to Stalin, 19 October 1944

My dear Marshal Stalin,

I have just received the two beautiful vases which you have given to me and my wife as a souvenir of this memorable visit to Moscow. We shall treasure them among our most cherished possessions.

I have had to work very hard here this time and also have received an Air Courier every day entailing decisions about our own affairs. Consequently, I have not been able to see any of the City of Moscow, with all its historic memories. But in spite of this, the visit has been from beginning to end a real pleasure to me on account of the warm welcome we have received, and most particularly because of our very pleasant talks together.

My hopes for the future alliance of our peoples have never stood so high. I hope you may long be spared to repair the ravages of war and lead All The Russias out of the years of storm into glorious sunshine.

Your friend and war-time comrade, Winston S. Churchill.

Chapter 8

Yalta and Potsdam: Triumph or Tragedy?

Not long after Churchill left Moscow Stalin had another important visitor: General Charles de Gaulle, the leader of the Free French. In his conversations with Roosevelt at Tehran Stalin had criticised de Gaulle for having illusions that he and the Free French represented the real France – a country that, in reality, had collaborated with the Germans and had to be punished – remarks of Stalin's that the Soviets expunged from their published record of the conference, which appeared shortly after the General returned to power in 1958.[1]

In April 1944 the French communists joined de Gaulle's French Committee of National Liberation and then agreed to serve in the provisional government the General now headed. Face to face with de Gaulle in Moscow in December 1944 Stalin oozed personal charm and expressed full understanding for France's position and aspirations. At his first meeting with the General, on 2 December, Stalin emphasised that he supported the restoration of France as a great power.[2]

De Gaulle's trip to Moscow was at his request and aimed to enhance liberated France's prestige by the conclusion of a Franco-Soviet pact similar to the 1942 Anglo-Soviet treaty of alliance. Stalin was happy to sign such a treaty, though he made sure Churchill and Roosevelt had no objections. Stalin tried to leverage some support from de Gaulle for the Soviet position on the Polish question. Molotov suggested to his French counterpart, Georges Bidault, that France exchange representatives with the Polish Committee of National Liberation (PCNL). Poland also loomed large in Stalin's second conversation with de Gaulle, on 6 December. In defence of the Soviet position on Poland, Stalin reminded de Gaulle that the Curzon Line had been supported by French Prime Minister Clemenceau after the First World War and pointed out that twice in the last 30 years Poland had been used as a corridor for a German invasion of Russia. Stalin also defended Soviet actions in relation to the Warsaw Uprising, saying that by the time the Red Army reached the Polish capital its offensive had penetrated to a depth of 600 kilometres and its artillery shells had to be shipped 400 kilometres to the front.

At their third and final meeting, on 8 December, de Gaulle raised the German question and Stalin warmed to his pet theme of the need to keep the Germans down, telling the General that he thought the British would take a hard line against Germany. When de Gaulle suggested that, judging by Versailles, Britain's commitment to a punitive peace would not last long, Stalin told him that this time around it would be possible to dismantle German industry and that the

British understood the importance of this. The question of French relations with the PCNL also came up and Stalin told de Gaulle that Churchill had suggested a tripartite pact involving Britain, rather than just a bilateral Franco-Soviet pact. De Gaulle did not like this idea; he wanted a bilateral agreement with Stalin on a par with the Anglo-Soviet pact. Stalin said that he would sign such a pact if de Gaulle would agree to exchange official representatives with the PCNL. 'Let the French do us a favour and we will do them one', Stalin told the General. At the end of the conversation de Gaulle came back to the Polish question and expressed great sympathy for the Soviet position. In relation to the PCNL he said that the French had already suggested an exchange of representatives with the Poles.

On 9 December Bidault told Molotov that de Gaulle was willing to exchange representatives with the PCNL in return for a Franco-Soviet pact. However, Molotov also wanted the French to publish a statement to this effect in the form of an exchange of letters between de Gaulle and the Chairman of the PCNL. This would have been tantamount to diplomatic recognition of the Lublin government – a step the Soviets had yet to take formally themselves. Bidault told Molotov that his proposal was unacceptable. It seems that discussions continued that night at the farewell dinner for the French delegation. Perhaps to oil the wheels of negotiation Stalin suggested to de Gaulle that they should 'bring out the machine guns. Let's liquidate these diplomats!'[3] Such drastic action was not necessary and the Franco-Soviet treaty of mutual aid was signed the next day. But the French got their way on the non-publication of a statement on the exchange of representatives with the PCNL and were able to present the deal to the British and Americans as a decision to exchange low-level representatives. Stalin, on the other hand, told the PCNL that it had been a hard-won concession and lambasted de Gaulle as a died-in-the-wool reactionary.[4]

The underlying reason for Soviet pressure on the French over the Polish question became apparent on 4 January 1945 when Moscow announced it was officially recognising the PCNL as the provisional government of Poland. This statement ended the prospect of any further negotiations with the exiled Poles in London about the formation of a united Polish government, although it did not rule out talks with the likes of former Premier Mikołajczyk. With the Red Army about to resume its march on Warsaw, Stalin had evidently decided to pursue his political goals in Poland through the pliable offices of the PCNL.

It was Roosevelt's idea to hold a second meeting of the Big Three and he originally hoped to hold the conference in Scotland in September 1944, but Stalin demurred about the date because of military commitments and then suggested a Black Sea port as a venue. Stalin hated flying and he could travel to the Black Sea coast by train. By this stage, however, the American presidential election was in progress and it was decided to postpone the conference until after Roosevelt's inauguration for his fourth term in January 1945. Eventually, agreement was reached on Yalta as the conference venue.

The Yalta, or Crimean Conference as the Soviets called it (4–11 February 1945), was an altogether grander affair than Tehran. The delegations were larger

(700 British and Americans alone), the agenda wider-ranging and many more decisions were taken. Tehran had been mainly about the war; Yalta focussed on the emerging post-war order.

The setting was Tsar Nicholas II's magnificent fifty-room Livadia Palace in the spa town of Yalta. It had been badly damaged by the Germans but was restored in time for the conference. The palace was several hours' drive from Saki airport where the Westerners' planes landed so they had a good opportunity to view the damage the peninsula had suffered as a result of war. 'Roosevelt, travelling in the lead car with his daughter, Anna Boettiger, marked the sights of the war with rising bitterness against the Germans', recalled Harriman. '"I'm more blood-thirsty than a year ago", he said to Stalin the following day.'[5] Apart from Soviet staff, Boettiger was one of only three women who attended the Yalta conference; the other two were Churchill's daughter, Sarah, and Harriman's daughter Kathleen, who was brought along to keep Anna company. Kathy wrote a series of letters about her experiences at Yalta. In one letter she recorded that her father had seen Churchill, who was

> all set for the worst. But maybe that mood will change ... At Chequers the P.M. holds forth and everyone listens, but here there's just general conversation ... Ave ... said he had never seen Stalin in such great form. He really was terrific. He enjoyed himself, was a splendid host ... At times Stalin just sat back and smiled like a benign old man, something I'd never thought possible. Anyway, I was much impressed. He toasted Churchill as the great leader who'd taken command when England was without fighting allies.[6]

There has been a lot of speculation and comment about the poor state of Roosevelt's health, much of it shaped by the knowledge that he died a few months later. However, in her letters from Yalta to Pamela Churchill, Kathy conveyed a different impression: 'The Pres is absolutely charming, easy to talk to on any subject ... [he's] getting a big kick out of presiding over meetings ... There was great rejoicing last night. They sold U.J. on Dumbarton Oaks. Very good indeed. At dinner the President was in great form.'[7]

As at Tehran, there were bilateral meetings among the Big Three as well as the tripartite plenary sessions. Stalin met with both Churchill (**Document 113**) and Roosevelt on the first day of the conference, 4 February. With Churchill he chatted about military matters and with Roosevelt continued the carping about de Gaulle they had begun at Tehran. The first plenary session began at 5.00pm that day with Stalin inviting Roosevelt to open the proceedings. The plenary then turned to an exchange of information and views about the military situation on the various fronts.[8]

At dinner that night, Churchill challenged Stalin's assertion that big powers like Britain, the United States and the Soviet Union could not be expected to submit to the judgement of small powers. Churchill argued that while there was no question of small states dictating to great powers, 'greatness carried with it a moral responsibility to exercise power with moderation and respect for the rights of weaker nations. "The eagle", said Churchill, "should permit the small birds to sing and care not wherefor they sang"".[9]

The first formal political discussion at Yalta took place at the second plenary session on 5 February. The topic was the future of Germany, and Stalin pushed again for definite commitments to dismember it. Referring to his discussions with Churchill in Moscow the previous October, Stalin noted that Roosevelt's absence meant it had not been possible to take decisions on the dismemberment of Germany, but 'had not the time come for decision on this question?' As the conversation developed, Stalin interrupted Churchill to ask 'when the question of the dismemberment of Germany would be put before the new people in Germany? The thing is this question is not in the conditions of capitulation. Perhaps a clause on the dismemberment of Germany should be added to the terms of surrender?' Responding to Roosevelt's suggestion that the matter should be referred to the three foreign ministers, Stalin said that while one could accept this 'compromise proposal', 'it was necessary to say directly that we consider it necessary to dismember Germany'. But Stalin conceded that it would be unwise to publicise dismemberment too far in advance since Nazi propagandists would use it to stiffen German resistance

When the discussion moved on to the question of whether or not France should be given a zone of occupation in Germany, Stalin opposed the move, arguing the French did not deserve it and that such a decision would lead to demands from other Allied countries for a share in the occupation: 'It is impossible to forget the past. In this war France opened the gate to the enemy. This cost the Allies colossal sacrifices in Europe. This is why we cannot place France on the same level as the three great allies.' Stalin relented only when it was made clear the French zone would be carved out of territories to be occupied by the British and Americans. But he continued to oppose the inclusion of France on the Allied Control Commission (ACC) for Germany, notwithstanding British arguments that it was illogical to allow the French an occupation zone but to deny them representation on the ACC.

Stalin was evidently not prepared to continue that discussion so he switched the debate to the more comfortable topic of reparations and announced that Maisky, who was sitting beside him, would make a presentation on the Soviet behalf. Maisky, who had been recalled from his ambassadorship in London to head the Foreign Commissariat's Reparations Commission, whispered to Stalin that they had yet to put a figure on Soviet reparations demands. Molotov, who was sitting on the other side of Stalin, intervened in this huddle and it was agreed on the spot to demand $10 billion in reparations rather than $5 billion, the low-end figure that had featured in Soviet internal discussions before the conference.[10]

Maisky duly gave his report outlining the principles of the Soviet reparations plan. First, reparations would be paid by Germany in kind, not money. Second, Germany would pay reparations in the form of lump withdrawals of factories, machinery, vehicles and tools from its national wealth at the end of the war and annual deliveries of goods thereafter. Third, Germany would be economically disarmed by reparations, leaving only 20 per cent of its pre-war heavy industry intact. Fourth, reparations would be paid over a 10-year period. Fifth, to implement the reparations policy the German economy would have to be strictly controlled by Britain, the United States and the USSR for a prolonged period. Sixth, all Allied countries damaged by Germany would be compensated by reparations, with those that had suffered most receiving the biggest payments. When it came to the compensation figure for the Soviet Union, Maisky played safe and spoke of at least $10 billion. He concluded by proposing the establishment of an Anglo-American-Soviet Reparations Commission that would meet in Moscow and negotiate the details of the plan.

In the ensuing discussion both Churchill and Roosevelt argued that the experience of the First World War cast doubt on the wisdom of trying to extract reparations from Germany, but they agreed to establish the Reparations Commission. At the end of the session Churchill, alluding to Karl Marx's slogan that socialism was based on the principle of 'from each according to his ability, to each according to his needs', quipped that he thought the reparations plan should be based on the principle of 'each according to their needs, and in Germany's case according to her abilities [to pay]'. Stalin said that he 'preferred another principle: each according to their deserts'.

At the third plenary session on 6 February the Big Three discussed the issue of the voting rights of the great powers in the proposed United Nations organisation. Stalin stressed that the agreed procedure had to be designed to avoid divergences among the great powers and the aim was to construct an organisation that would ensure peace for at least 50 years. This first discussion was inconclusive, but the voting issue was resolved amicably later in the conference by adoption of the great power veto principle that the UN Security Council retains to this day. It was also agreed that the states invited to the founding conference of the UN in San Francisco would include any country that declared war on Germany by the end of the month, a device designed by Churchill to allow Turkey to attend (Ankara declared war on Germany on 23 February 1945) but to exclude neutral states such as Ireland that had not been as cooperative as the British Prime Minister thought they should have been.

A much thornier issue, raised by Churchill at the session on 6 February, was the question of Poland; specifically, the question of recognising the pro-Soviet 'Lublin Poles' as the Polish Provisional Government (a misnomer, as by this time the PCNL had moved to Warsaw). Both Churchill and Roosevelt wanted the so-called Lublin government replaced by a broad-based provisional government that would reflect Polish public opinion. In response Stalin strongly defended the Soviet Union's Polish policy, pointing out that the reestablishment of a strong and independent but friendly Poland was a vital matter of security for the USSR. He argued, too, that 'the new Warsaw Government ... has no less a democratic basis than, for example, the government of de Gaulle' – a point that Churchill contested, saying that it had the support of less than a third of the Polish population.

In the discussion about Poland, Churchill and Stalin rehearsed their positions once again. For Churchill Poland's independence was a matter of honour because Britain had gone to war on its behalf, while for Stalin it was a matter of security, Poland having served yet again as a corridor for aggression against Russia.[11] When Churchill and Stalin had their second bilateral meeting, on 10 February, Poland was one of the main topics of conversation (**Document 114**).

After the third plenary session Roosevelt wrote Stalin a note making it clear the US would not recognise the Lublin government, proposing instead the formation of a new government consisting of Poles based in Poland and those living abroad, including former members of the London Government-in-Exile such as Mikołajczyk. In response, at the fourth plenary session on 7 February the Soviets tabled a proposal on Poland consisting of three main components: (a) recognition of the Curzon Line; (b) Poland's western border to run along the Oder–Neisse line; and (c) the enlargement of the Lublin government to include 'democratic leaders' from Poles living abroad. This proposal, essentially a variation on the position the Soviets had been pushing for a year or more, provoked much discussion, extending over several plenary sessions both of the Big Three and of the three foreign ministers – Eden, Molotov and Edward Stettinius (who had replaced Hull as American Secretary of State) – who were meeting separately as well as attending the plenaries. Eventually it was agreed that 'the Provisional Government which is now functioning in Poland' would be 'reorganised on a broader democratic basis with the inclusion of democratic leaders from Poland itself and from Poles abroad. This new Government should then be called the Polish Provisional Government of National Unity.' The Curzon Line was agreed as Poland's eastern frontier but the details of its western frontier with Germany were left open for further discussion at a future peace conference. Agreement on a government formula for liberated Yugoslavia proved much easier to reach and the decision was quickly taken that the communist leader Tito and the Yugoslav exile politicians should form a united government.

Equally congenial was the discussion about Soviet participation in the Far Eastern war, the subject considered by Stalin and Roosevelt at a bilateral meeting on 8 February. The agreement reached was that the USSR would abrogate the Soviet–Japanese neutrality pact of April 1941 and join the war in the Far East two or three months after the defeat of Germany. In return the Soviet Union would regain the territories and concessions Imperial Russia had lost to Japan as a result of defeat in the Russo-Japanese war of 1904–5. South Sakhalin would be returned, and the Kuril Islands handed over to the Soviet Union as well. Port Arthur on the Chinese mainland would be leased to the USSR as a naval base, while nearby Dairen would be internationalised and Soviet interests in the port safeguarded. A joint Soviet–Chinese company would be established to safeguard Moscow's railway transit rights through Manchuria.

Important to the success of the conference was the work of the Big Three's interpreters – Arthur Birse for Churchill, Charles Bohlen for Roosevelt and Vladimir Pavlov for Stalin. At the dinner he hosted on 9 February, Stalin proposed a toast to the interpreters. In response Churchill raised his glass and exclaimed: 'Interpreters of the world unite! You have nothing to lose but your audience.' 'This parody of the Communist Manifesto slogan so tickled Stalin's sense of humour', recalled Birse, 'that it was some time before he could stop laughing.'[12] At the same dinner Stalin proposed a toast to Churchill, the man without whom Britain would not have been able to stand up to Hitler. 'He could think of no other instance in history', said Stalin, 'where the future of the world depended on the courage of one man.'[13]

On 11 February 1945 the Big Three met for the last time to agree the communiqué issued at the end of the conference that announced the Big Three's policy on Germany, the United Nations, Poland and Yugoslavia. It also contained the text of a Declaration on Liberated Europe that committed Britain, the Soviet Union and the United States to the destruction of Nazism and fascism and the establishment of a democratic Europe based on free elections. In conclusion the three leaders pledged to maintain wartime unity and to create the conditions for a secure and lasting peace. As well as this statement of policy there was a confidential protocol setting out the decisions of the conference the Big Three did not want to make public, for example in relation to the USSR's entry into the Far East war.

Stalin had every reason to be pleased with the results of Yalta. On almost every policy issue the Soviet position had prevailed. The Big Three had got on well once again and Stalin had proved to be as effective a negotiator as he had been at Tehran. The only major concession to Western wishes was the Declaration on Liberated Europe. But the Soviet interpretation of this document emphasised its anti-fascist rather than its democratic character and, anyway, Stalin was confident his communist allies across Europe would form part of the broad-based coalition governments the declaration spoke of and would do very well in the elections that followed. Later, when Harriman congratulated him on the Red Army capturing Berlin, Stalin pointed out that Tsar Alexander I had got to Paris when he defeated Napoleon. But what Stalin had in mind was political, not military, expansion further west. As Harriman observed, Stalin only resorted to repression and outright domination of the states in central and eastern Europe that he controlled when it turned out that his leftist allies were not as popular as he expected them to be.[14]

Within a few weeks of Yalta, Stalin was in a more pessimistic mood about relations with Churchill and Roosevelt and at a reception for a visiting Czechoslovak delegation at the end of March 1945 complained about the Western Allies' kid-gloves treatment of Germany. Partly this reflected his disappointment with Churchill and Roosevelt's resistance to dismembering Germany. Compounding Stalin's bad mood was the so-called 'Berne crisis'. At the end of February General Karl Wolff, a high-ranking SS officer, had contacted US intelligence agents about arranging a ceasefire in Italy and had meetings with them in Switzerland. When told about these contacts the Soviets asked to be involved in any negotiations. The Americans did not think this was necessary but Moscow, suspecting a plot to facilitate transfer of German forces from Italy to the Russian front, was outraged by the rejection. The Wolff initiative soon fizzled out but not before it had caused considerable acrimony in Stalin's relations with Roosevelt.[15]

Then there was the interminable Soviet–Western dispute about the future of Poland. At Yalta it had been decided that a Polish commission consisting of Molotov, Harriman and the British ambassador, Clark Kerr, would implement the decision to reorganise the Lublin government and establish a new provisional government for Poland. The commission held its first meeting in Moscow on 23 February and initially the talks were quite friendly, but subsequent meetings degenerated into prolonged procedural wrangles. From the Soviet point of view what had been agreed at Yalta was that the so-called Lublin government would be enlarged by the inclusion of other Polish political leaders. The Soviets also insisted that only Poles who accepted the Yalta decisions on Poland could serve in the new government. This ruled out politicians like Mikołajczyk who refused to accept the Curzon Line as the Soviet–Polish frontier, at least not without further negotiation. For their part the British and Americans chose to interpret the Yalta declaration on Poland as meaning a completely new provisional government would be established. By early April the commission's talks were at an impasse. Roosevelt appealed to Stalin to break the logjam but the Soviet leader was unmoved. He was determined that Poland would have a government friendly to the Soviet Union and made it clear that the only way forward was acceptance of Moscow's interpretation of the Yalta agreement. If that was accepted, Stalin told Roosevelt, 'the Polish question can be settled in a short time'. Churchill weighed in strongly on the President's side (**Document 115**).

President Roosevelt died in the early hours of 13 April 1945 (Moscow time). Molotov immediately went to the American embassy to express his condolences. According to Harriman, Molotov 'seemed deeply moved and disturbed. He stayed for some time talking about the part President Roosevelt had played in the war and in the plans for peace, of the respect Marshal Stalin and all the Russian people had for him and how much Marshal Stalin had valued his visit to Yalta.' With regard to new President Harry Truman, Molotov expressed confidence in him because he had been selected as Vice-President by Roosevelt. 'I have never heard Molotov talk so earnestly', commented Harriman in his telegram to Washington. Harriman saw Stalin later that day: 'When I entered Marshal Stalin's office I noticed that he was obviously deeply distressed at the news of the death of President Roosevelt. He greeted me in silence and stood holding my hand for about 30 seconds before asking me to sit down.' Harriman told Stalin that he had come to see him because he thought the Soviet leader might have some questions about the situation in the United States following Roosevelt's death. Stalin, however, expressed confidence that there would be no change in US policy. 'President Roosevelt has died but his cause must live on', Stalin told Harriman. 'We shall support President Truman with all our forces and all our will.' In response Harriman suggested that to smooth Truman's path and reassure American public opinion Stalin should send Molotov to the United States to meet the new President and to attend the founding conference of the United Nations in San

Francisco. This was a personal suggestion of Harriman's but Stalin agreed on the spot to send Molotov to the US.[16]

Molotov had, in fact, been slated to go to San Francisco together with a high-powered government delegation, a decision, as Vladimir Pechatnov put it, designed 'to emphasise the USSR's special role in the founding of the United Nations as well as the great importance the Kremlin attached to the launch of this international organisation'. However, at the height of the Berne crisis Molotov's trip was cancelled and the delegation downgraded to lower-level officials.[17]

Molotov's trip to San Francisco was quite successful but his two meetings with Truman in Washington DC on 22 and 23 April did little to ameliorate the Polish problem. Famously, the new President supposedly told Molotov off, who complained 'I have never been talked to like that in my life'. To which Truman replied: 'Carry out your agreements and you won't get talked to like that', or so Truman claimed in his memoirs. However, neither the American nor the Soviet record of the Molotov–Truman talks contains any mention of such an acerbic exchange.[18]

But there was certainly some tough talking about Poland between the two men. While Molotov stuck to the Soviet interpretation of the Yalta agreement that the existing pro-communist regime in Warsaw should be broadened and reconstructed, Truman insisted that it meant there must be a new government in Poland. In their correspondence Churchill and Stalin restated the same positions and arguments (**Documents 122–5**). Truman's tough talking with Molotov was to no avail. Stalin stuck to the Soviet interpretation of the Yalta agreement on Poland and insisted in no uncertain terms that Moscow would not allow the formation in Warsaw of a government unfriendly to the USSR.

Truman blinked first over Poland. When the European war ended he decided that Harry Hopkins, Roosevelt's trusted confidant and a favourite with Stalin, should go to Moscow to broker a deal. Hopkins arrived in the Soviet capital on 25 May and the next day began a series of meetings with Stalin.[19] He told Stalin that American public opinion was disturbed by recent developments in US–Soviet relations, particularly the failure to implement the Yalta agreement on Poland. But, Hopkins reassured Stalin, Truman intended to continue Roosevelt's policy of cooperation with the USSR. In response Stalin employed one of his favourite debating tactics, blaming a third party, saying the problem was that while the Soviets wanted a friendly government in Poland, Great Britain was trying to revive the anti-Bolshevik cordon sanitaire of the post-First World War years.

At their meeting on 27 May Stalin expounded to Hopkins his own gripes about Soviet–American relations. As well as the Polish dispute, Stalin resented American manoeuvres to gain UN membership for Argentina – a neutral state that the Soviets saw as a wartime collaborator of the Germans. Then there was France's involvement in Allied discussions about reparations from Germany – which Stalin opposed – and the abrupt manner in which the United States had cut Lend-Lease shipments to the Soviet Union as soon as Germany surrendered. Stalin was also keen to secure a share of the German navy and merchant fleet and suspected the British and Americans might oppose this. Later in the conversation Stalin adopted a more conciliatory tone. He told Hopkins that the United States was a world power with worldwide interests and for this reason he accepted that the Americans had a right to be involved in the resolution of the Polish question. Stalin admitted that the Soviet Union had acted unilaterally in Poland but asked Hopkins to understand the reasons why. As to the future, Stalin proposed that four or five of the ministers in a reorganised Polish government could be chosen from the lists of favoured politicians drawn up by the British and Americans.

This suggestion of Stalin's soon led to a resolution of the Polish dispute. During the course of June 1945 a deal was struck that the communist-dominated Polish provisional government would be reorganised to include four pro-Western cabinet ministers, including Mikołajczyk who became one of two deputy premiers (the other was the Polish communist leader, Gomulka) serving under a left-wing socialist prime minster, Edward Osóbka-Morawski. This reorganised government was recognised by the British and Americans on 5 July.

Hopkins was gravely ill when he went on his last mission to Moscow (he died in January 1946) but he performed a very important service. His meetings with Stalin paved the way for a resolution of the Polish dispute and made possible the airing of grievances about a number of other issues in Soviet–American relations. Both sides signalled their intention to continue relations in the cooperative tradition established by Roosevelt. The scene was set for the repetition at Potsdam of the triumphal tripartism of Yalta, leading to a strengthening of relations between the Soviet Union and its wartime allies.

This rosy post-Yalta, pre-Potsdam scenario is not one that finds favour with all historians. Some prefer to emphasise the differences and divergences within the Grand Alliance at this time. Such interpretations tend to reflect the later impact of the Cold War and the influence exercised by protagonists such as Truman and Churchill who subsequently sought to distance themselves from the cooperative spirit of Yalta and Potsdam. A similar distancing from the Grand Alliance took place on the Soviet side after the outbreak of the Cold War, but Stalin's contemporaneous view of relations with the West was quite optimistic and the Soviet delegation set off for Potsdam confident that tripartite cooperation between Britain, the US and the USSR to achieve post-war security and a durable peace remained by far the best option for all.

It was Churchill who had pressed hardest for an early summit of the new Big Three and it was his was his idea to code-name it 'Terminal' – which was unfortunate give that the conference marked the end of his premiership. It was Stalin who suggested a meeting in the vicinity of Berlin, a location that would symbolise the Allied and, in particular, the Soviet victory over Nazi Germany. Berlin as well as Germany had been divided into Soviet and Western zones of military occupation, with the Americans, British and French in control of the west of the city and the Soviets the east. The Cecilienhof Palace in Potsdam was one of the few intact buildings left in greater Berlin. Potsdam was in the Soviet zone and Stalin's security forces prepared carefully for the conference. Seven NKVD regiments and 1,500 operatives provided three rings of protection. Stalin's train route to Berlin was guarded by thousands of troops and a 40-kilometre-wide zone cleared either side of the railway lines.[20]

Before the conference Churchill and Stalin exchanged several messages about a possible meeting with King George VI (**Documents 126–9**). Churchill was keen on a meeting between the King and the Big Three and the first draft of the Soviet response to the invitation to meet His Majesty – composed by Deputy Foreign Commissar Andrey Vyshinsky – said that Stalin 'would be glad to receive the King and you at the Soviet quarters'. However, Molotov thought otherwise and he advised Stalin that 'it won't do in my view. Churchill wants too much profit for the monarch and himself.' Stalin replied to Churchill, diplomatically, that while it wasn't part of his plans, he would meet the King if the Prime Minister thought it necessary. Sensing a lack of enthusiasm Churchill backed away from the invitation, explaining to Stalin that the King's plans had changed and he would now visit Ulster rather than tour Germany.[21] This episode may explain why when he talked to Churchill at Potsdam Stalin want out of his way to praise the King: 'no country needed a monarchy so much as Great Britain because the Crown was the unifying force throughout the Empire ... no one who was a friend of Britain would do anything to weaken the respect shown to the Monarchy' (**Document 131**).

The Potsdam Conference lasted for two weeks (17 July to 2 August),[22] far longer than the four days of Tehran and the week Churchill, Roosevelt and Stalin spent at Yalta. One reason for the length of the conference was a break at the end of July when Churchill flew home for the results of the British general election. He lost the election by a landslide and never returned to Potsdam; his and Eden's places at the conference table were taken by the new Labour Prime Minister, Clement Attlee, and his Foreign Secretary, Ernest Bevin (although Attlee, as Deputy PM, had accompanied Churchill to Potsdam). Another reason for the duration of the conference was the number and type of issues discussed at Potsdam. At Tehran the main theme had been the co-ordination of military action against Germany while at Yalta it was general perspectives on the post-war world that dominated the discussions. Potsdam was more like the Moscow conference of foreign ministers of October 1943 in that it focused on the resolution of specific issues: the future of Germany; peace treaties with enemy states; the revision of the Montreux Convention on access to the Black Sea; the formation of territorial trusteeships to govern Italy's former colonies; and the establishment of procedures for the future conduct of Soviet–Western relations within the Grand Alliance.

Stalin was keen to deal with all these questions as soon as possible because he worried that the benevolent glow of the common victory over Germany would not last much longer and that relations with his Anglo-American allies would become progressively more difficult after the war. Stalin also thought he had a trump card to play in the negotiations: the Red Army was needed to help finish off Japan.

In personal terms the relations between Churchill, Stalin and Truman never achieved the intimacy of Churchill, Roosevelt and Stalin at Tehran and Yalta. But the new Big Three were pretty friendly with each other and the conference records are full of good humour, jokes, laughter and of efforts to avoid confrontation and deadlock in negotiations. The Prime Minister was 'again under Stalin's spell', complained Eden. 'He kept repeating "I like that man"'. At the time Truman thought that Stalin was 'straightforward' and 'knows what he wants and will compromise when he can't get it'. Later, Truman recalled that he had been a 'Russophile' and thought he could live with Stalin; indeed he 'liked the little son of bitch'.[23]

Stalin was his usual charming self at the banquet he hosted. After a piano concert by leading Soviet artistes Truman got up and played some Chopin. According to Birse, the British interpreter, 'Stalin applauded with enthusiasm, remarking that he was the only one of the three with no talents; he had heard that Churchill painted, and now the President proved that he was a musician'.[24]

There were, of course, sharp political differences at Potsdam, prolonged negotiations and hard bargaining. Stalin also had to contend with the ever more marked tendency of the British and Americans to line up together against the Soviets in negotiations. But there were Anglo-American differences too. As James F. Byrnes, Truman's Secretary of State, joked at the conference:

> one gets the impression that when we agree with our Soviet friends, the British delegation withholds its agreement, and when we agree with our British friends, we do not obtain the agreement of the Soviet delegation. (Laughter).

Stalin's first meeting at Potsdam was with Truman on 17 July. Stalin began by apologising for arriving a day late at the conference. He had been detained in Moscow by negotiations with the Chinese and his doctors had forbidden him to fly to Berlin. After an exchange of pleasantries Stalin listed the issues he would like discussed at the conference: the division of the German fleet, reparations, Poland, territorial trusteeships, the Franco regime in Spain. Truman was happy to discuss these issues but said the United States had its own items for the agenda, although he did not specify what these were. To Truman's statement that there were bound to be difficulties and differences of opinion during the negotiations, Stalin responded that such problems were unavoidable but the important thing was to find a common language. Asked about Churchill, Truman said he had seen him yesterday morning and that the Prime Minister was confident of victory in the British general election. Stalin commented that the English people would not forget the victory in the war, in fact they thought the war was over already and expected the Americans and Soviets to defeat Japan for them. This provided Truman with an opening to remark that while there was active British participation in the war in the Far East, he still awaited help from the USSR. Stalin replied that Soviet forces would be ready to launch their attack on the Japanese by the middle of August. This led to the final exchange of the conversation in which Stalin indicated that he was sticking to the agreement at Yalta on the terms of

Soviet participation in the Far Eastern war and did not intend to demand anything more.[25]

Stalin's conversation with Truman was friendly enough though it did not match the bonhomie he had achieved with Roosevelt at Tehran and Yalta. But Truman was new to the job, was still feeling his way with Stalin and, unlike his predecessor, had not engaged in a long wartime correspondence with the Soviet leader prior to meeting him.

Stalin's private chats with Churchill were much cosier. At their first meeting, after the opening plenary session on 17 July, Stalin told Churchill that he had started smoking cigars and complained that he couldn't get to sleep before 4.00am even though the war was over and he didn't need to work so late. Churchill thanked Stalin for the hospitality that his wife had received on her recent visit to Russia and told him that Britain welcomed Russia as a great power, including a naval power (**Document 130**).

The bonhomie continued the next night at dinner. Stalin was confident Churchill would win the British general election and predicted a parliamentary majority of eighty for the Prime Minster. Churchill was equally effusive, saying that he would 'welcome Russia as a great power on the sea' and that the country had a right of access to the Mediterranean, the Baltic Sea and the Pacific Ocean. On Eastern Europe, Stalin repeated previous promises to Churchill that he would not seek its sovietisation, but expressed disappointment at Western demands for changes to the governments in Bulgaria and Romania, especially when he was refraining from interfering in Greek affairs. Churchill spoke of difficulties in relation to Yugoslavia, pointing to the 50–50 arrangement he had made with Stalin in October 1944, but the Soviet leader protested that the share of influence in Yugoslavia was 90 per cent British, 10 per cent Yugoslavian and 0 per cent Russian. Stalin continued that Tito had a 'partisan mentality and had done several things that he ought not to have done. The Soviet Government often did not know what Marshal Tito was about to do.' The positive tenor of the conversation was summed up by Churchill's remark towards the end of dinner that 'the Three Powers gathered round the table were the strongest the world had ever seen, and it was their task to maintain the peace of the world' (**Document 131**).

The next day Churchill told Lord Moran, his private doctor, that the Marshal was very amenable. I gave him a box of my cigars, the big ones you know. He smoked one of them for three hours. I touched on some delicate matters without any clouds appearing in the sky. He takes a very sensible line about the monarchy.' Churchill continued that he thought Stalin wanted him to win the election and that the dictator had given him 'his word that there will be free elections in the countries set free by his armies ... I told Stalin Russia was like a giant with his nostrils pinched. I was thinking of the narrows from the Baltic and the Black Sea. If they want to be a sea power, why not?'[26]

Potsdam was the last time Churchill and Stalin met. On 24 July, the day before he returned to Britain to receive the result of the general election, Churchill hosted a dinner party for the Big Three. Stalin 'was in good humour and seemed to enjoy himself ... He said that he liked these English dinners; they were simple and at the same time dignified ... At the end of the dinner [he] got up and went round the table with his dinner-card, collecting autographs.'[27]

Like the Tehran and Yalta conferences, Potsdam was primarily a Soviet-American show. At the first plenary session Truman was, as Stalin proposed, elected Chairman for the duration of the conference. The main item on the agenda was an exchange of views on what issues the three leaders wanted to discuss at the conference. Stalin's list was similar to the one he had presented to Truman at their bilateral meeting earlier that day. Again, the division of the German navy and merchant fleet was number one on his list, followed by reparations, the resumption of diplomatic relations with Germany's former satellites, and the position of the Franco regime in Spain. Stalin's order of priorities was interesting for a number of reasons.

First, it reflected his always keen desire to get a fair share of war booty and he suspected that the British, in particular, were trying to deny the Soviets their share of German shipping. Second, Stalin had asserted on a number of occasions during the war that one of the defining features of a great power was a big fleet and he was planning a significant post-war build-up of the Soviet navy. This required a share of the German as well as the Italian fleet (already agreed at Yalta) and port facilities in various parts of the world. The demand for a share of the German fleet reflected Stalin's view that now the war in Europe was over the Soviet Union should get its just rewards. 'We want no gifts', Stalin told Truman and Churchill later in the conference, 'but wish to know whether or not the principle is recognised, whether or not the Russian claim to a part of the German navy is considered legitimate.' Stalin displayed a similar attitude in relation to a number of other questions that came up at the conference. Justifying the Soviet demand for Königsberg he said:

> We consider it necessary to have at the expense of Germany one ice-free port in the Baltic. I think that this port must serve Königsberg. It is no more than fair that the Russians who have shed so much blood and lived through so much terror should want to receive some lump of German territory which would give some small satisfaction from this war.

A more serious issue of national pride concerned Soviet demands in relation to Turkey. In June 1945 the Soviet Union had demanded the return of the provinces of Kars and Ardahan to the USSR. These were areas of eastern Turkey with Armenian and Georgian populations and had been part of the Tsarist empire from 1878 to 1921, when a Soviet–Turkish treaty returned the two districts to Turkey. These Soviet territorial demands were prompted by a suggestion from the Turkish ambassador that the Soviet Union and Turkey should sign a treaty of alliance. Molotov responded that before such an agreement could be concluded the frontier dispute about Kars and Ardahan needed to be resolved and there had to be negotiations about the revision of the Montreux Convention and the establishment of Soviet military bases on the Dardanelles. At Potsdam the USSR tabled a demand for joint control of the Black Sea Straits with Turkey, including provisions for Soviet military bases. At the plenary session on 23 July Stalin defended the Soviet position on Kars and Ardahan on ethnic grounds, and in relation to the straits said:

> For a great power such as Russia the question of the Straits has great significance. The Montreux Convention was directed against Russia, it was an agreement hostile to Russia. Turkey was given the right not only to close the Straits to our shipping during war but when there exists a threat of war, as defined by Turkey. An impossible position! Turkey can always show that such a threat exists and she can always close the Straits. We Russians have the same rights in relation to the Straits as the Japanese Empire. This is laughable but it is a fact ... Imagine the uproar there would be in England if such an agreement existed in relation to Gibraltar, or in America if such an agreement existed in relation to the Panama Canal ... You consider that a naval base on the Straits is unacceptable. Very well, then give me some other base where the Russian fleet would be able to carry out repairs and re-equip and where, together with its allies, it would be able to defend Russia's rights.[28]

Stalin's allusion to a naval base elsewhere was a reference to another issue of prestige raised by the Soviets at Potsdam: the demand for Soviet participation in the administration of the Trusteeship Territories that were to supersede Italy's colonies in North Africa. The background to the Soviets' demand was a long-standing American proposal that the League of Nations' mandate system for overseeing the transition of former colonies to independence should be replaced by a trusteeship system. At the San Francisco conference in June 1945 there was correspondence between Ambassador Gromyko and Stettinius, the American Secretary of State, which indicated that the United States would support Soviet participation in the proposed trusteeship system. This was very encouraging for Moscow and at Potsdam the Soviets proposed there should be a discussion about whether territories taken into trusteeship should be managed collectively by the Big Three or by individual countries responsible for separate territories. Stalin and Molotov pressed for a discussion of this matter but it was agreed to refer the issue to the first meeting of the newly-created Council of Foreign Ministers, scheduled to meet in London in September.

After Potsdam Moscow hardened its position on the trusteeship issue and decided to demand that Tripolitania (western Libya) should become a Soviet trust territory, which meant Stalin would have been able to establish port facilities in the Mediterranean. The Soviets were quite open about their self-interested aims in relation to Tripolitania and saw nothing wrong with them, although they did stress that their intention was to establish merchant fleet facilities.

At Potsdam a number of questions were raised and then tabled for future discussion by the Big Three's foreign ministers. But there were some issues that had to be discussed and decided upon by the conference. First and foremost was Germany's future. This was a matter considered over several plenary sessions and by the foreign ministers and specialist working commissions of less senior officials. The most difficult issue was that of reparations. At Yalta it had been agreed in principle that the Soviet Union would receive reparations from Germany, the ball-park figure being $10 billion. The reparations were to be extracted in kind by the dismantling of German industry and infrastructure and by deliveries from current production. The difficulty was that German industry was mostly located in the Western-occupied areas of the country such as the Ruhr. The British and Americans, none too keen on reparations anyway, feared they would end up having to meet Soviet reparations demands by deliveries from their zones. Their preference was for the Soviets to extract reparations exclusively from their own zone of occupation in Germany and, if there were to be reparations deliveries from the west, these should be in exchange for agricultural products from the east. In the end agreement was reached that 10 per cent of German industry would be removed from the western zones in part payment of Soviet reparations and another 15 per cent would be dismantled and shipped east in exchange for food and raw materials. As important, from Stalin's point of view, was that the agreement provided for Germany's 'complete disarmament and demilitarization' and the elimination of its war potential. Stalin's views on the long-term danger of a German revival were well rehearsed and they came to the fore once again in an exchange with Truman on 21 July about the utility of shifting Poland's border with Germany as far west as possible:

> **Stalin**: Of course the proposal ... to shift the frontier westwards will create difficulties for Germany. I do not object to the claim that it will create difficulties for Germany. Our task consists in creating more difficulties for Germany ...
> **Truman**: But it is not good to create difficulties for the Allies as well.
> **Stalin**: The less industry in Germany, the greater the outlets for your goods. Germany will not be competing with your goods. Is that so bad? It seems very good to me. We put on its knees the state which threatens peace and peaceful competition ... There are difficulties for Germany here, but we must not be afraid of them.

Alongside the German question, the issue of Poland's western border with Germany gave rise to the most protracted discussion at Potsdam. At Yalta it had been agreed that Poland would be compensated for territorial losses to the Soviet Union by gains at Germany's expense. But no agreement had been reached on the precise frontier and there were differences about how far west the German–Polish border should be pushed. Those differences were compounded by the fact that the Soviets controlled all the German territory in question and they had handed it over to Polish administrative control. The Poles began resettling the area in anticipation that it would become part of Poland and there was a consequent mass exodus of Germans westwards, causing problems for the British and Americans in their zones of occupation in Germany.

By the end of the conference a demarcation line between Germany and Poland had been agreed and Polish administration of the German territories in question had been accepted by the British and Americans, 'pending the final determination of Poland's western frontier' at a future peace conference.

A third area of contention at Potsdam concerned Big Three relations with Germany's erstwhile allies during the Second World War – Italy, Bulgaria, Finland, Hungary and Romania. The scenario was that the British and Americans sought special treatment for Italy, while Stalin strove to protect the interests of those countries that fell within his sphere of influence in Eastern Europe. The argument began with a Western proposal that Italy be admitted as a member of the United Nations. The Soviets did not object but Stalin did not see why the other four ex-enemy states should not be treated in the same way. The British and Americans said they did not have diplomatic relations with those states and so could not consider their admission to the UN until peace treaties had been signed. The compromise finally agreed was to prioritise the negotiation and signing of a peace treaty between the Big Three and Italy that would lead to the country's admission to the UN. Soviet sensibilities were assuaged by a commitment from the British and Americans to consider recognising the governments of Bulgaria, Finland, Hungary and Romania.

The only really jarring note at Potsdam concerned the Soviet Union's entry into the war against Japan. At the conference Stalin told Truman that he would be ready to attack Japan by the middle of August. This pleased Truman. 'I've gotten what I came for', he confided to his wife on 18 July. 'Stalin goes to war August 15 with no strings on it … I'll say that we'll end the war a year sooner now, and think of the kids who won't be killed. That's the important thing.' The British record of Stalin's conversation with Churchill at dinner on 18 July (**Document 131**) states: 'it was evident that Russia intends to attack Japan soon after August 8. The Marshal [i.e. Stalin] thought it might be a fortnight later.' These indications were consistent with the commitment the Soviets had given at Yalta to enter war two or three months after the defeat of Germany and with Soviet military plans and preparations in the Far East, about which Stalin's Chief the General Staff, General Antonov briefed the British and American military.

The problem was that American interest in Soviet participation in the war against Japan was fading by the time of Potsdam. Militarily, it was no longer seen as vital as it had been and this view was reinforced by the successful A-bomb test on 17 July. Truman told Stalin about the test. According to Pavlov, Stalin's interpreter, who claimed to be the only witness to what happened, Truman told Stalin: 'Yesterday we tested a bomb of unusual power.' Stalin did not react at all to this news. Truman was dumbfounded and froze for several seconds as he watched Stalin walk away.[29] Stalin's lack of interest is explained, perhaps, by the presence of numerous Soviet spies in the Manhattan Project who kept him abreast of Anglo-American atomic research.

The changing American attitude to the Soviets in the Far Eastern context was indicated by Truman's handling of the Potsdam Proclamation of 26 July 1945. This was a public statement by Britain, China and the United States calling upon Japan to surrender unconditionally or face 'prompt and utter destruction'. In the original American draft of the declaration the Soviet Union was included among the signatories and there was a reference to the 'vast military might of the Soviet Union' having been added to the arsenals of Britain, China and the US. But on

26 July Byrnes sent Molotov a copy of a new text of the declaration that omitted these references. The Soviets immediately got to work producing their own draft declaration, which reinstated the USSR as a signatory and stated that 'the United States, China, Great Britain and the Soviet Union consider it their duty to come forward with joint decisive measures that ought to lead to an end to the war'.

Just before midnight the Soviets rang the American delegation to ask them to postpone publication of the Proclamation for three days. Fifteen minutes later, however, the Soviets were informed it had already been released to the press. The subsequent American explanation for this lack of consultation was that since the Soviet Union was still neutral it would not want to get involved in such a statement. This was a pretty lame excuse and Stalin showed his annoyance by pointedly referring at the plenary session on 28 July to the fact that 'he had not been informed beforehand of the call to surrender published by the British and American governments'. Even so, Stalin did not give up the idea of a public show of Allied solidarity in advance of the Soviet attack on Japan. He suggested to Truman that Britain and the United States should issue a statement inviting the Soviet Union to enter the war in the Far East. Truman responded by suggesting that the Moscow declaration on general security issued in October 1943 and the as yet unratified Charter of the United Nations provided sufficient formal grounds for Soviet entry into the war. This was hardly satisfactory from Stalin's point of view and when the Soviets did declare war on 8 August they used the pretext of Japan's failure to comply with the Potsdam Proclamation to justify their action.

At the conclusion of the conference the participants solemnly declared that it had 'strengthened the ties ... and extended the scope of their collaboration and understanding' and had renewed their confidence in their ability to deliver 'a just and enduring peace'. The conference communiqué went on to announce, first, the establishment of a Council of Foreign Ministers that would constitute a permanent forum of tripartite collaboration and, second, plans for post-war Germany, including policy on reparation payments. There followed the announcement of various other decisions such as the transfer of Königsberg to the USSR and the agreement on Poland's western border. The final communiqué also paved the way for the admission of more states to the United Nations, including countries that had remained neutral throughout the war. As well as the public communiqué an unpublished conference protocol dealt with matters such as the tripartite disposal of the German navy and merchant marine and the need to revise the regime governing the Black Sea Straits.

The Yalta and Potsdam conferences have generated a myriad of historical myths.[30] Yalta is seen, variously, as the place where Churchill and Roosevelt appeased Stalin, divided Europe into spheres of influence, and betrayed the freedom-loving peoples of Eastern Europe. In truth, while Stalin was appeased by the Western leaders, he was also the appeaser in his relations with Churchill and Roosevelt. An implicit division of Europe into spheres of influence did take place at Yalta but this reflected not deals made but the realities of the military course and outcome of the war. While both Soviets and Westerners interpreted the Yalta agreements in ways which suited their interests, the two sides continued to see the continent's future in pan-European terms and within the framework of a peacetime Grand Alliance.

The main myth about Potsdam is that the conference marked the beginning of the Cold War. But Soviet-Western relations did not deteriorate really badly until after Potsdam and even then it took two years for the Grand Alliance to collapse and the Cold War to break out, notwithstanding Churchill's fanning of the flames at Fulton, Missouri in March 1946. As Michael Neiberg has pointed out, in 1945 Soviet and Western leaders were not grappling with the problems of the coming Cold War – about which they had no knowledge. Their reference points were the failure of the post-Versailles international order and the experience and results of the war.[31] Viewed from that perspective, Yalta and Potsdam represented the end of one era rather than the beginning of another. As to the future, Yalta and Potsdam pointed in many different directions, towards an enduring Grand Alliance as well as to the Cold War. The same was true of the Churchill-Stalin relationship.

Documents 98–131

98. Churchill to Stalin, 16 November 1944

1. You will doubtless like to have some account of our visit to Paris. I certainly had a wonderful reception from about half a million Frenchmen in the Champs Elysees and also from the headquarters of the Resistance Movement at the Hotel de Ville. I also re-established friendly personal relations with de Gaulle.

2. I see statements that the French press and other sources are reporting that all sorts of things were decided by us in Paris. You can be sure that our negotiations about important issues proceeded on the basis that everything we talked about is subject to examination by the three Great Powers ...

4. [The French] pressed very strongly for a share in the occupation of Germany, not merely as sub-participants under British or Allied Command but as a French Command ...

5. I see a report from Reuters, no doubt emanating unofficially from Paris, that it was agreed that France should be assigned certain areas, the Ruhr, the Rhineland, etc., for her troops to garrison. This does not correspond to reality and it is clear that nothing can be decided except in agreement with the President and you. All I said to de Gaulle was that we had divided Germany into Russian, British and American spheres; roughly, the Russians had the East, the British the North, and the Americans the South. I further said, speaking for His Majesty's Government, that we would certainly favour the French taking over as large a part as their capacity allowed, but that all this must be settled at an inter-Allied table ...

6. It is clear, however, that there are a number of questions which demand decision at a level higher than that of the High Commands ... and this seems to reinforce the desirability of a meeting between us three and the French in the fairly near future. In that event, the French would participate in the discussion of some subjects but not others.

7. Generally, I felt in the presence of an organised government, broadly based and of rapidly growing strength, and I am certain that we should be most unwise to do anything to weaken it in the eyes of France at this difficult, critical time. I had a considerable feeling of stability and thought we could safely take them more into our confidence.

99. Stalin to Churchill, 20 November 1944

Thank you for keeping me posted about your talks with de Gaulle. I read your communications with interest. I have nothing against the proposal for a possible meeting between the three of us and the French if the President agrees, but we must first reach final agreement on the time and place of the meeting of us three.

Recently General de Gaulle expressed the wish to come to Moscow to establish contact with Soviet Government leaders. We replied that we agreed, and we expect the French in Moscow by the end of the month. They have not yet specified the points they would like to discuss. In any event, after the talks with de Gaulle I will tell you about them.

100. Churchill to Stalin, 25 November 1944

... I am glad that de Gaulle is coming to see you and I hope you will talk about everything. There has been some talk in the press about a Western bloc. I have not yet considered this. I trust first of all to our Treaty of Alliance and close collaboration with the United States as the mainstay of world organisation to ensure and impose peace upon a tortured world. Only after the creation of such an international organisation, and subordinate to it, can there be any arrangements for close and friendly European unity. In these matters we will have no secrets and we are certain that you will continue to tell us what you feel and need ...

101. Stalin to Churchill, 1 December 1944

As regards the Western bloc, so far I have little information about it, and the newspaper reports are contradictory. I am grateful to you for the promise to keep me informed about developments, and I myself am ready to reciprocate ...

102. Churchill to Stalin, 2 December 1944

I thank you most warmly for your very kind message upon my birthday, which a year ago I celebrated with you and the President of the United States at my side. Since then we have achieved enormous success, and we can hope that a continuance of all our efforts at the highest speed and with the utmost energy and devotion will see the final destruction of Hitlerism in the coming year. Especially welcome is the expression in your message of the wish that our comradeship and personal relations continue in the future, not only under the dangerous conditions of war but also in solving the problems of peace.

103. Stalin to Churchill, 2 December 1944

According to information, de Gaulle and his French friends, who have arrived in the Soviet Union, will raise two questions.

1. The conclusion of a Franco-Soviet pact of mutual aid similar to the Anglo-Soviet pact.

It would be difficult for us to object but I would like to know what you think and advise.

2. De Gaulle will probably suggest revising the eastern frontier of France and shifting it to the left bank of the Rhine. There is talk, too, about a plan for forming a Rhine-Westphalian region under international control. Possibly French participation in the control is likewise envisaged. Thus, the French proposal for shifting the frontier line to the Rhine will compete with the plan for a Rhineland region under international control.

I ask for your advice on this question ...

104. Churchill to Stalin, 3 December 1944

1. I have seen Mr Mikołajczyk, who has explained to me the reason for his resignation. Briefly, the position is that he could not count on the support of important sections of his cabinet for his policy and was, therefore, unable at this stage to conclude an agreement on the basis of the discussions between us at our recent Moscow meeting.

2. Attempts are now being made to form an alternative Polish Government, in which Mr Mikołajczyk, Mr Romer and the Ambassador, Mr Raczynski, have refused to participate. A change of Prime Ministers does not affect the formal relations between States. The desire of His Majesty's Government for the reconstitution of a strong and independent Poland, friendly to Russia, remains unalterable. We have practical matters to handle with the Polish Government, and more especially the control of the considerable Polish armed forces, over 80,000 excellent fighting men, under our operational command. These are now making an appreciable contribution to the United Nations' war effort in Italy, Holland and elsewhere. Our attitude towards any new Polish Government must therefore be correct, though it will certainly be cold. We cannot of course have the same close relations of confidence with such a government as we have had with Mr Mikołajczyk or with his predecessor, the late General Sikorski, and we shall do all in our power to ensure that its activities do not endanger the unity between the Allies.

3. It is thought that such a government, even when formed, will not last long. Indeed, after my conversations with Mr Mikołajczyk, I would not be surprised to see him back in office before long, with increased prestige and with the necessary authority to carry through the programme discussed between us in Moscow. This outcome would be all the more propitious because he would by his resignation, in a most convincing way, proclaim himself and his friends as a champion of Poland's good relations with Russia.

4. I hope, therefore, that you will agree that our respective influence should be used with the Poles here and with those in Lublin to prevent any steps on either side which might increase the tension between them and so render more difficult Mr Mikołajczyk's task when, as I hope, he takes it up again in the not too distant future. He feels optimistic and still very much wants a satisfactory settlement of

this question. I see no reason why he should not emerge from this crisis as a leader even more necessary than ever for the restoration of Poland.

105. Stalin to Churchill, 3 December 1944

The meeting with General de Gaulle provided the opportunity for a friendly exchange of views on Franco-Soviet relations. In the course of the talks General de Gaulle, as I had anticipated, brought up two major issues – the French frontier on the Rhine and a Franco-Soviet mutual aid pact modelled on the Anglo-Soviet Treaty.

As to the French frontier on the Rhine, I said, in effect, that the matter could not be settled without the knowledge and consent of our chief Allies, whose forces are waging a liberation struggle against the Germans on French soil. I stressed the complexity of resolving this question.

Concerning the proposal for a Franco-Soviet mutual aid pact, I pointed to the need for a thorough study of the matter and for clearing up the legal aspects, in particular the question of who in France in the present circumstances is to ratify such a pact. Hence the French will have to give a number of explanations, which we have yet to receive from them.

I would be grateful for a reply to this message and for your observations on these questions ...

106. Churchill to Stalin, 5 December 1944

1. Your telegram about General de Gaulle's visit and the two questions he will raise. We have no objection whatever to a Franco-Soviet pact of mutual assistance similar to the Anglo-Soviet pact. On the contrary His Majesty's Government consider it desirable and regards it as an additional link between us all. Indeed, we are also thinking that, possibly, it would be best if we were to conclude a tripartite treaty between the three of us which would include our existing Anglo-Soviet Treaty together with any improvements. In this way the obligations of each one of us would be identical and linked together. Please let me know if this idea appeals to you ...

2. The question of changing the eastern frontier of France to the left bank of the Rhine, or alternatively of forming a Rhenish-Westphalian province under international control, together with the other alternatives, should await settlement at the peace table. There is, however, no reason why, when the three heads of government meet, we should not come much closer to conclusions about all this than we have done so far. As you know, the President does not expect General de Gaulle to come to the meeting of the three. I would hope that this could be modified to his coming later, when decisions specially affecting France were under discussion ...

107. Stalin to Churchill, 7 December 1944

I have received your reply to my message about the Franco-Soviet pact and the French frontier on the Rhine. Thank you for your advice.

By the time your reply came we had begun talks on the pact with the French. I and my colleagues approve of your suggestion that a tripartite Anglo-Franco-

Soviet pact, improved in comparison with the Anglo-Soviet one, would be preferable. We have suggested a tripartite pact to de Gaulle but have had no reply so far ...

108. Stalin to Churchill, 8 December 1944

Your message on Mikołajczyk received.

It has become obvious since my last meeting with Mikołajczyk in Moscow that he is incapable of helping to resolve the Polish business. Indeed, his negative role has been revealed. It is now evident that his negotiations with the Polish National Committee are designed to cover up those who, behind his back, engage in criminal terror acts against Soviet officers and Soviet people generally on Polish territory. We cannot tolerate this state of affairs. We cannot tolerate terrorists, instigated by the Polish émigrés, assassinating our people in Poland and waging a criminal struggle against Soviet forces liberating Poland ...

Ministerial changes in the émigré Government are no longer of serious interest. It is the same marking of time by people who have lost touch with the national soil and have no contact with the Polish people. Meanwhile the Polish Committee of National Liberation has made serious progress in strengthening its national, democratic organisations on Polish territory, in implementing land reform in favour of the peasants and in expanding its armed forces, and it enjoys great authority among the population.

I think that our task now is to support the National Committee in Lublin and all who want to and are capable of cooperating with it. This is particularly important for the Allies, bearing in mind the task of accelerating the defeat of the Germans.

109. Stalin to Churchill, 10 December 1944

I informed General de Gaulle of your opinion that an Anglo-Franco-Soviet mutual aid pact was preferable and declared for your proposal. General de Gaulle, however, insisted on a Franco-Soviet pact, suggesting that a tripartite pact be the next stage, because the matter required preparation. Meanwhile we received a message from the President, saying that he had no objection to a Franco-Soviet pact. As a result, we agreed on a pact which was signed today. The text will be published when General de Gaulle reaches Paris.

I think de Gaulle's visit has yielded positive result and will not only strengthen Franco-Soviet relations, but will contribute to the common cause of the Allies.

110. Churchill to Stalin, 19 December 1944

I saw last night for the second time the film which you gave me called *Kutuzov*. The first time I greatly admired it but, as it was all in Russian, I could not understand the exact meaning of each situation. Last night I saw it with English subtitles, which made it all intelligible, and I must tell you that in my view this is one of the most masterly films I have ever seen. Never has the struggle between two strong characters been more clearly displayed. Never has the importance of commitment in commanders and men been more effectively shown in the cinema. Never has this art-form presented Russian soldiers and Russian people so gloriously to the British nation. Never have I seen the art of the camera better used ...

111. Stalin to Churchill, 25 December 1944

... I greatly appreciate your praise for the Kutuzov film and shall not fail to convey your comments to those who made it ...

112. Stalin to Churchill, 3 January 1945

You must know that the Polish National Council in Lublin has announced its decision to transform the National Committee into a Provisional National Government of the Polish Republic. You are well aware of our attitude to the National Committee, which, in our view, has already won great authority in Poland and is the legitimate expression of the will of the Polish people. The transformation of the Polish National Committee into the Provisional Government seems to us quite timely, especially now that Mikołajczyk has withdrawn from the émigré Government and that the latter has thereby lost all semblance of a government. I think that Poland cannot be left without a government. Accordingly, the Soviet Government has agreed to recognise the Provisional Polish Government.

I greatly regret that I have not succeeded in fully convincing you of the correctness of the Soviet Government's stand on the Polish question. But I hope that further developments will show that our recognition of the Polish Government in Lublin is in keeping with the interests of the common cause of the Allies and that it will help accelerate the defeat of Germany ...

113. Churchill-Stalin Meeting at Yalta, 4 February 1945, 15.00

Churchill expressed thanks for the comforts that had been made available to him.

Stalin replied that it was the duty of a host. Our people couldn't do more as they didn't have much time.

Churchill asked about news from the front.

Stalin replied that the news is not bad.

Churchill stated that on 8 February British forces together with 9th American Army will advance north.

Stalin said that it is good. The Germans have to be denied the possibility of moving their forces from one front to another.

Churchill said that at the meeting today General Marshall [Chief of Staff of the US Army] will present the plans of the Allies in the west. Churchill would like Field Marshal Alexander [Allied Commander-in-Chief in the Mediterranean] to talk about the situation at the front in Italy.

Stalin said that now Germany has lost the Silesian coal basin and if it loses the Ruhr – if it loses both its main supplies of coal – then as a result of a coal and grain deficiency there could be internal collapse before its military defeat.

Churchill replied that might happen.

Stalin stated that the Germans don't have any available reserves. The Germans built very strong defences on the east, but there were defended by fighters from the Volkssturm, not very reliable people.

Churchill stated that he agrees the Germans have no available reserves. In this connection he would like to ask Stalin what he thinks about Rundstedt's [Ardennes] offensive.

Stalin replied that Rundstedt was very stupid to begin his advance at a time when Germany has no forces. It happened because Germany still considers itself a great power, but it has ceased to be one. For new operations you need reserves and Germany doesn't have any.

Churchill said that Hitler had prepared a web but forgot to supply a spider. He asked what Stalin thought about Hitler as a strategist.

Stalin replied that as a strategist Hitler had lost it. Bock was much smarter. Hitler has now lost all his experienced generals.

(Further conversation took place in a room where there hung maps of different fronts.)

Field Marshal Alexander explained the situation at his front.

Stalin said that on the Italian front the Germans won't attack. Hence it would be desirable to leave some forces in Italy for defence while the rest moved across the Adriatic for a joint advance with the Red Army in Austria.

Alexander replied that at present he doesn't have any forces free for such an operation. Besides, he thinks it is now too late to start such a campaign.

114. Churchill-Stalin Meeting at Yalta, 10 February 1945

Churchill stated that he has come to Marshal Stalin about a pretty unpleasant matter. It concerns the last phrase in the agreement on the Polish question. But Churchill had just heard from Eden that the Soviet delegation has a new proposal.

Molotov, who is present at the meeting, handed Eden the text of Soviet proposal and clarifies that he gave the same text to Harriman for Stettinius.

Churchill and **Eden** familiarised themselves with the proposal, declared it satisfactory and said thanks.

Churchill declared that he will be honest. He doesn't know what's happening in Poland and in relation to information about events there he is completely dependent on the charity of the Polish Government in London. As a result the London Poles spread their own versions of events in Parliament. He would like to defend the general position. But how is he going to do that if he is not aware of the real state of affairs in Poland. He might be asked in Parliament to send people to Poland. He would have to say no. It would facilitate the Poles spreading rumours in England. Naturally, the British government would have approved the sending of a Soviet mission to any of the rear areas of the Allied forces, be it Greece, Italy or Flanders.

Stalin said that de Gaulle has his own representative in Lublin. Perhaps the British government could send its representative to Poland. You could send journalists to Poland. Up to this point the British Government has not put this issue before the Soviet Government. But he thinks that if the question is raised the Poles won't protest.

Churchill replied that he would like to send official representatives to Poland. They wouldn't interfere in military affairs but would be able to report to the British Government about the situation in the country. He has to convince Parliament and would like to use the best means. So he would like to send official representatives to Poland, not journalists, as the latter seem less desirable. Besides, as soon one journalist got into the country, more would ask to do the same.

Stalin said that if Churchill is not worried about offending the London Poles it would be best to send a British representative in an official capacity.

It could be done, **Churchill** replied, on condition that agreement is reached on the formation of new Polish government. Then the British government could decline to recognise the Polish Government in London and would acknowledge the newly formed united Polish Government.

Eden stated that after recognising the new Polish Government, the British Government would like to send to Poland its official representatives.

Stalin noted that the British Government would have an accredited ambassador to the Polish Government.

Eden stated that he and Churchill would like to include in the agreement a condition about the official representatives of the Allies being present in Poland to report to their governments about the implementation of the agreement. This absolutely vital, as the Polish Government in London could start a campaign of critique and propaganda.

Stalin asked if Churchill and Eden desired to send their representatives prior to the formation of the Polish Government?

Eden responded that the British Government wants to do this after the formation of the Polish Government.

Churchill said that one can imagine a Member of Parliament rising and quoting evidence from the London Polish Government that the Lublin Poles are killing and arresting members of the underground movement. He would have to reply that this evidence was incorrect and exaggerated. But he must support his argument with facts, and to do that it is necessary to have representatives in Poland.

Stalin stated that the British Government will have an ambassador and his aides in Poland.

Eden said that the British Government would like to be able to say in Parliament that after the formation of a new Polish government and until elections in the country the British Government will be fully informed about the events in Poland. Hence the necessity to include in the agreement that British representatives in Poland will keep the British Government informed.

Stalin replied that this is a given, since the British Government will have an ambassador and his aides in Poland.

Eden asked if the ambassador would have freedom of movement in Poland?

Stalin replied that the Red Army authority will not interfere with the ambassador's freedom of movement. As regards the Polish Government, they can be negotiated with.

Eden said that he would very much like to include in the agreement a formula that will calm the British people and not offend others. He thinks that the following addition to the last paragraph suggested by the Soviet delegation would be acceptable: 'and will exchange ambassadors who will inform their governments about the situation in Poland'.

Stalin responded that he agreed with the formula proposed by Eden.

Churchill and **Eden** thanked Stalin.

Churchill said that he would like talk about POWs. He has learned there are a large number of Russian POWs in Western Europe. The Germans treated them as slaves, and some were forced to take arms against the Allies.

Stalin said that the Soviet government requested that Soviet citizens captured by the Allies not be hurt and not forced to become traitors.

Churchill replied that there are no such cases. The British and Soviet governments have already agreed about the working conditions of the Soviet citizens in the hands of the Allies. Eleven thousand Soviet citizens have already returned to their country, with 7,000 more to be sent.

Stalin stated that among Soviet citizens there are people forced to work by the Germans, but there are also those who voluntarily took up arms against the Allies. Such people have to bear responsibility for their actions. The Allies have an absolute right to keep them in their camps. But he would like to stress that the Soviet Government considered both categories to be its citizens.

Churchill stated that the British government would like to return home both categories as soon as possible. The issue is shipping.

Stalin said that the Soviet Government also asks British Government to keep Soviet citizens separate from the Germans and not to treat them the same as the Germans.

Churchill replied that the British Government aims to satisfy the wishes of the Soviet Government. But it would like to know how many English POWs were liberated by the Red Army.

Stalin said that these particulars can be obtained from the fronts.

Churchill asked if the Soviet Government will allow specialist English officers to be sent to the camps to look after English POWs.

Stalin replied affirmatively.

Churchill asked if it would it be possible to send Red Cross parcels to the English POWs liberated by the Red Army.

Stalin replied affirmatively.

Churchill asked if it was possible to return the English POWs home on the same ships that will, in the near future, carry the 7,000 Soviet citizens.

Stalin said that of course it would be possible.

Stalin asked Churchill if the English are alarmed by the figures on reparations from Germany proposed by the Soviet delegation.

Churchill replied that he had received a telegram from the War Cabinet, which says that for the moment the British Government is against fixing a sum for reparations.

Eden said London doesn't have a reparations committee like the Maisky committee, therefore it can't assess the figure presented by the Soviet delegation. The British Government agreed in principle with reparations. Regarding the figure for reparations, in his opinion this question could be better studied by a reparations commission in Moscow.

Stalin remarked that Churchill seemed to feel sorry for the Germans.

Eden replied that the issue is not one of pity for Germans, but the sad experience of reparations which British Government had after the last world war.

Churchill said that he is resolutely in favour of the Russians getting German factories. This is profitable for the English as they will get the German exports.

Stalin said the Russians will expropriate the German plants when they get to them.

Churchill stated that there are many German generals in Soviet captivity. He would like to know if the Soviet government intends to use them only as propaganda or to use them in Germany too.

Stalin responded: 'God forbid!'

Churchill expressed satisfaction with Stalin's reply.

Churchill said that the Soviet Government didn't repay the 'Lena Goldfields' debts. In comparison with that toward the Americans, the attitude of Soviet Government to the English is unjust, as the Soviet Government pays the Americans.

Stalin said that he is not familiar with this matter and needs to familiarise himself with it.

Stalin said he would like to ask Churchill how things stand in relation to the revision of the Montreux convention.

Churchill replied that he considers the convention shouldn't continue to exist in its present form. In October it was agreed between him and Stalin that the Soviet Government will present its recommendations in respect of convention change.

Stalin asked Churchill what he thinks about him (Stalin) raising at today's meeting the question of revising [the Montreux convention] and proposing that the Foreign Ministers discuss it?

Churchill replied he agreed with this suggestion.

115. Churchill to Stalin, 1 April 1945

1. I trust that by now you have received the message from the President of the United States which he was good enough to show to me before he sent it. I consider it my duty on behalf of His Majesty's Government to assure you that the War Cabinet wants me to tell you that we fully endorse the President's message and that we associate ourselves with it in its entirety.

2. There are two or three points which I desire specially to emphasise. Firstly, we do not think we have retained in the Moscow discussions the spirit of the Yalta agreement, nor indeed, at points, the letter. It was never imagined by us that the Commission which we all three appointed with so much goodwill would not have been able to carry out their job swiftly and easily in a mood of give and take. We certainly thought that a Polish Government, 'new' and 'reorganised', would

by now have been in existence, recognised by all the United Nations. This would have shown the world our capacity and resolve to work together for its future. It is still not too late to achieve this.

3. In the Commission agreement was reached that Poles from inside Poland and from abroad would be summoned, not necessarily to take part in the government but merely for free and frank consultation, even before the forming of a new and reorganised Polish Government. Even this preliminary step cannot be taken because of the demand to veto any invitation, even to consultation, which the Soviet or Lublin Governments does not approve of. We can never agree to such a veto by anyone of us three. This veto reaches its supreme example in the case of Mr Mikołajczyk, who is regarded throughout the British and American world as the outstanding Polish figure outside Poland.

4. We also have learned with surprise and regret that Mr Molotov's proposal, made on his own initiative, to allow observers or missions to enter Poland has now been withdrawn. We are, therefore, deprived of all means of checking for ourselves information, often of a most painful character, which is sent us almost daily by the Polish Government in London. We do not understand why the situation in Poland should be shrouded in mystery. We offer fullest facilities to the Soviet Government to send missions or individuals to visit any of the territories under our military occupation. In several cases this offer has been accepted by the Soviets and visits have taken place to mutual satisfaction. We ask that the principle of reciprocity be observed in these matters, which would be a good foundation for our enduring partnership ...

6. ... If our efforts to reach agreement on Poland are doomed to failure I will have to confess that to Parliament when it returns from the Easter recess. No one has pleaded the cause of Russia with more fervour and conviction than I have tried to do. I was the first to raise my voice on 22 June 1941. It is more than a year since I proclaimed to a startled world the justice of the Curzon Line as Russia's western frontier and this frontier has now been accepted by both the British Parliament and the President of the United States. It is as a sincere friend of Russia that I make my personal appeal to you and to your colleagues to come to a good understanding about Poland with the Western democracies and not to spurn the hand of friendship in the future guidance of the world which we have extended.

116. Stalin to Churchill, 7 April 1945

I have received your message of 1 April on the Polish problem ... I must say the following:

1. The British and US Ambassadors – members of the Moscow Commission – do not want to reckon with the Polish Provisional Government and insist on inviting Polish leaders for consultation regardless of their attitude to the decisions of the Crimea Conference on Poland or to the Soviet Union. They insist, for example, on Mikołajczyk being invited to Moscow for consultations, and they do so in the form of an ultimatum, ignoring the fact that Mikołajczyk has openly attacked

the Crimea Conference decisions on Poland. However, if you think it necessary, I will try to persuade the Provisional Polish Government to withdraw its objections to inviting Mikołajczyk provided he publicly endorses the decisions of the Crimea Conference on the Polish question and declares in favour of establishing friendly relations between Poland and the Soviet Union.

2. You wonder why the Polish military theatre should be shrouded in secrecy. Actually, there is no secrecy at all. You forget that the Poles regard the despatch of British or other foreign observers to Poland as an affront to their national dignity, especially when it is borne in mind that the Polish Provisional Government feels the British Government has adopted an unfriendly attitude towards it. As for the Soviet Government, it has to take note of the Polish Provisional Government's negative view on sending foreign observers to Poland. Furthermore, you know that given a different attitude towards it, the Polish Provisional Government would not object to representatives of other countries entering Poland and would not put any difficulties in their way, as was the case, for example, with representatives of the Czechoslovak Government, the Yugoslav Government and others.

3. I had a pleasant talk with Mrs Churchill. She made a deep impression upon me. She gave me a present from you. Please accept my heartfelt thanks for it.

117. Churchill to Stalin, 14 April 1945

... I have been greatly distressed by the death of President Roosevelt with whom I had in the last five and a half years established very close personal ties of friendship. This sad event makes it all the more important that you and I are linked together by the many pleasant courtesies and memories even in the midst of all the perils and difficulties that we have surmounted.

... I must take the occasion to thank you for all the kindness with which you have received my wife during her visit to Moscow, and for all the care that is being taken of her on her journey through Russia. We consider it a great honour that she should receive the Order of the Red Banner of Labour on account of the work she has done to mitigate the terrible sufferings of the wounded soldiers of the heroic Red Army. The amount of money she collected is perhaps not great, but it is a love offering not only of the rich but mainly of the pennies of the poor who have been proud to make their small weekly contributions. The future of the whole world resides in the friendship of the masses of our peoples, in the mutual understanding of their governments and in the mutual respect of their armies.

118. Stalin to Churchill, 15 April 1945

Your message on the occasion of the death of President F. Roosevelt has reached me.

In President Franklin Roosevelt the Soviet people recognised an outstanding political leader and an unswerving champion of close cooperation between our three states.

President F. Roosevelt's friendly attitude to the Soviet Union will always be valued highly and remembered by our people.

As for myself, I am deeply touched by the loss of this great man, our common friend.

119. Churchill to Stalin, 15 April 1945

Mr Mikołajczyk came to see me today and after some conversation he issued the following declaration, which he wanted publicised immediately ...

1. I consider that close and lasting friendship with Russia is the cornerstone of future Polish policy within the wider friendship of the United Nations.

2. To remove all doubt as to my attitude, I wish to declare that I agree with the Crimea decision in regard to the future of Poland, its sovereign independent position and the formation of a provisional government representative of national unity.

3. I support the Crimea decision that a conference of leading Polish personalities be called with a view to constituting a government of national unity as widely and fairly representative of the Polish people as possible, which will receive recognition by the three major powers.

120. Stalin to Churchill, 18 April 1945

... Mikołajczyk's declaration is, of course, a big step forward, but it is not clear whether he accepts that part of the Crimea Conference decisions which relate to Poland's eastern frontier. It would be good, firstly, to have the full text of Mikołajczyk's declaration and, secondly, to receive from him elucidation as to whether he also accepts that part of the Crimea decisions which relate to Poland's eastern frontier.

121. Churchill to Stalin, 18 April 1945

My message of 16 April contained the full text of Mr Mikołajczyk's statement.

Since receiving your message I have made quite certain by explicit inquiry that Mr Mikołajczyk accepts the Crimea decisions as a whole, including that part which deals with the eastern frontiers of Poland. I should not indeed have thought it worthwhile to have forwarded his statement unless I had been sure that this was the case.

122. Churchill and Truman to Stalin, 18 April 1945

We are sending this joint reply to your messages of 7 April in regard to the Polish negotiations for the sake of greater clarity and in order that there will be no misunderstanding as to our position on this matter. The British and United States Governments have tried most earnestly to be constructive and fair in their approach and will continue to do so. Before putting before you the concrete and constructive suggestion which is the purpose of this message, we feel it necessary, however, to correct the completely erroneous impression which you have apparently received in regard to the position of the British and United States Governments ...

It is most surprising to have you state that the present government functioning in Warsaw has been in any way ignored during these negotiations. Such has never been our intention nor our position. You must know that our Ambassadors in

Moscow have agreed without question that the three leaders of the Warsaw Government should he included in the list of Poles to be invited to come to Moscow for consultation with the Polish Commission. We have never denied that among the three elements from which the new Provisional Government of National Unity is to be formed the representatives of the present Warsaw Government will play, unquestionably, a prominent part. Nor can it be said with any justification that our Ambassadors are demanding the right to invite an unlimited number of Poles. The right to put forward and have accepted by the Commission individual representative Poles from abroad and from within Poland to be invited to Moscow for consultation cannot be interpreted in that sense ... The real issue between us is whether or not the Warsaw Government has the right to veto individual candidates for participation in the conference ...

You mention the desirability of inviting eight Poles (five from within Poland and three from London) to take part in these first consultations, and in your message to the Prime Minister you indicate that Mikołajczyk would be acceptable if he issued a statement in support of the Crimea decision. We therefore submit the following proposals for your consideration in order to prevent a breakdown, with all its incalculable consequences, of our efforts to settle the Polish question. We hope that you will give them your most earnest and serious attention:

(1) That we instruct our representatives on the Commission to extend invitations immediately to the following Polish leaders to come to Moscow for consultation: Bierut, Osóbka-Morawski, Rola-Żymierski, Bishop Sapieha, one representative Polish political party leader not connected with the present Warsaw Government ... and from London Mikołajczyk, Grabski and Stanczyk.

(2) That once invitations to come for consultation have been issued by the Commission, the representatives of the Warsaw Provisional Government could arrive first if desired.

(3) That it be agreed that those Polish leaders called for consultation could suggest to the Commission the names of a certain number of other Polish leaders from within Poland or abroad who might be brought in for consultation in order that all the major Polish groups be represented in the discussions.

(4) We do not feel that we could commit ourselves to any formula for determining the composition of the new Government of National Unity in advance of consultation with the Polish leaders and we do not in any case consider the Yugoslav precedent to be applicable to Poland ...

123. Stalin to Churchill, 24 April 1945

I received the joint message from you and President Truman of April 18.

1. From this message it appears that you still regard the Polish Provisional Government, not as the nucleus of a future Polish Government of National Unity, but merely as a group on a par with any other group of Poles. It would be hard to reconcile this concept of the position of the Provisional Government and this attitude towards it with the Crimea decision on Poland. At the Crimea Conference the three of us, including President Roosevelt, proceeded from this –

that the Polish Provisional Government, as the Government now functioning in Poland and enjoying the trust and support of the majority of the Polish people, should be the core, that is, the main part of a new, reconstructed Polish Government of National Unity. It seems you disagree with this understanding of the issue. By turning down the Yugoslav example as a model for Poland, you confirm that the Polish Provisional Government cannot be regarded as a basis for, and the core of, a future Government of National Unity.

2. Another circumstance that should be borne in mind is that Poland borders on the Soviet Union, which cannot he said about Great Britain or the USA. Poland is to the security of the Soviet Union what Belgium and Greece are to the security of Great Britain. You evidently do not agree that the Soviet Union is entitled to seek in Poland a Government that would be friendly to it, that the Soviet Government cannot agree to the existence in Poland of a Government hostile to it. This is obligatory because, among other things, of the buckets of blood shed by the Soviet people on the fields of Poland liberating that country. I do not know whether a genuinely representative Government has been established in Greece, or whether the Belgian Government is a genuinely democratic one. The Soviet Union was not consulted when those Governments were being formed, nor did it claim the right to interfere in those matters, because it realises how important Belgium and Greece are to the security of Great Britain. I cannot understand why in discussing Poland no attempt is made to consider the interests of the Soviet Union in terms of security as well.

3. It is necessary to recognise as unusual a situation in which two Governments – those of the United States and Great Britain – reach agreement beforehand on Poland – a country in which the USSR is above all interested – and place Soviet representatives in an intolerable position, attempting to dictate terms to them ...

4. I am most grateful to you for kindly communicating the text of Mikołajczyk's declaration concerning Poland's eastern frontier. I am prepared to recommend to the Polish Provisional Government that they take note of this declaration and withdraw their objection to inviting Mikołajczyk for consultation on a Polish Government. The important thing now is to accept the Yugoslav precedent as a model for Poland. It seems to me that if this is done we shall be able to make progress on the Polish question.

124. Churchill to Stalin, 28 April 1945

1. Thank you for your message of 24 April. I have been much distressed at the misunderstanding that has grown up between us on the Crimea agreement about Poland. Of course, I went to Yalta with the hope that both the London and Lublin Polish Governments would be swept away and that a new government would be formed from among Poles of goodwill, among whom members of M. Beirut's government would be prominent. But you did not like this plan, and we and the Americans agreed, therefore, that the Bierut government should not be removed but that instead it should become a 'new' government 'reorganised on a broader democratic basis with the inclusion of democratic leaders from

Poland itself and from Poles abroad'. For this purpose, Mr Molotov and the two Ambassadors were to meet in Moscow and try to form such a government by consultations with members of the present Provisional Government and with other Polish democratic leaders from within Poland and from abroad.

2. The Commission then would have to set to work to select Poles who were to come for the consultations. We tried in each case to find representative figures and we were careful to exclude those who in our view were extremists and unfriendly to Russia ...

3. The candidates for invitation from within Poland and from abroad were proposed by us and the Americans with aim of helping the process ... Please note that those named were not to be members of a reorganised Polish Government but merely participants in the round table negotiations provided for in the Crimea declaration, the result of which would be to forward the formation of a united provisional government, representative of the main elements of Polish society and prepared to work on friendly terms with the Soviet Government, and also of a kind which we and the whole world could recognise. That was and still is our desire. This provisional government was then, in accordance with our joint decision in Crimea, to pledge itself to hold 'free and unfettered elections as soon as possible on the basis of universal suffrage and secret ballot' in which 'all democratic and anti-Nazi parties shall have the right to participate and put forward candidates'. Alas! Neither the first nor the second is any further forward.

4. In paragraph 1 you speak of accepting 'the Yugoslav precedent as a model for Poland'. You have always wished that our private personal series of telegrams should be frank and outspoken. I must say at once that the two cases are completely different. In the case of Poland, the three Powers reached agreement about how we should arrange the organisation of a new government ... In the case of Yugoslavia there was nothing of this kind ...

5. I must also say that the way things have worked out in Yugoslavia certainly does not give me the feeling of a fifty-fifty interest as between our countries. Marshal Tito has become a complete dictator. He has proclaimed that his prime loyalties are to the Soviet Union. Although he allowed members of the Royal Yugoslav Government to enter his government they number only six as against 25 of his own nominees. We have the impression that they are not being consulted on matters of high policy and that it is becoming a one-party regime. However, I have not made any complaint or comment about all this, and both at Yalta and at other times I have acquiesced in the settlement reached in Yugoslavia ...

6. We could not, however, accept 'the Yugoslav model' as a guide to what should happen in Poland. Neither we nor the Americans have any military or special interest in Poland ... We are all shocked that you suppose we would work for a Polish Government hostile to the USSR. This is the opposite of our policy. But it was on account of Poland that the British went to war with Germany in 1939 ... The British people do not, as is sometimes thought, go to war for calculation, but for sentiment ... they can never feel this war will have ended rightly unless Poland

has a fair deal in the full sense of sovereignty, independence and freedom on the basis of friendship with Russia. I thought this was what we had agreed at Yalta.

7. Side by side with this strong sentiment for the rights of Poland, which I believe is shared in at least as strong a degree throughout the United States, there has grown up throughout the English-speaking world a very warm and deep desire to be friends on equal and honourable terms with the mighty Russian Soviet Republic and to work with you, making allowances for our different systems of thought and government, in the long and bright years for all the world which we three Powers alone can make together. I, who in my years of great responsibility, have worked methodically for this unity, will certainly continue to do so by every means in my power, and in particular I can assure you that we in Great Britain would not work for or tolerate a Polish Government unfriendly to Russia. Neither could we recognise a Polish Government that did not truly correspond to the description in our joint declaration at Yalta with proper regard for the rights of the individual as we understand these matters in the Western world.

8. With regard to your reference to Greece and Belgium, I recognise the consideration which you gave me when we had to intervene with heavy armed forces to quell the EAM-ELAS attack upon the centre of government in Athens. We have given repeated instructions that your interest in Romania and Bulgaria is to be recognised as predominant. However, we cannot be excluded altogether, and we dislike being treated by your subordinates in these countries so differently from the kind manner in which we at the top are always treated by you ...

9. As to Belgium we have no conditions to demand, though naturally we would not be happy if they started putting in place rockets pointed at us, and we hope they will, under whatever form of government they adopt by popular decision, enter into a general system of defence to prevent Germany striking westward. Belgium, like Poland, is a theatre of war and a corridor of communication, and everyone must recognise the force of these factors ...

10. As to your third paragraph, it is true that we and the Americans have arrived at a definite line of action in relation to Poland. This is because we agree naturally upon the subject, and both sincerely feel we have been rather ill-treated by the way the matter has been handled since the Crimea Conference. No doubt these things seem different when looked at from the opposite point of view. However, we are absolutely agreed that the pledge we have given for a sovereign, free, independent Poland, with a government fully and adequately representing all democratic elements among the Poles, is for us a matter of honour and duty ...

11. .... There is no part of our occupied or liberated territory into which you are not free to send delegations, and people do not understand why you object to similar visits by British delegations to foreign countries liberated by you.

12. There is not much comfort in a future where you and the countries you dominate, plus the Communist parties in many other states, are all drawn up on one side, and those who rally to the English-speaking nations and their allies or Dominions, are on the other. It is quite obvious that their quarrel would tear the

world to pieces and that we, the leaders on both sides … would be shamed before history. Even embarking on a long period of suspicions, of abuse and counter-abuse and of opposing policies would be a disaster hampering the great develop-ment of world prosperity for the masses which is attainable only by the unity of our trinity. I hope there is no word or phrase in this outpouring of my heart to you which unwittingly gives offence. If so, let me know. But do not, I beg you, my friend Stalin, underrate the divergences which are opening about matters which you may think are unimportant to us but which are symbolic of the way the English-speaking democracies look at life.

125. Stalin to Churchill, 4 May 1945

I am in receipt of your message of April 28 on the Polish question.

I must say that I cannot agreed with the arguments put forward in support of your position.

1. You are disposed to regard the proposal that the Yugoslav precedent be accepted as a model for Poland as renunciation of the procedure agreed between us for setting up a Polish Government of National Unity. With this I cannot agree. I think that the Yugoslav example is important because it shows the way to the most expedient and practical solution of the problem of forming a new United Government …

2. I cannot subscribe to that part of your considerations on Greece where you suggest three-Power control over elections. Such control over the people of an Allied country would be seen as an affront and as a gross interference in their internal affairs. Such control is out of place in relation to former satellite countries which subsequently declared war on Germany and ranged themselves with the Allies, as demonstrated by electoral experience, for example, in Finland, where the election was held without outside interference and yielded positive results.

Your comments on Belgium and Poland as war theatres and communication corridors are perfectly justified. As regards Poland, it being a neighbour of the Soviet Union makes it essential for a future Polish Government to seek friendly relations between Poland and the USSR, which is also in the interest of all other freedom-loving nations … We insist, and will continue to insist, that only people who have demonstrated by deeds their friendly attitude to the Soviet Union, who are honestly and sincerely willing to cooperate with the Soviet state, should be consulted about the formation of a future Polish Government …

4. It is evident from your message that you are unwilling to consider the Polish Provisional Government as a basis for a future Government of National Unity, or to accord it the place in that Government to which it is entitled. I must say frankly that this position precludes the possibility of an agreed decision on the Polish question.

126. Churchill to Stalin, 15 June 1945

During our conference, from July 15 onwards, King George will be travelling in France and Germany inspecting his troops, and he will probably visit American Headquarters. He would like very much to have an opportunity of meeting you and some Soviet Generals. He would, therefore, like to come to Berlin on a day when we will all be together. He would, of course, take no part in the business of the conference. He would stay in the British sector. He would be very glad if you invited him to come to luncheon with you at Soviet Headquarters. He would, in the evening, give a dinner in the British sector to which he would invite yourself and other Soviet leaders and also President Truman and members of his delegation ... During his visit to Berlin he would, no doubt, confer British honours on British, Russian and American commanders ... I hope it would be a demonstration of goodwill and a cause for celebration which would be helpful in other respects ...

127. Churchill to Stalin, 22 June 1945

I had another conversation with the King yesterday and he suggested it might be better if he arrived at Berlin on the day arranged and simply gave luncheon to you and President Truman, together with suitable guests, and then departed in the afternoon to continue his inspection. It occurred to me this might be more convenient to you. Please let me know exactly how you feel and be assured no offence will be caused in this.

128. Stalin to Churchill, 23 June 1945

Your message of June 22 about the King visiting Berlin, and your previous message on the same subject, have reached me.

My plan did not envisage a meeting with the King. I had in mind a conference of the three of us, on which you, the President and myself had exchanged messages earlier. However, if you think it necessary that I should meet the King, I have no objection to your plan.

129. Churchill to Stalin, 1 July 1945

Thank you so much for your most kind telegram about the proposal that the King should visit Berlin during the conference, I greatly appreciate your answer. However, the King now finds it impossible for him to make his tour of Germany at the present time, as so many secret agents and special service officers will be required for the conference of the three. He has now informed me of his wish to visit Ulster at this time ...

130. Churchill-Stalin Meeting at Potsdam, 17 July 1945

The Generalissimo said that as his party was leaving Moscow, an unaddressed message was delivered [to him] through the Japanese Ambassador Sato. It was assumed that the message was intended for either the Generalissimo or President Kalinin or other members of the Soviet Government. It was from the Emperor of Japan who stated that 'unconditional surrender' could not be accepted by Japan, but if it was not insisted upon, Japan might be prepared to compromise with regard to other terms. The Emperor was making this suggestion in the interests of all concerned.

The Generalissimo had not spoken of this message to anyone except the Prime Minister, but he wanted to bring it up at the next session of the Conference.

The Prime Minister thought the Generalissimo should send [President Truman] a note on the subject in order to warn him before the next session.

The Generalissimo pointed out that he did not wish the President to think that the Soviet Government wanted to act as an intermediary, but he would have to no objection if the Prime Minister mentioned it to the President.

The Prime Minister agreed to do so pointing out that he also did not wish the President to feel that we were not at one with the United States in their aim of achieving complete victory over Japan. America had helped us enormously in the war against Germany and we intended to help her now to the full. At the same time people in America were beginning to doubt the need for 'unconditional surrender'. They were saying: was it worthwhile having the pleasure of killing ten million Japanese at the cost of one million Americans and British?

The Generalissimo remarked that the Japanese realised our strength and were very frightened. Unconditional surrender in practice could be seen here in Berlin and the rest of Germany.

The Prime Minister asked: where was Germany?

The Generalissimo said Germany was nowhere and everywhere.

The Generalissimo went to say that he could not understand German up-bringing. The Germans were like sheep and always needed a man who could give them orders. They never thought for themselves.

The Prime Minister agreed and said that the Germans had always believed in a symbol. If a Hohenzollern had been allowed to reign after the last war, there would have been no Hitler. They certainly were like sheep.

The Generalissimo said that the need for a symbol applied only to the Germans.

To illustrate the German sense of justice, the Generalissimo then spoke of an incident which had recently occurred in Berlin. An SS man had fired at a Russian soldier from a house. Soviet troops immediately surrounded the house. A crowd of Germans approached the troops and said that they had heard that, in retaliation, their rations would be stopped for a week. Instead of stopping their rations they offered 40 or 50 hostages. When the Russians refused the hostages, the Germans immediately entered the building and seized the SS man and handed him over. The Generalissimo observed that there were several questions he would like to discuss with the Prime Minister and it was agreed that they should meet at the Generalissimo's house at 8.30pm on July 18th.

The Generalissimo told the Prime Minister that he had taken to smoking cigars.

The Prime Minister replied that if a photograph of the Generalissimo smoking a cigar could be flashed across the world it would cause an immense sensation.

On the subject of working late hours, **the Generalissimo** said he had become so accustomed to working at night that now that the need had passed he could not get to sleep before 4am.

The Prime Minister thanked the Generalissimo for the welcome which Mrs Churchill had received during her visit to Russia.

The Generalissimo replied that the visit had been a great pleasure to him.

The Prime Minister spoke of the women workers in Stalingrad whom Mrs Churchill had seen and who had said they were glad to work hard as they were reconstructing the city for their husbands who would soon be coming home.

The Generalissimo appeared to be touched.

The Prime Minister said that Britain welcomed Russia as a Great Power and in particular as a Naval Power. The more ships that sailed the seas the greater chance there was for better relations.

The Generalissimo replied that he also wanted good relations. As regards Russia's fleet it was still a small one, nevertheless, great or small, it could be of benefit to Great Britain.

The Prime Minister asked Marshal Stalin whether in future he should call him Premier, Marshal or Generalissimo. Stalin replied that he hoped the Prime Minister would call him Marshal as he had always done in the past.

131. Churchill-Stalin Meeting at Potsdam, 18 July 1945

The following is a very fair summary of some of the salient points. The conversations lasted from 8.30pm till 1.30am and were thoroughly informal and genuinely friendly. It did not seem that any notes were taken by M. Pavlov to help him in his translation.

1. General Election in England. **Marshal Stalin** suggested that the Prime Minister would have a majority of 80. He thought the Labour Party would receive 220–230 seats. **The Prime Minister** was not sure how the soldiers had voted, but the Marshal said that an Army preferred a strong government and would therefore vote for the Conservatives.

Marshal Stalin asked why King George was not coming to Berlin, and **the Prime Minister** replied that it was because his visit would add to the security problem.

Marshal Stalin then volunteered the following: that no country needed a Monarchy so much as Great Britain, because the Crown was the unifying force throughout the Empire, and that no one who was a friend of Britain would do anything to weaken the respect shown to the Monarchy.

2. **The Prime Minister** said he would be going home for one day after the meeting on July 25.

The Prime Minister asked what Marshal Stalin thought of President Truman as Chairman of the Conference. He himself thought the President was doing well. **Marshal Stalin** replied that it was too early to say.

3. Japan. **Marshal Stalin** showed the Prime Minister the Soviet Government's reply to the Mikado's message. In their reply, the Soviet Government stated that as the Mikado's message had been in general terms and contained no concrete proposals, the Soviet Government could take no action.

From Marshal Stalin's further statements, it was evident that Russia intends to attack Japan soon after August 8. (The Marshal thought it might be a fortnight later.)

4. **The Prime Minister** said that it was his policy to welcome Russia as a great power on the sea. He wished to see Russian ships sailing across the oceans of the world. Russia had been like a giant with his nostrils pinched: this referred to the narrow exits from the Baltic and the Black Sea.

The Prime Minister brought up the question of Turkey and the Dardanelles. He said the Turks were very frightened. **Marshal Stalin** explained what had happened: the Turks had approached the Russians with regard to a treaty of alliance. In reply the Russians had said that there could be a treaty only if neither side had any claims. Russia however claimed Kars and Ardahan, which had been taken away from her at the end of the last War. The Turks then said that they could not discuss this claim. Russia then raised the question of the Montreux Convention. Turkey said she could not discuss it, so Russia replied that she could not discuss a treaty of alliance.

The Prime Minister said that he personally would support an amendment to the Montreux Convention, throwing out Japan and giving Russia access to the Mediterranean. He repeated that he welcomed Russia's appearance on the oceans, and this referred not only to the Dardanelles but also to the Kiel Canal, which should have a regime like the Suez Canal, and to the warm waters of the Pacific. This was not out of gratitude for anything Russia had done, but his settled policy.

The Marshal brought up the question of the German Fleet. He said that a share of it would be most useful for Russia, who had suffered severe losses at sea. He was grateful to the Prime Minister for the ships delivered in connection with the surrender of the Italian Navy, but he would like his share of the German ships.

5. **Marshal Stalin** spoke of Greek aggression on the Bulgarian and Albanian frontiers. He said that there were elements in Greece which were stirring up trouble.

The Prime Minister said that the situation on the frontiers was confused, and that the Greeks were grievously alarmed at the Yugoslav and Bulgarian attitude. He had not heard of any fighting worthy of the name. He thought that the Conference should make its will plain to these small Powers, and that none should be allowed to trespass or fight. They should be told this plainly and that any alteration in the frontier lines could only be settled at the Peace Conference. Greece was to have a plebiscite and free elections, and he suggested that observers should be sent to Athens by the Great Powers. **Marshal Stalin** thought that the presence of observers would show a want of confidence in the honesty of the Greek people. He thought that the Ambassadors of the Great Powers should report on the elections.

6. **Marshal Stalin** asked what were the Prime Minister's views about Hungary? **The Prime Minister** replied that he was not sufficiently informed upon the subject to give a view on the immediate situation, but he would enquire of the Foreign Secretary.

Marshal Stalin said that in all the countries liberated by the Red Army, the Russian policy was to see a strong, independent, sovereign State. He was against

Sovietization of any of those countries. They would have free elections, and all except Fascist parties would participate.

7. <u>Yugoslavia</u>. **The Prime Minister** spoke of the difficulties in Yugoslavia, where we had no material ambitions, but there had been the 50–50 arrangement. It was now 99–1 against Britain. **Marshal Stalin** protested that it was 90 per cent British, 10 per cent Yugoslavian, and 0 per cent Russian interests. In reply to the Prime Minister's remarks, he said that Marshal Tito had the partisan mentality and had done several things he ought not to have done. The Soviet Government often did not know what Marshal Tito was about to do.

8. <u>Roumania</u>. **Marshal Stalin** said that he had been hurt by the American demand for a change of Government in Roumania and Bulgaria. He was not meddling in Greek affairs, so he thought it was unjust of the Americans to make the present demand. **The Prime Minister** said he had not before seen the American proposals. **Marshal Stalin** explained that in the case of countries where there had been an émigré government, he had found it necessary to assist in the creation of a home government. This of course did not apply in the case of Roumania and Bulgaria. Everything was peaceful in those two countries. **The Prime Minister** asked why the Soviet Government had given an award to King Michael. **The Marshal** thought King Michael had acted bravely and wisely at the time of the coup d'etat.

9. **The Prime Minister** spoke of the anxiety felt by some people with regard to Russia's intentions. He drew a line from the North Cape to Albania, and named the capitals east of that line which were in Russian hands. It looked as if Russia were rolling on westwards. Marshal Stalin said he had no such intention. On the contrary, he was withdrawing troops from the West. Two million men would be demobilized and sent home within the next four months. Further demobilization was only a question of adequate railway transport.

10. **Marshal Stalin** mentioned that Russian losses during the War had amounted to 5 million killed and missing. The Germans had mobilized 18 million men apart from industry, and the Russians 12 million.

11. **The Prime Minister** hoped that agreement would be reached both as regards the questions connected with the frontiers of all European countries as well as Russia's access to the seas, including the division of the German Fleet, before the Conference ended. He said that the Three Powers gathered round the table were the strongest the world had ever seen, and it was their task to maintain the peace of the world.

It was agreed that, although satisfactory to us, the German defeat had been a great tragedy. But the Germans were like sheep. The Prime Minister told the story of young Lieutenant Tirpitz. **Marshal Stalin** spoke of his experience in Germany in 1907, when two hundred Germans missed a Communist meeting because there was no-one to take their tickets at the station barrier.

12. **Marshal Stalin** apologised for not having officially thanked Great Britain for the help in the way of supplies during the War. This would be done.

13. **Marshal Stalin**, in reply to a question, explained the working of Collective and State farms. It was agreed that both in Russia and Britain there was no fear of unemployment. The Marshal said that Russia was ready to talk about Anglo-Russian trade. The Marshal said that the best publicity for Soviet Russia abroad would be the happiness and well-being of her people. The Marshal spoke of the continuity of Soviet policy. If anything were to happen to him, there would be good men ready to step into his shoes. He was thinking thirty years ahead.

Chapter 9

Churchill's 'Operation Unthinkable'

Not declassified until 1998 and dated 22 May 1945, 'Operation Unthinkable' was a scenario for war with Russia drawn up by the British Chiefs of Staff Joint Planning Staff. It is not clear when Churchill ordered his military planners to devise such a scenario but it must have been no later than April 1945. Evidently, Churchill was thinking about the possibility of war or some kind of military conflict with the USSR even before the final defeat of Nazi Germany by the Soviet-Western coalition. 'Operation Unthinkable', it should be noted, predates the testing of the first atomic bomb in July 1945, so it was a feasibility study and contingency plan – perhaps the last of its kind – for a conventional world war, not a nuclear one.

'Operation Unthinkable' was concocted at a low point in Anglo-Soviet relations. The Soviets and the British and Americans were in the midst of the prolonged post-Yalta dispute about creating a new Polish government. The Allied invasion and occupation of Germany was in full swing but, following the 'Berne incident', Moscow suspected its Western Allies might sign truces with German forces in Italy and elsewhere that would facilitate a last-gasp redeployment of troops to the Soviet-German front. Churchill was frustrated by the American refusal to use Western military power on the ground to extract further political concessions from Stalin. Marshal Tito was excluding British influence from Yugoslavia while the Greek communists were challenging for power in a country deemed vital to Britain's strategic position in the Mediterranean. Above all, there was the shadow of Roosevelt's death in April 1945 and how that and the appointment of a new US President – Harry S. Truman – might impact on the future of British-American as well as Soviet-American relations. Moreover, it was unclear what would happen when the United States redeployed its military forces to finish off Japan following the Allied victory in Europe.

Churchill's mood at this time is captured by what he wrote to his Foreign Secretary, Anthony Eden, in early May 1945:

> I fear terrible things have happened during the Russian advance through Germany to the Elbe. The proposed withdrawal of the United States Army to the occupational lines arranged with the Russians ... would mean the tide of Russian domination sweeping forward 120 miles on a front of 300 or 400 miles. This ... event ... would be one of the most melancholy in history ... Poland would be completely engulfed and buried deep in Russian-occupied lands ... the territories under Russian control would include the Baltic Provinces, all of Germany to the occupational line, all Czechoslovakia,

a large part of Austria, the whole of Yugoslavia, Hungary, Romania, Bulgaria, until Greece in her tottering condition is reached. It would include all the great capitals of middle Europe ... This constitutes an event in the history of Europe to which there has been no parallel ... these matters can only be settled before the United States Armies in Europe are weakened. If they are not settled before the US Armies withdraw from Europe ... there are no prospects of a satisfactory solution and very little of preventing a Third World War.[1]

Apart from Jonathan Walker's book, 'Operation Unthinkable' has been little discussed by historians. It is not mentioned at all in Martin Gilbert's eight-volume official biography of Churchill. According to British historian David Dilks, the document was purely exploratory, while for Churchill expert David Reynolds it constitutes evidence that after the exertions of five years of war, Churchill was mentally and physically ill.[2]

'Operation Unthinkable' was drawn up in utmost secrecy; staff officers in the various service ministries were not even consulted about its contents. The plan and its associated documents may be found in the National Archives of Great Britain. The cover sheet, on Ministry of Defence headed notepaper, has written on it 'Russia Threat to Western Civilisation'.[3]

The political goal of the projected operation was 'to impose upon Russia the will of the United States and the British Empire'. As the document pointed out, even if the 'will' of the two countries was limited to a 'square deal for Poland' that would not limit the military commitment involved in going to war with Russia: 'a quick success might induce the Russians to submit to our will ... but it might not. That is for the Russians to decide. If they want total war, they are in a position to have it.'

As stated by the planners, 'Operation Unthinkable' was based on the following assumptions. Firstly, that it would have the support of Anglo-American public opinion, hence the morale of British and American troops would be high. Secondly, there would be assistance from Polish armed forces serving in Anglo-American armies. German manpower and industrial capacity would also be utilised. Thirdly, Russia – at that time still neutral in the Far Eastern war – would ally itself with Japan. Fourthly, hostilities would begin on 1 July 1945.

The scenario sketched in 'Operation Unthinkable' was only a few pages long but the document, together with its extensive appendices, contained a lot of detail about the strength and disposition of the opposing forces, not just in Europe but globally. The USSR was to be defeated much like Hitler had envisioned – by the occupation of 'metropolitan Russia' and the 'decisive defeat of the Russian forces in the field'. The document was signed by Captain Guy Grantham (Director of Plans at the Admiralty), Brigadier Geoffrey Thompson (Director of Plans at the War Office) and Air Commodore Walter Lloyd Dawson (Director of Plans for the Air Staff), who concluded:

(a) If we are to embark on war with Russia we must be prepared to be committed to a total war, which will be both long and costly.

(b) Our numerical inferiority on land renders it extremely doubtful whether we could achieve a limited and quick success, even if the political appreciation considered that this would suffice to gain our political objective.

On 24 May the Joint Planners had a meeting with the British Chiefs of Staff and gave them a copy of their plan. That evening, the Chairman of the Chiefs of Staff Committee, Field Marshal Sir Alan Brooke, recorded in his diary:

I went carefully through the Planners' report on the possibility of taking on Russia should trouble arise in our future discussions with her. We were instructed to carry out this investigation. The idea is of course fantastic and the chances of success quite impossible. There is no doubt that from now onwards Russia is all powerful in Europe.[4]

On 31 May, when the British Chiefs of Staff discussed 'Unthinkable' with their Joint Planners, Brooke noted in his diary that 'we are more convinced than ever that it is unthinkable'.[5]

Churchill followed up the 'Operation Unthinkable' document with a request to his Chiefs of Staff to consider 'our potential ability to exert pressure on Russia by the threat or use of force'. They responded on 8 June with a pithy memo that summarised the balance of forces. General Hastings Ismay, Churchill's military advisor, who forwarded the report to the Prime Minister, noted that the Chiefs felt that 'the less that was put on paper on this subject the better'.

The key estimate in the Chiefs' report was that the Soviets had at their disposal 264 divisions including 36 armoured, while the Western Allies had only 103 divisions with just 23 armoured. The Chiefs of Staff concluded that 'it is clear from the relative strength of the respective land forces that we are not in a position to take the offensive with a view to achieving a rapid success ... once hostilities began it would be beyond our power to win a quick but limited success and we should be committed to a protracted war against heavy odds. These odds, however, would become fanciful if the Americans grew weary and indifferent and began to be drawn away by the magnet of the Pacific War.'

Churchill was nothing if not persistent and he responded to the Chiefs' memo by asking his Joint Planners how Great Britain could be defended from a Russian advance in event of an American withdrawal to the Pacific. A minute, drafted in Churchill's name and dated 9/10 June, observed that 'by retaining the codeword 'UNTHINKABLE', the Staffs will realise that this remains a precautionary study of what, I hope, is still a purely hypothetical contingency'.

The Joint Planners were more optimistic in relation to defending against a possible Soviet attack on Britain than they were about an offensive war against Russia. While Soviet armies would undoubtedly be able to reach the shores of the North Sea and the Atlantic they did not have the naval strength to threaten Britain's sea communications, let alone successfully invade the British Isles. The Soviet Air Force was geared to tactical support for land campaigns rather than strategic bombing of industries and cities so the RAF should be able to parry Russian aerial attacks on Britain. But the Soviets could attack Britain with rockets and pilotless aircraft (as the Germans had done with their V1 and V2 attacks in 1944–5). The planners concluded: 'It is only by the use of rockets and other new weapons that the Russians could develop any serious threat to the security of this country in the initial stages. Invasion or a serious attack on our communications could only be undertaken after a period of preparation which must last some years.'

By the time this document was composed in mid-July the British General Election had been held and Churchill was on the verge of an historic defeat at the hands of the Labour Party. Counting of the votes was delayed while awaiting receipt of ballots from British military personnel serving overseas. It was this delay that enabled Churchill to attend the first part of the Potsdam conference in the second half of July. When he heard the news from Truman about the successful atomic bomb test Churchill's interest in the feasibility of 'Operation Unthinkable' was reignited but his departure from office meant there was no further work on the operation. While the plans were consigned to the archives, the post-war period saw a mushrooming of Western preparations for war with Russia as the Grand Alliance collapsed and the Cold War intensified.

The documents on 'Operation Unthinkable' prompt two questions. First, was the Red Army in 1945 preparing or planning for the contingency of an offensive that would project its forces to the shores of the Atlantic and the North Sea? The answer is no because on 23 June 1945 the USSR passed a law on the demobilisation of its army and navy. Demobilisation began on 5 July and ended in 1948. The army and navy were reduced from eleven million to less than three million. The State Defence Committee and the Headquarters of the Supreme Command that had been established in July 1941 were abolished. The number of military districts decreased from thirty-three to twenty-one. The number of troops in East Germany, Poland and Romania was significantly reduced. In September 1945, Soviet troops were withdrawn from northern Norway, in November from Czechoslovakia, in April 1946 from Bornholm (Denmark) and from Bulgaria in December 1947. The main task of the Red Army in the Soviet defence plan of 1947 was not offensive action in the event of war but securing the USSR's borders. Only in 1949, when NATO was established, did the Soviet Union inaugurate an accelerated programme of rearmament.[6]

Second, did the Soviet leadership know about British plans for war against the USSR? The answer to this question is yes. The first information about 'Operation Unthinkable' arrived in Moscow on 18 May 1945 under the unusual rubric of 'Extremely Urgent',[7] which meant the message was very important and required immediate delivery to the addressee.

The information was from Agent X in London – whose identity remains classified – who reported that at Churchill's behest a plan for a sudden attack by the Anglo-Americans on the Soviet forces in Germany was under development. The agent reported that preparation of the plan by the Joint Planning Staff had begun on 15 May. On that day Brigadier Thompson had announced to a meeting of the planners that the plan would be prepared in absolute secrecy and that Churchill wanted to teach Stalin a lesson, 'to drive the Russians east of the Curzon Line and then make peace'.

Agent 'X' also reported that 'Unthinkable' entailed a surprise attack by two army groups – one from the north of Germany, and the other from the Leipzig region into the centre of Poland. It would be accompanied by powerful air raids on crucial communications centres and on the most important cross-river railway bridges. Subsequently, there would be an offensive south of the Linz-Vienna axis. The possibility of dispatching Special Forces to the Black Sea and the bombing of the Caucasian oil refineries were being considered, as were sea and air operations against Leningrad.

This information on 'Operation Unthinkable' was reported to Stalin and Molotov by the Chief of Soviet military intelligence, Lieutenant-General I.I. Il'ichev. The reactions of the Soviet leadership to 'Unthinkable' remain unknown but on 29 May Stalin and his Chief of Staff, General A.I. Antonov, signed a directive ordering reorganisation of the 1st Belorussian Front and the establishment on 10 June of a Group of Soviet Occupation Forces in Germany with Marshal G.K. Zhukov as its commander-in-chief. On 9 July 1945 the State Defence Committee issued a decree on the armouring and mechanisation of the Red Army that gave priority to strengthening troops in the western direction.[8] Such precautions were entirely understandable.

Given the enormous sacrifices of the Red Army and the Soviet people in defeating Nazi Germany, 'Operation Unthinkable' was a rather distasteful episode in the history of the Grand Alliance. While it did not negate the positive pages in its history, it did besmirch the great coalition that had just beaten Hitler after such a titanic struggle. It also pointed towards the post-war problems and mentalities that would beset the Grand Alliance, not least the role that Churchill would play in promoting a Cold War against his erstwhile comrade-in-arms, Joseph Stalin.

Chapter 10

Aftermath: Churchill, Stalin and the Cold War

Less than a year after the end of the war the two comrades-in-arms who had done so much to defeat Hitler clashed publicly in an episode that is often seen as the harbinger of the decades-long Soviet-Western Cold War.

When Stalin met Churchill at the Potsdam conference, he confidently predicted an eighty-seat Tory majority when they counted the votes from the recent British General Election. Much to Stalin's surprise, if not Churchill's, the result was a landslide victory for the Labour Party. Churchill remained leader of the Conservative Party but after all the excitement and glories of the war, he did not relish sitting on the House of Commons' opposition benches. He missed the power and the limelight and craved publicity. An opportunity to return to public prominence came with an invitation from Westminster College in Fulton, Missouri to give a speech and receive an honorary degree. Missouri was President Truman's home state and his presence on the platform at the conferring ceremony on 5 March 1946 added political weight and ensured the event received mass coverage by the American media.

Churchill's Fulton speech was rather pompously titled 'The Sinews of Peace' – a reference to the need for a robust post-war peace settlement. Captured by iconic newsreel footage, the most famous section of the speech was this:

> From Stettin in the Baltic to Trieste in the Adriatic an iron curtain has descended across the Continent. Behind that line lie all the capitals of the ancient states of Central and Eastern Europe. Warsaw, Berlin, Prague, Vienna, Budapest, Belgrade, Bucharest and Sofia, all these famous cities ... lie in what I must call the Soviet sphere, and all are subject in one form or another, not only to Soviet influence, but to a very high and, in some cases, increasing measure of control from Moscow ... The Communist parties ... have been raised to pre-eminence and power far beyond their numbers and are seeking everywhere to obtain totalitarian control.

Churchill went on to talk about the communist threat in Western Europe and to highlight anxieties provoked by Soviet policies in relation to Turkey, Iran and the Far East. Churchill's moral was that Western democracies had to stick together and take a strong stand in defence of their principles. The Russians had no respect for weakness, Churchill told his audience, and he drew a parallel with the appeasement that had allowed Hitler to unleash war. To prevent that happening again 'a good understanding' should be reached with Russia.

Churchill was by means uniformly hostile to the Soviet Union. As well as warning of the dangers of the 'iron curtain' he spoke about extending the term of the 1942 Anglo-Soviet treaty of alliance from 20 to 50 years (a proposal that British Foreign Secretary Ernest Bevin had put to Stalin in December 1945). 'We aim at nothing but mutual assistance and collaboration with Russia', said Churchill, and he expressed

> strong admiration and regard for the valiant Russian people and for my war-time comrade, Marshal Stalin. There is deep sympathy and goodwill in Britain ... towards the people of all the Russias and a resolve to persevere through many differences and rebuffs in establishing lasting friendships. We understand the Russian need to be secure on her western frontiers by the removal of all possibility of German aggression. We welcome Russia to her rightful place among the leading nations of the world. We welcome her flag upon the seas.[1]

Churchill saw the speech as the most important of his career but not because of the 'iron curtain' reference. It was because of a section of the speech that introduced an equally enduring idea – the Anglo-American 'special relationship'. Churchill believed that a strong British-American alliance was essential to create a stable post-war order – a stance that stemmed from his wartime realisation that only the Americans could save Britain from Hitler and only the United States had the power to preserve the values of the English-speaking world.

The anti-Soviet theme of Churchill's speech was generally welcomed in the United States but his call for an Anglo-American alliance was criticized as a species of dangerous power politics that could marginalize the newly-created United Nations, a body designed to ensure peace and security for all states.[2]

Churchill was heavily criticized in *Pravda* and *Izvestiya* but both papers carried long summaries and extracts from the speech, including his remarks about the 'iron curtain' – a concept that Hitler's propaganda chief, Joseph Goebbels, had used during the war to characterise the Red Army's liberation of Eastern Europe from German occupation.

On 14 March Stalin responded to the Fulton speech with a ferocious personal attack on Churchill. In an interview with *Pravda* he accused Churchill of being a warmonger who had adopted 'a war position, a call for war on the USSR'. He also compared Churchill to Hitler as an advocate of the racialist theory of the superiority of English-speaking nations. Stalin did not mention the 'iron curtain' but he frankly asserted the USSR's right to have friendly regimes in Eastern Europe, given the role these states had previously played in providing a platform for German aggression against the Soviet Union. Stalin unashamedly talked up the post-war growth of communism:

> The increased influence of communism cannot be considered fortuitous ...
> The influence of the communists has grown because in the years of the rule of Fascism in Europe the communists showed themselves trusty, fearless, self-sacrificing fighters ... Mr Churchill in his speeches sometimes recalls

the plain people ... These plain people have views of their own, a policy of their own, and they know how to stand up for themselves. It was they, the millions of these plain people, that defeated Mr Churchill and his party in Britain.

In conclusion, Stalin alluded to Churchill's role in the anti-Bolshevik coalition that had intervened in the Russian civil war and promised that if 'Churchill and his friends' succeeded in organising a 'new march against "Eastern Europe"' they 'will be beaten again as they were beaten in the past'.[3]

Stalin's tart response to Churchill's Fulton speech was a sign of the drastic deterioration in Soviet relations with Britain and the United States that occurred immediately after the end of the war. The Yalta and Potsdam promise of a peace-time Grand Alliance remained unfulfilled. Instead there was prolonged wrangling about the terms of peace treaties to be imposed on ex-enemy states, clashes in relation to Iran, Turkey and Japan, Western complaints about Soviet ideological expansionism and Soviet complaints about American military globalism. Still, it was a year or more before the Cold War broke out. More decisive in precipitating the final collapse of the Grand Alliance than Churchill's remarks about the 'iron curtain' was Truman's containment speech of March 1947 in which the US President proclaimed to Congress that America's global mission should be the defence of the 'free world' against further totalitarian encroachments.

Notwithstanding Stalin's venomous attack on him, Churchill was happy to send the Soviet dictator birthday greetings in December 1946, to which Stalin replied: 'my warm thanks for your good wishes on my birthday'. In January 1947 Field Marshal Montgomery visited Moscow and Stalin took the opportunity to give Monty a message for Churchill saying that he had the happiest memories of working with Britain's great war leader. Churchill responded on 3 February 1947:

I always look back on our comradeship together, when so much was at stake, and you can always count on me where the safety of Russia and the fame of its armies are concerned ... Your life is not only precious to your country, which you saved, but to the friendship between Soviet Russia and the English-speaking world.[4]

By the time he returned to power as British Prime Minister in 1951 Churchill had shed the mantle of Cold Warrior bestowed on him by the Fulton speech and rein-vented himself as a peacemaker who preferred 'jaw-jaw to war-war'. In February 1950 he had called for a 'parley at the summit' with the USSR, thus introducing another new word to the international political lexicon. Churchill's call for the resumption of top-level meetings with Soviet leaders did bear fruit, but not until after Stalin's death from a stroke in March 1953. In June 1953 Churchill himself suffered a debilitating stroke and it was his Foreign Secretary and successor as Prime Minister, Anthony Eden, who played the starring role in a series of Soviet-Western summits in 1954–5. The main Soviet participant in these summits was Vyacheslav Molotov, who had lost his job as Soviet foreign minister in 1949 but returned to the post when Stalin died. Molotov's mission at these summits was much the same as the role he had played during the war – to find an acceptable basis for Soviet collaboration with the West. Such a task was all the more pressing now that both the United States and the USSR possessed hydrogen bombs – nuclear weapons of mass destruction that threatened the very existence of humankind.

When Stalin died Churchill reputedly said that 'he had found Russia working with wooden ploughs and is leaving her equipped with atomic piles'. Actually, the attribution is a myth.[5] Churchill admired Stalin as a great war leader but disdained his dictatorial rule and was not overly impressed by socialist economic construction. Indeed, Churchill said nothing publicly when Stalin died; he did not even send a condolence card. But in years to come he was keen to stress that whatever his other faults, Stalin's word was his bond.

According to the Yugoslav communist, Milovan Djilas, Stalin reportedly told him in 1945 that 'Churchill is the kind of man who will pick your pocket of a kopeck if you don't watch him'.[6] Stalin may well have said something along those lines: he liked to impress his comrades with tough talk about the capitalist enemy. But this book has provided abundant evidence that while Stalin never forgot the fundamental political gulf that separated him from Churchill, he did not allow such differences to preclude cooperation with even as militant an anti-communist as his wartime comrade-in-arms.

Winston Churchill: Wartime Traveller
By Ged Martin

Winston Churchill was Britain's prime minister through five years of war in Europe, from 10 May 1940 to VE Day on 8 May 1945. In that time, he made a remarkable 25 foreign trips, spending no fewer than 369 days – more than one year of the five – out of the country. Even if we discount short cross-Channel excursions – five in May and June 1940 to stiffen French morale and seven more to Normandy and the advancing front into Germany in 1944–5 – we still have an itinerary of foreign travel astonishing in a man who turned 70 in the last year of the war.

Churchill crossed the Atlantic six times to lobby Roosevelt, whom he also met at Casablanca in Morocco. There were two journeys to Moscow to see Stalin, both involving long and cumbersome detours through the Mediterranean, the second undertaken in October 1944 to assure 'Uncle Joe' that Britain and the United States were not plotting against him. Then there were the meetings of the Big Three at Tehran in 1943 and Yalta in 1945. (A third gathering, of Churchill, Stalin and Truman at Potsdam, is excluded from this survey as it took place after the Nazi surrender.) In addition, Churchill flew from Casablanca in January 1943 to seek help from the Turks, and in Christmas week 1944 travelled to Athens to preach peace to the Greeks – noble but hopeless excursions. The mobile premier sought to mediate between Serbs and Croats, monarchists and Communists, and Charles de Gaulle and the rest of humanity. To an amazing degree, Churchill's wartime leadership was peripatetic.

Winston Churchill had always been a great traveller. He had spent his 21st birthday under fire in Cuba, and before turning 30 he had seen warfare in India, the Sudan and South Africa. His political career had never been Whitehall-bound. Within months of receiving his first political job, at the Colonial Office, he was off to inspect Britain's empire in East Africa. In October 1914, as First Lord of the Admiralty, he tried to take charge of the defence of Antwerp. Yet his Second World War travels were unprecedented. By September 1943, Churchill's staff calculated that he had travelled 111,000 miles, and spent 339 hours in the air. Public opinion had admired Chamberlain's courage – if not his diplomacy – in flying across Germany to meet Hitler in Munich. In five years of war, Churchill notched up the equivalent of a journey three-quarters of the way to the Moon.

Many of Churchill's journeys were vital for the waging of war. One of the earliest politicians to win pilot's wings, it was fitting that Winston Churchill should become the world's first practitioner of summit and shuttle diplomacy.

Churchill came as close to persuading the French to fight on in 1940 as any out-sider could have done. His meeting with Roosevelt off the coast of Newfound-land in August 1941 was far-reaching in its consequences, both in demonstrating the determination of the United States to resist the Nazis, and in committing both countries to the principles of the Atlantic Charter. Churchill's personal partnership with FDR remains one of the key elements of the story of the Second World War. It may also be argued that his attempts to win the trust of Stalin were bold and that his epic journeys to meet 'Uncle Joe' were perhaps the only way that the dictator's suspicions of the Western Allies could be blunted.

Churchill sought to build personal relationships. On his first visit to the White House, he stepped from his bath and – as was his habit – immediately began dictating memoranda to a secretary (male, of course). Unexpectedly, Roosevelt entered the room, to find his guest utterly naked. 'You see, Mr President', said the nonchalant Churchill, 'I have nothing to hide from you.' Roosevelt once said – perhaps as a politeness – that it was fun to live in the same decade as Churchill. Stalin, too, could give the impression of entering into the spirit of comradeship. When someone at a Moscow dinner in 1944 referred to the leaders of the three Great Powers as the Holy Trinity, Stalin joked that Churchill must be the Holy Spirit, 'He flies around so much'.

Churchill's epic journeys were also part of his inspirational hold on the British people. Learning of his intention to fly to Cairo in 1942, Oliver Harvey was moved by the 'energy and gallantry of the old gentleman'. On his return, *Punch* – in an allusion to the popular film *The Lion Has Wings* – published a cartoon of him as a flying bulldog. 'It will make a great effect that Winston at the age of 70 should fly out on Christmas Day to Athens', wrote Harold Nicolson – not always an admirer – of the mission to Greece in 1944. There is evidence, too, that the unexpected appearance of Churchill put heart into servicemen and embassy staffs as they did their bit for Britain far from home.

Yet there is another side to the story of Winston the wartime traveller. Churchill as historian portrayed his relationship with Roosevelt as the almost idyllic partnership of the Grand Alliance of English-speaking peoples, a view that Sir Martin Gilbert largely endorses. Other scholars, such as Warren F. Kimball and Christopher Thorne, see a less sentimental marriage of convenience, with Roosevelt battling to overcome a personal dislike for the 'Former Naval Person' which went back to his own days as Assistant Secretary for the Navy under Woodrow Wilson. Amiable or not, nobody can doubt that their relationship was one between needy client and powerful patron, as Churchill himself admitted. 'No man ever studied every whim of his mistress as I did those of President Roosevelt', he recalled in 1948. Stalin, too, of Georgian origins, made sure that Churchill came to pay court at the Kremlin, ignoring suggestions in 1942 that they meet in the Caucasus, and so adding 1,600 miles to the round trip from Cairo. Even the argument that visits from the winged Winston were inspirational to those on the front line can be questioned: was this really the best use of a leader's time? It is, after all, the task of generals and ambassadors to keep up the morale of soldiers and diplomats overseas. Had Churchill been killed on one of his foreign tours, the effect on morale would have been devastating.

Churchill's wartime travels were certainly dangerous. U-boats were a threat in the North Atlantic: in 1943, Churchill insisted on having a machine gun fitted to a lifeboat so that he might resist capture if torpedoed. Even without the Germans, bad weather could make an Atlantic voyage unpleasant: Churchill described his crossing on HMS *Duke of York* in December 1941 as 'the longest week I have lived since the war began', and he suffered even more from hot weather in September 1944, when the *Queen Mary* was forced to take a southerly route to avoid U-boats.

There are some amusing glimpses of Churchill running the war from the high seas. D-Day was rehearsed in a bath in his suite on the *Queen Mary*, in 1943, with senior officers churning the water to simulate waves. One of the most bizarre scenes of the war occurred on HMS *Ajax*, off Athens on Christmas Day 1944. Archbishop Damaskinos, seen as the only possible peacemaker among the Greeks, was ushered aboard in his full canonicals, including a mitre which reminded one of Churchill's staff of a chef's hat. There was an awkward moment when the Archbishop ran into a raucous party of sailors celebrating Yuletide in fancy dress, who thought that the prince of the Church had come to join in the fun.

On his transatlantic voyages, radio silence often kept Churchill out of contact with London for long periods, which would have been highly inconvenient in a sudden crisis. Although Churchill had assured the King that it would be possible to fly home 'in a few hours', his first transatlantic flight took over 26 hours. The first generation of airliners were neither comfortable nor very safe. They were not pressurised, and en route to Cairo in 1942, Churchill insisted that his oxygen mask be adapted to accommodate a cigar. Key personnel were lost in air crashes on their way to or from Newfoundland in 1941, Casablanca in 1943 and Yalta in 1945. Brooke, Tedder and Wavell had a close escape from disaster travelling to Moscow in 1942. Harold Macmillan was seriously injured in a crash-landing in North Africa. Churchill's Boeing flying boat survived a lightning strike in mid-Atlantic in 1943.

Returning without fighter escort from France in June 1940, Churchill had a brush with the Luftwaffe. The pilot of the de Havilland Flamingo – it shook passengers like 'salad in a colander manipulated by a particularly energetic cook' – dived to wave-top height to avoid two German fighters. Others were not so lucky. In August 1942, Churchill flew into Cairo, again without escort, to appoint General Gott as commander of the Eighth Army. Two days later, Gott was killed when his plane was attacked as it tried to land at the same airfield. On the day Churchill flew home from Gibraltar in June 1943, the actor Leslie Howard was killed when a Boeing Clipper was shot down over the Bay of Biscay.

Returning from Bermuda in January 1942, Churchill was briefly at risk from both friend and foe. His flying boat strayed from its route, an error only noticed five minutes' flying time from the coast of occupied France. The plane was turned north for Plymouth, only to be identified by radar as a hostile bomber. Six Hurricanes were scrambled to intercept the intruder. 'However', Churchill curtly noted, 'they failed in their mission.' In October of that year, Churchill's doctor, Sir Charles Wilson briefed the King's private secretary, 'Tommy' Lascelles, on Churchill's adventures. Lascelles noted that Wilson 'made my hair stand on end by his account of how nearly they have ended in disaster on more than one occasion'.

There were huge security risks in Churchill's travels, and several near-disasters. Tehran was a nightmare choice for a summit: the Shah's government lined the road from the airfield with uniformed cavalrymen, whose presence attracted large crowds whom they were unable to control. The danger of assassination was enormous, not only there but in Malta in 1943, when thousands turned out to welcome Churchill, or in any of his five visits to Cairo, where the British pro-consul, Lord Moyne, was murdered by the Zionist Stern Gang in 1944 (though Churchill himself supported Zionist aspirations). When Churchill visited the Blue Grotto at Capri in 1944, nobody seemed to have realised that the tourist trade had continued in full swing throughout the war, and the location had been especially popular with the occupying Germans. A Scotland Yard detective who reviewed the security situation in Paris advised the postponement of a planned visit in November 1944. The British Ambassador, Duff Cooper, successfully pointed out that Paris would be just as dangerous in the weeks ahead.

Security precautions were often lax and sometimes non-existent. The French prime minister, Reynaud, referred to Churchill's plans to fly to Tours in June 1940 over an open telephone line. British codes were less than ingenious: 'Christmas' for Turkey and 'Mr Cocktail' for Molotov were little more than schoolboy efforts, while 'Abraham' for Quebec would hardly have fooled any intelligence operative who knew that General Wolfe had captured the city on the Heights of Abraham. Churchill's own staff thought the device of sending telephone messages to General Ismay in Hindi – 'Pug' was an old India hand – was too clever by half, especially when peppered with allusions such as 'Lord President Sahib'. Nor were the risks imaginary. German radio broadcast news that Churchill and Roosevelt were about to meet somewhere in the western hemisphere the day before their rendezvous off Newfoundland in 1941. When Churchill crossed the Atlantic on the *Queen Mary* in May 1943, he and his high-powered entourage shared the liner with around 5,000 German prisoners of war, on their way to internment in Canada. Most had probably lost their enthusiasm for heroic gestures, but it seems amazing that nobody considered the risks of a mass mutiny. Yet Churchill could make light of elementary precautions. 'I mustn't tell you on the open line how we shall be travelling', he said to Roosevelt as he telephoned to announce his return from Florida in January 1942, 'but we shall be coming by puff-puff.'.

Far from avoiding danger, Churchill seemed to seek it out. Observers noted his excitement at any prospect of danger by sea or air. Lascelles noted 'there isn't a soul in the cabinet, or anywhere else, who will undertake to dissuade him'. This was not quite true: Eden talked him out of visiting Egypt after the fall of Tobruk, arguing that he would simply get in Auchinleck's way. 'You mean like a great blue-bottle buzzing over a huge cowpat!' Churchill challenged him, at which Eden quietly agreed. Only the pleading of George VI prevented the 69-year-old prime minister from taking part in D-Day, despite the misgivings of senior commanders. Churchill's plan to experience the bombardment of the beaches from HMS *Belfast* would have taken him away from the nerve-centre of government at a crucial moment and made him vulnerable to possible counter-attack – while the 14,000-yard range of the cruiser's guns would have meant that he would have seen nothing of the actual landings. Yet even three days before the invasion, Churchill's intentions remained unclear, and the King even considered driving through the night to forbid his prime minister's embarkation. The concession was made grudgingly: 'as Prime Minister & Minister of Defence, I ought to be allowed to go where I consider it my duty', he complained to his sovereign.

By way of compensation, Churchill positioned himself off the south of France to watch the Anvil landings two months later, even though he disapproved of the sideshow. His visits to Normandy in the weeks after D-Day were high-risk exercises in fact-finding. On D+6, he was lunching with Montgomery just three miles from the fighting when a casual enquiry revealed that there was in fact no continuous front line. On his third visit, as the Germans counter-attacked at Mortain, on 7 August, even Churchill sensed that his presence was inopportune, and he left after an hour. By the end of the year, he had managed to get himself close to fire both in Italy and the Vosges. Entering one Italian village to find rubble strewn about, his host, General Alexander, asked when the bombardment had stopped. Churchill was delighted with the reply: 'About a quarter of an hour ago.'

In March 1945, a pardonably triumphant Churchill joined British forces as they pushed into Germany. At one point, he wandered off from Alanbrooke's headquarters, and was later located with 'a boyish look of contentment' after achieving the personal goal of urinating into the Rhine, thus exposing himself in more than one way. (Some weeks previously, he had made a point of retaining a full bladder in order to perform a similar salute on the Siegfried Line: sadly, accompanying photographers were barred from immortalising the moment.) He was also determined to be among the first across the Rhine. Montgomery escorted him to the west bank the day after the first troops had crossed. 'Why don't we go across and have a look at the other side?', Churchill asked, and Monty unexpectedly agreed. For half an hour, in bright sunshine and accompanied by a mere handful of armed men, the prime minister and the field marshal strolled along the east bank, happily unmolested. Later, the American General Simpson took a firmer line, insisting that he could not guarantee his guest's safety from sniper attack. Churchill was 'like a small boy being called away from his sand-castles on the beach'.

Churchill's wartime travels were not only a risk to his safety but also a danger to his health. He was not a young man, and his lifestyle was never conducive to the longevity that he so mysteriously attained. When he became prime minister in May 1940, cabinet colleagues insisted that he accept Sir Charles Wilson (later Lord Moran) as his personal physician. Moran soon found that his 'thankless task' involved not simply medical but political decisions. At the White House on 26 December 1941, Churchill reported pains in his chest. In a split second, Moran diagnosed angina and decided to say nothing. Professionally, this was very risky: had Churchill succumbed to a heart attack, Moran would have been held responsible for failing to advise him. On the other hand, the obvious treatment, six weeks of total rest, would have torpedoed the Washington mission and announced to the world that Britain's leader 'was an invalid with a crippled heart and a doubtful future'. 'Forget your damned heart', he told his patient when the subject came up again after their arrival in Ottawa three days later. The gamble worked. Churchill went on to make one of his finest speeches ('Some chicken! Some neck!') to the Canadian parliament.

In caring for his patient, Moran had to fend off amateur intrusions into the medical sphere. When Churchill went to Italy in August 1944, Moran was determined that he should take the anti-malarial drug, mepacrine. His defiant patient invoked first the King, who had recently visited Italy without ill effects, then Alexander, who rated the risks of infection as slight and warned that the pills had unpleasant side-effects. Moran replied that refusal to take mepacrine in Italy was a court-martial offence, adding that 'General Alexander's views on medical matters have the same value as mine on military affairs'. Churchill disarmingly 'hoisted the yellow flag', but the pills – which had to be continued for four weeks after the visit – were still making him groggy as he travelled to the second Quebec conference.

By 1944, however, Moran was right to lay down the law. Repeated travelling had taken its toll. Churchill's return from Casablanca in February 1943 was followed by a bout of pneumonia. On Moran's advice, he travelled by sea to Washington three months later rather than subject his lungs to the hazards of flying. Nonetheless, Churchill was briefly felled by a fever and ran a temperature of 103 degrees. At the end of the year, returning from Tehran, he collapsed at Eisenhower's headquarters in Tunisia with a further bout of pneumonia. Fearing a heart attack, Moran ('that bloody old man', his patient called him) was soon summoning specialists from Britain. With an eye to history, Churchill pictured himself 'stranded among the ruins of Carthage'. His more practically-minded wife, Clementine, was more concerned that he was within two hours' flying time of German bases in Italy. After a dangerous flight through the Atlas Mountains, Churchill convalesced at Marrakesh. In total, he was away from Britain for over two months.

The risks that Churchill ran were not just physical, but political as well. Had he been killed, his obvious replacement was Anthony Eden, 'the outstanding Minister in the largest political party in the House of Commons', Churchill called him in June 1942, when he designated Eden to the King as his successor. But Eden's own health was precarious, and he too engaged in dangerous overseas missions. Beyond Eden, there was little potential leadership talent among the coalition government's Conservative ministers, few of whom would have been palatable to Labour anyway. Palace thinking was reflected in the interest shown by Lascelles in August 1943 in a suggestion that Viscount Cranborne should be regarded as second-in-line to the premiership. But 'Bobbety', heir to the Marquess of Salisbury and already a member of the House of Lords, hardly embodied the Britain that people thought they were fighting for, while his celebrated inability to artic-ulate the letter R (it emerged as a W) would have made him a laughing stock on the radio. In January 1945, on the eve of flying to Yalta with Eden, Churchill advised that, if both were killed, the King should commission one of the great 'Who?' figures of British political history, Sir John Anderson. A former civil servant and governor of Bengal, Anderson was an efficient Chancellor of the Exchequer. As MP for the Scottish Universities, he had the advantage of sitting in the Commons as an Independent. He could thus be plausibly nominated as a neutral, if presumably transitional, head of a coalition cabinet whose component parts were already looking towards post-war political conflict. Whether this Edinburgh Scot could have risen to inspirational national leadership may be doubted. Once, when both the prime minister and his deputy were out of the country at the same time, Churchill assured Attlee that they could safely entrust the government machine 'for a day or two to the automatic pilot'.

What did Churchill achieve in his travels? As already argued, in his dealings with Roosevelt and Stalin, he was doing no more than accept the responsibilities of leadership. Sometimes his personal diplomacy came unstuck, as with the 'half-sheet of paper' which he offered to Stalin in October 1944 as a basis for dividing Eastern Europe. The 'Percentages Agreement' (or 'naughty document') was a genuine attempt to agree policy between Britain and Russia on a post-war Europe from which the Americans were expected to withdraw. Yet there were risks in carrying on negotiations far from the support of civil servants and their files, espe-cially for somebody whose ideas could be so imaginative – or mercurial. During the Quebec conference in 1944, Churchill had to be briefed in his bath before talking to Roosevelt about the division of Germany into zones of occupation. There is something charming about the vignette of Churchill aboard HMS *Renown* on his way home from Halifax in 1943, using a box of matches to re-fight the battle of Omdurman, where he had served under Kitchener in 1898. Less pleasant, perhaps, is the thought of Churchill using matches in a late-night talk with Stalin at Tehran to demonstrate how the frontiers of Poland might be moved westwards. Away from home, Churchill was apt to push some of his pet ideas – such as the invasion of northern Norway or the seizure of a foothold in Sumatra. At Tehran, he astonished Eden – who was, after all, his foreign minister – by suddenly sug-gesting the transfer of southern Germany to a Danubian confederation. He was also liable to fall under the influence of travelling companions such as Beaver-brook or even his son Randolph, 'a dreadful young man' as Cadogan called him after an encounter in Cairo.

Unfortunately, Churchill the traveller could control neither the agenda nor the events around him. His last-gasp visit to France in June 1940 was actually turned against his own intentions: Churchill was not told that the divided French cabinet had gathered at a nearby chateau in the hope of meeting him. On learning that their ally had flown home without seeing them, the French ministers felt abandoned and swung towards surrender. Similarly, on his last night in Moscow in 1942, Churchill had planned to talk to the Polish leader, General Anders. Stalin, however, threw a surprise feast and ensured that there was no time for a proper discussion. Roosevelt was full of sympathy when news of the surrender of Tobruk reached Churchill in the White House in June 1942. Stalin, we may be sure, would have been less generous had news of such a disaster accompanied Churchill to Moscow.

Face-to-face meetings did not in themselves guarantee effective communication. Roosevelt and Mackenzie King were both part of the English-speaking world (although community of language did not ensure agreement with Australia's John Curtin). Talking to Stalin was a different matter, and there were interpretation problems at their first meeting in 1942. Churchill's confidence in his own ability to speak French could be a complication. On one occasion in 1940, the distracted French prime minister Reynaud actually called for Churchill's comments which had been delivered in French to be translated.

Translation problems reached high farce in January 1943, when Churchill met the Turkish cabinet in a railway carriage at Adana. Churchill had prepared a survey of the world scene, which a member of the British Embassy staff was briefed to translate into French, still the language of international diplomacy. When the young diplomat converted 1,500 miles into 2,500 kilometres, he was silenced by Churchill who launched into a gallant attempt at a literal translation delivered in an English accent. The mystified Turks were too polite to laugh.

The half-comic episode at Adana is a key to assessing Churchill's wartime travels. He was right to accept the responsibility and face the dangers of journeying to meet Roosevelt and Stalin, to ensure the effective functioning of an alliance of Great Powers. Only the leaders, for instance, could have authorised work on the atomic bomb. Yet his almost demonic mobility devalued the Churchillian currency. Shuttling through North Africa, he could not avoid entanglement in the petty quarrels of the Free French, even to the point – bizarre though it may seem – of leaving himself open to a snubbing from de Gaulle. Had Churchill, like Stalin, stayed at the centre of his empire and forced lesser chieftains to come to him, such a nonsense could never have happened.

The author of the Dardanelles campaign was hardly likely to persuade the Turks to enter the war against Germany, and even his own cabinet tried to dissuade him from the attempt. Faced in that railway carriage with the importunity of one of the world's greatest statesmen, it is little wonder that the Turkish cabinet felt important enough to await a better offer. When Churchill and Anthony Eden tried to solve the Greek quarrels in the thick of Athens street-fighting, even the devoted Brendan Bracken likened them to two housemaids, scurrying to answer every bell. The Greek Communists had come reluctantly to the negotiating table – an achievement in itself, as one of them had to be persuaded to part with his Mauser rifle at the door of the conference chamber. Unfortunately, they raised their terms 'astronomically', as one observer put it. If the mighty Churchill had come to meet them, surely they should not sell themselves cheap?

The Conservative Chief Whip consoled himself with the hope that if the party had to fight a general election while Churchill was away at Potsdam, voters would be encouraged to support him as a world leader. If anything, Churchill's frequent wartime journeys probably conveyed the message that Britain was safe in the hands of his deputy, Labour leader Clement Attlee. By the last year of the German War, party politics were returning, and Churchill's private comments show that he was well aware that an election was close, and that he was in combat with both 'Atler' and 'Hitlee'. Yet from mid-July 1944 to the end of March 1945, only once did Churchill spend as much as five consecutive weeks in Britain. Both his personal staff and his cabinet ministers worried that he was losing his grip on government business.

From 1943 onwards, as the tide turned against the Nazis, both on national and on party grounds, Churchill might well have heeded the wartime austerity slogan: 'Is your journey really necessary?' Yet for many, the spirit of Churchill the wartime traveller will be summed up in the story that Harold Nicolson gleefully recorded of that Christmas visit to strife-torn Athens. On being shot at by a sniper, Winston Churchill's characteristic comment was, 'Cheek!'

Table of Documents

1941

1. Churchill to Stalin, 7 July
2. Churchill to Stalin, 9 July
3. Stalin to Churchill, 18 July
4. Churchill to Stalin, 20 July
5. Churchill to Stalin, 25 July
6. Churchill to Stalin, 28 July
7. Churchill and Roosevelt to Stalin, 14 August
8. Stalin to Churchill, 3 September
9. Churchill to Stalin, 6 September
10. Stalin to Churchill, 13 September
11. Stalin to Churchill, 3 October
12. Stalin to Churchill, 8 November
13. Churchill to Stalin, 21 November
14. Stalin to Churchill, 23 November
15. Eden-Stalin meeting in Moscow, 16 December
16. Eden-Stalin meeting in Moscow, 17 December
17. Eden-Stalin meeting in Moscow, 18 December
18. Eden-Stalin meeting in Moscow, 20 December

1942

19. Churchill to Stalin, 9 March
20. Stalin to Churchill, 14 March
21. Stalin to Churchill, 22 April
22. Molotov-Churchill meeting in London, 21 May
23. Molotov-Churchill meeting in London, 22 May
24. Molotov-Churchill meeting at Chequers, 22 May
25. Churchill to Stalin, 23 May
26. Stalin to Churchill, 24 May
27. Molotov-Churchill meeting in London, 25 May
28. Stalin to Churchill, 27 May
29. Stalin to Churchill, 28 May
30. Molotov-Churchill meeting in London, 9 June
31. Molotov-Churchill meeting in London, 10 June
32. Churchill to Stalin, 21 June
33. Stalin to Churchill, 23 July
34. Churchill-Stalin meeting in Moscow, 12 August
35. Stalin to Churchill, 13 August
36. Churchill to Stalin, 14 August
37. Churchill-Stalin meeting in Moscow, 13 August
38. Dinner in Honour of Churchill and Harriman, 14 August
39. Churchill-Stalin meeting in Moscow, 15 August
40. Churchill-Stalin conversation in Stalin's Kremlin apartment, 15–16 August
41. Stalin to Churchill, 27 November
42. Churchill to Stalin, 3 December
43. Stalin to Churchill, 6 December

1943

44. Stalin to Churchill and Roosevelt, 30 January
45. Churchill to Stalin, 9 February
46. Stalin to Churchill, 16 February
47. Stalin to Churchill, 15 March
48. Stalin to Churchill, 21 April
49. Churchill to Stalin, 24 April
50. Stalin to Churchill, 25 April
51. Churchill to Stalin, 25 April
52. Churchill to Stalin, 30 April
53. Stalin to Churchill, 4 May
54. Churchill to Stalin, 12 May
55. Stalin to Churchill and Roosevelt, 11 June
56. Churchill to Stalin, 19 June

Notes

Introduction

1. Cited in Geoffrey Roberts, *Stalin's Wars: From World War to Cold War, 1939–1953* (London, 2006), p. 314.
2. Frank Costigliola, *Roosevelt's Lost Alliances: How Personal Politics Helped Start the Cold War* (Princeton, 2012), p. 98.
3. William Averell Harriman Papers on Special Envoy to Churchill and Stalin, 1941–1946, Rare Book & Manuscript Library (Butler Library), Columbia University MS0557, box 1, file 4. This collection contains material used by Elie Abel, the co-author of Harriman's memoir-history *Special Envoy to Churchill and Stalin, 1941–1946* (London, 1976). It includes the transcripts of interviews that Abel conducted with Harriman in the 1970s and by Herbert Feis with Harriman in the 1950s. By no means all the transcript material made it into the book. Hereafter it is called the Abel Archive in order to distinguish it from the Harriman Papers in the Library of Congress. The quote here is from a Feis interview in 1953.
4. David Reynolds, *In Command of History: Churchill Fighting and Writing the Second World War* (London, 2005), p. 468.
5. The Communist Information Bureau (Cominform) was established as a successor to the Comintern (Communist International) which had been abolished by Stalin in 1943, partly as a sop to his Western capitalist allies. The Cominform's function was to fight the ideological battles of the Cold War. It was disbanded in 1956.
6. Oleg Rzheshevsky, *War and Diplomacy: The Making of the Grand Alliance* (Amsterdam, 1996); *Voina i Diplomatiya* (Moscow, 1997); *Stalin i Cherchill'* (Moscow, 2004).
7. All the documents in this book are translations of Russian archival records with the exception of Documents 64, 130 and 131, which are from the British Foreign Office. There are no known Soviet records of these conversations.
8. Stalin's correspondence with Churchill (and Roosevelt) was first published in *Perepiska Predsedatelya Soveta Ministrov SSSR s Prezidentami SShA i Prem'er-Ministrami Velikobritanii vo vremya Velikoi Otechestvennoi Voiny 1941–1945 gg*, 2 vols (Moscow, 1957). An English edition was also published by the Foreign Languages Publishing House, Moscow, in the same year. On the genesis of this publication see G. Roberts, 'Stalin, the Pact with Nazi Germany and the Origins of Post-war Soviet Diplomatic Historiography', *Journal of Cold War Studies*, Vol. 4, No. 4 (Fall 2002), and V. Pechatnov, 'How Soviet Cold Warriors view World War II: the Inside Story of the 1957 edition of the Big Three Correspondence', *Cold War History*, Vol. 14, No. 1 (2014). In 2015 Vladimir Pechatnov, together with I.E. Magadeev, published a new Russian edition of the correspondence, which contains extensive analysis of the processing and preparation of the correspondence by the Soviets: *Perepiska I.V. Stalina s F. Ruzveltom i U. Cherchillem v gody Velikoi Otechestvennoi Voiny*, 2 vols (Moscow, 2015). See further Pechatnov's essay 'How Stalin and Molotov Wrote Messages to Churchill', *Russia in Global Affairs*, Vol. 7, No. 3 (July–September 2009). All the letters published in this book are translated from the Russian-language versions written or read by Stalin. For the English-language versions of the letters read or written by Churchill see the online database associated with D. Reynolds and V. Pechatnov (eds), *The Kremlin Letters: Stalin's Wartime Correspondence with Churchill and Roosevelt* (London, 2018). Note that in the present book the letters are dated day of dispatch; and that in some cases the letters were not received until a day or two later.
9. In 2015, on the 70th anniversary of the Allied victory over Nazi Germany, the archives section of the Russian Foreign Ministry published an online digital archive on Soviet relations with Britain,

France and the United States during the war. It contains some 3,900 files on Soviet diplomatic relations with those countries, including the digital images of the original archive reports (in Russian) on Eden's meetings with Stalin in December 1941, Molotov's conversations with Churchill in May–June 1942 and Stalin's talks with Churchill in August 1942. The archive also contains the files on Churchill's visit to Moscow in October 1944, However, the pages with the reports on Stalin's conversations with Churchill are listed as missing from those files. But the Soviet records of the October 1944 talks are available in the state archive (known as RGASPI) that contains Stalin's personal papers. The relevant section of the foreign ministry archive may be accessed online (http://agk.mid.ru/fonds/sovetsko-britanskie-otnosheniya/).

Chapter 1. Big Game: Churchill and Stalin before Barbarossa

1. Cited by Geoffrey Roberts, *Stalin's Wars: From World War to Cold War, 1939–1953* (London, 2006), p. 38.
2. Gabriel Gorodetsky (ed), *The Maisky Diaries* (London, 2015), pp. 230–3, hereafter cited as Maisky diaries; in Russian: *Ivan Mikhailovich Maiskii: Dnevnik Diplomata, London 1934–1943*, 2 vols (Moscow, 2009), Vol. 2, pp. 28–31 (hereafter *Dnevnik Diplomata*).
3. Arkhiv Vnesheni Politiki RF F. 059. Op. 1, P. 326, D. 13, L. 4, hereafter cited as AVPRF. See also *Vestnik Arkhiva Prezidenta Rossiiskoi Federatsii: SSSR-Germaniya, 1933–1941* (Moscow, 2009).
4. U. Cherchill', *Vtoraya Mirovaya Voina*, Vol. 1 (Moscow, 1955) p. 496; A. Kerillis Frankais, *Voici la ve'rite!* (New York, 1942), p. 102.
5. J. Bardoux, *Journal d'un témoin de la troisième* (Paris, 1957), pp. 203–4.
6. UK National Archives, CAB., 80/4 pp. 294–7.
7. *The Ironside Diaries 1937–1940* (London, 1962), p. 190.
8. *Velikaya Otechestvennaya Voina, 1941–1945 godov*, Vol. 2 (Moscow, 2012), pp. 354ff.
9. M. Gamelin, *Servir*, Vol. 3 (Paris, 1947), p. 199.
10. Maisky diaries, pp. 287–8 (in Russian: *Dnevnik Diplomata*, p. 201).
11. Dokumenty Vneshnei Politiki Vol. 22, Book 1, Moscow 1992, pp. 399–400, hereafter cited as DVP.
12. Ibid., pp. 394–9.
13. Llwellyn Woodward, *British Foreign Policy in the Second World War*, Vol. I (London, 1970), pp. 468–70.
14. Cited by Roberts, *Stalin's Wars*, p. 57.
15. Maisky diaries, pp. 317–18 (in Russian: *Dnevnik Diplomatiya*, Vol. 2, p. 286). A.A. Vyshinky was one of Molotov's Deputy Foreign Commissars.
16. DVP Vol. 23, Book 1, Moscow 1995, pp. 704–5.
17. Alexander Chubarian, *Kanun Tragedii: Stalin i Mezhdunarodnyi Krizis, Sentyabr' 1939–Iun' 1941g* (Moscow, 2008), pp. 389, 391.
18. AVPRF F. 059. P. 353. D. 2409. L. 54.
19. *Moskva-Washington: Politika i Diplomatiya Kremlya, 1920–1941*, Vol. 3 (Moscow, 2000), pp. 719–20.
20. A. Martirosyan, *22 Iunya: Blitzkrig Predatels'stva: Ot Istokov do Kanuna* (Moscow, 2012), p. 55.
21. *Izvestiya*, 14 June 1941.
22. G. Roberts, *Stalin's General: The Life of Georgy Zhukov* (New York, 2012), p. 98.
23. Maisky diaries, pp. 360–1 (in Russian: *Dnevnik Diplomata*, Vol. 2, pp. 407–8).
24. W. F. Kimball (ed), *Churchill and Roosevelt. The Complete Correspondence* (Princeton, 1984), pp. 208, 211.
25. *The New York Times*, 25 June 1941.

Chapter 2. Comrades-in-Arms: Churchill and Stalin at War

1. John Charmley, *Churchill. The End of Glory* (London, 1993); David Carlton, *Churchill and the Soviet Union* (Manchester, 2000).
2. Robin Edmonds, *The Big Three* (London, 1991); David Reynolds, 'Churchill, Roosevelt and the Stalin Enigma', in *From World War to Cold War. Churchill, Roosevelt and the International History of*

the 1940s (Oxford, 2006), pp. 235–48; Martin Kitchen, 'Winston Churchill and the Soviet Union During the Second World War', *Historical Journal* 30 (1987), pp. 415–36.

3. David Stone, *War Summits. The Meetings That Shaped World War II and the Post-war World* (Washington DC, 2005), pp. xiii, 247, 271.

4. Charmley, *End of Glory*, p. 605; Edmonds, *Big Three*, pp. 454–5; Elisabeth Barker, *Churchill and Eden at War* (London, 1978), pp. 128–31, 136.

5. Carlton, *Churchill and the Soviet Union*, pp. 23–6.

6. Max Hastings, *Finest Years. Churchill as Warlord 1940–1945* (London, 2009), p. 328.

7. Geoffrey Roberts, *Stalin's Wars. From World War to Cold War, 1939–1953* (New Haven, 2006); Vladislav Zubok and Constantine Pleshakov, *Inside the Kremlin's Cold War. From Stalin to Khrushchev* (Cambridge, MA, 1996); Caroline Kennedy-Pipe, *Stalin's Cold War 1943–1956. Soviet Strategies in Europe* (Manchester, 1995); O.A. Rzheshevksy, *War and Diplomacy. The Making of the Grand Alliance. From Stalin's Archives* (Amsterdam: 1996. Trans. T. Sorokina).

8. Ilya Gaiduk, 'Stalin. Three Approaches to One Phenomenon', *Diplomatic History* 23 (1999), p. 119; Barker, *Churchill and Eden at War*, p. 221.

9. Milovan Djilas, *Conversations with Stalin* (New York, 1962), p. 115.

10. R. Edmonds, 'Churchill and Stalin', in R. Blake and W. Louis (eds), *Churchill* (London, 1993), p. 311.

11. Carlton, *Churchill and the Soviet Union*, pp. 55–7; David Reynolds, *In Command of History: Churchill Fighting and Writing the Second World War* (Cambridge, 2004), pp. 243–4.

12. Edmonds, 'Churchill and Stalin', p. 311; Charmley, *End of Glory*, p. 316; *Daily Mirror* 13 July 1939; Barker, *Churchill and Eden*, p. 225. Gabriel Gorodetsky, *The Maisky Diaries. Red Ambassador to the Court of St James's 1932–1943* (New Haven, 2015), p. 50 and Maisky diaries for 16 November 1937.

13. Reynolds, *From War to Cold War*, pp. 243–4; Carlton, *Churchill and the Soviet Union*, pp. 55–7.

14. Maurice Hankey, 'Note of a Conversation with Mr Winston Churchill on Sunday, 19th April, 1936' CAB21/435, British National Archives, Kew (TNA). All document references are for TNA unless otherwise stated.

15. Neville to Ida Chamberlain 26 March 1939, in Robert Self (ed.), *The Neville Chamberlain Diary Letters. Volume 4. The Downing Street Years* (Aldershot, 2005), p. 396.

16. *Daily Mirror* 13 July 1939 – see M. Gilbert, *Winston S. Churchill* Vol. 5 (London, 1976), p. 1088, also pp. 1010, 1037, 1044 and 1067.

17. Neville to Hilda Chamberlain 1 October, 1939, Self, *Neville Chamberlain Diary Letters*, p. 453.

18. Robert Boothby to Lloyd George 18 September 1939, Lloyd George papers G/3/13, House of Lords Record Office; Martin Gilbert, *Winston S. Churchill, Vol. 6, Finest Hour* (London, 1983), pp. 44, 49, 98, 100–1.

19. Churchill radio broadcast 1 October 1939, Winston Churchill, *Into Battle* (London, 1941), p. 108. Interestingly, Churchill found the key to the enigma to be the hard-headed pursuit of national interest, not ideology.

20. Channon diary, 12 March 1940, R. Rhodes James (ed.), *'Chips'; The Diaries of Sir Henry Channon* (London, 1967).

21. Churchill radio broadcast 20 January 1940, C.G. Eade (ed.), *The War Speeches of the Rt. Hon. Winston S. Churchill* Vol. 1 (London, 1951), p. 137.

22. Carlton, *Churchill and the Soviet Union*, p. 73.

23. Cripps diary, 4 October 1939, cited in C. Cooke, *The Life of Richard Stafford Cripps* (London, 1957).

24. Hugh Dalton diary 17 May 1940, Ben Pimlott (ed.), *The Second World War Diary of Hugh Dalton* (London, 1986); Lockhart diary 21 May 1940, Kenneth Young (ed.), *The Diaries of Sir Robert Bruce Lockhart, Vol. ii, 1939–1965* (London, 1980).

25. Cabinet meeting WM(40)123rd 15 May 1940 CAB65/7. The Beaverbrook papers were already floating the idea of sending an envoy of left-wing persuasion to Moscow, Lockhart diary 4 May 1940.

26. Fitzroy Maclean (Foreign Office) letter to Lascelles (Moscow) 24 May 1940 FO371/24847/N5648.

27. War Cabinet meetings WM(40)138th 25 May 1940, WM(40)149th 31 May 1940 CAB65/7; Sargent (Foreign Office) minute 24 May, Halifax minute 25 May 1940 FO371/24847/N5660.
28. Maclean minute 19 June 1940 FO371/24844/N5888.
29. Churchill note 25 June 1940 PREM3/395/1. The wording was largely the Foreign Office's, Maclean draft 22 June, telegram to Cripps 25 June 1940 FO371/24844/N5853. See also Winston Churchill, *The History of the Second World War, vol 2, Their Finest Hour* (London, 1949), pp. 119–20.
30. Cripps conversation with Stalin 1 July 1940, Cripps to Foreign Office 2 July 1940 FO371/24844/N5937; War Cabinet paper WP(40)254 CAB66/9.
31. Dominions Office to Field Marshal Smuts 1 November 1940 FO371/24845/N7046. For the meetings, see Geoffrey Roberts, *Molotov. Stalin's Cold Warrior* (Dulles, VA, 2012), pp. 42–5.
32. Winston Churchill, *History of the Second World War, Vol. 3, The Grand Alliance* (London, 1950) pp. 227–8, 643.
33. DO(40)39th 31 October 1940 CAB69/1.
34. F.H. Hinsley, *British Intelligence in the Second World War*, Vol. 1 (Cambridge 1979), pp. 432, 437, 440.
35. WM(41)20th Confidential Annexe 24 February 1941 CAB65/21.
36. Churchill to Inönü 31 January 1941 PREM3/309/1; Gilbert, *Finest Hour*, p. 1006.
37. Churchill broadcast 9 March 1941; Churchill, *Grand Alliance*, pp. 317, 319; Hinsley, *British Intelligence*, Vol. 1, p. 450.
38. Hinsley, *British Intelligence*, p. 451. Gabriel Gorodetsky, *Stafford Cripps' Mission to Moscow 1940–42* (Cambridge, 1984), pp. 116–18 suggests Churchill reacted slowly, and was actually influenced by a warning from Cripps that Germany would attack and other materials as well as the Enigma decrypt.
39. Churchill to Eden 30 March 1941 PREM3/395/16.
40. Churchill to Cripps 3 April 1941 PREM3/403/4.
41. Churchill to Pownall and Deakin 25 May 1948 Ismay Papers, Liddell Hart Centre, King's College, London.
42. Cripps to Foreign Office 3 April 1941 FO371/24965/N1386.
43. Cripps to Foreign Office, aide-memoire to Vyshinsky, 19 April 1941 FO371/29479/N1716 and FO371/29480/N1848.
44. Cripps described Churchill's message as fragmentary and less emphatic than his own approach; Cripps to Foreign Office 12 April 1941 FO371/29479/N1573.
45. Churchill to Eden 30 April 1941 PREM3/396/16.
46. Churchill minute 14 October 1941 PREM 3/403/4, 403/5. See H. Hanak, 'Sir Stafford Cripps as Ambassador in Moscow, June 1941-January 1942', *English Historical Review* (1982), p. 69. Gabriel Gorodetsky has come to Cripps' defence, and argues that he was not firmly instructed to deliver the message directly to Stalin; Gabriel Gorodetsky, 'Churchill's Warning to Stalin: A Reappraisal', *Historical Journal* 29 (1986), p. 981. See, however, Churchill to Eden 15 April and 18 April 1941 FO371/29479/N1573.
47. Eden to Cadogan 29 March 1941 FO371/29464/N1360. Attlee had raised the issue in Cabinet, WM(41)33rd mtg CAB65/18. Eden had made his own approach to Maisky on 16 April FO371/29464/N1386.
48. Churchill to Cadogan 3 April 1941, 5 April 1941 FO371/29271/N1323. Churchill was acting Foreign Secretary at the time (Eden was in the Mediterranean).
49. Churchill to Eden 22 April 1940 PREM 3/395/16.
50. This was a view Stalin had advanced back in 1927, Stephen Kotkin, *Stalin. Vol. 1. Paradoxes of Power* (New York, 2014), p. 639.
51. As Gorodetsky has pointed out, Stalin's suspicions that the British wished to get the Soviets involved in war with Germany received a little further confirmation from the message, and even more from Cripps' veiled threats about a British 'separate peace', Gorodetsky, *Stafford Cripps' Mission*, p. 124.
52. Maisky had influenced the contents of the communiqué, but then became convinced by the intelligence Cadogan summarised to him, that a German attack was imminent, Maisky diaries 13 June, conversation with Cadogan 15 June, Cripps 18 June 1941, Maisky diaries, p. 355.

53. Churchill, *Grand Alliance*, p. 330.
54. J. Colville, *The Fringes of Power. Downing Street Diaries*, Vol. 1 (London, 1985), diary 21 June 1941. Colville noted that Churchill felt the USSR would 'assuredly' be defeated.
55. Eden conversation with Maisky 22 June 1941 PREM3/401/1; Cripps luncheon with Maisky 19 June 1941 FO371/29466/N3099.
56. For conflicting accounts by Beaverbrook, Cripps and Eden as to who influenced Churchill, see Bruce Lockhart diary 20, 23 and 25 June 1942.
57. Eade (ed.), *War Speeches*, pp. 450–4.
58. Churchill to Roosevelt 14 June 1941 PREM3/230/1; Duff Cooper to Eden 28 June 1941 Ministry of Information Papers INF1/913; War Cabinet minutes WM(41)64th meeting 30 June 1941 CAB65/18. Colville observed a spirited conversation along similar lines immediately after the broadcast, as Churchill shared drinks with Beaverbrook, Eden and Cripps. Carlton notes Colville described this late-night discussion as hilarious, and concludes that Churchill took the Soviet entry into the war rather frivolously, because he thought Soviet resistance would be short-lived and because all his hopes for the war were pinned on the USA. However, the line Colville says Churchill took (along with Cripps) reflected the tone of the broadcast: Carlton, *Churchill and Soviet Union*, p. 85; Colville diary 22 June 1941.
59. Cripps to Foreign Office 27 June 1941 FO371/29466/N3232.
60. Hanak, 'Sir Stafford Cripps as Ambassador in Moscow', p. 334.
61. Churchill to Stalin 7 July 1941 **Document 1**.
62. Churchill added, 'I do not want to be alone in Europe with the bear'. Barrington-Ward diary 29 March 1943, Donald McLachlan, *In the Chair, Barrington-Ward of* The Times, *1927–1948* (London, 1971), p. 205.
63. Cripps to Foreign Office 8 July 1941 FO371/29467/N3528.
64. Churchill to Stalin 10 July 1941 **Document 2**.
65. Stalin to Churchill 18 July 1941 **Document 3**, Churchill to Stalin 20 July 1941 **Document 4**.
66. Gorodetsky, *Stafford Cripps' Mission*, pp. 188–9.
67. Eden diary 11 October 1944 Avon papers AP20/3/09, Birmingham University Library.
68. Churchill to Stalin 28 July 1941. **Document 6**. John Harvey (ed.), *The War Diaries of Oliver Harvey, 1941–1945* (London, 1978), 28 July 1941, hereafter Harvey diary.
69. Each had the advice of an ambassador (Maisky until mid-1943, Clark Kerr from March 1942) who himself developed significant personal contact with the other leader: both treated this advice inconsistently and did not regard it as more authoritative than their own gut instinct.
70. Maisky diaries 30 August 1941: also entries for 21 July 1942 and 5 February 1943.
71. Stalin to Churchill 3 September 1941 **Document 8**.
72. According to Churchill he could not restrain himself from answering the taunt from Maisky at the start of September that the USSR had been fighting virtually alone for the past eleven weeks, saying 'Remember that only four months ago we in this island did not know whether you were not coming in against us on the German side. Indeed, we thought it quite likely that you would … Whatever happens, and whatever you do, you of all people have no right to make reproaches to us.' Maisky's diary does not confirm this, and he did not include any such statement in his despatch to Molotov. Churchill, *Grand Alliance*, p. 406; Lawrence Rees, *World War II: Behind Closed Doors. Stalin, the Nazis and the West* (London, 2008), p. 103; Maisky diaries 4 September 1941.
73. Churchill to Stalin 6 September 1941 FO371/29490/N5113.
74. Cripps to Foreign Office 7 September 1941 FO371/29490/N5113. Cripps noted '[T]here was some return to old attitude of suspicion and distrust, which had been absent recently'.
75. Churchill to Cripps 5 September 1941 PREM3/401/1.
76. Harvey diary 29 August 1941; Joan E. Beaumont, *Comrades in Arms. British Aid to Russia 1941–1945* (London, 1980), pp. 27, 31, 33–4.
77. Stalin to Churchill 13 September 1941 **Document 10**; Maisky told Eden on 16 September that the message he had delivered to Churchill (on 15 September) was very important, and emphasised the need for a substantial British force to be sent to the southern sector of the Soviet front, plus perhaps some Canadians, used to the climate, to Arkhangelsk, Eden to Cripps 16 September 1941

FO371/29490/N5397. Maisky told Eden on 17 September that Stalin would assume from Churchill's reply that the idea was rejected: Eden pointed out that Churchill had said 'we will study with you any other form of useful aid', and took that to include consideration of help to the Caucasus, for instance, taking into account Turkish needs and the supply routes through Iran, Eden to Churchill 18 September 1941 – Churchill replied to Eden, 'All is governed by shipping. There is no objection to studying any plan: but we must not encourage delusions that any large armies can be sent from Great Britain to fight in Russia', minute 19 September 1941, message to Stalin 17 September 1941 (presented to Stalin by Cripps on 19 September) FO371/29490/N5421.

78. Hastings, *Finest Years*, p. 201, Maisky-Eden conversation 19 September 1941 FO371/29490/N5501. Molotov told Cripps on 22 October he did not wish for British troops in the Caucasus, as there was no fighting there, Cripps to Foreign Office 22 October 1941 FO371/29492/N6068. When Beaverbrook mentioned troops for the Caucasus, with Stalin, he was told the need for them was in Ukraine. Beaverbrook had said this might be done, and Stalin said he had faith in Churchill's military judgment, Foreign Office to Cripps 31 October 1941 FO371/29492/N6135.

79. Churchill, *Grand Alliance*, pp. 68–9.

80. Churchill to Beaverbrook 30 August 1941 BBK D/94: Harold Balfour diary 26 September 1941, Inchyre papers, House of Lords Record Office; Kenneth Young, *Beaverbrook and Churchill. A Study in Friendship* (London, 1966), pp. 204–5.

81. Churchill to Cripps 28 October 1941 FO371/29471/N6583: while telling Cripps not to make such points to the Soviets, Churchill happily reprinted this jeremiad in 1949, in Churchill, *Grand Alliance*, p. 420.

82. Churchill draft message to Cripps 3 October 1941 FO371/29491/N5679; Churchill to Stalin 12 October 1941 FO371/29492/N6026. This example of 'guff' accompanied the tactless offer to take over Soviet occupation duties in Iran.

83. Eden paper, 'Forthcoming Discussions with the Soviet Government', 26 November 1941, WP(41)288, FO371/29472/N6835; Eden conversation with Winant, 4 December 1941, FO371/29472/N6893; Winant to Hull, 4 December 1941, State Department Papers, National Archives, Record Group 59 (RG59), 740.0011/17085.

84. WM(41)102nd 13.10.41 CAB65/19.

85. Maisky conversations with Eden 17 October 1941, 27 October 1941 FO371/29469/N6059, N6228.

86. WM(41)104th 20 October 1941 CAB65/19, Churchill to Cripps 28 October 1941 FO371/29471/N6583.

87. See Churchill draft to Cripps 15 November 1941 FO371/29493/N6544, superseded by an Eden version.

88. Stalin to Churchill 8 November 1941 **Document 12**. Maisky delivered the message on 11 November: the embassy's translation is in FO954/24B. In the Foreign Office, part of the brusque tone was ascribed to possible shoddy translation in the Embassy: direct analysis of the original text suggests the tone was not changed by translation; Warner (Foreign Office) long minute assessing the message, 12 November 1941 FO371/29471/N6540. Warner wondered also if the shift in tone compared to that in Stalin's previous messages was down to Maisky, who had objected to a paragraph in the original draft of Churchill's message that had implied he was not representing Stalin's views.

89. WM(41)111thCA 11 November 1941 CAB65/24.

90. Cripps to Churchill telegrams 109, 110 15 November 1941 FO371/29471/N6605, N6606.

91. Eden conversation with Maisky 12 November 1941 FO371/29470/N6288. Eden said Churchill and the Cabinet were surprised and pained by the tone and contents of the message. Maisky seemed himself to regret the tone, and, as he often did, then 'spoke off the record': implying that he was then giving personal and heterodox views, though invariably his comments were actually a reiteration of the Party line and often special pleadings about Soviet sensitivities and suspicions, always, in Maisky's account, completely justified, even as he posed as a sincere friend of Britain concerned to present some home truths. He therefore, while appearing to agree with Eden, merely depicted Stalin's suspicions as justified. The message, however, seems to have got through, as subsequent conversations showed. Maisky note of conversations with Beaverbrook and Eden,

diary 12 November 1941. Cripps summarised the ploy that was being attempted, as it had been explained to him: 'provided Soviet Ambassador can extract from Stalin an explanatory light in his original message (intention being, I assume, that he should moderate its frankness) … you will be able to come out here … to discuss both Stalin's points with him', telegram to Eden 19 November 1941 FO371/29471/N6750.

92. Eden conversations with Maisky 18 November, 20 November 1941 FO371/29471/N6660, N6704.

93. Harvey diary 21 November 1941.

94. Churchill to Stalin 21 November 1941 FO371/29472/N6750. Churchill, *Grand Alliance*, pp. 471–2. It was delivered on 22 November, hence the date in the Soviet records, **Document 13**. Churchill referred to Stalin's message as 'just received', even though it had been in British hands for ten days and it was fourteen days between Stalin writing it, and his getting the reply.

95. Stalin to Churchill 23 November 1941 **Document 14.**

96. Stalin to Churchill 30 November 1941, USSR Ministry of Foreign Affairs, *Stalin's Correspondence with Churchill and Attlee 1941–1945* (New York, 1965), p. 36, hereafter cited as *Stalin's Correspondence*.

97. Cadogan diary November 28 1941 in David Dilks (ed.), *The Diaries of Sir Alexander Cadogan 1938–1945* (London, 1971), hereafter cited as Cadogan diary.

98. Ismay to Churchill 5 December 1941, and Churchill marginal note FO954/24B.

99. War Cabinet paper WP(41)238 8 October 1941 CAB66/19; Eden memorandum 4 December 1941, *Foreign Relations of the United States 1941*, Vol. I, pp. 192–4; War Cabinet meeting 4 December 1941 WM(41)124th mtg Confidential Annexe CAB65/24.

100. Eden conversations with Stalin, 16–22 December 1941 **Documents 15, 16, 17** and **18**. British records are in WP(42)8 5 January 1942 FO954/25A.

101. Churchill to Attlee 20 December 1941 while *en route* to the US PREM 3/399; Churchill to Eden 7 January 1942 PREM3/399 and 8 January 1942 FO371/32874/N108.

102. War Cabinet meeting 6 February 1942 WM(42)17th CAB65/29.

103. War Cabinet meeting 25 February 1942 WM(42)24th CAB65/29; Beaverbrook paper 'Controversy Over Russia', 3 March 1942 FO954/25A.

104. Churchill to Stalin 12 March 1942 **Document 19**.

105. Carlton, *Churchill and the Soviet Union*, p. 97; Eden at War Cabinet, WM(42)1st mtg 1 January 1942 CAB65/29.

106. General Alan Brooke diary 17 April 1942 published in Alex Danchev and Daniel Todman (eds), *War Diaries 1939–1945. Field Marshal Lord Alanbrooke* (London, 2001), hereafter Brooke diary.

107. War Cabinet meeting 25 March 1942 WM(42)37th CAB65/29; Churchill to Roosevelt 7 March 1942 FO371/32877/N1174; Cadogan minutes 4 March 1942 FO371/32876/N1156, and 7 May 1942 FO371/32881/N2524. Harvey diary 6 March 1942; Brooke diary 5 March 1942.

108. Roosevelt to Churchill 18 March 1942, in Warren Kimball (ed.), *Churchill and Roosevelt. The Complete Correspondence* (Princeton: Yale University Press, 1984), Vol. 1, p. 421.

109. Harvey diary 17 March 1942. Maisky had a long discussion with Churchill at Chequers on 15 March, but did not note in his diary that Churchill had suggested this, Maisky diaries 16 March 1942.

110. Cadogan diary 7 May 1942.

111. Maisky diaries 20 July 1941. The message from Stalin is **Document 3.**

112. Aide memoire to Molotov 10 June 1942 CAB120/684; Lord Avon, *The Reckoning* (London, 1965), p. 330; Harvey diary 10 June 1942.

113. Molotov talk with Churchill 21 May 1942 **Document 22.**

114. Churchill-Stalin conversation 12 August **Document 34.**

115. Molotov-Churchill meeting 22 May 1942 **Document 24.**

116. Molotov-Churchill meeting 9 June 1942 **Document 30.**

117. Churchill to Stalin 27 May 1942 **Document 28.**

118. Combined Chiefs of Staff Conference 22 July 1942 CAB99/190; WM(42)94th mtg 22 July 1942 CAB65/31; Brooke diary 24 July 1942. Churchill much preferred an attack on the Germans in

North Norway, code-named Operation Jupiter, which he was to propose to Stalin in August. The COS consistently opposed the idea as a diversion of resources.

119. On the day of his telegram to Churchill, Stalin recalled to Moscow the commander of the Southern Front, Marshal Timoshenko, with his forces retreating in disarray, and on 28 July issued the 'no step back' order threatening death to any commander who allowed unauthorised retreat.

120. Stalin to Churchill 23 July 1942 **Document 33**.

121. Churchill to Stalin 18 July 1942 CAB120/856.

122. Hastings, *Finest Hour*, pp. 321–2.

123. Roberts, *Stalin's Wars*, p. 136.

124. Maisky diaries 23 July, 24 July 1942.

125. Clark Kerr had described Stalin as 'just my cup of tea'. They had been forced into each other's company for an extended period in the Kremlin air-raid shelter, and had filled the time talking on a range of subjects, including tobacco and women, Clark Kerr to Cripps 26 April 1942 FO800/300.

126. Clark Kerr to Cadogan 28 July 1942 PREM3/76A/1. Eden noted, 'Took the telegram round to Winston, and he jumped at it', diary 30 July 1942 in Avon, *The Reckoning*, p. 338.

127. Churchill to Stalin 31 July 1942 CAB120/856.

128. Winston Churchill, *The Second World War, Vol. 4, Hinge of Fate* (London, 1951), p. 428; Harriman and Abel, *Special Envoy*, p. 125; Churchill told the War Cabinet that he would give Stalin an account of the Anglo-American discussions (thereby ensuring Stalin got Churchill's side of the story first) and their plans for 1942, War Cabinet 30 July 1942 WM(42)100th CAB65/27; Churchill told his wife, 'I am not looking forward to this part of my mission because I bear so little in my hand, and sympathise so much with those to whom I go'. Martin Gilbert, *Road to Victory. Winston S. Churchill 1941–1945* (London, 1986), pp. 161, 169, 170.

129. Stalin to Churchill 20 June 1942, *Stalin's Correspondence*, p. 51.

130. The aircraft carrying Cadogan and the generals experienced engine trouble and had to return to Teheran. They arrived the following day.

131. Clementine Churchill letter 4 August 1942, cited in Gilbert, *Road to Victory*, p. 161.

132. Graham Ross analysed the mission most fully, but did not focus on the issue of the reasons for the mission, beyond breaking the news about the second front, nor did he consider in detail how Churchill's approach to the mission fitted in to the developing Big Three relationship; Graham Ross, 'Operation Bracelet: Churchill in Moscow, 1942' in David Dilks (ed.), *Retreat from Power*, Vol. 2 (London, 1981), pp. 101–19.

133. Churchill-Stalin meeting 12 August 1942 **Document 34**. Stalin was accompanied by two of his closest comrades, Molotov and Marshal Kliment Voroshilov.

134. He discussed the tactic of breaking the worst news directly and immediately and then revealing what the Anglo-Americans were going to do, in his initial meeting with the ambassador; Clark Kerr manuscript journal of Bracelet conference, 12 August 1942 FO800/300.

135. Notes of meeting with Stalin, Kremlin 7pm 12 August 1942 CAB127/23.

136. Stalin-Churchill conversation 12 August 1942 **Document 34**.

137. Clark Kerr Bracelet journal 12 August 1942 FO800/300.

138. Churchill to Attlee 13 August 1942 FO800/300; Jacob diary 13 August 1942, published in Charles Richardson, *From Churchill's Secret Circle to the BBC. The Biography of Lieutenant-General Sir Ian Jacob* (London, 1991), hereafter Jacob diary; Sir Charles Wilson (later Lord Moran) told Clark Kerr that Churchill had said to him after the first meeting 'I want that man to like me', Clark Kerr Bracelet journal 13 August 1942 FO800/300.

139. Lord Tedder, *With Prejudice* (London, 1966), p. 330.

140. Churchill conversation with Molotov 13 August 1942 PREM3/76A/12; Records of Bracelet Conference FO800/402. Churchill at one point described relations between de Gaulle and the Vichy regime as like those between Reds and Whites in Russia in 1918–20. He and Molotov also engaged in verbal sparring over the Crimean War.

141. Stalin to Churchill 13 August **Document 35**.

142. Churchill-Stalin meeting 13 August 1942 **Document 37**, cf British minutes of meeting at Kremlin 11.15pm 13 August 1942 CAB127/23. Gilbert, *Road to Victory*, p. 185; Jacob diary 13 August 1942; Ross, 'Operation Bracelet', p. 111; John W. Wheeler-Bennett (ed.), *Action this Day: Working with Churchill* (London, 1968), p. 215. Churchill's intended agenda for his second meeting with Stalin covered shipping losses on the Russian convoys, further statements about growing Allied air strength, post-war cooperation, Soviet contingency planning in the Caucasus and Caspian region and Japan; memorandum for meeting with Stalin, 13 August 1942 PREM3/76/11.

143. Churchill to Attlee 14 August 1942 PREM3/76A/9.

144. Clark Kerr Bracelet journal 14 August 1942 FO800/300.

145. Churchill to Attlee 14 August 1942 PREM3/76A/9.

146. Maisky diaries 21 July 1942.

147. Maisky memorandum 7 August 1942 in Anatoli Filev, 'New Documents about Winston Churchill from Russian Archives', *International Affairs* (Moscow), 47 (2001), pp. 131–5.

148. Stalin-Churchill conversation 13 August 1942 **Document 37**.

149. Churchill to Attlee 14 August 1942 PREM3/76A/9; Jacob diary 13 August 1942.

150. Harriman note to Churchill 13 August 1942 PREM3/76/11; Jacob diary 13 August 1942.

151. Clark Kerr Bracelet journal 14 August 1942 FO800/300.

152. Clark Kerr Bracelet journal 15 August 1942 FO800/300. Clark Kerr thought Churchill's garment 'dreadful', since it resembled mechanic's overalls or a child's romper suit. By a strange inversion, the capitalist imperialist Churchill was garbed in proletarian clothing, while the Communist Party officials were all in bourgeois evening dress or uniform.

153. Dinner in Honour of Churchill and Harriman 14 August 1942 **Document 38**. Churchill described the food to Wilson as 'filthy', Wilson diary 14 August 1942 in Lord Moran, *Churchill at War 1940–45* (London, 2002) and see pp. xx–xxix (hereafter Moran diary). Some accounts follow Churchill in ignoring his bad mood at the dinner and subsequently: Churchill's account to the War Cabinet glossed over his unhappiness during the dinner, Churchill to Attlee 15 August 1942 CAB120/67. Gilbert suggests Churchill was depressed by bad news concerning the Malta convoy, and was not angry – Clark Kerr's notes confirm Churchill's bad temper earlier in the day. John Colville observed that 'Moran [Wilson] was seldom, if ever, present when history was made: but he was quite often invited to dinner afterwards', Wheeler-Bennett (ed.), *Action this Day*, pp. 10, 30–6, 110–12. This was not quite accurate: Churchill's habit of declaiming on weighty issues last thing at night, while stripping for his bath, regardless of who was present, meant that Wilson, in attendance in his official capacity, was indeed often there when Churchill was thinking out loud.

154. Clark Kerr Bracelet journal 15 August 1942 FO800/300; Jacob diary 14 August 1942. Cadogan had reported to Molotov on the morning of the dinner that Stalin's truculence at the second meeting had had a bad effect, Clark Kerr to Foreign Office 16 August 1942 PREM3/76A/11; Moran diary 14 August 1942; Harriman and Abel, *Special Envoy*, p. 161.

155. Clark Kerr Bracelet journal 14 August 1942 FO800/300; Brooke diary 14 August 1942; Moran diary 14 August 1942.

156. Clark Kerr Bracelet journal 15 August 1942 FO800/300; Moran diary 15 August 1942. Leslie Rowan, Churchill's private secretary, writing in the volume refuting Wilson's book, saw Churchill to be deliberately countering Stalin's rudeness; it was 'not bad temper, it was a calculated response to a calculated move', Rowan in Wheeler-Bennett (ed.), *Action This Day*, p. 255. On the other hand, Wilson's and Clark Kerr's accounts describe Churchill's bad temper and querulousness on 14 and 15 August in some detail.

157. Jacob diary 15 August 1942. Arthur H. Birse, *Memoirs of an Interpreter* (London, 1967), pp. 94–7.

158. Carlton describes Churchill's repeated indiscretions within microphone range as 'unprofessional', and speculates that some of them, such as his comment that the Russians were 'orangutans', were made while drunk; Carlton, *Churchill and the Soviet Union*, p. 100.

159. Clark Kerr Bracelet journal 16 August 1942 FO800/300.

160. Svetlana Alliluyeva (transl. Patricia Johnson McMillan), *Twenty Letters to a Friend* (London, 1967), p. 185; Ross, 'Operation Bracelet', p. 115; Clark Kerr Bracelet journal 16 August 1942 FO800/300.

161. Churchill-Stalin meetings 15–16 August **Documents 39 and 40**. Michael Ellman, 'Research Note: Churchill on Stalin: A Note', *Europe-Asia Studies* 58 (2006), pp. 965–71 points out that Churchill's account in his memoirs of what Stalin said about the kulaks is at odds with these records, while also noting that the official records, compiled by the interpreters, were written after the event.

162. Birse notes of Churchill-Stalin talks, Kremlin 7pm 15 August 1942 FO800/300.

163. Churchill-Stalin meeting 15 August 1942 **Document 39**, Edmonds, *Big Three*, p. 303.

164. Churchill-Stalin conversation 15–16 August 1942, notes by Pavlov **Document 40**. Churchill, *Hinge of Fate*, pp. 446–9; Churchill to Attlee 16 August 1942 PREM3/76A/11. Stalin once said of such drinking bouts: 'When great affairs of state are at stake, alcohol tastes like water and one's head is always clear', Hastings, *Finest Years*, p. 327 – *à propos* of this, Harry Truman noted that at Potsdam Stalin's preferred drink was a watered-down wine, rather than the hard spirits the Soviets liked to press on their foreign visitors: so Stalin made sure his aphorism applied to himself, if no-one else.

165. Cadogan to Halifax 29 August FO1093/247.

166. Clark Kerr noted 'the P.M. began to chuckle and to kick a pair of gay legs in the air. I can't remember the words he used, but it had all been grand. He had cemented a friendship with Stalin. My God! he was glad that he had come. Stalin had been splendid … What a pleasure it was to work with "that great man". The glee of the P.M. was a pleasure to see. He was like that dog with two cocks.' Clark Kerr Bracelet journal 16 August 1942 FO800/300.

167. Churchill to Attlee 16 August 1942 PREM3/76A/11.

168. Jacob diary 16 August 1942.

169. Martin Kitchen, *British Policy Towards the Soviet Union During the Second World War* (London, 1986), p. 140.

170. RAF officers went to Moscow later in the year to discuss arrangements for this, code-named Operation Velvet, but the Soviets were no longer keen, and eventually said they preferred to be supplied with aircraft, not operational squadrons, Kitchen, *British Policy*, p. 144.

171. Birse, *Memoirs of an Interpreter*, p. 103.

172. Churchill-Stalin conversation 15–16 August 1942, notes by Pavlov **Document 40**.

173. Churchill to Attlee and War Cabinet 14 August 1942 FO800/300. David Stone, who generally depicts Stalin as a manipulative genius, always cunningly getting his way, suggests Stalin stage-managed these events to set himself off in the best light, with the additional motive of testing the strength and cohesion of the Anglo-American partnership, Stone, *War Summits*, pp. 59, 61. For more on the theory of two or more schools within Soviet foreign policy-making circles, see Martin H. Folly, *Churchill, Whitehall and the Soviet Union, 1940–45* (London, 2000), pp. 80–6, and Reynolds, *From World War to Cold War*, pp. 243–5, part of a perceptive and balanced account of Roosevelt and Churchill's wartime perceptions of Stalin.

174. Churchill to Stalin 30 December 1943, Gilbert, *Road to Victory*, p. 630. Stalin said in his reply on 2 January, 'I fully agree with you about frequent meetings'. Maisky to Molotov 20 August 1942, Molotov to Maisky 22 August 1942, in Filev, 'New Documents', pp. 137–8. See also Molotov's memorandum on the meetings, in *Soviet-British Relations During the Great Patriotic War*, Vol. 1 (Moscow, 1983), Document 132.

175. Cadogan to Halifax 29 August 1942 FO1093/247.

176. Martin H. Folly, 'Friends – of a Kind: America and Its Allies in the Second World War', *Journal of American Studies* 40, 3 (2006), pp. 633–44.

177. Harriman and Abel, *Special Envoy*, p. 164.

178. Hansard, *House of Commons Debates*, Vol. 383, p. 95.

179. Churchill to Stalin 9 October 1942 CAB120/856.

180. Churchill to Roosevelt 24 October 1942 FO954/25B.

181. Churchill, *Hinge of Fate*, pp. 581–2.

182. Stalin telegram to Maisky 19 October 1942, in *Soviet-British Relations*, Vol. 1, Document 147. Maisky bravely contested Stalin's more extreme assertion, though his own reports had encouraged the fundamental assumption, Maisky diaries, p. 463.

183. Stalin to Maisky 28 October 1942 in Filev, 'New Documents', pp. 138–9; Roberts, *Stalin's Wars*, p. 141. The backdrop to this was a disagreement over the treatment of war criminals.

184. Stalin speech 6 November 1942 FO371/32923/N5782.

185. Churchill to Stalin 24 November CAB120/856, Stalin to Churchill 27 November 1942 **Document 41**.

186. Churchill to Stalin 4 December, Stalin to Churchill 6 December 1942 **Documents 42** and **43**.

187. Sargent minute 11 January, Cadogan note 13 January, Eden minute 14 January 1943 FO371/33154/R8820. Foreign Office despatch 56 to Moscow 4 February 1943 FO371/35338/U321.

188. Churchill 26 February note on Clark Kerr telegram FO371/35338/U888.

189. Stalin letter contained in Clark Kerr to Foreign Office telegram 113 25 February 1943 FO371/35338/U888.

190. Warner to Clark Kerr 16 March 1943 FO800/301.

191. Warner to Clark Kerr 26 March 1943 FO800/301: Harvey diary 26 February 1943.

192. Clark Kerr to Foreign Office telegram 105 25 February 1943 FO181/973/20.

193. Churchill to Attlee, Cyprus, 1 February 1943 PREM4/30/2. Except for Cadogan, who was traveling with him, Churchill had consulted no-one in the Foreign Office, not even Eden, before producing this document. Churchill, *Hinge of Fate*, pp. 636–7. Churchill wished to base future British influence as a great power on leading Europe through a regional council: the Foreign Office and Eden felt that this would prompt the US to retreat into isolation, leaving Britain to run Europe, and restrain Germany, on its own if the Soviets were not cooperative, Klaus Larres, *Churchill's Cold War: The Politics of Personal Diplomacy* (New Haven, 2002), pp. 73–81.

194. Churchill to Stalin 1 February, Stalin to Churchill 6 February 1943 *Stalin's Correspondence*, pp. 90–3.

195. Cadogan to Churchill 25 March 1943 PREM4/30/1.

196. Churchill minute to Cadogan 26 March 1943, Cadogan telegram to Clark Kerr 27 March 1943 PREM4/30/1.

197. Stalin to Churchill 30 January 1943 **Document 44**.

198. Churchill to Stalin 9 February 1943 **Document 45**. Maisky diaries 9 February 1943 – Churchill did prepare some ground by complaining about the slow rate of American build-up of divisions in Britain.

199. Churchill to Stalin 11 March 1943, CAB120/856, Stalin to Churchill 15 March 1943 **Document 47**; Vladimir Pechatnov, 'How Stalin and Molotov Wrote Messages to Churchill. Following Stalin's Archives', *Russia in Global Affairs* 7 (2009), p. 166

200. Stalin to Churchill 29 March 1943, Churchill to Stalin 30 March 1943 CAB120/856, Maisky conversation with Churchill 31 March 1943; Stalin to Churchill 2 April 1943, *Stalin's Correspondence*, p. 112; Pechatnov, 'How Stalin and Molotov', p. 166.

201. Stalin to Churchill 21 April 1943 **Document 48**.

202. Cadogan diary 15 April 1943.

203. Churchill to Stalin 24 April, 25 April 1943 **Documents 49** and **51**.

204. Stalin to Churchill 25 April 1943 **Document 50**.

205. Churchill to Stalin 30 April, Stalin to Churchill 4 May 1943 **Documents 52** and **53**.

206. Churchill to Stalin 2 May 1943 CAB120/856; Harvey diary, 4 May 1943.

207. Stalin to Churchill 4 May 1943 **Document 53**.

208. Stalin to Churchill and Roosevelt 11 June 1943 **Document 55**.

209. Stalin to Churchill 24 June 1943 **Document 57**. See also Churchill to Stalin 19 June 1943 **Document 58**.

210. Churchill to Stalin 27 June 1943 **Document 59**; Pechatnov, 'How Stalin and Molotov', p. 168.

211. Stalin to Churchill and Roosevelt 22 August 1943 **Document 59**; Harriman and Abel, *Special Envoy*, p. 225.

212. Folly, *Churchill, Whitehall and the Soviet Union*, pp. 97–9.

213. Stalin to Churchill and Roosevelt 24 August 1943 **Document 66**. See also Harvey diary 25 August 1943. Actually two SS panzer divisions had been withdrawn from the Kursk front in response to the Allied landing in Sicily in July.

214. Harriman's note of a dinner at Quebec, August 1943 in Harriman and Abel, *Special Envoy*, p. 226.

215. Pechatnov, 'How Stalin and Molotov', pp. 162–73.

216. Stalin to Churchill 8 September, Stalin to Churchill and Roosevelt 12 September 1943 **Documents 61** and **62**. Churchill commented 'on this meeting of the three of us ... may depend not only the best and shortest method of finishing the war, but also those good arrangements for the future of the world which will enable the British and American and Russian nations to render a lasting service to humanity'; to Stalin 10 September 1943 *Stalin's Correspondence*, p. 161.

217. Harvey diary 6 October 1943.

218. Stalin to Churchill 13 October 1943 *Stalin's Correspondence*, pp. 171–3.

219. Molotov told Gusev 'We consider the return of the envelope simply as another of Churchill's hysterical gestures'. Hastings, *Finest Years*, pp. 398–9; Cadogan diary 18 October 1943.

220. Churchill to Roosevelt 16 October 1943, Kimball (ed.), *Churchill and Roosevelt. The Complete Correspondence*, p. 533.

221. Pechatnov, 'How Stalin and Molotov', p. 169.

222. See Avon, *The Reckoning*, pp. 411–18 and Harriman and Abel, *Special Envoy*, pp. 234–48.

223. Moran diary 25 November 1943.

224. Churchill to Lady Violet Bonham-Carter on returning from Teheran, TV interview with Kenneth Harris, 13 April 1967, *The Listener*, 17 August 1967, quoted in Wheeler-Bennett, *Action this Day*, p. 96n.

225. Keith Sainsbury, *The Turning Point* (Oxford, 1986), pp. 227–33.

226. Ibid., pp. 231–2, 242–7.

227. Moran (Sir Charles Wilson) diary, 29 November 1943; Sainsbury, *Turning Point*, pp. 247–9.

228. Churchill-Stalin conversation 30 November 1943 **Document 65**.

229. Though Cadogan believed personal relations had been excellent and that Anglo-Soviet relations would have been improved by Stalin's insight into Churchill's character as one without duplicity (Cadogan was wrong) and noted 'UJ [Uncle Joe, i.e. Stalin] has a good sense of humour and is very adept at pulling Winston's leg', letter to Halifax, December 1943, Dilks, *Diaries of Sir Alexander Cadogan*, p. 586.

230. Winston S. Churchill, *History of the Second World War vol 5 Closing the Ring* (London, 1951), pp. 358–9.

231. Wheeler-Bennett (ed.), *Action this Day*, p. 90.

232. Sainsbury, *Turning Point*, p. 247.

233. Fraser J. Harbutt, *Yalta 1945. Europe and America at the Crossroads* (Cambridge, 2010), p. 144.

234. Churchill to Eden 16 January 1944 PREM3/399/6. For the 'convergence hypothesis' see Geoffrey Roberts, 'Churchill, Roosevelt and Stalin: The Role of the Personal Factor in the Success and Failure of the Grand Alliance' in Military Leaders Club of the Russian Federation (eds), *The Co-operation of the Anti-Hitler Coalition* (Moscow, 2014), p. 169.

235. WM(44)11th mtg Confidential Annexe (CA) 25 Jan. 1944 CAB65/45.

236. Churchill to Stalin 24 January, Eden minute 28 January 1944 PREM3/396/11.

237. Brooke diary 24 January 1944.

238. Churchill to Stalin 24 January 1944 PREM3/396/11.

239. Churchill to Stalin 1 February 1944 **Document 66**.

240. Stalin to Churchill 4 February 1944 **Document 67**.

241. Carlton, *Churchill and the Soviet Union*, pp. 108–10; Pechatnov, 'How Stalin and Molotov', pp. 169–70.

242. Churchill to Stalin 27 February 1944 **Document 68**. Churchill bizarrely justified the Soviet demand for Königsberg with reference to the battles the Russian army fought in that area in 1914, saying that he regarded this war against German aggression as one thirty-years war.

243. Nicolson diary 22 February 1944, N. Nicolson (ed.), *Harold Nicolson Diaries and Letters, Vol. 2, 1939–45* (London, 1967), hereafter Nicolson diary.

244. Stalin to Churchill 3 March, Churchill to Stalin 7 March 1944 **Documents 69** and **70**.

245. Harvey diary 2 March 1944.
246. Harvey diary 10 March 1944.
247. Churchill to Stalin 21 March 1944 **Document 72**.
248. Stalin to Churchill 23 March 1944 **Document 73**.
249. Ibid.
250. Harriman Memorandum of conversations in London 2–5 May 1944 Harriman papers box 172, Library of Congress. See also Churchill's minute to Eden concerning his fear of Soviet ambitions in the Balkans and even Italy, 4 May 1944 FO371/43636/R7380.
251. Halifax to Foreign Office 28 March 1944 FO371/43304/N1908.
252. Churchill to Eden 1 April 1944 FO371/43304/N2128. Churchill had just received a curt message from Stalin on the Polish issue, Stalin to Churchill 23 March 1944 **Document 73**, Pechatnov, 'How Stalin and Molotov', p. 170.
253. Ivan Porter, 'Some Notes on Operation Autonomous: Romania, 1944' in W. Deakin, E. Barker and J. Chadwick (eds), *British Political and Military Strategy in Central, Eastern and Southern Europe in 1944* (London, 1988), pp. 162–79.
254. Churchill to Molotov 2 May 1944 FO371/43999/R7106.
255. Clark Kerr to Foreign Office 6 May, Molotov to Churchill 10 May 1944 FO371/43999/R7287, Eden to Churchill 15 May FO371/44000/R7830.
256. Clark Kerr to Foreign Office 2 May 1944 FO371/43686/R7102.
257. Molotov to Churchill 22 April, Clark Kerr to Foreign Office 23 April 1944 FO371/43686/ R6642, R6530, R6672.
258. Eden conversation with Gusev 18 May 1944 FO371/43636/R7903.
259. FO to Halifax 25 May 1944 FO371/43636/R7903.
260. Churchill to Halifax 8 June 1944 FO371/43646/R8988.
261. Churchill to Roosevelt 700 11 June 1944, Roosevelt to Churchill 560 13 June 1944 FO371/ 43646/R9472, R9514. Churchill to Roosevelt 23 June 1944 *FRUS1944* V, p. 126; Churchill to Stalin 12 July, Stalin to Churchill 15 July 1944; Gilbert, *Road to Victory*, pp. 1069–71; Elisabeth Barker, *British Policy in South-East Europe in the Second World War* (London, 1976), p. 144; A. Filitov, 'The Soviet Union and the Grand Alliance: The Internal Dimension of Foreign Policy', in Gabriel Gorodetsky (ed.), *Soviet Foreign Policy 1917–1991 A Retrospective* (London, 1994), pp. 99–100; Silvio Pons, 'Stalin and the European Communists after World War Two', *Past and Present* supplement 6 (2011), p. 123; Geoffrey Roberts, 'Stalin and the Grand Alliance: Public Discourse, Private Dialogues and the Direction of Soviet Foreign Policy, 1941–1947', *Slovo* 13 (2001), pp. 8–10.
262. Martin H. Folly, 'The Red Air Force in Italy, 1944: A Case Study in the Formation of British Policy to the Soviet Union in World War II', *Diplomacy and Statecraft* 11 (2000), pp. 121–4; Harbutt, *Yalta*, pp. 139–40.
263. Harriman and Abel, *Special Envoy*, pp. 328–9.
264. Reynolds, *From World War to Cold War*, p. 131. Compare Churchill's comments at War Cabinet 11 May WM(44)63rd mtg CA with those of 11 April WM(44)47th mtg CA CAB65/46.
265. Stalin to Churchill 9 June, 11 June **Documents 74** and **75**.
266. WM(44)157th 27 November 1944 CAB65/48.
267. Gabriel Kolko, *Politics of War. The World and United States Foreign Policy, 1943–1945* (New York, 1968), pp. 119–20.
268. Stalin had actually pressed Marshals Zhukov and Rokossovsky to attempt a Vistula crossing, but they insisted they were unable to do so, Simon Sebag-Montefiore, *Stalin: the Court of the Red Tsar* (London, 2003), p. 475. The Soviet armies were aligned for advance northwards along the east bank of the river, and were not in a position to switch direction, in addition to being close to exhausted after continuous fighting since 22 June 1944.
269. Reynolds, *From War to Cold War*, p. 246.
270. Antony Polonsky (ed.), *The Great Powers and the Polish Question* (London, 1976), pp. 213–20.
271. Harbutt describes the outcome as the Anglo-Soviet 'Moscow Order': Harbutt, *Yalta*, pp. 154–82.
272. Moran diary 9 October 1944.

273. Stalin to Roosevelt 8 October 1944. It was Roosevelt's advisor Harry Hopkins who had pointed out to the President that Stalin might assume Churchill spoke for both of them, at a time when the Americans were suspicious about Churchill's intentions in the eastern Mediterranean and interest in spheres of influence, Susan Butler (ed.), *My Dear Mr Stalin. The Complete Correspondence of Franklin D. Roosevelt and Joseph V. Stalin* (New Haven, 2005), pp. 260–4.
274. Stalin-Churchill meeting 9 October 1944 **Document 87**. The British record is in PREM3/434/2.
275. Stalin-Churchill meeting 9 October 1944 **Document 87**.
276. The document can be seen in PREM3/66/7.
277. The report to Roosevelt was very vague: Churchill and Stalin to Roosevelt 10 October 1944 **Document 88**.
278. Molotov-Eden meeting 10 October 1944 PREM3/434/2.
279. Churchill-Stalin meeting 18 July 1945 **Document 131**: see also Churchill to Stalin 28 April 1945 **Document 124**.
280. Harriman and Abel, *Special Envoy*, pp. 357–8.
281. Winston Churchill, *The History of the Second World War, Vol. 6, Triumph and Tragedy* (London, 1953), pp. 201–4: Reynolds, *In Command of History*, p. 461.
282. Churchill-Stalin meeting 9 October 1944 **Document 87**. They did have a discussion about Italy, on Churchill's initiative, including the activities of the Italian communists, but relative influence was not mentioned.
283. R. Garson, 'Churchill's "Spheres of Influence": Rumania and Bulgaria', *Survey* 24 (1979), pp. 145, 153, 157, suggests that Churchill hoped recognition of the legitimacy of Soviet influence would invite some concessions in return from the Soviets. The Bulgarian issue was particularly important because Churchill was concerned to get assurance that Bulgaria would return the Greek territory it had been granted by Hitler – which gave it a coastline on the Aegean. When Molotov gave an assurance with regard to this issue, the final Bulgarian percentage, a significant shift from Churchill's original figure, was now deemed acceptable.
284. Churchill-Stalin meetings 14 and 16 October, Churchill to Stalin 17 October 1944 **Documents 91, 93** and **94**.
285. Harvey diary 13 October 1944; Avon, *Reckoning*, p. 486, Churchill-Stalin meeting 16 October 1944 **Document 93**.
286. Stalin-Churchill meetings with Polish Government in London representatives and representatives of the Polish Committee of National Liberation 13 October 1944, **Documents 89** and **90**: S. Mikołajczyk, *The Pattern of Soviet Domination* (London, 1948), pp. 93–9.
287. Birse, *Memoirs of an Interpreter*, pp. 171–5; Moran diary, 10 October 1944.
288. Eden described the first meeting in his diary as 'friendly and easy'. While his 10 October meeting with Molotov, where they haggled over the Hungary and Bulgaria percentages, 'didn't go well', he found things then went smoothly, with his achieving 90 per cent of his aims, making clear the main British concern was ensuring Bulgarian withdrawal from Greek and Yugoslav territory, diary 9, 10, 11 October 1944 Avon papers, Birmingham University Library, AP20/3/09.
289. Harvey diary 16 October 1944, Brooke diary 12 and 14 October 1944.
290. Churchill to Stalin 17 October 1944 **Document 94;** Moran diary 16 October 1944
291. Moran diary 16 and 18 October 1944: see also entry for 30 October.
292. Edmonds, 'Churchill and Stalin', pp. 320–1.
293. Churchill to Stalin 2 December 1944 **Document 102**; Churchill to Eden 3 December 1941 (re. Switzerland), Churchill, *Triumph and Tragedy*, p. 616; Churchill to Eden 11 December 1944 (re. Spain) PREM 8/106.
294. Stalin to Churchill 2, 3 and 7 December 1944 **Documents 103, 106** and **108**.
295. Churchill to Stalin 19 December 1944 **Document 110**.
296. Stalin to Churchill 8 December 1944, 3 January 1945 **Documents 108** and **112**.
297. Churchill-Stalin conversation 4 February 1945 **Document 113**.
298. Churchill-Stalin meeting 17 October 1944 **Document 95**.
299. Churchill-Stalin conversation 10 February 1945 **Document 114**.
300. Ibid.

301. Letter from Cadogan to his wife, 11 February 1945, Dilks (ed.), *Diaries of Sir Alexander Cadogan*, pp. 708–9.
302. Churchill to Stalin 17 February 1945 PREM4/78/1.
303. Marginal note in Dalton diary, 23 February 1945.
304. Churchill, *Triumph and Tragedy*, pp. 312, 316. He noted, 'I had never expected that he could be so expansive'.
305. Nicolson diary 27 February 1945.
306. Churchill to Roosevelt, 13 March 1945, Kimball (ed.), *Churchill and Roosevelt. The Complete Correspondence*, vol. 3, pp. 564–6.
307. Churchill to Roosevelt 11 April 1945, Kimball (ed.), *Churchill and Roosevelt. The Complete Correspondence*, vol. 3, pp. 603–5; Gilbert, *Road to Victory*, pp. 1274–5.
308. Stalin to Roosevelt, 3 April 1945, Butler (ed.), *Dear Mr Stalin*, pp. 312–13. Churchill to Stalin 1 April 1945 **Document 115**.
309. Roosevelt to Churchill 12 April 1945, Kimball (ed.), *Churchill and Roosevelt. The Complete Correspondence*, vol. 3, pp. 595–7, 630; Churchill, *Triumph and Tragedy*, p. 398.
310. Stalin to Churchill 15 April 1945 **Document 118**.
311. W.D. Miscamble, 'Anthony Eden and the Truman-Molotov Conversations, April 1945', *Diplomatic History* 2 (1978), pp. 86–7; Geoffrey Roberts, 'Sexing up the Cold War: new Evidence on the Molotov-Truman Talks of April 1945', *Cold War History* 14 (2004), pp. 108–15.
312. Churchill to Stalin 14 April 1945 **Document 117**.
313. Eden minute to Churchill 24 March 1945 and Churchill note 25 March PREM3/346; Churchill kept silent for all of five days, Churchill to Stalin 1 April 1945 **Document 115**.
314. Churchill to Roosevelt 19 March 1945 PREM3/356/9; Reynolds, *In Command of History*, pp. 470–1.
315. Churchill to Stalin, 28 April, Stalin to Churchill 4 May 1945 **Documents 124** and **125**; Churchill, *Triumph and Tragedy*, p. 435.
316. Churchill to Truman, 6 May 1945, Churchill, *Triumph and Tragedy*, p. 437.
317. Cadogan diary 11 May 1945.
318. See W. Strang, *Home and Abroad* (London, 1956), pp. 213–14. Strang was UK delegate on the European Advisory Commission, set up to deal with such problems. Also Cadogan diary 21 July 1945.
319. Churchill to Truman 12 May 1945, Churchill, *Triumph and Tragedy*, p. 498.
320. Carlton, *Churchill and the Soviet Union*, p. 137.
321. Churchill to private office 4 June 1945 PREM3/396/12.
322. Clark Kerr note of Churchill luncheon with Gusev 18 May 1945 PREM3/396/12.
323. Richard Aldrich, *The Hidden Hand. Britain, America and Cold War Secret Intelligence* (London, 2001), p. 58; Operation Unthinkable, 22 May 1945 CAB120/691. Despite the assumed mobilisation of hundreds of thousands of US, British and German soldiers, and the probable war-weary state of the Red Army (whose discipline was asserted to have collapsed into looting and drunkenness), the authors of this staff study were extremely dubious of success. The Chiefs of Staff thought the idea entirely unrealistic, Brooke diary 24 May, 31 May 1945.
324. Cadogan diary 18 June and 5 July 1945.
325. Brooke diary 11 June 1945.
326. Churchill to Stalin 28 April 1945 **Document 124**; Cadogan diary 18 July 1945.
327. Churchill-Stalin meetings 17 July, 18 July 1945, Stalin to Churchill 4 May 1945 **Documents 130, 131** and **125**.
328. Eden diary 17 July 1945, cited in Avon, *Reckoning*, p. 535.
329. Churchill-Stalin meeting 18 July 1945 **Document 130**; Moran diary 19 July, 22 July 1945, Dixon diary 19 July 1945 in P. Dixon (ed.), *Double Diploma: the Life of Sir Pierson Dixon, Don and Diplomat* (London, 1968). Churchill had made similar remarks in Moscow: Stalin-Churchill conversation 9 October 1944 **Document 87**.
330. Moran diary, 20 July 1945, Dixon diary 20 July 1945.
331. Brooke diary 23 July 1945 and later note. For the whole issue of Churchill and the bomb, see Kevin Ruane, *Churchill and the Bomb in War and Cold War* (London, 2016).

332. Cadogan diary 24 July 1945, Moran diary 24 July 1945.
333. Dixon on 21 July noted; 'There has been much closer liaison this time between our Delegation and the Americans. At Yalta the distances precluded this ... There has been a satisfactory air of reality about the meetings. Both at the plenary and the Foreign Secretaries' meetings, both we and the Americans have voiced plainly our misgivings about Soviet policy in various spheres.'
334. Churchill-Stalin meetings 17 July, 18 July 1945 **Documents 130** and **131**.
335. Zubok and Pleshakov, *Inside the Kremlin's Cold War*, p. 25.
336. Churchill to Stalin 24 January PREM3/396/11, Stalin to Churchill 29 January 1944, *Stalin's Correspondence*, pp. 191–2.
337. Both at times referred explicitly to the frank tone that they were themselves using and which they regarded as acceptable to each and necessary. Neither handled his correspondence with Roosevelt in the same way.
338. Stalin-Churchill conversation 12 August 1942 **Document 34**.
339. See Stalin's remarks to Field Marshal Montgomery in 1947: in 1951, Churchill was to describe Stalin as an 'amazing and gigantic personality', Reynolds, *From War to Cold War*, p. 264.

Chapter 3. Allying with the Devil: Forging the Grand Alliance, 1941–1942

1. Albert Resis (ed), *Molotov Remembers* (Chicago, 1993), p. 39.
2. Dokumenty Vneshnei Politiki Vol. 24 (Moscow, 2000) doc. 2, hereafter cited as DVP.
3. As recalled by John Colvillle, at the time Churchill's Assistant Private Secretary, in J. Wheeler-Bennett (ed), *Action this Day: Working with Churchill* (London, 1968), p. 89.
4. DVP doc. 87.
5. Abel Archive (for details of this archive see n. 3 of Introduction), box 2, file 28, Harriman interview with Herbert Feis, February 1954.
6. See Mark Harrison, *Soviet Planning in War and Peace, 1938–1945* (Cambridge, 1985) and idem, *Accounting for War: Soviet Production, Employment and the Defence Burden, 1940–1945* (Cambridge, 2005).
7. DVP doc. 228.
8. Abel Archive, box 1, file 5, Harriman interview with Feis, October 1953.
9. Harriman's report on the dinner in Harriman Papers, Library of Congress Manuscript Division, container (c.) 160, chronological file (cf.) 1–3/10/41.
10. Balfour's diary in Harriman Papers c. 164.
11. DVP, Vol. 25 (Moscow, 2010) doc. 131.
12. On Molotov and his trip to London and Washington see G. Roberts, *Molotov: Stalin's Cold Warrior* (Washington DC, 2012), pp. 59–63.
13. Oleg Rzheshevsky, *War and Diplomacy: The Making of the Grand Alliance* (Amsterdam, 1996) doc. 28.
14. Ibid., doc. 38.
15. Ibid., doc. 112.
16. 'New Documents about Winston Churchill from Russian Archives', *International Affairs*, Vol. 47, No. 5 (2001), pp. 131–4.

Chapter 4. Into the Ogre's Den: Churchill in Moscow, August 1942

1. Abel Archive, box 1, file 12, interview with Herbert Feis, October 1953.
2. UK National Archives, CAB 127/33 n. 29.
3. Abel Archive, box 1, file 12. Harriman document entitled 'Trip to Moscow with the Prime Minister, August 1942', p. 7. The document is undated but seems to be based on a diary by Harriman and to have been composed shortly after the trip.
4. W. Harriman and E. Abel, *Special Envoy to Churchill and Stalin, 1941–1946* (London, 1976), p. 157.
5. UK National Archives, CAB 127/33 n. 30.
6. Harriman, 'Trip to Moscow with the Prime Minister, August 1942', p. 7.
7. Harriman's notes on talks with Stalin at dinner, 14 August 1942, Harriman Papers, c. 162, cf. 14–15/8/42

8. Abel Archive, box 2, file 14, interview with Herbert Feis, November 1953.
9. A.H. Birse, *Memoirs of an Interpreter* (London, 1967), p.101.
10. Birse's report may be found in the Harriman Papers, c.162, cf. 14–15/8/42.
11. 'Avtobiograficheskie Zametki V.N. Pavlova – Perevodchika I.V. Stalina', *Novaya i Noveishaya Istoriya*, no.4, 2000.
12. Harriman Papers, c.162, cf. 14–15/8/42.
13. Harriman, 'Trip to Moscow with the Prime Minister, August 1942', p.8.
14. John W. Wheeler-Bennett (ed.), *Action this Day: Working with Churchill* (London, 1968), p.255.
15. 'New Documents about Winston Churchill from Russian Archives', *International Affairs*, Vol.47, No.5 (2001), pp.137–8.
16. *Sovetsko-Angliiskie Otnosheniya vo Vremya Velikoi Otechestvennoi Voiny, 1941–1945*, Vol.1 (Moscow, 1983) doc.147.
17. O.A. Rzheshevsky, *Stalin i Cherchill'* (Moscow, 2004), doc.157.
18. Ibid., doc.158.

Chapter 5. The Rocky Road to Tehran

1. See G. Roberts, 'Stalin and the Katyn Massacre' (available online at academia.edu).
2. The Soviet records of the conference were published in *Moskovskaya Konferentsiya Ministrov Inostrannykh Del SSSR, SShA i Velikobritanii* (Moscow, 1984).
3. *Sovetsko–Angliiskie Otnosheniya vo Vremya Velikoi Otechestvennoi Voiny 1941–1945* Vol.1 (Moscow, 1983) doc.295.
4. I. Stalin, *O Velikoi Otechestvennoi Voine Sovetskogo Souza* (Moscow, 1946), pp.108–9.
5. An English translation of the Soviet transcripts of the plenary sessions of the Tehran, Yalta and Potsdam conferences was published as *The Tehran, Yalta and Potsdam Conferences* (Moscow, 1969). The Russian-language volumes on the conferences are much fuller and include the reports on Stalin's bilateral conversations with his Western counterparts.
6. Abel Archive, box 2, file 28. Harriman memorandum of conversations at Tehran, dated 28/11/43.
7. Oleg Rzheshevsky, *War and Diplomacy: The Making of the Grand Alliance* (Amsterdam, 1996) doc.82.
8. *Tegeranskaya Konferentsiya Rukovoditelei Trekh Souznykh Derzhav – SSSR, SShA i Velikobritanii* (Moscow, 1984) doc.57.
9. W. Harriman and E. Abel, *Special Envoy to Churchill and Stalin, 1941–1946* (London, 1976), pp.273–4.
10. The British record of this conversation may be found at PREM3/136/11. In his memoirs (p.159) Birse indicates that he was the only interpreter at this meeting and translated both ways. However, there is a Soviet record of the meeting, written by Valentin Berezhkov, who sometimes substituted for Pavlov – Stalin's regular interpreter.
11. *Tegeranskaya Konferentsiya* doc.59.
12. Arthur H. Birse, *Memoirs of an Interpreter* (London, 1967), p.160.
13. Finland joined the German attack on the USSR in June 1941 in what the Finns call the 'Continuation War' i.e. the continuation of the Winter War with Russia in 1939–40.
14. See the British record of this discussion: PREM 3/136/11/75892, p.16.
15. See G. Roberts, 'Stalin at the Tehran, Yalta and Potsdam Conferences', *Journal of Cold War Studies*, Vol.9, No.4 (Fall 2007).
16. PREM 3/136/11/75892, pp.19–20.
17. AVPRF, F.0555, Op.1, Pap.12, D.24, L.101.
18. 'Izlozheniye Otdel'nykh Voprosov Obsuzhdavshikhsya na Konferentsii v Tegerane', RGASPI, F.558, Op.11, D.234, LL.99–104.

Chapter 6. Crossing the Frontier: Poland and the Warsaw Uprising

1. Antony Polonsky (ed.), *The Great Powers and the Polish Question, 1941–1945* (London, 1976), doc.82.
2. *Vneshnyaya Politika Sovetskogo Souza v Period Otechestvennoi Voiny* Vol.2 (Moscow, 1946), pp.59–61.
3. Harriman Papers c.171, cf. 1–15/1/44.

4. *Vneshnyaya Politika Sovetskogo Souza v Period Otechestvennoi Voiny* Vol. 2 (Moscow, 1946), pp. 339–40.
5. Harriman Papers, c. 171, cf. 16–21/1/44.
6. Ibid. cf. 1–8/3/44.
7. Ibid. c. 175, cf. 22–29/2/44.
8. *Stalin and the Cold War, 1945–1953: A Cold War International History Project Documentary Reader* (1999), p. 3.
9. Ibid., pp. 9, 15–16.
10. *Sovetskii Faktor v Vostochnoi Evrope, 1944–1953*, Vol. 1 (Moscow, 1999), doc. 9.
11. Polonsky, *The Great Powers and the Polish Question*, doc. 102.
12. *Sovetskii Faktor v Vostochnoi Evrope*, doc. 11.
13. Polonsky, *The Great Powers and the Polish Question*, doc. 102.
14. Harriman Papers, c. 173, cf. 13–15/8/44. For Vyshinskii's record of this conversation: *Sovetsko–Amerikanskie Otnosheniya, 1939–1945* (Moscow, 2004) doc. 251.
15. Harriman Papers, cf. 16–18/8/44; *Sovetsko–Amerikanskie Otnosheniya, 1939–1945*, doc. 252.
16. Polonsky, *The Great Powers and the Polish Question*, doc. 107.
17. Abel Archive, box 3, file 33. Harriman's published memoir of the Warsaw uprising may be found in *Special Envoy to Churchill and Stalin, 1941–1946*, Chap. XV.
18. See G. Roberts, *Stalin's General: The Life of Georgy Zhukov* (New York, 2012), pp. 205–7.
19. Harriman Papers, c. 174, cf. 1–5/9/44.
20. Sergey Shtemenko, *The Soviet General Staff at War, 1941–1945*, book 2 (Moscow, 1973), pp. 102–4; A. Chmielarz, 'Warsaw Fought Alone: Reflections on Aid to and the Fall of the 1944 Uprising', *Polish Review*, Vol. 39, no. 4 (1994), p. 421.
21. Harriman and Abel, *Special Envoy*, p. 348.

Chapter 7. With Bow against Bear: Churchill in Moscow, October 1944

1. W.S. Churchill, *The Second World War* Vol. 6 (London, 1954), pp. 194–5. The famous piece of paper may be found here: https://images.nationalarchives.gov.uk/assetbanknationalarchives/action/viewFullSizedImage?id=30941&size=800.
2. 'Zapis' Besedy s Prem'e-Ministrom Velikobritanii Cherchillem, 3 Iunya 1953 goda', *Istochnik* No. 2 (2003), p. 55.
3. Cited by David Carlton, *Churchill and the Soviet Union* (Manchester, 2000), p. 120.
4. G. Ross (ed.), *The Foreign Office and the Kremlin: British Documents on Anglo-Soviet Relations 1941–1945* (Cambridge, 1984) doc. 30.
5. O.A. Rzheshevsky, *Stalin i Cherchill* (Moscow, 2004) doc. 162.
6. See G. Roberts, 'Moscow's Cold War on the Periphery: Soviet policy in Greece, Iran and Turkey, 1943–1948', *Journal of Contemporary History*, Vol. 46, No. 1 (January 2011).
7. Abel and Harriman, *Special Envoy*, p. 360.
8. Lord Moran, *Winston Churchill: The Struggle for Survival, 1940–1965* (London, 1968), p. 218.
9. Arthur H. Birse, *Memoirs of an Interpreter* (London, 1967), p. 175.
10. Harriman Papers, c. 174, cf. 15–16/10/44. Pamela Churchill had an affair with Kathy's father during the war and in the 1970s married him and became Pamela Harriman.
11. J.M. Siracusa, 'The Meaning of Tolstoy: Churchill, Stalin and the Balkans, Moscow, October 1944', *Diplomatic History* (Fall 1979), p. 449.
12. Abel and Harriman, *Special Envoy*, p. 363.
13. On the ethnic dynamics of Stalin's foreign policy see Alfred J. Rieber, *Stalin and the Struggle for Supremacy in Eurasia* (Cambridge, 2015).
14. The photograph was on display at an exhibition about Stalin's *lichnyi fond* (personal archive) in Moscow in September 2018.

Chapter 8. Yalta and Potsdam: Triumph or Tragedy?

1. See G. Roberts, 'Stalin at the Tehran, Yalta and Potsdam Conferences', *Journal of Cold War Studies*, Vol. 9, No. 4 (Fall 2007).

2. Soviet records of Stalin's conversation with de Gaulle in December 1944 may be found in *Sovetsko-Frantsuzkie Otnosheniya vo Vremya Velikoi Otechestvennoi Voiny, 1941–1945* Vol. 2 (Moscow, 1983).

3. Harriman Papers, c. 175, cf. 8–14/12/44.

4. *Stalin and the Cold War, 1945–1953: A Cold War International History Project Documentary Reader* (1999), p. 103.

5. W. Harriman and E. Abel, *Special Envoy to Churchill and Stalin, 1941–1946* (London, 1976), p. 391.

6. Harriman Papers, H.176, cf.1–5/2/45.

7. Kathleen Harriman letters to Pam, 7/8/2/45, in the Pamela Harriman Papers, Library of Congress Manuscript Division.

8. Soviet records of the plenary sessions at Yalta may be found in *The Tehran, Yalta and Potsdam Conferences* (Moscow, 1969). Many more Soviet documents on the conference are printed in *Krymskaya Konferentsiya Rukovoditelei Trekh Souznykh Depzhav – SSSR, SShA i Velikobritanii* (Moscow, 1984).

9. Harriman and Abel, *Special Envoy*, p. 396.

10. Rzheshevsky, *Stalin i Cherchill'* doc. 175.

11. Harriman and Abel, *Special Envoy*, pp. 406–7.

12. Arthur H. Birse, *Memoirs of an Interpreter* (London, 1967), pp. 184–5.

13. Lord Moran, *Winston Churchill: The Struggle for Survival, 1940–1965* (London, 1968), p. 252.

14. Abel Archive, box 3, file 41, interview with Abel. See further E. Mark, *Revolution by Degrees: Stalin's National-Front Strategy for Europe, 1941–1947*, Cold War International History Project, Working Paper No. 31, Febrary 2001.

15. Harriman and Abel, *Special Envoy*, pp. 432–9.

16. Harriman Papers c. 178, cf. 10–13/4/45.

17. V.O. Pechatnov, 'Averell Harriman's Mission to Moscow', *The Harriman Review* (June 2003), p. 25.

18. See G. Roberts, 'Sexing up the Cold War: New Evidence on the Molotov-Truman Talks of April 1945', *Cold War History*, Vol. 4, No. 3 (April 2004).

19. On Hopkins' discussions with Stalin: *Foreign Relations of the United States: The Conference of Berlin* Vol. 1 (US Government Printing Office: Washington DC, 1960).

20. V.O. Pechatnov, 'The Soviet Union at the Potsdam Conference' in Christoph Koch (ed), *Das Potsdamer Abkommen, 1945–2015* (Frankfurt am Main, 2017).

21. Ibid., p. 186.

22. Soviet records of the plenary sessions at Potsdam may be found in *The Tehran, Yalta and Potsdam Conferences* (Moscow, 1969). Many more Soviet documents on the conference are printed in *Berlinskaya (Potsdamskaya) Konferentsiya Rukovoditelei Trekh Souznykh Derzhav – SSSR, SShA i Velikobritanii* (Moscow, 1984).

23. Cited by Geoffrey Roberts, *Stalin's Wars: From World War to Cold War, 1939–1953* (London, 2006), p. 273.

24. Birse, *Memoirs of an Interpreter*, p. 208.

25. *Berlinskaya (Potsdamskaya) Konferentsiya* doc. 62. This Soviet document is the only extant record of this conversation. The US record got lost in the American bureaucracy because it was classified as containing military secrets i.e. the discussion about the coming Soviet attack on the Japanese.

26. Moran, *Winston Churchill: The Struggle for Survival, 1940–1965* , p. 299.

27. Birse, *Memoirs of an Interpreter*, p. 209.

28. On Soviet policy towards Turkey: G. Roberts, 'Moscow's Cold War on the Periphery: Soviet Policy in Greece, Iran and Turkey, 1943–1948', *Journal of Contemporary History* (January 2011).

29. 'Avtobiograficheskie Zametki V.N. Pavlova – Pervodchika I.V. Stalina', *Novaya i Noveishaya Istoriya*, no. 4 (2000).

30. See G. Roberts, 'Antipodes or Twins? The Myths of Yalta and Potsdam' in Koch (ed.), *Das Potsdamer Abkommen, 1945–2015*.

31. Michael Neiberg, *Potsdam: The End of World War II and the Remaking of Europe* (New York, 2015), pp. 247–56.

Chapter 9. Churchill's 'Operation Unthinkable'

1. Cited by Jonathan Walker, *Churchill's Third World War: British Plans to Attack the Soviet Empire, 1945* (Stroud, 2013), loc. 114 (Kindle edition).
2. David Dilks, *Churchill and Company: Allies and Rivals in War and Peace* (London, 2012), pp. 204–6; David Reynolds, *From World War to Cold War: Churchill, Roosevelt, and International History of the 1940s* (Oxford, 2007), p. 253.
3. UK National Archives, CAB 120/691/109040. All citations and references to the 'Operation Unthinkable' documents are from this source.
4. Walker, *Churchill's Third World War*, loc. 1950 (Kindle edition).
5. Ibid., loc. 2025.
6. See further Matthew Evangelista, 'Stalin's Post-war Army Reappraised' in S.M. Lynn-Jones et al. (eds), *Soviet Military Policy* (Cambridge, Mass. 1989).
7. The literal translation of the Russian would be 'very lightning'.
8. V.I. Lota, *RKS (Razvedyvatel'nyi Klub Souznikov)* (Moscow, 2016); RGASPI, F. 644, Op. 2, D. 514, L. 1–2; Yu. Gor'kov, *Gosudarstvennyi Komitet Oborony Postanovlyaet* (Moscow, 2002), p. 526.

Chapter 10. Aftermath: Churchill, Stalin and the Cold War

1. https://winstonchurchill.org/resources/speeches/1946-1963-elder-statesman/the-sinews-of-peace/
2. See Philip White, *Churchill's Cold War: The 'Iron Curtain' Speech That Shaped the Post-war World* (New York, 2012).
3. https://www.marxists.org/reference/archive/stalin/works/1946/03/x01.htm.
4. D. Reynolds & V. Pechatnov, *The Kremlin Letters: Stalin's Wartime Correspondence with Churchill and Roosevelt* (London, 2018), p. 594.
5. The idea derives from Isaac Deutscher in *Russia after Stalin* (London, 1953, 1969), who wrote that Stalin 'drove a nation of 160–200 million people to jump the chasm which separated the epoch of the wooden plough from that of the atomic pile' (p. 73).
6. Milovan Djilas, *Conversations with Stalin* (London, 2014), p. 53.

Index

Page numbers appearing in *italics* refer to maps.

Dodecanese, 85, 91, 159
Duke of York, HMS, 287
Dumbarton Oaks conference, 207, 211, 236
Dunkirk evacuation, 4, 121, 124
Dunlop, Charles, 33, 35, 129, 130

Eastern European states federation, 43, 86, 88, 172, 204
economic unity for Europe, 232
Eden, Anthony: about, xiii, 290; aid to the Soviets, 25, 26, 48, 300–1n77, 301–2n91; Anglo-Soviet agreement, 21, 22, 75; Churchill, 47, 62–3, 245, 288; Foreign Minister's Conference, 152; German invasion of Soviet Union, 19, 21; Molotov-Churchill meetings, 116, 125; Poland, 65, 163, 259–60; post-war planning, 42–3; Potsdam Conference, 65; second Moscow meeting, 56, 199, 229–30; Soviet-Western summits of 1950s, 283; Tehran Conference, 173; Yalta Conference, 259–60, 261; Yugoslav situation, 17. *See also* Eden-Stalin meetings
Eden-Stalin meetings, 83–105; background, 27, 73–4, 83–4; 16 December discussion, 84–91; 17 December discussion, 92–7; 18 December discussion, 97–100; 20 December discussion, 101–5
Egypt, 31, 134, 147
Eisenhower, Dwight D., 46, 62, 175
ELAS, 53, 55, 268
elections of 1945, British, 245, 246, 272, 279, 281, 293
Ercoli, 210
Estonia, 2, 5, 27, 92–4, 96, 100, 109
European Advisory Commission, 48, 152, 157